Jobs for Development

Jobs for Development

Challenges and Solutions in Different Country Settings

Edited by
Gordon Betcherman and Martin Rama

OXFORD
UNIVERSITY PRESS

OXFORD
UNIVERSITY PRESS

Great Clarendon Street, Oxford, OX2 6DP,
United Kingdom

Oxford University Press is a department of the University of Oxford.
It furthers the University's objective of excellence in research, scholarship,
and education by publishing worldwide. Oxford is a registered trade mark of
Oxford University Press in the UK and in certain other countries

Published in the United States of America by Oxford University Press
198 Madison Avenue, New York, NY 10016, United States of America

British Library Cataloguing in Publication Data
Data available

Library of Congress Control Number: 2016935367

ISBN 978–0–19–875484–8

Printed in Great Britain by
Clays Ltd, St Ives plc

Links to third party websites are provided by Oxford in good faith and
for information only. Oxford disclaims any responsibility for the materials
contained in any third party website referenced in this work.

The findings, interpretations, and conclusions expressed in this work are entirely those of
the authors and should not be attributed in any manner to the World Bank, its Board of
Executive Directors, or the governments they represent.

Acknowledgments

The chapters in this volume were originally commissioned as background papers for the 2013 edition of the *World Development Report* (WDR), the flagship publication of the World Bank. The preparation of this edition, entitled *Jobs*, was led by Martín Rama, with Gordon Betcherman as a member of the core team.

The country case studies in this volume were selected as good illustrations of the diverse range of jobs challenges identified by the WDR. Each of the original papers had a member of the WDR core team as its coordinator. Kathleen Beegle was the focal person for Mozambique, Gordon Betcherman for Tunisia, Samuel Freije-Rodríguez for Mexico, Jesko Hentschel for Ukraine, and Martin Rama for Bangladesh and Papua New Guinea. A case study on South Sudan, coordinated by Dena Ringold, could not be included in this volume because of difficulties conducting further research. The chapter on St Lucia in this volume was launched subsequent to the WDR.

Generous funding for the preparation of these country case studies was provided by bilateral donors. The Government of Denmark, through its Royal Ministry of Foreign Affairs, supported the work on Mozambique and Tunisia. The Australian Agency for International Development (AusAID) assisted with Papua New Guinea; Canada's International Development Research Centre (IDRC) with Mexico; the Government of Denmark, through its Royal Ministry of Foreign Affairs, with Mozambique and Tunisia; and the Japan International Cooperation Agency (JICA), through the JICA Institute, with Bangladesh. Additional funding was generously provided by the Development Economics Group at the World Bank, under the Knowledge for Change program.

The authors benefited from early discussions held at a workshop at the World Bank in Washington, DC in December 2012. In particular, we would like to acknowledge the contributions made by the workshop discussants: Pradeep Mitra, Reema Nayar, Louise Fox, Pablo Acosta, Diego Angel-Urdinola, David Newhouse, Manohar Sharma, Polly Jones, Sonia Plaza, Ihsan Ajwad, Erwin Tiongson, Aline Coudouel, and Gladys Lopez-Acevedo.

Insightful comments on a draft version of this volume by two anonymous referees are gratefully acknowledged as well.

Finally, the editors and contributors appreciate the encouragement, guidance, and support provided by Adam Swallow, Aimee Wright, and the editing and production team at OUP.

Table of Contents

List of Figures

List of Tables

List of Boxes

Notes on Contributors

Nelly Aguilera is the Chief of the Economic Analysis Unit at the Ministry of Health of Mexico. She holds a PhD in Economics from the University of Chicago. Her research interests are health, pensions, and social programs.

Marjorie Andrew holds an MPhil in Development Studies from the University of Sussex. Her professional career started in Papua New Guinea's Department of National Planning, but she has since worked as an independent consultant on issues such as human resource development, social protection, and good governance. She is currently Deputy Director of the PNG Institute of National Affairs, which is a privately funded think tank engaged in policy dialogue with the PNG government.

Rim Ben Ayed Mouelhi received her doctoral degree in Economics from the University of Dijon, France. She is currently Professor of Economics at the University of Manouba, Tunisia, and Research Fellow of the Economic Research Forum (ERF Egypt). Her research focuses on firm productivity analysis and the impact of public policies on labor demand. Rim is a Tunisian citizen.

Ezra Jn Baptiste has an MSc degree in Sociology and is a professionally qualified and highly experienced social development analyst and program/project manager with extensive knowledge and skills in social impact analysis, beneficiary assessment, program/project planning and management, and public sector administration, gained from working with public sector institutions in St Lucia and international organizations. He is the Principal Consultant of the consulting firm Social Development Solutions Inc. As a qualitative researcher, his main interests are social capital focusing on bonding, bridging, and linking social capital and its role in community based development in rural communities.

Gordon Betcherman is a Professor at the School of International Development and Global Studies at the University of Ottawa. His research interests are in labor economics, demography, social policy, and the economics of development. His most recent publications are on the impacts of labor market regulation in developing countries, youth employment in sub-Saharan Africa, and poverty trends in Vietnamese fishing villages. Dr Betcherman was a co-author of the World Bank's 2013 World Development Report on Jobs. He is a Research Fellow at the Institute for Labor Studies (IZA) in Germany. He joined the University of Ottawa in 2009 after eleven years at the World Bank. Dr Betcherman holds a PhD from the University of California at Los Angeles.

Andrew S. Downes holds a BSc and MSc in Economics from the University of the West Indies and a PhD in Economics from the University of Manchester. He is presently

Professor of Economics and Pro Vice Chancellor for Planning and Development at the University of the West Indies. He specializes in labor/human resources economics, applied econometrics, and development economics and has published extensively in these areas. He was formerly Director of the Sir Arthur Lewis Institute of Social and Economic Studies.

Abdel-Rahmen El Lahga received his doctoral degree in Economics from the University of Louis Pasteur, Strasbourg, France. He is currently Associate Professor of Economics at the University of Tunis, Tunisia. He is also a Research Associate at the Economic Research Forum (ERF, Egypt). His research fields are family economics and the analysis of inequality and poverty in the Arab World. AbdelRahmen is a Tunisian citizen.

Colin Filer holds a PhD in Social Anthropology from the University of Cambridge. He has been undertaking research on the social, economic, and political impacts of major resource projects in Papua New Guinea for more than thirty years, and has provided advice on this subject to a wide variety of organizations involved in the assessment and management of such impacts. He is currently an Associate Professor at the Crawford School of Public Policy at the Australian National University.

Mahabub Hossain was widely regarded as one of the leading agricultural economists in the Asian region. He passed away in January 2016. Dr Hossain was the President of the Asian Agricultural Economic Association. He was formerly the Head of Social Sciences Division at IRRI and, prior to that, Director General of the Bangladesh Institute of Development Studies (BIDS). In recent years, he played an active role in institution building, as a development practitioner, having served as the Executive Director of BRAC—the largest development NGO in the world. He pioneered long-term panel studies at the village and household level in Bangladesh. Dr Hossain wrote a number of books on rural development and technological change and contributed to more than 100 publications in academic journals and edited books. Dr Hossain received his PhD in Economics from Cambridge University.

Benedict Y. Imbun holds a PhD in Employment Relations and Human Resource Management from the University of Western Sydney. The main focus of his academic research has been industrial relations, technical education, and human resource management, with specific reference to the extractive industry sector in Papua New Guinea. He is currently a Senior Lecturer in the School of Business at the University of Western Sydney University.

Phillipa Jenkins is a doctoral candidate at the Crawford School of Public Policy at the Australian National University. Her doctoral research has been concerned with the politics of mine closure and sustainability planning at the Ok Tedi mine in Papua New Guinea's Western Province.

Sam Jones is an Associate Professor in Development Economics at the University of Copenhagen, Denmark. Sam specializes in research in applied macroeconomics, foreign aid effectiveness, labor markets, and education quality, with a special focus on sub-Saharan Africa. Previously, Sam worked for the Bank of England and spent seven years supporting the Government of Mozambique in the Ministry of Finance and Planning and the Ministry of Planning.

Olga Kupets is an Associate Professor at the Economics Department of the National University of Kyiv-Mohyla Academy (Kiev, Ukraine). She has also been working as a local consultant to the World Bank and the International Labour Organization. Olga received her PhD (Candidate of Economic Sciences Degree) from the Institute of Demography and Social Studies of the Ukrainian National Academy of Sciences. Previously, she obtained her MA in Economics from the Master Program founded by the Economics Education and Research Consortium in Kyiv (now Kyiv School of Economics) and MA in Mathematics and Computer Science from Cherkasy National University (Ukraine). Olga's research interests include population aging and its consequences; youth and long-term unemployment; education, skills, and their employability; international and internal labor migration; analysis of employment, education, and social policies; and transition economics.

Mohamed Ali Marouani is Associate Professor of Economics at Paris1-Panthéon-Sorbonne University and Director of the Master Program "Economic Expertise in Development Policies." He is also Research Fellow of the Economic Research Forum (ERF Egypt), Research Associate of DIAL, and Secretary General of the Cercle des économistes Arabes. His research focuses on the impact of public policies on employment, on the interactions between trade policy and development, on the determinants of structural change, and on the interactions between economic research and policy making. Mohamed Ali is a Tunisian citizen.

Gabriel Martinez is the Director of the Public Policy Program at ITAM, in Mexico City. He holds a PhD in Economics from the University of Chicago. His research interests are labor economics and economics of regulation.

Martha Miranda is a Professor of Development and Social Policy at the State University of Puebla (ICGDE-BUAP). She holds a PhD in Economics from the University of Essex (UK). Her research interests are social protection systems, financing of public pensions and public health insurance, and impact evaluation of social policies.

Martin Rama, a Uruguayan citizen, is the Chief Economist for the South Asia region of the World Bank, based in Delhi. Before that he was the Director of the World Development Report (WDR) 2013, on Jobs. Previously, for eight years, he was the Lead Economist for Vietnam, based in Hanoi. Before moving to operations, he spent ten years with the research department of the World Bank, working mainly on labor issues. His professional career started in CINVE, Uruguay's largest think tank. He was also Visiting Professor at the graduate program in Development Economics at the Université de Paris I until 2005. Martin Rama gained his degree in Economics from the Universidad de la República (Uruguay) and his PhD in Macroeconomics from the Université de Paris I (France).

Bill F. Sagir holds a PhD in Social Anthropology from the Australian National University. He has worked as a community affairs officer and consultant on social issues in Papua New Guinea's extractive industry sector for many years. He is currently a Senior Lecturer at the School of Humanities and Social Sciences at the University of Papua New Guinea.

Yasuyuki Sawada is a Professor of Economics at the University of Tokyo. His main research interests are in the broad area of development economics, applied micro-econometrics, poverty dynamics, and experimental economics. He has co-edited two books on income dynamics, poverty, and disability, and contributed to more than thirty publications in international academic journals. Dr Sawada received his PhD in Economics from Stanford University.

Binayak Sen is currently a Research Director at the Bangladesh Institute of Development Studies (BIDS). Previously, he was a Senior Economist at the World Bank and a Visiting Fellow at the Institute for Development Policy and Management at the University of Manchester. He has taught economic development at BRAC University and the North South University. His main research areas cover poverty, income distribution, human development, labor markets, gender, inclusive growth, and economic history. Dr Sen has contributed to more than sixty publications in academic journals and edited books. Binayak Sen received his MA in Political Economy from Moscow State University and his PhD in Economics from the Institute of Oriental Studies at the Soviet Academy of Sciences.

Edwin St Catherine holds a MA Degree in Economics from the University of Cambridge. From 1993 to the present, he has been the Director of the Central Statistical Office of St Lucia. Mr St Catherine has served on and chaired several UN Statistical Division Expert Groups including the review of the World Demographic Yearbook and the development of the UN principles for Censuses. He is a registered expert with the IMF on Inflation Measurement and he has been Consultant Statistician to the CDB on labor force surveys, multi-dimensional poverty, and living conditions assessments in most Caribbean countries for the past fifteen years.

Finn Tarp is Director of UNU-WIDER and Professor at the University of Copenhagen. He has some thirty-seven years of experience in academic and applied development economics research and teaching. His field experience covers more than twenty years of in-country work in thirty-five countries across Africa and the developing world more generally, including longer-term assignments in Swaziland, Mozambique, Zimbabwe, and Vietnam. Finn Tarp has published almost ninety articles in international academic journals, alongside five books, fourteen edited book volumes and special journal issues, and more than forty book chapters. He is presently a member of the World Bank Chief Economist's fifteen-member "Council of Eminent Persons" advising the Chief Economist.

1

The Job Creation Challenge

Across Developing Country Settings

Gordon Betcherman and Martin Rama

Jobs are a pressing issue everywhere. Still struggling in the wake of the global financial crisis, around 200 million people are unemployed worldwide. But the challenges go far beyond this. Quality is a huge concern. About half of the people working in developing countries are in self-employment or farming, where incomes tend to be low and erratic and benefits are rare. While there have been substantial gains over the past two decades, 30 percent of workers in these countries still live on less than US$2 per day (ILO 2014). Safe conditions and basic rights in the workplace remain elusive for many. Access to jobs and employment income is very uneven, with certain groups—such as young people, women, and the disabled—facing particular barriers in many countries. And future prospects can seem daunting. Over 600 million new jobs will need to be created over the next fifteen years just to keep employment rates at today's levels, with the bulk of these jobs in low-income countries where populations are still young.

Policy-makers seem to be responsive to the jobs issue. Just listen to the discourse in political campaigns or read national planning documents. The country doesn't matter: employment is framed as a priority, often as the number one priority. However, actual *jobs strategies* are hard to find. When employment plans and policies are carefully examined, they usually turn out to be something else. Often, these strategies are really growth strategies—based either on deregulation and low taxes or substantial state intervention, depending on the ideology of the designers. Or, they are actually education strategies built on the assumption that jobs will come to a skilled labor force. While considerations like fiscal policy, the business climate, and education are fundamentally important, they capture only part of what is needed for a jobs strategy that meets the needs of individuals and supports the development of society within a particular country context.

The 2013 World Development Report, Jobs (World Bank 2012), departs from these conventional approaches and proposes a framework that shifts the way we might think about jobs and job strategies. The starting point is the centrality of jobs in the development process. Jobs are more than just the by-product of growth. They can actually drive development by raising living standards, enhancing productivity, and strengthening social cohesion. But not all jobs are equal from a development perspective. Jobs obviously bring private returns to the people who hold them, but they can also have social returns (that is, beyond the individual) that are important to take into account. Some jobs do more for society than others in the sense that they have higher social returns, or positive development spillovers. These are called "good jobs for development" in the lexicon of the Jobs WDR. These may be "good jobs" according to conventional thinking, such as formal wage employment with high earnings and generous benefits. But this may not necessarily be the case. Depending on the country context, jobs with positive development spillovers could take a variety of forms.

The policy implications of the Jobs WDR framework extend conventional notions. On the one hand, it retains traditional concerns for strong growth fundamentals like sound macro policy, a regulatory framework that encourages investment, and a good education system as well as labor institutions that balance protection with flexibility. However, the innovation is that the framework calls also for policies to support country priorities—that is, actions that will encourage the creation of more good jobs for development, which may not always be generated in sufficient numbers because of market or institutional failures. So countries can reap development payoffs if they take actions to alleviate whatever constraints exist in the creation of these jobs. This could involve a range of policy sectors that are not usually considered in jobs strategies.

What are these good jobs for development and what policies can encourage their creation? Not surprisingly, the Jobs WDR concludes that this depends on the country context. Countries differ in terms of where the development payoffs from jobs are greatest and the report creates a typology of eight "jobs challenges" to illustrate these diverse agendas. Certainly, the level of development matters. The jobs challenges countries face are different in *agrarian economies* than in *urbanizing societies*, which are different, in turn, from more advanced *formalizing economies*. But good jobs for development are not dictated solely by the stage of development. Demography may be a decisive factor, such as in *countries with high youth unemployment* or in *aging societies*.

Natural endowments, including geography, can also create unique jobs challenges; for example, in *resource-rich countries* and *small-island nations*. Finally, jobs agendas can also be defined by the strength of a country's institutions, with an extreme case being *conflict-affected countries*. These types are not mutually exclusive; it is not hard to think of countries that face more than one of these challenges. But focusing on these diverse types can help to identify how jobs can drive development depending on the context.

The different types of jobs challenges discussed in the Jobs WDR (specifically in Chapter 6) were informed by a series of country case studies that were commissioned as background research for the report. These case studies represented a first effort to apply the Jobs WDR framework at the country level. Since the release of the report, the authors—all acknowledged experts in the countries they were studying—have continued their research and more systematically applied the Jobs WDR's framework to jobs in their countries (Figure 1.1).[1] The result is this volume.

The overarching objective of this project has been to learn more about how this framework to think about jobs can be usefully applied at the country level. This has involved two related tasks. The first has been to explore how the development of different countries can be interpreted through the core concepts of the framework—how jobs have contributed to living standards, productivity, and social cohesion; identifying "good jobs for development"; constraints on the creation of more of these jobs; and interventions that might alleviate these constraints. This covers what the authors have been asked to address in their chapters, but they have been free to analyze these issues in their own way.

This brings us to the second objective of the volume: to learn more about what research methods and data can be used to operationalize the framework. Some authors have relied on the traditional tools of labor economists—quantitative data from household surveys, analysis of the impacts of labor policies and programs, and so on. In other cases, less conventional approaches have been used, drawing on both quantitative and qualitative data, and analytical techniques taken from fields not normally considered in the study of employment, such as poverty analysis, public finance, rural and urban development, and conflict studies. In addition to generating a rich body of country-specific analysis, then, the book can also be seen as a "practitioner's guide" to implement the concepts developed in the Jobs WDR.

---

[1] St Lucia was not included in the background research for the Jobs WDR and was added to have a small-island nation case for this volume. Some analysis for South Sudan, as a conflict-affected country, was included in the Jobs WDR but a chapter was not prepared for this volume because of difficulties accessing data and other relevant information.

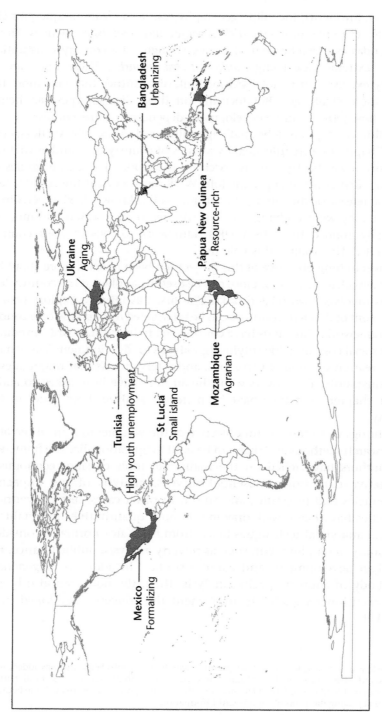

Figure 1.1. Countries included in volume

1.1 The Development Payoffs to Jobs

Jobs are multidimensional, as suggested by the range of words used to describe them, even within the same language. In English, for example, the word "job" may indicate the nature of the activity being performed, evoking the skill or expertise that is required from the worker. But it may also imply the existence of a contractual relationship with an employer, involving mutual obligations and a certain degree of stability. "Labor" hints at the volume of human inputs used in production, suggesting images of effort and conveying a sense of physical exertion. "Employment" is associated with the number of people engaged in economic activity, in an almost statistical sense. In some languages, the word for jobs designates the place where the person works, or at least a slot in a production process. This multiplicity of words shows that jobs may be difficult to characterize through a single measure or indicator.

The main analytical toolkit to think about jobs, and the contribution they make to society, is labor economics. This is a coherent body of theories explaining how households make decisions related to work, how firms set their employment levels, and how labor markets function. Over the years, an impressive body of empirical evidence has developed thanks to the growing availability of household surveys, establishment surveys, and administrative records, combined with rapidly expanding computational power. As a result, labor economists have been able to estimate with relative precision key parameters influencing household and firm decisions, to identify the nature of frictions in labor markets and, to assess the impact of policy interventions. In light of these strengths, labor economics is the natural starting point to analyze the relationship between jobs and development.

At the same time, a mechanical reliance on labor economics may lead to important features of jobs in developing countries being ignored. For example, "employment" and "the labor market" are often used as interchangeable expressions. Yet, a majority of the people at work in developing countries are farmers and self-employed, who work for themselves and sell their products directly, rather than selling their work to a firm. The labor economics toolkit also focuses attention on potential gaps between labor supply and labor demand. Not surprisingly, discussions about jobs in developing countries are often centered on unemployment rates and skills mismatches, despite these notions losing some of their relevance when vast swathes of the population cannot afford to be out of work or are not in an employee–employer relationship. In a similar spirit, issues about voice are often framed in the context of collective bargaining between workers and employers, but the relevant counterparts for many workers in developing countries are urban authorities and the local police.

Labor economics usually considers two measures of the contribution jobs make to society. One of them, seen from the perspective of the workers and their households, is the value of the earnings and benefits associated with a job (w). The other, from a production viewpoint, is the output created by the job (y). In equilibrium, these two variables equalize. Indeed, in a well-functioning labor market, the marginal product of labor is equal to the earnings and benefits of the marginal worker ($y = w$). The level of employment, hence the volume of job creation, is implicitly determined by this equilibrium condition: jobs will be created up to the point where the additional output is entirely offset by the additional labor earnings.

From this perspective, job creation is not a government objective in itself, and nor should it be. Policies may aim at making workers more productive; for instance, by increasing their human capital. Or they may support firms in becoming more productive in the use of their workers; say, by improving logistics or reducing red tape. And they can certainly ensure that the labor market operates efficiently, through better labor regulations and improved matching between job-seekers and vacancies. But all this may not necessarily result in more jobs. For instance, more educated and better paid workers could prefer to have more leisure time, or keep their offspring in school for longer, such that actual employment levels would decline.

The Jobs WDR does not at all question the validity of this robust and well-tested analytical framework. In fact, it fully endorses its policy implications, namely the need for strong fundamentals—macroeconomic stability, human capital, and the investment climate—and for appropriate labor policies. If anything, it finds that while labor policies have an important role, they are usually not the central factor in a country's jobs successes or failures. In most countries, they affect distributional outcomes but do not have a significant impact on economic efficiency and overall employment.

The main methodological innovation of the Jobs WDR is to introduce one more measure of the contribution jobs make to development, namely their societal value (v). This societal value may differ from the value jobs have from an earnings (w) or an output (y) perspective due to their potential spillovers on other aspects of the economy and society.

Perhaps the most obvious way to visualize these spillovers is through the example of environmental impacts. Some jobs pollute more than others. The net value added of a polluting job, once the cost of emissions is deducted, is less than the value added as seen from the point of view of the firm or the worker ($v < y$ *and* w). Similarly, a job can affect interactions at the household level, and hence the wellbeing of others beyond the worker. For instance, paid employment for women is often associated with greater household investments in health and education. The societal value of paid employment for women could thus be higher than the direct earnings their jobs provide or the direct output they generate ($v > w$ and y). Importantly, jobs shape who we are and how we interact with each other. If jobs are associated with greater trust, or with greater engagement in collective decision-making, fewer resources may be wasted in confrontational forms of collective decision-making. Thus a job that reduces the risk of violent extremism is more valuable to society than the output or the earnings associated with it would suggest ($v > y$ and w).

The potential gaps between the societal and the private measures of the contribution jobs make to development are at the center of the Jobs WDR framework. The examples above refer to consumption spillovers from jobs in the example of paid employment for women, production spillovers in the case of polluting jobs, and social spillovers when jobs affect trust or engagement in collective decision-making. As shorthand, the Jobs WDR framework refers to these spillovers under the *living standards*, *productivity*, and *social cohesion* headings.

Spillovers of this sort may not always be present. In many cases the social value of jobs is likely to be close to their value to the jobholders and their employers, implying that the traditional labor economics framework is sufficient to guide policy-making. But spillovers from jobs are likely in countries where market imperfections and governance failures are common, as well as in periods of dramatic economic transformation.

1.2 Priorities for Job Creation

This analytical framework brings the thinking about jobs and development closer to public economics. In public economics, policy intervention is justified when individual incentives are not well aligned with social goals. In this particular case, there is a justification for intervention when there are untapped development payoffs to jobs. Again, pollution provides a straightforward illustration of this idea. There is a clear case for policy interventions reducing the number of jobs that seriously damage the environment. Similarly, there is a justification to support the development of paid employment for women in patriarchal societies, or to focus on job creation—especially for young men—in conflict-affected countries.

More generally, the gap between the societal value of jobs and their private value makes it possible to think rigorously about job creation as an explicit goal of public policy. Job creation should be encouraged to the point where the two values coincide. But the examples above suggest that the creation of just any jobs is likely to be sub-optimal, and the focus should be on the types of jobs that have high development payoffs ($v > w$ and y).

It does not follow that untapped development payoffs exist in all circumstances. Some countries may just do fine by adopting a growth strategy, and letting markets handle the level and composition of employment. But development spillovers from jobs cannot be ruled out in all cases. The multi-dimensional nature of jobs makes them a vehicle to connect people and firms not only through labor markets, but also through non-market interactions. The presumption is that the nature of the untapped payoffs from jobs varies across countries, calling for different jobs strategies depending on the nature of the jobs challenge faced.

When viewed from this perspective, several recent WDRs were implicitly about jobs strategies. The 2009 WDR, Reshaping Economic Geography (World Bank 2008) was on the contribution jobs in cities make to economic development. The 2011 WDR, Conflict, Security and Development (World Bank 2010), argued that justice, security, and jobs were critically important to defuse conflict. And the 2012 WDR, Gender Equality and Development (World Bank 2011), saw paid employment as a key driver of agency among women. The Jobs WDR integrates these perspectives by claiming that the country context determines which are the relevant jobs challenges or, put differently, where the main untapped development payoffs from jobs lie.

Paid employment for women, polluting jobs, and jobs fostering trust are only telling examples of the potential development payoffs (positive or negative) from jobs. But the list of potential spillovers is actually longer. Most development economics, when viewed through a jobs lens, is arguably about such spillovers. The Jobs WDR reviews the development literature, reinterpreting the main findings from various schools of thought as evidence of development payoffs from jobs that even well-functioning labor markets would be unable to internalize.

Development payoffs associated with living standards include the following:

- *Earnings of others.* Taxpayers and consumers may be negatively affected when specific jobs are supported through transfers and market distortions.
- *Household allocations.* Bringing earnings home can change the status of the jobholder and result in a greater say in household decision-making.
- *Poverty reduction.* Since jobs are the main avenue out of poverty, there is social value in the availability of jobs for the poor.

There are also several development payoffs of jobs associated with aggregate productivity:

- *Agglomeration and congestion.* There is more learning and a better matching of skills in urban environments, although more urban jobs can also result in greater congestion.
- *Global integration.* Firms that engage in export markets tend to become more productive and, in doing so, they push other less-productive firms out of business.

- *Environmental effects.* Jobs have negative impacts on aggregate productivity when they damage the environment or lead to an overuse of scarce resources.

Finally, there are several ways in which jobs can affect social cohesion:

- *Social identity.* Jobs can influence the values and behavior of those who hold them in ways that affect society at large.
- *Networks.* Jobs connect people to each other; they convey information and can increase interactions across social and ethnic backgrounds.
- *Sense of fairness.* A perceived absence of fairness in the access to job opportunities, even beyond one's own job, can undermine the sense of belonging in society.

The typology of jobs challenges considered by the Jobs WDR framework is meant to help identify the most likely spillovers from jobs in each case. Table 1.1 provides an inventory of the spillovers that emerged from the country studies.

The Jobs WDR framework also offers guidance on the most conducive policies for job creation. Once a gap between the societal and the private value of jobs is identified, the next question is what lies behind it. Because the gap is between v and either y or w, and not between y and w, most likely the cause is outside the labor market. Poor infrastructure development may prevent the creation of more jobs in cities; protectionist policies may get in the way of having more jobs connected to world markets; tax evasion and explicit subsidies may convert some jobs into a burden for others; and so on and so forth.

This is why, in addition to strong fundamentals and appropriate labor policies, the Jobs WDR also calls for policy priorities guided by the nature of the jobs challenges faced by each country. Because some jobs may do more for development than others, it is necessary to understand where good jobs for development lie, given the country context. More selective policy interventions are justified when incentives are distorted, resulting in too few of those jobs. If this is the case, policies should remove the market imperfections and institutional failures that prevent the private sector from creating more good jobs for development.

1.3 Good Jobs for Development

The chapters in this volume illustrate the different jobs challenges identified in the Jobs WDR, challenges that are determined by the country's level of development, demography, physical endowments, and institutions. The

Table 1.1. Spillovers from jobs in country cases

	Bangladesh	Mexico	Mozambique	PNG	St. Lucia	Tunisia	Ukraine
Earnings of others	Jobs in unsafe manufacturing plants (–)	Some jobs in the informal sector (–)				Jobs in protected sectors (–)	Jobs in protected sectors (–)
Household allocations	Jobs for women in light manufacturing (+)						
Poverty reduction			Jobs in non-farm household enterprises (+)	Jobs in resource sector that remit income (+)		Unskilled (or no) jobs for educated youth (–)	Jobs that extend work-life of older workers (+) Jobs in foreign firms (+)
Global integration	Jobs in export-oriented RMG sector (+)	Formal jobs in export-oriented sectors (+)		Jobs that expats take in foreign resource operations (+)	Service sector jobs connected with regional economy (+)		
Agglomeration and congestion				Jobs that drive up land and housing prices in urban areas (–)			
Environmental effects				Resource jobs that damage surrounding environment (–)			
Social identity		Segmentation between covered and uncovered jobs (–)	Scarcity of urban jobs for youth (–)				
Networks					Urban jobs for rural migrants with loss of supporting community (–)		
Sense of fairness						Jobs for youth not based on privilege or insider connections (+)	Jobs not based on privilege or insider connections (+)

Notes: (+) and (–) indicate direction of the spillover.
Source: authors' compilation based on chapter cases.

country's context, and the jobs challenges it faces, determine what kinds of jobs have the greatest development payoff in terms of contributing to living standards, productivity, and social cohesion.

This said, the Jobs WDR framework is an ambitious one to implement operationally. Chapters apply the framework very differently and with varying degrees of exactness. This diversity is not surprising since these case studies are the first attempt at applying these concepts to concrete country situations. Not only was there no guidance from earlier studies on how to do this, but the specific country histories and contexts, the available data, and the orientation of the researchers all contribute to the variety of approaches. From the point of view of the objectives of the book, this lack of uniformity is useful since it sets out the range of possibilities for applying the Jobs WDR framework that can then be evaluated by the reader.

While approaches may vary, the chapters all consider a set of common issues related to the contribution of jobs to development, what are good jobs for development, and policy actions that could encourage their creation. Depending on the country's needs, the transformative role of jobs may be most important for living standards, or productivity, or social cohesion.

Chapter 3 by Hossain, Sen, and Sawada on Bangladesh highlights how development can happen through jobs in the context of *urbanization*. After its independence in 1971, Bangladesh's prospects were assessed as dismal, reflecting its high population density, malnutrition, limited resources, frequent natural disasters, and the legacies of its political struggles. Forty-five years later, there is good reason for cautious optimism: economic growth has been steady if not exceptional; poverty has declined substantially; human development indicators have been notable for a low-income country; and despite bouts of political disorder and a young population, social peace has generally been maintained. Moreover, these advances have occurred despite governance failures manifested, for example, in the rights violations and industrial accidents that the country experiences.

The authors see the emergence of large numbers of low-skilled jobs in Bangladesh's urban areas—especially in light manufacturing and, more particularly, in ready-made garments—as the key driver of this success story. They show how the proliferation of urban jobs not only benefited migrants but had positive feedback effects on rural areas as well, through linkages that enhanced productivity growth in non-farm activities and improved incentives for human capital investments, such as girls' education. Urban jobs in Bangladesh involve hard work, relatively low pay, and difficult conditions. But these jobs are usually preferable to jobs in agriculture. Importantly, the massive creation of low-skilled jobs in manufacturing has resulted in growing female labor force participation, in contrast with the experience of most other countries in South Asia. The associated empowerment of women may be one of the reasons why Bangladesh's human development indicators stand out.

Chapter 6 on Mexico by Martinez, Aguilera, and Miranda considers the challenge of *formalization*, which is relevant for a number of emerging economies. Despite a substantial middle class, high productivity gains in some industries, and improvements in its human capital, Mexico has a persistently large share of jobs outside the formal social protection system. Its pension, health, and now unemployment insurance programs are modeled on those in richer countries, but roughly half of the workforce remains outside those programs, with virtually no gains in formalization over the past twenty-five years.

And yet there is a higher societal value to formal sector jobs, not necessarily in terms of earnings or productivity, but as a mark of social inclusion. Martinez, Aguilera, and Miranda identify a number of adverse social consequences from lacking social protection coverage, including persisting damage to households from events that should have only temporary effects. This segmentation is all the more harmful given Mexico's large population and ethnic diversity. The authors see universal social security as a cornerstone of social cohesion. While in other developing countries, the ambition to create a sufficient number of formal sector jobs would most likely be unattainable, in Mexico this should not be an unrealistic goal, given that half of the workforce is already covered. In this context, the authors argue, it is hard to overstate the case of social protection as the key to good jobs for development.

In Chapter 2, Jones and Tarp examine the case of Mozambique, an *agrarian* economy that has emerged successfully from conflict and has been among the fastest-growing developing countries. Yet, Mozambique is still one of the poorest countries in the world, and the decline in poverty has not been nearly as rapid as GDP growth rates would have led one to anticipate. Over 80 percent of workers are still in agriculture, with smallholder farming as the norm, and the ratio has been relatively stable since the 1990s. Urban economies are undeveloped and only a very small share of the workforce is engaged in wage employment in industry or services. The analysis undertaken by Jones and Tarp demonstrates that poverty rates are highest among households relying on agriculture, where yields have remained mainly stagnant.

As they note, a superficial interpretation of their evidence would be that good jobs for development in Mozambique would be outside agriculture and the country's job strategy should focus on shifting resources out of this sector, ideally to wage employment where poverty rates are lowest. However, this is not their message. Simulations they carry out suggest that improving agricultural productivity is critical for raising rural incomes and for promoting job creation in the other sectors, as well as enhancing social cohesion. Their projections show that employment outside agriculture will continue to represent only a small minority of jobs for at least a generation, so cannot be the sole solution to Mozambique's job challenges. Thus, Jones and Tarp argue, more productive smallholder farming jobs in agriculture are good jobs for development in agrarian societies like Mozambique.

Chapter 4 by Filer, Andrew, Imbun, Jenkins, and Sagir considers the jobs challenges Papua New Guinea (PNG) faces as a *resource-rich* country where minerals and oil and gas account for a quarter of GDP and almost 80 percent of exports. But, like many countries with abundant physical resources, PNG has found it difficult to translate this wealth into broadly based social and economic development though jobs. Its human development index ranking is among the lowest in the Asia-Pacific region. While GDP growth has been strong since 2007, most people are no better off. In fact, the proportion of the population below the national poverty line was actually higher in 2010 than it had been in 1996. Development is slow in many of the rural areas where the bulk of the population lives and, while earnings have risen in cities, urban poverty has actually increased because of rapid rises in the cost of living.

The authors use various pieces of quantitative and qualitative evidence to try to overcome a dearth of national statistical data. Based on this admittedly partial empirical evidence, they conclude that the number of jobs created directly and indirectly by the resource sector is larger than is commonly assumed and has grown considerably. Filer and colleagues argue that the jobs generated by this resource-based economy likely have a more positive development impact than is generally believed. But such jobs are scarce in vast swathes of the country. Most of the job creation is in the project areas, and even after a project has been in operation for ten or twenty years, many of the people living in the affected areas show little or no improvement in their standards of living. In sum, many of the jobs created by the resource boom may be good jobs for development, but there are simply not enough of them.

St Lucia, like other *small-island* nations, faces unique development challenges due to its small scale and its physical separation from potential economic partners. It is also vulnerable to shocks that would be relatively minor in larger, more connected countries but can have major impacts when economic activity and jobs are concentrated and alternatives are scarce. St Lucia has struggled with such a disruption with the decline since the 1990s of the banana industry that historically dominated the island's production and exports. In Chapter 5, Downes, St Catherine, and Baptiste show that St Lucia is characterized by high unemployment (around 20 percent) and a large informal sector which accounts for about 60 percent of all employment. Unemployment and informality are significantly correlated with poverty. In addition to negatively affecting living standards, the decline of jobs in the banana sector has eroded social cohesion by initiating a drift of workers to the cities where social networks and norms are often weaker than they were in the countryside.

According to Downes and colleagues, St Lucia's job challenge is to identify and facilitate the structural transformation to a post-banana economy that will inevitably be service based. What services jobs will be good for the country's development? Government plans have identified various service industries for growth, including tourism, information technology, and finance. As the authors note, these industries would be desirable in that they would connect the island to the global economy, which would have productivity spillovers for St Lucia. They also emphasize the payoffs that would come from jobs that rebuild social networks, since social cohesion is especially important for economic resilience in small, isolated nations that are vulnerable to shocks.

While some chapters demonstrate how specific jobs can have a transformative role, a number of other chapters show how difficult it can be for countries to create jobs that address their specific development challenges. One example is the account in Chapter 7 by El Lahga, Marouani, and Mouelhi of Tunisia, a country facing the challenge of *high youth unemployment*. Tunisia has been unable to generate sufficient employment—both in terms of quantity and quality—to meet its labor supply. Like many countries in the Middle East and North Africa, this jobs deficit is most chronic for its large youth cohort, where the unemployment rate for the 15–29 age group has been well above 25 percent in recent years. This group accounts for about 60 percent of total unemployment. El Lagha, Marouani, and Mouelhi catalog various economic and social consequences of this situation, including depressed incomes, low morale, delayed family formation—which creates frustration, weakened collective identity, and the reinforcement of a sense of inequality of opportunity. And, though difficult to quantify, Tunisia is incurring longer-term economic costs by not taking advantage of the full potential of its young people, who risk being scarred by their early labor market experiences.

Jobs for educated youth are thus good jobs for development in the Tunisian context. Usual explanations for their scarcity tend to focus on demographics or education failures. But not all countries have had problems absorbing large youth bulges. And, while Tunisia may have room to improve the quality and relevance of its education system, it is striking that unemployment rates are much worse for university graduates than for other young people. Ultimately, El Lagha, Marouani, and Mouelhi argue that issues on the demand side are the decisive ones. In short, the economy is not generating skilled jobs to take advantage of the human capital of the country's educated youth. High-productivity sectors are not creating jobs. Small firms do not grow, even when they are as productive as larger ones. Ultimately, the productivity, income, and employment gains from structural change do not exist in Tunisia like they do in more dynamic economies.

Kupets in Chapter 8 considers what good jobs for development are in Ukraine, a country that faces the challenges of *aging*. Ukraine's share of population that is 65 and over is projected to increase from about 15 percent to over 25 percent in the next half century, while the working-age population, already in decline, will decrease by a further 12 million over this period. If not managed well, this combination of growing numbers of elderly people with pension and health needs and a shrinking cohort to create the required wealth could lead to economic adversity and social discord. Compared to high-income aging countries, Ukraine has fewer financial resources, poorer economic fundamentals, and weaker institutions to mitigate potential negative consequences of aging. Kupets argues that Ukraine's jobs challenge will be to encourage jobs that boost productivity, support the participation of more of the population able to work, and ensure the long-term sustainability of public finances and social programs that can provide for the needs of the elderly.

Kupets offers examples of jobs that would have significant development impacts for an aging Ukraine. One is employment in foreign companies. These jobs have high individual returns with good salaries and benefits. But they also have high social returns, since they contribute to the budget and to social protection programs, offer the potential for learning spillovers and technology transfer, and encourage the strengthening of institutions. Creating better farming jobs for the rural population would also contribute to higher living standards and productivity in parts of the country where current outcomes are poor but where Ukraine has comparative advantages and where social returns could be high. A third example cited by Kupets is jobs created by small entrepreneurs among return migrants. These would increase employment, boost productivity and investment through the productive use of accumulated earnings and new skills brought from abroad, and expose Ukrainians to democratic values and institutions from abroad.

1.4 Addressing the Jobs Challenge

The Jobs WDR identifies three layers of policies to meet a country's jobs challenge. The first two are firmly anchored in traditional labor economics: they are conventional categories of interventions in the sense that they are commonly considered by policy-makers concerned with employment. One is what can be thought of as the fundamentals, which include policies to support macroeconomic stability, an enabling business environment, the rule of law, and human capital accumulation. These fundamentals apply to all countries and are necessary to improve the general environment for job creation. The case studies highlight the importance of fundamentals, which come into play in virtually every chapter.

The second layer, labor policies, includes regulations, employment programs, collective bargaining, and social insurance. This layer does not figure too prominently in most countries included in this volume. In the following chapters, labor policies play a role—though it is almost consistently secondary.

The unique aspect of the Jobs WDR framework concerns what the report calls "priorities"—actions that will remove constraints on the creation of good jobs for development. These go beyond what is typically considered in jobs policies. This third layer of actions can include a wide range of areas, depending on the country's particular job challenge and the barriers it faces in the creation of jobs with development payoffs. Where these barriers are removed or bypassed because of the policy intervention, the country can expect positive social returns through some combination of enhanced living standards, productivity, and social cohesion. The chapters are rich in their identification of different actions to address the range of jobs challenges covered in each country.

Hossain, Sen, and Sawada draw on historical, economic, social, and cultural factors to explain how Bangladesh was able to support the creation of so many large numbers of low-skilled jobs in urban areas. They highlight three important and interrelated developments: the modernization of agriculture, the growth of a labor-intensive urban economy, and supportive social policies.

The modernization of the rural sector has been driven by the adoption of high-yielding variety seed technology in rice production and a pro-poor transition from sharecropping to land tenancy arrangements. The results of these changes have been increases in agricultural productivity and incomes and the release of large supplies of unskilled labor. Rural-to-urban and international migration provided destinations for this workforce, with migration costs partly handled through Bangladesh's trademark microfinance. The authors outline the various factors that contributed to the emergence of a labor-intensive urban economy. These included institutional innovations that improved financing and logistics to facilitate exporting, as well as continuous learning from abroad. The third theme highlighted by Hossain, Sen, and Sawada is progressive social policies, perhaps surprising for a traditional, low-income country. These policies, delivered by government and a vibrant NGO sector, have enhanced social inclusion through the provision of basic health and education that, in particular, have encouraged female participation and advancement.

Bangladesh has experienced unexpected success in meeting the urbanizing challenge of creating non-agricultural jobs for low-skilled labor. The authors argue that the resulting payoffs in higher living standards, productivity, and social cohesion can continue for some time in the future. However, sustaining the dynamism of cities and the emergence of new export sectors in addition to ready-made garments will require larger investments in urban infrastructure and connectivity, as well as improvements in access to urban land. Bangladesh will need to grapple with new challenges if it is going to build on its past achievements.

Martinez, Aguilera, and Miranda ask themselves why, in Mexico, there are so many informal jobs and so little progress in formalization. They conclude that two factors are particularly important. One is the preponderance of microenterprises with very low productivity; formalization is strongly correlated with firm size in Mexico, with 90 percent of workers in large firms insured but fewer than 10 percent in micro ones. The other is what the authors call "social segmentation," whereby households with access to formal jobs have different characteristics than those without access due to long-term constraints on human capital accumulation or to discrimination. Moreover, these latter households have higher-than-average fertility rates, which could have significant implications for the long-term evolution of social security coverage. They project trends in coverage and conclude that even significant economic growth and a gradual formalization of the economy will leave a large number of families without formal protection in the long term.

Given this social segmentation and the concentration of informality in the large microenterprise sector, Martinez and his colleagues are dubious that standard policy prescriptions based on tax and benefit reform will have a major impact. In their view, only strategic choices on social insurance reform will likely have a substantial impact on the challenge of formalization in Mexico.

Jones and Tarp identify three priorities to alleviate poverty in agriculture and spark the process of structural change in Mozambique. The first is to foster the dynamism of the non-farm, informal sector through growth-friendly regulations and reforms that improve access to finance. The second is support for export-oriented, labor-intensive industries and services, which are essential for aggregate growth. Specific measures would include a spatial industrial policy and the leveraging of natural resource revenues to improve infrastructure and logistics services along key value chains. The third priority is to improve the low levels of productivity in agricultural jobs. According to the authors, agricultural policy reforms are the most important action for making substantial progress on reducing poverty.

In PNG, the optimal policy response would be to use the royalties from the resource boom to finance the development of infrastructure and the accumulation of human capital across the country. Filer and colleagues conclude that the challenges faced in doing so have more to do with failures related to urban management, education, and governance than the country's resource riches. The conventional wisdom is that the natural resource sector potentially can destroy job prospects elsewhere because of Dutch Disease. And, since benefits are not widely distributed and may be contested, resources are often seen as a divisive element from a social perspective. Filer and his colleagues assess this narrative in the case of PNG. While acknowledging that Dutch Disease has been an issue when the sector is booming, they believe that government mismanagement and misappropriation of revenues has been a more serious problem.

Downes and colleagues highlight the challenges St Lucia faces to create jobs that could drive development in the post-banana era. Ensuing structural transformation towards a service economy will require education and training reforms in order to improve human capital and retool the workforce. But the creation of jobs with positive development payoffs will also depend on a process of "self-discovery" to identify services that reduce poverty and restore social cohesion. The authors of the St Lucia chapter argue that this will require a national planning process and formal social dialogue.

Tunisia's youth unemployment problem would be alleviated somewhat by better labor regulations and by making the postsecondary education system more relevant. But, ultimately, the authors argue that the most binding constraints are on the demand side, specifically Tunisia's anti-competitive formal and informal rules and practices. These reduce innovation and dynamism and choke off enterprise growth in high-productivity sectors. The result is that that there is little demand for educated young people. Governance and product market reforms are keys to relieving Tunisia's youth unemployment problems. The authors point to non-competitive practices in product markets and failures in the judicial and financial systems that create barriers for the growth and upgrading of firms. Until reforms address these issues, the creation of jobs that will meet the aspirations of Tunisia's large and educated youth cohort will remain elusive.

In Ukraine, the shortage of good jobs for development is the result of a collective action program: people are individually better off withdrawing from the labor force and collecting a pension than they are working and contributing to the financing of the social protection system. The individual choice is self-reinforcing, leading to a growing burden on the social protection system as the population ages. Acknowledging this difficult starting point puts the spotlight on the organization of the social protection system and the incentives to remain informal or stay out of the labor force altogether. Kupets does not shy away from recognizing that it will be a formidable task to meet this challenge.

These and the other cases illustrate the breadth of actions that can constitute a jobs strategy. Actions can encompass familiar policies to ensure that a country's fundamentals and labor rules and programs are properly aligned for the creation of jobs. In addition, the chapters highlight the wide range of policy priorities that can encourage the creation of good jobs for development. Many of these involve sectors that are not normally part of jobs strategies.

But, depending on the country's particular challenges, they can encourage jobs that have high social returns in terms of gains in living standards, productivity, and social cohesion.

References

ILO (International Labour Organization) (2014). World of Work 2014: Developing with Jobs. Geneva: ILO.

World Bank (2008). World Development Report 2009: Reshaping Economic Geography. Washington, DC: World Bank.

World Bank (2010). World Development Report 2011: Conflict, Security, and Development. Washington, DC: World Bank.

World Bank (2011). World Development Report 2012: Gender Equality and Development. Washington, DC: World Bank.

World Bank (2012). World Development Report 2013: Jobs. Washington, DC: World Bank.

2

Mozambique

Jobs and Welfare in an Agrarian Economy

Sam Jones and Finn Tarp

2.1 Introduction

This chapter examines the nature and functioning of the labor market in Mozambique. There is little disagreement that the country has achieved remarkable success over recent decades, particularly when viewed at the aggregate level. Over nearly twenty years, Mozambique has boasted one of the world's highest rates of GDP growth and has successfully moved from post-conflict stabilization and reconstruction into a more mature developmental phase. While the country remains a predominantly agrarian economy, in the sense that most workers rely on agriculture for a living, policy attention has largely been elsewhere. Recent discoveries of large natural gas deposits, plus investments in the coal sector, mean that Mozambique may become a significant global player in these commodities over the next twenty-five years.

Addressing the potential tension between agriculture and other drivers of growth is an ongoing challenge. Indeed, the country's recent development record is not unblemished. There is growing evidence that macroeconomic success has not delivered unambiguous socio-economic benefits at the household level. Mozambique remains one of the poorest countries in the world, ranked on the UNDP's 2014 Human Development Index at 178 out of 187 countries, below so-called failed states such as Haiti (168) and Afghanistan (169). It is also increasingly recognized that Mozambique's growth has become less pro-poor over time, meaning that consumption poverty rates have remained persistently high (DNEAP 2010; Arndt et al. 2012b). This is especially true in the rural sector, suggesting a widening urban–rural gap and upward pressure on income inequality. Social tensions have also been rising, spilling over into isolated incidences of unrest, and reflecting concerns over the high cost of living in urban areas as well as a scarcity of good-quality employment opportunities.

These challenges motivate a closer examination of trends in Mozambique's labor market. A key determinant of the extent to which macroeconomic growth produces gains in social welfare is the quality of jobs that an economy generates. Where productivity is increased by reallocating workers from lower- to higher-productivity activities, by adopting new technologies and practices in laggard sectors, or by creating new jobs in higher-productivity sectors (and thus absorbing underemployed labor), we should expect growth to have a strong positive effect on individual and social welfare. In light of the above, this chapter seeks to shed light on three main questions:

- What has happened to jobs (the labor market) in Mozambique over the past fifteen years?
- What has been the nature of the link between jobs and development outcomes?
- Where should Mozambican policy-makers focus to create more good jobs for development?

The rest of the chapter is structured as follows: Section 2.2 begins by discussing some of the analytical challenges involved in building an understanding of the nature and functioning of the Mozambican labor market. Household surveys (microdata) are the most reliable and comprehensive evidence source, and one contribution of this chapter is to place a series of four nationally representative household surveys on a consistent basis for the purpose of deriving coherent labor market information. Section 2.3 introduces the case of Mozambique. It starts with a broad overview of recent economic performance, followed by a closer examination of the principal characteristics of the labor market and its evolution over time. This description indicates that Mozambique's labor market shares many similar features with other low-income (sub-Saharan African) countries. More importantly, it suggests there has been little transformation in how labor is deployed throughout the economy for many years.

Section 2.4 digs deeper into the linkages between jobs and development outcomes. To do so we draw on the framework of the 2013 World Development Report (hereafter Jobs WDR; see World Bank 2012). Our focus is on jobs that contribute most to development outcomes not only from an individual perspective, but also for society as a whole. As per the Jobs WDR, we seek to analyze the nature and strength of links between jobs and outcomes in three domains: living standards, productivity, and social cohesion. We encounter specific and distinct challenges in each domain. In particular, we highlight that the prevalence and persistence of low-productivity smallholder agricultural jobs, alongside capital-intensive (and lumpy) industrial expansion, is essential to understanding both the lack of structural transformation in the labor market and the fragile connection between aggregate growth and poverty reduction.

In order to clarify the policy implications of these insights, Section 2.5 undertakes an econometric analysis of the determinants of household jobs choices. The aim is to identify relevant incentives (pull factors) and constraints (push factors) that influence household labor market behavior. Interpretation of our econometric results, which are based on a multinomial logit model of jobs choice probabilities, is aided by estimation of the relative importance of different sets of factors and a number of simple simulations. We find that agricultural activities are frequently a default or residual choice in which households are constrained, both due to a lack of endowments and due to external impediments, such as weak demand. This reflects an absence of sustained productivity growth in this sector.

Section 2.6 considers the policy implications. The main message is that raising returns in agriculture must be a priority to achieve sustained improvements in living standards across the population. Indeed, spillovers from agriculture to other sectors are potentially large and will be vital to support a vibrant manufacturing sector. However, promotion of non-farm activities, as well as providing expanded formal-wage employment opportunities in modern export sectors, will also be key. The latter is particularly important to strengthen social cohesion and fulfill the aspirations of more-educated urban youth. Section 2.7 concludes.

How does this chapter contribute to the literature, including the Jobs WDR framework? First, we demonstrate how microeconomic survey data can be used to provide a diagnostic assessment of jobs challenges in a low-income country. Second, we go beyond the identification of *which* jobs are good for development and consider *why* households participate in certain kinds of activities and not in others. This analysis demonstrates how models of occupational choice (e.g., French and Taber 2011) can be used to deepen insights based on the framework of the Jobs WDR. In contrast to most existing studies of jobs choices, a distinctive feature of our approach is that we take households rather than individuals as the appropriate unit of analysis. Third, we emphasize the salience of agricultural jobs and particularly the fundamental importance of a significant increase in agricultural productivity in sub-Saharan Africa. Although this message is not new, it brings to light the relevance of seeing jobs challenges from a macroeconomic and general equilibrium perspective.

2.2 Data and Methods

As set out in the Jobs WDR, the concept of jobs encompasses the full range of economic activities—ranging from family agriculture to employment in modern corporations. An immediate analytical constraint is that official stat-istics on employment are neither easily available nor particularly informative in many low-income countries. Rather, official data typically only refer to workers who have formal contracts with registered economic entities. As will be substantiated below, the size of the informal (non-registered) sector in both rural and urban areas in Mozambique renders such official labor force statistics of limited value. Instead, it is necessary to assemble the chosen measures directly from microdata, such as household surveys or censuses.

In this chapter we rely primarily on a set of three nationally representative household budget surveys. These are the two "Inquéritos aos Agregados Familiares" (IAFs) of 1996/97 and 2002/03, and the "Inquérito ao Orçamento Familiar" (IOF) of 2008/09. The three surveys provide information about the labor services supplied by each member of the household (e.g., employment status, sector of activity, type of work performed), the main sources of income for the household, and detailed information about household expenses. Importantly, these surveys have also constituted the information base for Mozambique's official national poverty assessments (DNEAP 2010); as such, a link can be made between jobs and welfare outcomes at the micro level.

In addition, we use the (one-off) dedicated labor force survey of 2004/05 (Inquérito à Força de Trabalho, IFTRAB), which collected more detailed infor-mation on labor force activity at the household level but did not include complementary information on household expenses from which consump-tion poverty measures could be built. Despite this drawback, the IFTRAB represents a valuable cross-check on the labor market information derived from the living standards surveys, and also fills an important temporal gap in the overall microdata series, thereby allowing us to identify trends with greater confidence.

Use of these surveys to derive labor market information is not without its challenges. These include discrepancies in questionnaire design (and subsequent coding), which makes it rather painstaking to derive consistent measures over time; and the treatment of family domestic work, which is problematic because there is frequent straddling between domestic and pro-ductive work, especially where the household has access to agricultural assets. The conceptual challenge of how to deal with individuals who straddle different labor market positions is not exclusive to part-time domestic work-ers. Many individuals in the surveys report having more than one job. However, on grounds of practicality and simplicity, we only report results for the stated principal occupation of each working-age person. Also, consid-erable effort has been made to place the surveys on a consistent footing; however, imperfections remain, which implies that caution should be exer-cised in interpretation.

2.3 Mozambique in Context

2.3.1 *Economy*

Mozambique's recent macroeconomic performance stands in sharp contrast to that of the 1980s. At independence from Portugal in 1975, Mozambique faced huge economic challenges including a dearth of skilled personnel and a poorly diversified economy. Despite some early achievements, sustained economic development was jeopardized by regional tensions that culminated in a prolonged armed conflict. After much loss, human and economic, a ceasefire was declared in 1992 and the first multi-party elections were held in 1994. With peace established, economic recovery quickly followed. In part reflecting its very low starting point, the rate of real GDP growth averaged over 7 percent per annum from 1994 to now, meaning that national real income has approximately tripled in twenty years. This places Mozambique among the best-performing countries in the world according to this metric. As reviewed elsewhere (e.g., Tarp et al. 2002; Fox et al. 2005; Arndt et al. 2007; Clement and Peiris 2008), three related factors have been behind these gains. They include maintenance of peace and political stability, supportive external relations (particularly with the donor community, but also with international investors), and sound economic governance, such as careful management of the government budget.

Despite sustained progress overall, colonialism and conflict continue to have persistent effects. Under Portuguese rule, the vast majority of Mozambicans had no access to education or professional training. During the recent post-conflict period, rehabilitation and expansion of the school system has been a major policy objective, supported by large amounts of foreign aid. However, aggregate measures of human capital only change slowly. Table 2.1 indicates how average years of education have changed over time across cohorts of workers. It shows that while skills have clearly improved, they remain very low. In all of the subgroups (as well as broad economic sectors), the average worker does not have a completed primary education (equal to seven years of schooling). Unsurprisingly, rural workers have the lowest average level of education at less than three years. Also, youth are now significantly better educated than adults, especially among females and in rural areas. This is pertinent as the employment aspirations of youth are likely to be conditioned by existing labor market structures and institutions.[1]

---

[1] Indeed, researchers have noted a concern that: "young Africans are increasingly reluctant to pursue agriculture-based livelihoods, which could have major implications for continent-wide initiatives to revitalise the agriculture sector"(Future Agricultures 2010: 3), which has been linked to perceptions of agriculture as a low-skill, distasteful occupation. See Perry (2009) for discussion of the complex cultural issues surrounding the employment of young men in a rural Senegalese context.

Table 2.1. Average years of education by gender and location of workers, 1996/97 to 2008/09

Age group	Year	Urban		Rural	
		Male	Female	Male	Female
Youth	96/97	4.91	3.56	2.45	1.42
	02/03	4.69	2.36	1.65	0.77
	04/05	4.72	3.83	3.21	1.94
	08/09	6.13	5.05	4.70	3.02
	Diff.	1.22	1.49	2.25	1.60
Adult	96/97	4.90	2.35	2.25	0.64
	02/03	5.21	2.29	1.59	0.34
	04/05	6.19	3.36	3.02	1.06
	08/09	6.13	3.70	3.27	1.26
	Diff.	1.23	1.35	1.03	0.62
Adult/Youth	08/09	1.00	0.73	0.70	0.42

Notes: Youth are aged 15–24; Adults are aged 25–64; "Diff." gives the absolute difference in years of education between 2008/09 and 1996/97 for each subgroup; "Adult/Youth" is the ratio of years of education of adults to youths in 2008/09.

Source: authors' estimates from household survey series.

Another legacy is widespread poverty. Household survey data indicate that consumption poverty rates fell relatively quickly from 68.5 percent in 1996/97 to 54.1 percent in 2002/03. Since then, the latest available estimates from 2008/09 point toward a stagnation in poverty rates at the national level. This chapter does not seek to directly examine why growth has failed to be associated with more rapid poverty reduction. This topic is addressed in detail by Arndt et al. (2012b), who identify a combination of factors including shocks to fuel and food prices over the period of the latest survey. However, aside from external vulnerabilities, the authors highlight the fundamental contribution of weak productivity growth in the smallholder agricultural sector. This points to the key role that jobs can play in connecting macroeconomic and microeconomic development processes. In turn it motivates the focus here on what has happened to jobs, particularly those in the agricultural sector.

In terms of the aggregate structure of the economy, the services sector (which includes government administration) is most important from a value-added perspective. These firms can be labeled as operating in the tertiary sector and currently contribute around 50 percent of aggregate GDP, compared to approximately 60 percent since the early 1990s.[2] Primary sector activities, which include agriculture and extractive industries, contribute around 30 percent of GDP. Secondary sector activities (i.e., manufacturing and processing industries) contribute the remaining 20 percent, up from around 10 percent in 1992. While this indicates that secondary industries have grown relatively

---

[2] See Jones and Tarp (2012) for details of GDP trends and its composition.

more rapidly than other sectors, much of this is owed to capital-intensive mega-projects established by international investors, such as the Mozal aluminum smelter (Arndt and Tarp 2009).

The spatial distribution of economic activity is also of interest. The capital city, Maputo, is located in the far southern tip of the country close to South Africa. Originally, the city was developed by the Portuguese precisely to facilitate the export of industrial goods from its neighbor, being the closest deep-water port to the Witwatersrand area. At the same time, the southern zone of Mozambique is comprised largely of arid and semi-arid agro-ecological zones, which are prone to drought and typically associated with lower soil fertility. The central and northern regions of Mozambique, which are separated from the capital city by more than 1,000 km, are generally more favorable to rain-fed and irrigated crops, including cash crops such as tobacco, cotton, and coconut. A key challenge is that transport links between the south and other regions essentially rely on a single main road, leading to high transport costs. This limits the potential for positive linkages to operate from agriculture to cheaper urban-wage goods, as well as from urban demand to agriculture (Arndt et al. 2012a). It also limits the scope for growth of agro-processing focused on domestic markets, as the locus of such demand is distant from regions with the most productive potential. Indeed, the substantially better-off urban south has been heavily reliant on South African agricultural imports, a trend bolstered by the recent expansion of large South African supermarket chains in the Maputo region.

Looking ahead, Mozambique is presently entering a qualitatively new phase in its developmental trajectory. The post-conflict challenges of reconstruction and stabilization have been largely overcome. The priority now is to ensure that economic growth remains robust and is made more inclusive. Over the medium term, prospects for growth are good. Multi-billion dollar investments in the natural resources sector have recently taken place and more are likely following discoveries of large reserves of natural gas.

2.3.2 Labor Market

A simple but fundamental starting point for any analysis of the labor market is the demographic structure of the workforce. Mozambique's population is young, predominantly rural, and is growing rapidly. Presently a little under 50 percent of the population is of working age (defined as aged between 15 and 64), meaning that there is more than one dependent to each potential worker. The urbanization rate is approximately 30 percent, which is low in global terms but not exceptional for low-income African countries in which agriculture is a widespread occupation. The rate of urban growth also appears to be relatively slow, meaning that the share of population residing in rural

Table 2.2. Labor force participation rates, by location and gender, 1996/97 to 2008/09

Age group	Year	Urban		Rural	
		Male	Female	Male	Female
Youth	96/97	52.0	49.2	74.2	90.1
	02/03	48.5	54.3	67.7	86.2
	04/05	51.2	58.0	79.0	92.0
	08/09	50.2	57.1	77.1	89.3
Adult	96/97	91.3	74.8	96.8	97.5
	02/03	97.1	85.4	99.6	99.2
	04/05	90.5	86.5	95.8	97.7
	08/09	90.5	88.2	97.6	97.6

Source: authors' estimates from household survey series.

areas has remained broadly unchanged since 1996/97.[3] A critical implication of this demographic structure is that the working-age population will continue to grow relatively rapidly over the next twenty-five years. In itself this generates a huge set of jobs policy challenges, which we come back to in Section 2.6.

As is common in other low-income countries where social security systems have limited coverage, rates of labor force participation are high in Mozambique. That is, virtually everyone of working age is economically active. This can be seen from Table 2.2, from which three important patterns can be highlighted. The first is that participation rates are consistently higher in rural compared to urban areas, among both youths and adults. This reflects lower participation in full-time education, as well as almost non-existent rates of unemployment in rural areas (see also Table 2.3). Second, female participation rates are high. Even in urban areas where access to training and exclusive domestic work is more common, around 80 percent of all adult women are economically active. Thus, female workers play a fundamental role in the Mozambican economy, especially in rural areas. Third, while participation rates among men have remained broadly stable over the period of the surveys, female participation appears to have increased in urban areas. This pattern would be consistent with evidence of tightening livelihood conditions as intimated by the evolution of poverty rates (see Section 2.3.1).

Table 2.3 provides a further decomposition of the working-age population according to their labor force status. Critically, only around 50 percent of the active labor force is fully employed, equal to 40 percent of a working-age population of 11 million. Although some of this is because a growing share of

---

[3] One reason for this may simply be due to the fact that the urban/rural classification used in the 1997 census was not updated for the 2007 census. As Cunguara et al. (2011) note, based on an urban agglomeration index, urbanization has increased from 15 to 21 percent over the same period. Whatever the correct measure, the key point is that the degree of urbanization remains low.

Table 2.3. Distribution of employment status of working-age population by location, 1996/97 to 2008/09

		96/97	02/03	04/05	08/09	Δ
Urban	Fully employed	36.4	30.1	34.6	36.6	0.2
	Underemployed	26.3	30.9	24.7	26.1	−0.3
	Work & study	0.6	4.4	4.8	5.7	5.1
	Unemployed	6.3	9.1	10.4	6.6	0.3
	Inactive	30.4	25.5	25.5	25.0	−5.4
	Working-age pop. (millions)	2.3	3.2	3.2	3.7	1.4
Rural	Fully employed	25.1	33.6	34.8	40.1	14.9
	Underemployed	63.8	53.4	52.4	45.7	−18.1
	Work & study	0.5	3.0	5.4	7.0	6.5
	Unemployed	2.6	2.5	0.8	0.4	−2.2
	Inactive	7.9	7.7	6.6	6.8	−1.1
	Working-age pop. (millions)	5.6	6.0	6.0	7.1	1.4

Notes: the final column indicates the absolute difference between 2008/09 and 1996/97 in percentage points; total working-age population gives the numbers of people aged 15–64, in millions; underemployed is defined as working under 40 hours per week.
Source: authors' estimates from household survey series.

individuals combine work and study (as shown in the table), a large share of workers are underemployed—defined as working less than 40 hours per week—particularly in rural areas.[4] At the same time, narrow or open unemployment has hovered at around 10 percent of the active workforce and is predominantly confined to urban areas. Looking over time, the only significant change in the urban labor market appears to have been a shift of workers from underemployment to combining work and study, which would be consistent with individuals investing spare time to raise their skills in order to secure a higher-productivity (full-time) occupation. In contrast, the same evidence on hours worked points to a gradual tightening of the rural labor market. Rates of underemployment have fallen from around 64 percent to 46 percent of the rural working-age population over the period and, correspondingly, full employment rates have risen from 25 percent to 40 percent. These changes are consistent with per capita consumption gains that have been primarily driven by increased hours worked rather than by a significant improvement in (agricultural) productivity, such as via the introduction of new technology or capital accumulation.

Another way of looking at the labor market is according to who buys labor services. Figure 2.1 classifies workers into three broad groups: those receiving a wage, the self-employed, and unpaid family workers.[5] Assuming the informal

---

[4] Data on hours worked should be treated with some caution given the prevalence of the informal sector and particularly because there are numerous missing values. Even so, these results are consistent with the overall pattern in the labor market described in this section.

[5] These categories are internally diverse. For instance, salaried workers includes a wide range of types and conditions of jobs, ranging from (frequently) low-paid agricultural work to higher-paid, non-farm occupations.

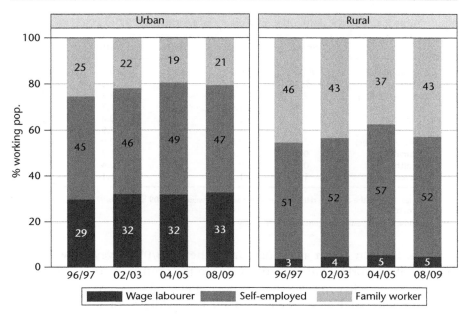

Figure 2.1. Distribution of workers, by type of employment and location, 1996/97 to 2008/09

Source: authors' calculations from household survey series.

sector broadly corresponds to the last two groups, we see that these are by far the most important sources of employment in both rural and urban areas. In rural areas, only 5 percent of jobs are plausibly located in the formal sector; this rises to a little over 30 percent in urban areas. At an aggregate level, the scarcity of wage work is startling. Only 12 percent of all workers report receiving a wage, of which almost 80 percent are men. As the figure shows, the proportion of workers found in each of these categories has remained stable over time, despite rapid economic growth. This indicates there has been no particular tendency for the economy to generate new jobs in the formal sector over the past fifteen years. As wage jobs remain a minority, it follows that job creation has occurred predominantly in the informal sector.

Trends in the sectoral allocation of labor similarly reveal only small movements over time. Table 2.4 indicates that agriculture remains the predominant occupation, employing over 80 percent of workers. In light of this it should be noted that there are very few large-scale commercial agricultural operations in Mozambique; this means that the vast majority of all agricultural work is undertaken by smallholders on family farms. According to data from agricultural surveys, in 2008 the average farm size was 1.5 hectares (DNEAP 2010). Employment in manufacturing has essentially stagnated in relative terms at under 4 percent of all workers, a trend which is not uniquely driven by rural

Table 2.4. Percent distribution of workers by sector, 1996/97 to 2008/09

	96/97	02/03	04/05	08/09	Δ
Agriculture	85.2	79.9	80.7	80.6	−4.6
Mining	0.5	0.5	0.2	0.2	−0.3
Manufacturing	2.7	3.6	2.8	2.7	0.0
Construction	1.4	1.6	1.4	1.7	0.3
Transport	1.1	1.1	0.8	0.8	−0.2
Commerce	4.0	7.3	7.8	7.9	4.0
Services (other)	2.7	2.8	2.9	2.9	0.2
Education	0.8	1.6	1.6	1.7	0.9
Health	0.5	0.5	0.5	0.4	−0.1
Government	1.2	1.2	1.2	1.1	−0.2

Notes: Δ gives the absolute difference in sector share between 2008/09 and 1996/97; each column sums to 100.

Source: authors' estimates from household survey series.

workers. Even in urban areas, data from the 2008/09 survey show that 46 percent of all workers are primarily active in the primary sector (agriculture), 42 percent are active in the tertiary sector, and only 11 percent in the secondary sector. In rural areas there is much less evidence of non-agricultural activities—around 95 percent of the workforce is active in the primary sector, a figure unchanged since 1996/97. Thus, the small relative shift that has occurred out of agriculture, shown in Table 2.4, can be understood primarily as an urban phenomenon, with the preferred destination sector being some form of services, typically (petty) commerce.

2.4 Connecting Jobs and Development

The previous section identified the main features of the jobs landscape in Mozambique. These include a preponderance of agricultural and informal jobs, high rates of underemployment (but low unemployment), and limited changes over time in the allocation of labor across sectors. Rapid rates of macroeconomic growth have not been associated with any significant transformation in how labor is deployed in production. At the same time, these findings do not illuminate the connection between jobs and key development outcomes. To see these more clearly, the framework of the Jobs WDR is helpful. The framework advocates that jobs connect to social and economic development along three distinct pathways, namely: (i) living standards, (ii) productivity, and (iii) social cohesion. "Good jobs for development" (hereafter, "good jobs") are those jobs that have the largest social spillovers in these dimensions, as opposed to merely generating higher private returns. It follows that an examination of how jobs have been associated with variations in these three dimensions over time can provide insight into the quality of jobs the economy has been generating, as well as relevant jobs policy challenges. The rest of this section considers each of these dimensions individually.

2.4.1 *Jobs and Living Standards*

The primary economic asset held by the poor is their labor power. Consequently, improvements in living standards are typically associated with jobs events, such as gaining access to more regular or better-paid employment (Inchauste et al. 2012). What, then, is the nature of the relationship between jobs and living standards in Mozambique? Although this may appear a straightforward question, an important theoretical concern is what kind of jobs classification is most informative. On the one hand, a tradition in labor economics has been to take the individual as the relevant unit of analysis, according to which the occupational sector or labor market position of workers is a natural focus (c.f., Tables 2.4 and 2.3 respectively).[6] On the other hand, traditions in other fields of development economics point to the household as the appropriate unit. This is motivated by the observation that a large share of production occurs within households (i.e., it is households rather than firms that organize economic production) and that the consumption decisions of households are typically not separable from production decisions (e.g., see de Janvry et al. 1991; Benjamin 1992; Le 2010).[7] Although a focus on households is most frequently applied in the analysis of rural production, the evidence presented in Section 2.3 indicates that household-based production is also a norm in urban areas of Mozambique. This is in keeping with evidence from other low-income sub-Saharan African countries that shows "non-farm household enterprises" are widespread and frequently operate as a crucial source of economic dynamism (e.g., Gulyani and Talukdar 2010; Fox and Pimhidzai 2011; Fox and Sohnesen 2012).[8] It also echoes the more established literature on rural livelihoods that points to non-farm income diversification as an important means to exit poverty (e.g., Ellis 2008; Haggblade et al. 2010).

To get a sense of the distinction between employing individuals or households as the analytical unit, Table 2.5 describes the link between living standards and jobs using both classifications. For the former, panel (a) classifies individuals by their broad occupational sector of employment; and panel (b) classifies the same individuals by their employment status. For households, a four-way classification of jobs portfolios is adopted based on the discussion in Jones and Tarp (2012). Shown in panel (c), this focuses on a central distinction between agricultural and

---

[6] For example, see Magnac (1991) and Günther and Launov (2012).
[7] One downside of focusing on households is that we miss intra-household distributional issues, as well as distinctive gender roles.
[8] These enterprises also have been called (non-farm) nano- or micro-enterprises elsewhere.

Table 2.5. Consumption poverty rates by employment sector, employment status, and household livelihood, urban and rural, 1996/97 to 2008/09

		Urban				Rural			
		96/97	02/03	08/09	Δ	96/97	02/03	08/09	Δ
(a)	*Employment sector:*								
	Primary	70.8	55.5	58.2	2.7	66.3	51.6	52.8	1.2
	Secondary	52.8	41.1	44.8	3.6	65.4	46.2	51.5	5.3
	Tertiary	48.5	37.7	36.2	−1.6	51.5	33.8	41.1	7.3
	All workers	60.7	46.8	47.4	0.5	65.9	50.7	52.2	1.6
(b)	*Employment status:*								
	Family worker	69.4	55.2	58.5	3.3	69.4	53.1	55.4	2.3
	Self-employed	63.8	49.2	48.2	−1.0	63.1	49.5	50.9	1.3
	Wage laborer	48.1	37.4	39.0	1.6	59.7	40.5	38.4	−2.1
	All workers	60.7	46.7	47.4	0.6	65.9	50.7	52.2	1.6
(c)	*Household livelihood category:*								
	Ag	79.4	64.1	65.0	0.9	72.4	58.7	59.0	0.3
	AgNf	64.9	53.9	57.5	3.7	69.7	47.3	52.3	5.1
	NfE	52.5	47.2	40.4	−6.8	34.8	51.2	58.3	7.1
	NfW	44.9	35.9	34.3	−1.5	36.2	41.2	25.5	−15.7
	All households	62.2	51.4	49.6	−1.8	71.4	55.6	57.1	1.5

Notes: Δ gives the percentage point difference in poverty between 2008/09 and 2002/03; panels (a) and (b) are calculated at the individual level (over all workers); panel (c) classifies working households as follows: "Ag" are exclusively reliant on agriculture, "AgNf" mix agriculture and non-farm activity, "NfE" operate exclusively in the non-farm sector and have some household production, and "NfW" are reliant on non-farm wage income; households with no active workers are excluded from panel (c).

Source: authors' estimates from household survey series.

non-agricultural activities (incomes), as well as the extent to which households are reliant on a single type of activity. The categories and corresponding abbreviations (used hereafter) are: "Ag"—households exclusively reliant on agriculture, the vast majority of which employ only family labor; "AgNf"—households that mix agriculture and any non-farm activity;[9] "NfE"—households that operate exclusively in the non-farm sector and at least partly undertake some household production (some but not all household members may be engaged in non-farm wage labor); and "NfW"—households exclusively engaged in non-farm wage labor. Living standards are measured according to consumption poverty; other metrics such as asset poverty yield similar results.

What do we learn from the table? On the one hand, there are large differences in poverty rates between alternative jobs. This holds regardless of the jobs classification or survey year considered. In particular, the average agricultural or unpaid family laborer (Ag household) is significantly more likely to be poor than the average wage worker (NfW household). Indeed, in 2008/09 around 60 percent of

---

[9] Note that the definition of non-farm activity includes commercial livestock farming—that is, selling either animal produce or live animals in the market. Strictly speaking this could be considered agriculture, but the data reveal that this is a higher-value activity, and it is therefore helpful to introduce this distinction to provide a more nuanced differentiation between households, particularly in rural areas.

rural households exclusively engaged in agriculture (Ag) were classified as poor compared to a little over 30 percent of urban wage-earning households (NfW). Considering that the majority of workers reside in rural areas, the persistence of high rates of poverty is clearly driven by (although is not entirely attributable to) jobs in the agricultural sector. (See Section 2.7 for further discussion.)

On the other hand, distinctions between jobs *within* the large informal sector do not emerge clearly from the individual-level jobs classifications. For instance, panel (b) suggests few differences in poverty rates between rural and urban jobs given their employment status. In contrast, the household-level categorization suggests more nuanced distinctions. Specifically, urban households with an agricultural income stream are typically worse off than rural households in the same categories. This underlines that urban agricultural activities are a kind of default strategy. Moreover, in urban areas, non-farm enterprise households appear qualitatively different to households with any agricultural activity. Not only do these NfE households achieve average poverty rates that are more comparable to households reliant on wage labor (NfW), but NfEs have also been more dynamic—achieving a 6.8 percentage point reduction in poverty since 2002/03. Thus, the informal sector must be considered heterogeneous, and wage work should not be considered uniquely capable of raising living standards.

Finally, differences in living standards between alternative jobs classifications are also substantially more acute when households are taken as the analytical unit. For instance, in 2008/09, the difference in average poverty rates between primary and tertiary rural workers was around 12 percentage points; however, the difference in rates between rural Ag and NfW households was 33 percentage points. This reflects the importance of income diversification for poor households, in accordance with the literature (Barrett et al. 2001), as well as the significance of differences in demographic structure. Neither of these features is captured when one retains a focus on individuals.

2.4.2 *Jobs and Productivity*

Although aggregate productivity and living standards are often positively correlated, the strength of this association can vary substantially within and between economic sectors. As such, if sectoral productivity growth is driven by a small number of isolated or capital-intensive firms, the average worker in these sectors may not benefit. For the same reason, the creation of new positions in higher-productivity enterprises and/or the reallocation of jobs from lower- to higher-productivity firms does not necessarily go hand-in-hand with productivity improvements. Policy-makers should also be sensitive to potential spillover effects from changes in productivity. Linkages between sectors and economies of agglomeration, both of which are typically associated with clusters of urban enterprises, can generate strong economic multiplier effects from relatively small innovations.

Analysis of productivity in Mozambique is hampered by a lack of comprehensive enterprise data. Although enterprise surveys have been conducted in Mozambique, these typically focus only on the (small) manufacturing sector, with limited coverage of informal firms. Nonetheless, evidence from these surveys indicates that the productivity of Mozambique's manufacturing firms is low compared to its low-income peers and geographical neighbors. This is revealed in Appendix Table 2A.1, which reports estimates of sales and value added (per worker) for a representative small food-processing firm. The point to note is that despite nominal wages being at a similar level to its peers, productivity in Mozambique measured in value-added terms is just over half that in other countries.

To get a broader picture of trends in productivity, aggregate data on sectoral value added (taken from national accounts) can be mapped to total hours worked, estimated from the microdata sources. This yields estimates of the mean value added contributed by one hour of labor service in different sectors. Aggregated to the primary/secondary/tertiary industrial sectoral classification previously applied, these estimates are depicted in Figure 2.2, stated in constant international dollars (per hour).[10]

Three main points can be highlighted. First, overall levels of productivity are low—on average Mozambican workers generate less than one dollar of value added per hour of work. Second, there are large productivity differences between sectors. The primary sector, dominated by agriculture, has by far the lowest labor productivity. Based on estimates from 2009, labor productivity is almost seven times higher in the tertiary sector and ten times higher in the secondary sector. This supports the evidence from Section 2.4.1 concerning significantly higher rates of poverty among (family) agricultural workers. Other sources of data further indicate that agricultural yields have remained stagnant over the post-conflict period. For instance, using data from successive agricultural surveys, DNEAP (2010) shows that crop productivity fell marginally over the period 2002–08, whether measured as calories produced per hectare under cultivation or as calories produced per head of rural population. This can be traced to the persistence of extremely rudimentary technologies (e.g., absence of fertilizers, lack of access to extension information, etc.), a reliance on rain-fed crops, and poor rural infrastructure. Indicative statistics in this regard are found in Appendix Table 2A.2.

Third, the gap between the primary and secondary sectors has widened over the period shown. This can be traced to the jump in productivity associated with a

---

[10] We arrive at international dollars by first converting from 2003 constant values in New Mozambican Meticais (US$1 = 23.7 Meticais) and then apply the PPP conversion factor of 2.5 from the World Bank's International Comparison Programme, yielding a PPP-adjusted exchange rate of 11.8 to the dollar. The resulting story from these figures is highly consistent with alternative labor productivity measures, such as those based on the numbers of individuals working in each sector.

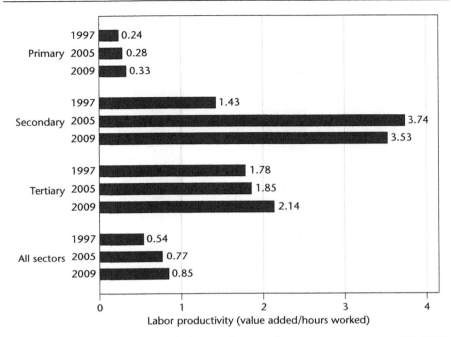

Figure 2.2. Estimates of average labor productivity by economic sector, 1997, 2005, and 2009

Notes: values are stated in real international dollars (2003 prices) per hour worked.

Source: authors' calculations from household survey series.

small number of capital-intensive "mega-projects" developed by foreign investors. However, as previously shown in Table 2.4, this jump has not been associated with a significant employment boost. The implication is that while this foreign investment has been good for growth, it has not had a major impact on jobs. At the same time, Figure 2.2 shows that productivity growth in the secondary sector has slowed over recent years. This further indicates these investments have been lumpy and isolated from the rest of the economy. In other words, there is no clear evidence of sustained positive dynamics in this sector.

2.4.3 Jobs and Social Cohesion

A vital aspect of jobs is their contribution to social cohesion. Where employment is scarce or vulnerable, social cohesion becomes frayed, particularly where there are sudden shocks to living standards. Over the past few years Mozambique has suffered isolated incidents of social unrest. The first occurred in February 2008, largely in response to rises in the cost of collective transportation linked to fuel prices. The second occurred in September 2010, also due

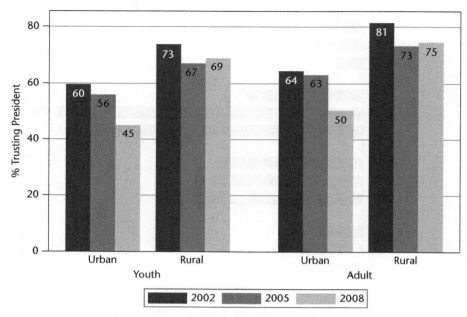

Figure 2.3. Share of rural/urban age cohorts trusting the President, 2002, 2005, and 2008

Notes: youth are defined as 18–24; adults are above 24 years old.

Source: authors' calculations from AfroBarometer surveys 2002, 2005, and 2008.

to rising utility, transport, and food prices. However, an underlying aspect of these events is persistent poverty and perceptions of rising inequality (Hanlon 2009).

What is the link between jobs and social cohesion in Mozambique? This is complex terrain, but some guidance comes from an analysis of the AfroBarometer opinion surveys, undertaken in Mozambique based on (small) nationally representative samples of the adult population in 2002, 2005, and 2008.[11] The results indicate that concerns around lack of access to employment are most acute among the urban youth. Almost 50 percent of all urban adults below 45 years of age consider a lack of jobs to be a problem; however, this view is shared by less than 30 percent of rural respondents. A closer look at the data shows rising rates of mistrust of high-level authorities among urban youth, particularly those who claim to receive some form of cash or wage remuneration.[12] This is shown in Figures 2.3 and 2.4, based on the perceived

---

[11] For an overview of the AfroBarometer surveys, see Mattes (2008); reference material can be found at http://www.afrobarometer.org.

[12] The particularly low level of trust in 2008 is consistent with tensions due to spikes in food prices that were most acute in 2008 and 2009 (Hanlon 2009).

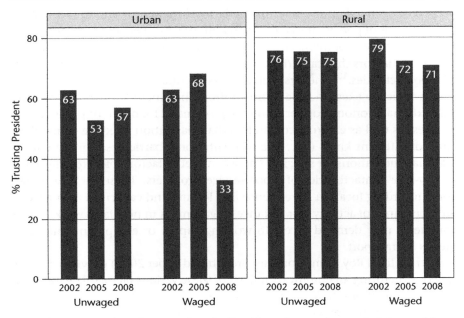

Figure 2.4. Share of workers trusting the President, by employment status and location, 2002, 2005, and 2008

Notes: "waged" refers to receiving some form of cash remuneration from sale of labor services.

Source: authors' calculations from AfroBarometer surveys 2002, 2005, and 2008.

degree of trust in the President as asked in the questionnaire. The implication is that the greatest threats to social cohesion are likely to emerge from younger urban cohorts, reflecting frustration from unmet expectations of finding stable, quality employment. Moreover, given that the lowest levels of trust are found among younger cohorts that receive some form of cash remuneration (Figure 2.4) and thus are relatively better off (see Section 2.4.1), it follows that there is not a perfect association between absolute poverty and weaker social cohesion. Thus, social cohesion represents a jobs challenge that is distinct from addressing concerns around living standards.

2.5 Determinants of Jobs Choices

2.5.1 *Methodology*

The previous sections provided a description of the characteristics of jobs in Mozambique and how they do (or often do not) connect to positive development processes. However, it remains to be explored what determines jobs choices at the household level. Understanding these factors is required to deepen our general understanding of jobs in Mozambique and to identify the specific kinds of policy interventions that may be most effective in supporting good jobs for development. In this regard it is helpful to distinguish between two sets of factors that can drive access to and participation in different kinds of labor activities.[13] The first refers to (structural) conditions over which agents typically exercise little or no control. They include the range of available external economic opportunities (e.g., demand for different products and services) as well as external constraints that may ration effective demand for labor of different kinds (e.g., due to institutional barriers, screening effects, seasonal fluctuations, or shocks). The second set of factors refers to internal or supply-side characteristics of labor service providers. These include preferences regarding location of residence and leisure, and capacities to engage in different kinds of activity. For instance, engagement in non-farm work such as commerce may demand access to working capital or equipment, such as a means of transport.

A generalized Roy framework (see French and Taber 2011) provides a useful way of structuring an empirical analysis of these various factors. The intuition is that agents (households) act to maximize expected utility given their relevant characteristics, external opportunities, and constraints. Thus, we observe that an agent supplies labor to activity (job) j when the utility expected from j is no lower than the utility expected from engaging in all other possible activities. Utility is an abstract concept that cannot be measured directly; even so, it can be treated as a latent variable from which a probability model can be derived and as such is amenable to econometric estimation (e.g., see Bourguignon et al. 2007).

Box 2.1 describes the specific methods used to implement this general approach and Appendix Table 2A.3 summarizes the variables employed to implement the model (equation (2.1)). Our choice of these is determined by information that is consistently available from the household survey series. For instance, we include a set of dummy variables that capture the durable productive assets owned by the household. These are ownership of (access to) agricultural land for crops or other forms of cultivation, livestock, means of transport, and communications technology (telephone, radio, TV are used). Human capital at the household level is captured by the (log.) number of workers, the share of workers with different levels of education, and the age and literacy of the household head. Household preferences are reflected through various aspects of the household's demographic structure, such as the percentage of workers who are young men.

---

[13] This follows an established literature. See, for example, Cook (1999); Verme (2000); Barrett et al. (2001); Haggblade et al. (2010).

Box 2.1 METHODOLOGY TO EVALUATE DETERMINANTS OF CHOSEN HOUSEHOLD JOBS PORTFOLIO

We assume that households are the relevant decision-making units (see Section 2.4.1). Thus, individual jobs choices are embedded within (and thus subject to) prior household-level labor-allocation decisions. For simplicity, we also presume that the four-way classification of household jobs portfolios (Ag, AgNf, NfE, NfW) is informative and can be applied to rural and urban areas separately. In order to model the determinants of entry into these alternative portfolios, a linear specification of latent utility is assumed. Ignoring household-specific indexes, for each portfolio ($j \in P$) this is given by:

$$Y_j^* = x'a_j + z'\beta_j + v'\gamma_j + \eta_j \tag{2.1}$$

where x is a vector of household characteristics (such as its demographic composition), z is a vector of household productive assets (capacities)—including human and physical capital endowments—and v is a vector of variables reflecting proxies for external labor market conditions. Under the assumption that $\forall j \in P$ each respective η_j is normal and identically Gumbel distributed, the above specification can be estimated via a multinomial logit model, which gives estimates of the contribution of these variables to the overall probability of observing a given household in each portfolio.

With respect to the vector of proxies for local conditions, three subsets of measures are included. The first seeks to capture differences in local productive conditions, such as infrastructure and transaction costs. To do so, we use the median degree of access to electricity, communications technology, and other public goods at the level of the primary sampling unit (typically a village). The second set seeks to capture the diversity and "thickness" of the local labor market, including the availability of opportunities across the jobs portfolios we have defined. To do so, we calculate the proportion of households engaged in each of the four portfolios at the regional level. These averages are included directly in the specification (with the Ag portfolio excluded to avoid collinearity). From these average shares we also construct a Herfindahl concentration index (Rhoades 1993), which takes a value of 1 if all households in the region adopt the same portfolio. This can be read as a metric of the degree of labor market specialization in the region where the household resides. The third set is dummy variables for broad geographical regions and dummy variables for each survey year (in all cases excluding a base category). These capture wider (unspecified) fixed effects such as those due to localized economic shocks (positive or negative).

2.5.2 Results

The model described in the previous subsection is run separately for rural and urban households, based on data from both the 2002/03 and 2008/09 surveys.

These surveys are not linked, meaning that only a static cross-sectional analysis is possible. The results of the estimation are summarized in Appendix Table 2A.4, which reports average marginal effects for a selection of the principal variables.[14] Four main results can be highlighted. First, demographic variables affect the propensity to select each of the portfolios, but in a relatively complex way. In both urban and rural areas, larger households are more likely to engage in some non-agricultural work. However, households that are uniquely reliant on wage labor tend to have smaller numbers of workers active in the household. There is also a clear tendency for males to seek non-farm work, and young men residing in urban areas are least likely to be active in agriculture. Similarly, and particularly in urban areas, wage work appears to be strongly skewed towards households dominated by male workers.

Second, household capacities affect the portfolio choice propensities in different ways. The negative direction of the vast majority of marginal effects for the pure agriculture portfolio (Ag) indicates that few factors appear to attract households into this portfolio in the sense of making it a positive choice. Households with higher capacities or endowments (e.g., more education or economic assets) are significantly less likely to be exclusively reliant on agricultural jobs. Both rural and urban households containing workers with at least a complete primary education are more likely to adopt non-farm jobs (AgNf or NfW). Particularly with regard to wage work, this suggests that a complete primary education operates as a minimum threshold to enter certain (modern) jobs. In urban areas, however, even an incomplete primary education (compared to none) is associated with a higher propensity to adopt the non-farm agricultural portfolio (AgNf), underlining that an Ag urban portfolio is very much a residual choice. On the other hand, adoption of the household enterprise portfolio (NfE) is not significantly driven by differences in education. A plausible explanation is that this portfolio comprises households that have proactively adopted this strategy as well as others that do so by default (e.g., having no access to productive land).

Third, proxies for local labor market conditions (see Appendix Table 2A.3) are statistically significant, indicating that external constraints do matter. The proportion of households engaged in non-farm portfolios, which captures the availability of outside opportunities, is negatively associated with the propensity to choose a pure agriculture portfolio, especially in urban areas. For example, a 10 percentage point increase in the proportion of urban households engaged in a non-farm enterprise reduces a given household's propensity to adopt the Ag portfolio by around 8 percentage points. Again this confirms that the Ag portfolio is predominantly a residual choice, driven by low levels of asset accumulation and scarce outside options. The choice of

---

[14] Full details are available on request from the authors.

an exclusively wage jobs portfolio, on the other hand, is strongly and positively associated with the prevalence of these types of jobs in the same region. This points to potential spillovers from the emergence of thicker labor markets, characterized by higher levels of demand and supply of labor of different types, which can enable a more efficient matching of workers to enterprises (Duranton and Puga 2004).

The reporting of marginal effects as per Appendix Table 2A.4 is useful; in particular, it reveals broad patterns in the direction and magnitude of individual variables (holding others constant) on the propensity to choose different jobs portfolios. Even so, it has limitations. Due to the nonlinear nature of the underlying econometric model, the predicted effect of a marginal change in a single variable varies according to each household's observed value of the same variable. Since there are systematic differences in the characteristics of households in different portfolios, (average) marginal effects could be calculated over multiple groups of households, potentially yielding quite different interpretations.[15] Furthermore, as in all regression models, marginal effects do not provide guidance as to the relative importance of different factors in the context of the overall model. In the present case the latter information would be especially useful to indicate which groups of factors are most (least) important in explaining observed jobs choices.

Table 2.6 therefore presents measures of the relative importance of different sets of variables (see Appendix Table 2A.3). Following the discussion

Table 2.6. Relative importance of variables in explaining households' jobs choices

	Variable set	Ag	AgNf	NfE	NfW	All
				Household type		
Urban	Demographic chars.	15.7	10.3	1.7	15.2	10.2
	Human capital	19.3	6.7	4.7	26.8	13.3
	Physical capital	21.6	5.4	24.7	0.0	12.5
	External	21.7	8.8	8.7	0.0	9.5
	Overall fit (%)	70.1	57.9	62.0	60.8	62.8
Rural	Demographic	15.4	1.0	0.2	2.6	8.4
	Human capital	14.6	3.3	0.7	28.7	9.3
	Physical capital	11.0	10.9	14.4	12.3	9.6
	External	15.6	1.0	9.5	5.9	8.8
	Overall fit (%)	92.0	33.2	29.4	63.2	72.0

Notes: metric of relative importance is the average percentage point change in model goodness-of-fit when factors are included first or last; the full model goodness-of-fit, defined as the share of households correctly allocated by the model to the observed portfolio, is given by the "overall fit" row; see Section 2.5.1 for model description; see Appendix Table 2A.3 for definition of variable sets.

Source: authors' estimates from household survey series.

[15] There are other ways to calculate marginal effects, but they suffer from similar problems. For a discussion of how marginal effects are calculated in probability models, see Bartus (2005).

in Grömping (2006), one way to assess this is to evaluate the change in model goodness-of-fit when a set of regressors is entered (together). Presuming there is some correlation between different sets of variables, as almost always occurs in practice, this measure will depend on which other variables have already been entered in the model. To get around this, we take the average change in the model's goodness-of-fit based on: (i) when a given set of variables enters the model first; and (ii) when the same set enters last. Respectively, these give the upper and lower bound on the relative importance of the given set of variables. The overall goodness-of-fit for the model is calculated for each jobs portfolio separately as the share of households that are correctly allocated to the portfolio in which they are observed. Thus, if the model indicates that portfolio Ag is given the highest predicted probability for a given household, then the prediction is deemed correct only if the household was indeed observed to have chosen that portfolio. When a set of variables is entered first, relative importance is based on the corresponding goodness-of-fit compared to a naïve model. When the set is entered last, relative importance is measured as the difference in goodness-of-fit between the full model and the model excluding the same set of variables.

The findings of Table 2.6 are complementary to the marginal effects analysis. Five results merit comment. First, according to the above definition, the overall model goodness-of-fit is relatively strong in urban and rural areas, where 63 percent and 72 percent of households are allocated to their observed portfolio respectively (compared to around 25 percent and 50 percent based on a naïve model). Second, for exclusively agricultural households (Ag), no single set of factors dominates. One interpretation is that for these households, the explanatory variables are strongly associated with one another, meaning that once any one set of factors enters the model, other factors provide little new information. This would arise where poverty traps are in operation, such as the coexistence of very low levels of human and productive capital. Third, lack of access to physical capital is a critical impediment to pursuing non-farm activities. In rural areas, these factors are the most important for choosing the AgNf and NfE portfolios. In urban areas, access to physical capital is most important for households to operate a non-farm enterprise. Fourth, human capital is an overriding factor explaining which households select a pure wage labor portfolio (NfW). Fifth, in the majority of cases external factors are material. The primary exception is for those that have already gained access to exclusive wage portfolios in urban areas. Recall that the measure of importance is based on the share of households correctly allocated to their observed portfolio. Thus, the fact that external factors exhibit a very low relative importance for actually observed NfW households indicates that these factors do not "pull" households into this choice but rather limit other households from doing so. This would be consistent with rationed access to wage jobs due to low effective demand.

2.5.3 Simulations

A final step considers what would happen to jobs choices if different factors, such as household endowments, were to improve. In doing so, we hold fixed the estimated model parameters, which among other things implies that expected returns to alternative choices remain constant. This is not intended to be especially realistic, but simply helps clarify some of the main policy implications of the analysis. Following the simulation-type approaches employed elsewhere (e.g., Abowd and Killingsworth 1984), we consider how each household's "preferred" jobs portfolio choice varies in response to simulated exogenous changes in the levels of the various explanatory variables. Given the welfare ordering of the portfolios (see Section 2.4.1), we focus here only on the implications of exogenous improvements for the Ag and AgNf households. To do so, for a simulation of changes in response to a given variable x, we hypothesize that each household observed in either of these portfolios faces the new value:

$$x_{ij}^* = \text{Max}(x_{ij}\bar{x}_k + \Phi_{xk}) \qquad (2.2)$$

where $\bar{x}_k$ indicates the mean value of x faced by the NfE and NfW portfolios, S_{x_k} is its standard deviation, and Φ is a random draw from a standard normal distribution. (A minimum function is imposed for those variables where increased values are associated with a higher propensity to access non-farm portfolios.) Values observed for households in either of the two non-agricultural portfolios are maintained fixed throughout. Also, as before, urban and rural households are treated separately.

The results of the simulations are reported in Table 2.7. Again, we do not consider changes in variables one by one, but alter sets of variables simultaneously. Thus, for each variable set, the cells report the predicted absolute change in the proportion of households expected to select a given portfolio relative to the baseline model (estimated in the previous subsection) when these factors are exogenously changed. For instance, if urban Ag and AgNf households came to face approximately similar external conditions to the two non-agricultural portfolios, we would expect an 18 percentage point reduction (from 27.3 percent in the baseline model) in the share of households adopting the Ag portfolio, a 3.4 percentage point increase in the share of households adopting the AgNf portfolio, and a further 8.4 and 6.2 percentage point increase in the share of households adopting the NfE and NfW portfolios respectively. These results not only emphasize that weak demand conditions for wage jobs effectively "push" households into alternative coping strategies, but they also highlight that the size of these effects is substantial in economic terms.

Table 2.7. Simulated effects on job choices of changes in job-choice factors, by household type

		Household type			
	Factors simulated	Ag	AgNf	NfE	NfW
Urban	Demographic chars.	−5.1	−3.0	4.6	3.5
	Human capital	−4.4	−2.2	0.7	5.9
	Physical capital	−3.1	4.5	−1.4	0.0
	External	−18.0	3.4	8.4	6.2
	All factors	−23.3	−16.6	4.6	35.3
Rural	Demographic chars.	−4.4	2.2	2.1	0.1
	Human capital	−6.8	7.1	0.1	−0.4
	Physical capital	−17.3	11.4	6.0	−0.1
	External	−3.1	0.2	1.1	1.8
	All factors	−44.5	24.6	14.8	5.1
Urban	Baseline model	27.3	25.4	29.9	17.5
Rural		78.6	13.8	6.3	1.3

Notes: cells report the predicted absolute percentage point change in the proportion of households expected to select a given portfolio relative to the baseline model for exogenous simulated improvements in the group of factors indicated by the row title (holding others constant); predicted allocations under the baseline model are reported in the final two rows (as percent of all households); the sum of changes across all households sums to zero (for each simulation); "all factors" indicates simulated exogenous improvements in all factors simultaneously.

Source: authors' estimates from household survey series.

The simulations further underscore the importance of physical capital accumulation to enable the rural poor to gain access to non-farm activities. However, the role of improvements to human capital is more ambiguous. On the one hand, where rural Ag households receive an exogenous boost to their human capital, a material shift out of the Ag portfolio (−6.8 points) into the AgNf portfolio (+7.1 points) is predicted. This reveals that a lack of education (or general skills) constitutes a barrier to realizing non-farm incomes. Even so, changes in human capital alone are insufficient to permit households to adopt the wage labor portfolio, thereby indicating that complementary factors (e.g., demographic and external) play a crucial role. Indeed, when all factors are simulated (improved) together, denoted by the row "All factors," the expected shift into the NfW portfolio is much larger than the sum of the set-specific simulations.

The final point to consider is that all the simulations indicate that households (on average) would prefer to shift out of exclusive agricultural work. On the one hand, this reinforces the status of the Ag portfolio as a residual or passive choice for many households, fundamentally reflecting a generalized condition of low agricultural returns. However, even if widening opportunities to non-farm activities is sensible (see Section 2.6), it is helpful to reflect on what actually would be required to achieve any significant decline in agricultural work as a share of all jobs. The magnitude of the exogenous improvements simulated under Table 2.7 is large, and could not be achieved over anything short of a very long time horizon across the population. For instance, the human capital simulation imposes an exogenous increase in the share of current Ag households with at least a complete primary schooling from 16 percent to 36 percent of the workforce, excluding population growth. Also, from a demographic perspective the simulations impose a reduction in the average number of workers per household, which is consistent with what we see among exclusive wage earners. Both of these simulations therefore implicitly demand that some labor is released from agriculture (e.g., to study), a realistic prior condition for which would be an increase in per worker agricultural productivity.

2.6 Policy Implications

2.6.1 *What are Good Jobs for Development in Mozambique?*

Drawing the analysis together, we can now address what are likely to constitute good jobs for development in Mozambique. Following Section 2.4, these jobs refer to activities that yield the highest payoffs across society in terms of living standards, productivity growth, and social cohesion. This chapter has frequently highlighted the complex and significant nature of jobs challenges surrounding smallholder agriculture. In particular, Section 2.5 highlighted that households often exclusively engage in agriculture as a default strategy, reflecting a low level of accumulation of physical and human capital as well as external demand constraints. A superficial reading of this evidence is that good jobs (from both an individual and social perspective) are uniquely located in non-farm sectors. We do not believe this interpretation is correct. As the jobs simulations show, rural households are more able to diversify their portfolio of jobs when they accumulate physical capital. This is only likely to occur on a significant scale if agricultural productivity is enhanced, permitting farmers to consistently realize a surplus. Moreover, experiences of other developing economies, such as Vietnam (de Janvry and Sadoulet 2010), point to the essential supportive role that successful agricultural development has played. This stems from the strong positive multiplier effects typically associated with agricultural productivity growth, which in turn can promote job creation in other sectors and reinforce social cohesion. Promoting good jobs within the agriculture sector is therefore vital to address poverty "where it is" and promote a more vibrant rural economy that has positive spillovers to other sectors.

Simple demographic projections give added force to this argument. It is reasonable to expect that changes in rural endowments and external conditions will be achieved gradually, implying that agriculture will remain a

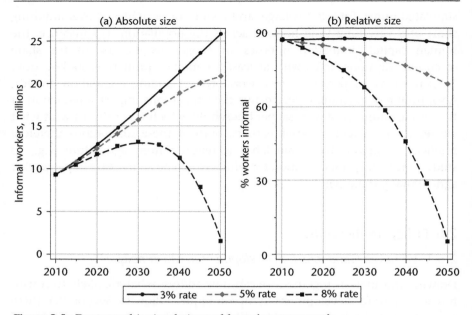

Figure 2.5. Demographic simulations of formal sector growth

Notes: the figure shows relative and absolute projected size of the informal sector (non-wage employment) based on hypothetical annual growth rates of wage employment; underlying demographic projections are based on 2012 UN baseline forecasts (see Jones and Tarp 2012).

Source: authors' calculations.

predominant activity even under rapid (rural) growth and development scenarios. Figure 2.5 takes the baseline UN population projections for Mozambique and estimates the absolute and relative size of the informal sector (i.e., principally agriculture) under alternative hypothetical rates of growth in the number of available formal employment positions. The assumption is that the informal sector will absorb all residual new entrants to the labor market; thus, if the size of the formal (wage) sector remained stagnant in absolute terms, then the informal sector is assumed to absorb all growth in the workforce. Historically, the annual growth rate of the formal sector has been positive but below 5 percent, and appears to have slowed to around 3 percent over the most recent period (2002/03–2008/09), consistent with a stagnant relative size of the formal sector in total employment. Figure 2.5 shows that if these historically observed growth rates continue, then the informal sector will grow rapidly in absolute terms. In a "worst case" scenario of 3 percent growth, the informal sector doubles in size in about twenty-five years (2010–35); at the (hardly pessimistic) 5 percent growth rate, the informal sector would double its present size in forty years (2010–50) and would still be growing in 2050. The optimistic scenario of an 8 percent sustained growth rate in formal wage employment would not lead to an immediate decline in the absolute size of the informal sector; however, over the simulated time frame it would be sufficient to largely formalize the productive economy. The fundamental implication is that the vast majority of all new jobs will be created in the informal sector over at least a generation. It is therefore unrealistic to presume that any feasible solution to the present set of jobs challenges lies uniquely in creating modern wage-sector jobs, to the exclusion of rural agriculture.

Despite the above, given the present very low level of agricultural productivity, even large improvements in that sector are unlikely to substantially raise aggregate levels of productivity. Moreover, a growing share of the population resides in urban areas where aspirations, particularly among youth, do not coincide with exclusive agricultural labor. This suggests that while there is scope to achieve transformation in the agricultural sector, agriculture cannot be the sole focus of jobs-based policy initiatives. The analysis of Sections 2.4 and 2.5 indicated that the urban non-farm informal sector is heterogeneous and that non-farm household enterprises have operated as a crucial means to improve living standards, particularly for households with some skills and productive assets to hand. It is also evident that significant hurdles must be overcome for households to become reliant on wage income. In particular, a complete primary education can be considered a minimum skills threshold to enter wage employment. This threshold is not met by a majority of current workers and rates of primary school completion (as opposed to enrolment) remain low in Mozambique, being less than 50 percent in some regions. Indeed, as the jobs simulations show, improvements in external (demand) conditions may be sufficient to induce households to set up a non-farm enterprise but insufficient to assure access to formal employment. Thus, as in many other low-income sub-Saharan African countries (Fox and Sohnesen 2012), the jobs challenge is to support and nurture dynamic non-farm household enterprises as engines for growth rather than default coping strategies.

Finally, although the informal sector will remain a key source of jobs over the medium term at least, formal jobs cannot be ignored. A stylized fact of successful economic development is structural transformation of the labor market, whereby workers move out of agriculture and into higher productivity (manufacturing) industries (e.g., see Rodrik 2007; Page 2012a). In Mozambique, we have seen that wage employment, much of which is in the formal sector, is associated with significantly higher living standards. However, despite encouraging macroeconomic performance, formal employment growth remains tepid and structural transformation elusive.[16] This appears to be a

---

[16] Other authors (e.g., Cunguara et al. 2011; Page 2012b) provide additional evidence in this regard. It should also be noted that Mozambique is hardly exceptional. McMillan and Rodrik (2012) argue that employment changes observed in Africa and Latin America have broadly been

source of frustration that has boiled over into isolated bouts of violent discontent. Policy attention to formal sector employment is recommended for other reasons. Midstream and downstream operations linked to the natural resource sectors, as well as general service activities, represent significant potential opportunities for local firms. However, these firms must meet minimum criteria, including being formally registered. Similarly, due to their association with foreign investment and know-how, the formal sector is a main locus of higher value-added activities and aggregate productivity expansion. These jobs therefore are essential for long-term growth, especially in the secondary and tertiary sectors. However, given the scale of the jobs challenge facing Mozambique, it is desirable that incentives are created to promote labor- as opposed to capital-intensive enterprise growth. Moreover, for the dual reasons that domestic demand is limited by the size of the market and that export industries have enhanced incentives to reach the technological frontier, export-oriented activities should be given specific support.[17]

2.6.2 Recommendations

Moving from the reporting of research findings to the making of specific policy recommendations is rarely straightforward. At an overall level, however, a primary objective must be to leverage forthcoming natural resource revenues to stimulate a pro-jobs structural transformation of the economy. A focus on creating good jobs for development is fundamental precisely because of the economic shift Mozambique is now starting to experience toward capital-intensive natural resource extraction.[18] Both international and local experience show that these mega-projects generate few sustained employment posts (Arndt and Tarp 2009; Rosenfeld 2012) and, in the absence of countervailing policy measures, tend to appreciate the real exchange rate.[19] The risk is that such projects will shift economic incentives (and policy attention) away from smallholders toward activities that are intensive in

growth reducing, because labor has not moved from lower- toward higher-productivity sectors, but rather has moved from low-productivity rural agriculture to even lower-productivity urban activities (or unemployment), contributing no growth gain on aggregate. See also Page (2012a).

[17] See Feder (1983); Alvarez and López (2008) for further reasons to explicitly support the export sector.

[18] A full discussion of the jobs challenges associated with future resource investment scenarios is beyond the scope of this chapter. It should be pointed out, however, that the precise scale and timing of any resource boom in Mozambique remains largely speculative, especially in the current environment of low commodity prices. As of April 2016, no final investment decisions have been made to develop natural gas fields. Also, existing investors in coal extraction are facing significant challenges due to infrastructure constraints. Rio Tinto, in particular, has sold its operations after incurring large losses.

[19] This is shown by evidence of employment generated by foreign investment projects in Mozambique over the past ten years. Rosenfeld (2012), for instance, estimates that massive investments in the coal sector will generate around 7,500 jobs for Mozambicans over the long run.

capital and imports, making transformation of the rural sector more difficult to achieve. The opportunity of a natural resources-led boom, however, is that it may loosen immediate budget constraints and place economic governance firmly in the hands of the government. Thus, there may be greater financial and policy space to make large, long-term, credible public investments and policy commitments.

The previous section indicated that good jobs in Mozambique include work in high(er)-productivity smallholder agriculture, complementary non-farm rural activities, jobs in dynamic non-farm enterprises, and labor-intensive modern enterprises linked to the global economy. To put these more concretely, they translate into three main complementary policy objectives, namely to: (i) achieve a step-increase in agricultural productivity across the rural sector (comprising both small family farms and larger commercial operations); (ii) foster the non-farm informal sector as a source of entrepreneurship and growth; and (iii) aggressively support the expansion of labor-intensive secondary and tertiary industries with export potential.

Taking each objective in turn, some more specific recommendations can be made. A starting point for agriculture is to recognize previous failings in policy coherence and implementation. Greater clarity and focus is required to ensure that the needs of both smallholders and larger commercial investors are addressed. A specific area for action is to promote positive and mutually beneficial interactions between existing local smallholders and external investors. Past experiences in smallholder outgrower (contract farming) schemes in cash crops in Mozambique, such as with tobacco, cotton, and sugar, suggest that a combination of foreign investment (bringing know-how, provision of inputs, and access to markets) with local land and labor can be highly productive (Benfica et al. 2002; Benfica 2007; Boughton et al. 2007). However, despite a surge of external interest in land acquisitions and instances of land conflicts, there is no explicit set of incentives or regulatory regime which proactively supports and protects the development of such schemes.

In addition to the above, we would suggest further measures to support agriculture. Following the evidence of Section 2.5 that external conditions are material, the first is to undertake large-scale investments in rural infrastructure, including water storage, water management (e.g., irrigation), transport, and electrification; these are fundamental to stimulate productive value chains (in new and old crops) and have been frequently identified as key constraints at the local level (Section 2.5). Indeed, Arndt et al. (2012a) argue that the absence of rural infrastructure, among other things, means that agricultural multipliers in Mozambique have been lower than those in Vietnam. Second, recognizing the present scarcity of access to extension services and improved inputs in the smallholder rural sector (Arndt et al. 2007;

Cunguara and Moder 2011), the government must draw in private sector energy and creativity, not least to allow a sustainable exit from support of the sector over the longer term. Targeted public–private partnerships (PPPs) (e.g., using performance-based subsidies) to deliver open pollinated high-yielding seed varieties represent just one example of a range of possible schemes that are likely to bring large welfare gains at relatively low cost. The policy challenge is to design appropriate economic governance structures for such PPPs in agriculture, which reward genuine outcomes while recognizing that these initiatives are inherently risky and some will fail.[20] Third, we recommend interventions on the demand side to loosen cash constraints and open up opportunities for diversification into small-scale processing and non-farm activities. Interventions in these areas, which may include expansion of rural financial services and products, are complex. Further research and rigorous evaluation of potential interventions is recommended.

What can be done to stimulate dynamic non-farm household enterprises? Here the evidence base is weak. This reflects the fact that these activities have more often been seen as a problem for the formal sector. Aside from a concern to promote enterprise formalization and expand access to banking services, public policy has largely been silent on how this sector (which remains distinct from small- and medium-sized enterprises) can be nurtured. Ahlers et al.'s (2013) case study of informal providers of water connections in Maputo provides a case in point. The authors show that rather than provide a supportive and facilitative regulatory framework, and perhaps enhanced access to training and finance, government policy has been to treat them as a temporary nuisance to be rendered obsolete by existing utility companies (whose coverage is limited). The point is that a more coherent strategy to address and nurture "informal space" is warranted. As Krause et al. (2010) argue, this requires smart regulation and committed implementation, not just a lower legal regulatory burden (see also Altenburg and von Drachenfels 2008).

Evidence from this chapter and elsewhere (e.g., Fox and Kweka 2011; Fox and Sohnesen 2012) indicates a few other areas that should be given attention. First, basic business inputs remain costly. Despite recent improvements, low-income users of pre-paid mobile phones in Mozambique face costs that are more than three times those found in Ethiopia and Kenya, ranking Mozambique the 25th most expensive country out of 46 in sub-Saharan Africa (ICT Africa 2012). Access to land and housing is also extremely problematic (Allen et al. 2010). This reflects a large number of factors including highly

---

[20] For further discussion of the potential role of these vehicles in the agricultural sector in Africa, see Poulton and Macartney (2012).

complex and inefficient ownership and transfer rules. These force the majority of transactions into a non-transparent black market and severely limit access to finance for all but the largest formal enterprises. The latter also speaks to the need for enhanced and effective urban planning, which is increasingly critical in Maputo where congestion, crime, and general living costs have increased notably over recent years (e.g., see Paulo et al. 2008).

With respect to how export-oriented manufacturing might be stimulated, a range of sensible suggestions can be found in Page (2012b). A key recommendation is to pursue spatial industrial policy, which refers to measures that stimulate the agglomeration of specific types of industries and tasks in particular geographical areas. This goes beyond a generic "Doing Business" agenda, which tends to focus on the formal content of regulations, but rather places emphasis on putting in the hard and soft infrastructure necessary for the private sector to compete at an international level. Thus, a leap forward in logistics capacity, transport links, customs administration, and reliability of core public services such as electricity and water in specific areas are required.

Four other areas merit attention. In light of the importance of human capital in gaining access to wage employment, Mozambique must not falter in its support for education at all levels. This will involve reducing dropout rates, enhancing quality, and extending technical education as a meaningful alternative to (standard) secondary schools. Indeed, significant investments in technical skills are vital to ensure that firms can access a sufficiently large pool of competent workers that are able to quickly add value in industrial occupations. Second, mechanisms to quality-certify and coordinate small- and medium-sized firms would help to effectively link them to larger firms, particularly, but not exclusively, in the natural resources sector. These are core public goods that no individual operator has any interest in supplying. Third, the current tax system remains overly complex and riddled with tax exemptions, particularly for capital investments, which tend to favor large (foreign) firms relative to smaller local operators (Byiers et al. 2010). The greater budget space that should slowly emerge from exploration of natural resources could be leveraged to level the tax playing field and strengthen the social compact between public authorities and small local firms.[21]

---

[21] Rosenfeld (2012) provides some estimates of the revenue implications of recent coal mining investments. Assuming infrastructure constraints are overcome and global prices remain buoyant, he suggests the government could receive around US$12 billion in revenues from now to 2030. If developed, large reserves of natural gas would yield even larger revenues over the much longer term.

2.7 Conclusions

Mozambique faces a number of acute jobs challenges. Impressive aggregate economic growth over the past twenty years has not been accompanied by sustained, rapid improvements in welfare at the household level. The majority of Mozambicans earn a living from smallholder agriculture, and the low productivity of these activities is a main reason why absolute poverty is widespread. Population growth remains high, which means that over the medium term more than 300,000 individuals will enter the labor market each year, likely increasing to 500,000 new entrants by 2025. Additionally, Mozambique's economic structure is shifting, but in a direction that may not be favorable toward job creation. Capital-intensive natural resource extraction is becoming the predominant target of investment and export growth. As is well known, this entails large socio-economic risks and must be carefully managed to avoid "resource curse" effects; in particular, that of constricting growth in other sectors of the economy.

In light of these challenges, this chapter took a close look at the Mozambican labor market. Employing survey microdata as our primary evidence base, the analysis proceeded in three main steps. First, we reviewed the broad contours of the labor market, yielding a descriptive profile of how Mozambique works and how jobs have evolved over the post-war period. This painted a fairly gloomy picture; although similar characteristics are found in other low-income African countries (e.g., see African Development Bank 2012). There is little evidence of a positive process of transformation in the jobs landscape. Underemployment is rife and a majority of Mozambicans continue to work in smallholder agriculture or the urban informal sector.

Second, drawing on the framework of the Jobs WDR, we analyzed links between jobs and development outcomes in three key domains: living standards, productivity, and social cohesion. This revealed that levels of labor productivity are generally low, and that they also are highly divergent across sectors. Moreover, different household jobs portfolios (livelihood strategies) are associated with marked differences in average living standards. Thus, a fundamental jobs challenge was identified—namely, stagnant productivity in the agricultural sector (in terms of caloric production per person), which is linked to very limited access to improved inputs and technologies (e.g., less than 5 percent of farms use fertilizer or pesticide). This accounts for much of the disconnect between (strong) aggregate growth and (slow) poverty reduction. However, distinct challenges were also noted in the urban sector, particularly among younger cohorts, where the failure to generate higher quality (modern) jobs is a source of rising frustration.

Third, we went beyond an identification of jobs challenges and undertook an econometric analysis of factors that determine household jobs choices.

This represents an important contribution to the Jobs WDR framework. Our findings indicated that agricultural activities, in both rural and urban areas, are frequently a default rather than proactive choice, driven by low household endowments and weak local demand while also reflecting their lower productivity. Gaining access to non-farm jobs, however, depends on various factors including external conditions, accumulation of economic assets by the household, and, in the case of wage work, surpassing a minimum education threshold (completed primary education).

Overall, our analysis of the Mozambican labor market points to three jobs priorities. These cover different sectors precisely because the jobs challenges are pervasive and actions in one sector are unlikely to be sufficient. The first priority is to foster the non-farm informal sector as a source of dynamism and entrepreneurship. Our analysis showed that many non-farm jobs offer living standards on a par with formal wage employment—that is, good jobs are not just in the formal sector. However, the Mozambican government currently tends to see these informal activities as a source of unhealthy competition for the formal sector. Thus, they face serious barriers to expansion and access to finance.

Second, we recommend that government aggressively supports the growth of labor-intensive secondary and tertiary industries with export potential. These are essential to aggregate productivity expansion and longer-term growth. Spatial industrial policy and leveraging of natural resource revenues to substantially improve infrastructure and logistics services along key value chains need to be given attention.

Third, and most importantly, low levels of agricultural productivity must be addressed. The rationale here is simple: to make substantial progress on poverty reduction, progress must be made in transforming agricultural jobs. This is urgent. Given the sheer weight of this sector in the volume of employment and the limited endowments of these households, only over the very long term is it reasonable to expect large numbers of existing (or future) rural households to accumulate sufficient assets to lift themselves into non-farm work and out of poverty. Thus, rather than agriculture being a last-resort activity, higher rates of productivity should act as a positive incentive to engage in the sector and also should deliver benefits to other sectors, both via multiplier-type effects and through competitive food prices.

In sum, jobs challenges in Mozambique are acute. While there are clear opportunities to make progress, policy-makers must take linkages between sectors into account. The point is that politically visible jobs challenges in the urban sector are unlikely to be uniquely solved via urban policy interventions. For Mozambique it is difficult to envisage a developmental trajectory that addresses jobs challenges without achieving significant increases in agricultural productivity.

Appendix 2A: Additional Tables

Table 2A.1. Comparative manufacturing performance metrics, 2008

	Sales/worker (annual)	VA/worker (annual)	Wage (US$ month)
Mozambique	11,932	3,516	53
Indonesia	13,200	6,535	56
Malawi	24,686	7,754	50
Angola	24,053	8,476	139
Zambia	22,948	8,725	69
South Africa	84,373	28,653	467

Notes: numbers refer to a small company in the food industry; the estimates for each country come from different sources and thus cannot be compared directly; they are nonetheless indicative.

Source: World Bank (2009).

Table 2A.2. Percentage of farms adopting agricultural technologies

	2002	2003	2005	2006	2007	2008	Δ
Receipt of extension info.	13.5	13.3	14.8	12.0	10.1	8.3	−5.2
Use of chemical fertilizer	3.8	2.6	3.9	4.7	4.1	4.1	0.3
Use of pesticides	6.8	5.3	5.6	5.5	4.2	3.8	−3.0
Use of irrigation	10.9	6.1	6.0	8.4	9.9	8.8	−2.1
Receipt of credit	−	2.9	3.5	2.9	4.7	2.6	−
Used animal traction	11.2	10.9	9.3	12.4	11.5	14.3	3.1
Membership of association	3.7	4.8	6.4	6.5	8.3	7.4	3.7
Hired permanent labor	2.2	1.9	1.8	2.2	2.6	3.0	0.8
Hired seasonal labor	15.5	15.3	17.6	23.8	20.8	19.6	4.1

Notes: Δ gives the absolute difference in each indicator between 2008 and 2002.

Source: DNEAP (2010) and authors' calculations using agricultural survey (TIA) data.

Table 2A.3 Summary of variables employed in regression estimates

Set	Variable	Description
Demographic chars.	Dependency ratio	Share of household members aged 0–14 or 65+
	Household size	No. of household members (log.)
	Household head female	Equals 1 if household head is female
	Adult males (% workers)	Share of workers that are males aged 25–64
	Young males (% workers)	Share of workers that are males aged 15–24
	Young females (% workers)	Share of workers that are females aged 15–24
Human capital	Log working members	Number of workers in household (log.)
	Household head literate	Equals 1 if household head is literate (0 otherwise)
	Household head age	Age of the household head
	Experience	Av. years of work experience of household's workers
	Incomplete lower primary	Share of workers with 1–4 years of education
	Complete lower primary	Share of workers with 5–6 years of education
	Complete primary	Share of workers with 7–9 years of education
	Lower secondary or above	Share of workers with >9 years of education
Physical capital	Asset: radio	Household owns a radio (dummy variable)
	Asset: telephone	Household owns a telephone (dummy variable)
	Asset: land	Household owns land (dummy variable)
	Asset: livestock	Household owns livestock (dummy variable)
	Asset: transport	Household owns means of transport (dummy variable)
	Non-labor income	Household receives non-labor income (dummy variable)
External conditions	Region: access to electricity	Share of PSUs in strata where median household has access to electricity
	Region: access to transport	Share of PSUs in strata where median household has means of transport
	Region: public sector posts	Share of PSUs in strata where public sector workers observed
	Region: % AgNf households	Share of households in strata observed in AgNf portfolio
	Region: % NfE households	Share of households in strata observed in NfE portfolio
	Region: % NfW households	Share of households in strata observed in NfW portfolio
	Region: specialization	Herfindahl portfolio concentration index (by strata)

Table 2A.4. Factors affecting the choice of different household jobs portfolios (average marginal effects from multinomial logit estimates)

	Urban				Rural			
	Ag	AgNf	NfE	NfW	Ag	AgNf	NfE	NfW
Dependency ratio	0.05***	-0.04***	0.01	-0.01**	0.01	-0.02	0.00	-0.00
	(4.4)	(-3.9)	(1.0)	(-2.3)	(0.9)	(-1.0)	(0.3)	(-0.4)
Household size	-0.24***	0.07**	0.13***	0.03	-0.13**	0.11*	0.02	-0.00
	(-6.0)	(2.0)	(3.9)	(1.2)	(-2.2)	(1.9)	(0.5)	(-0.4)
Household head female	-0.03	-0.08***	0.05***	0.05***	-0.03	-0.03	0.05***	0.01**
	(-1.6)	(-4.3)	(2.9)	(4.6)	(-1.3)	(-1.5)	(3.4)	(2.1)
Adult males (% workers)	-0.15***	-0.01	-0.03	0.19***	-0.11***	0.07*	0.04	0.01***
	(-5.6)	(-0.3)	(-1.0)	(11.1)	(-3.2)	(1.9)	(1.1)	(3.2)
Young males (% workers)	-0.13***	-0.09**	0.06	0.16***	-0.05	0.00	0.04	0.00
	(-3.8)	(-2.3)	(1.5)	(6.5)	(-1.2)	(0.1)	(1.2)	(0.7)
Young females (% workers)	0.00	0.02	-0.01	-0.01	0.00	0.06*	-0.05**	-0.00*
	(0.2)	(0.7)	(-0.4)	(-0.4)	(0.1)	(1.8)	(-2.3)	(-1.6)
Log working members	0.07	0.23***	0.08**	-0.38***	-0.04	0.07	-0.01	-0.02***
	(1.4)	(4.7)	(2.0)	(-10.8)	(-0.5)	(0.9)	(-0.2)	(-3.2)
Household head literate	-0.06***	-0.02	0.04*	0.04***	-0.05***	0.05***	-0.01	-0.00
	(-3.9)	(-1.1)	(1.9)	(3.0)	(-3.0)	(3.6)	(-0.5)	(-0.4)
Household head age	0.00***	0.00	-0.00***	0.00***	-0.00	0.00	-0.00	-0.00
	(3.0)	(0.3)	(-5.3)	(4.6)	(-0.8)	(0.9)	(-0.1)	(-0.1)
Experience	0.00	0.00	0.00	-0.00**	-0.00	-0.00	0.00	-0.00
	(0.7)	(0.2)	(0.8)	(-2.5)	(-0.0)	(-0.1)	(0.3)	(-1.1)
Incomplete lower primary	-0.04**	0.07**	-0.02	-0.00	-0.01	0.02	-0.00	0.00
	(-2.5)	(2.4)	(-0.7)	(-0.1)	(-0.8)	(0.9)	(-0.3)	(0.7)
Complete lower primary	-0.10***	0.07**	0.00	0.03	-0.06*	0.06*	-0.00	0.01**
	(-4.4)	(2.3)	(0.1)	(1.0)	(-1.8)	(1.8)	(-0.2)	(2.1)
Complete primary	-0.15***	0.07**	0.02	0.06**	-0.22***	0.18***	0.03	0.02***
	(-5.7)	(2.3)	(0.5)	(2.5)	(-4.6)	(4.2)	(0.9)	(3.9)
Lower secondary or above	-0.22***	0.04	-0.04	0.22***	-0.60***	0.53***	0.05	0.03***
	(-6.3)	(1.0)	(-1.0)	(8.9)	(-6.6)	(7.1)	(0.8)	(6.0)
Asset: radio	-0.01	0.02	-0.00	-0.00	-0.01	0.01	-0.00	0.00*
	(-1.1)	(1.4)	(-0.2)	(-0.3)	(-1.2)	(1.2)	(-0.2)	(1.8)

Asset: telephone	-0.07***	0.01	0.03*	0.03**	-0.03	-0.01	0.04**	0.00***
	(-5.1)	(0.7)	(1.9)	(2.4)	(-1.3)	(-0.2)	(2.1)	(2.6)
Asset: land	0.14***	0.12***	-0.21***	-0.05***	0.14***	-0.06*	-0.07*	-0.01***
	(5.9)	(5.4)	(-16.9)	(-5.5)	(2.9)	(-1.7)	(-1.9)	(-5.0)
Asset: livestock	-0.06***	-0.05**	0.11***	-0.00	-0.39***	0.10***	0.29***	-0.00***
	(-3.0)	(-2.3)	(4.4)	(-0.0)	(-33.5)	(7.8)	(17.3)	(-3.1)
Asset: transport	0.00	0.04***	-0.03**	-0.01	-0.04***	0.07***	-0.02**	-0.00
	(0.0)	(3.3)	(-2.1)	(-1.1)	(-3.3)	(5.1)	(-2.1)	(-1.5)
Non-labor income	0.04***	-0.01	-0.01	-0.01	-0.04**	0.01	0.03***	-0.00
	(3.1)	(-0.5)	(-1.0)	(-1.5)	(-2.3)	(0.5)	(2.7)	(-0.8)
Region: access to electricity	-0.08	0.05	0.01	0.02	-0.72	0.62	0.27	-0.17**
	(-0.7)	(0.3)	(0.1)	(0.2)	(-0.9)	(0.7)	(0.4)	(-2.5)
Region: access to transport	-0.07	0.04	0.01	0.02	0.15*	-0.16*	0.02	-0.02*
	(-0.7)	(0.4)	(0.1)	(0.3)	(1.7)	(-1.9)	(0.3)	(-1.9)
Region: % AgNf households	-0.82***	0.54*	0.15	0.13	-0.40	0.78**	-0.44*	0.06*
	(-3.7)	(2.0)	(0.6)	(0.6)	(-1.1)	(2.2)	(-1.8)	(1.9)
Region: % NfE households	-0.77*	0.31	0.78	-0.32	0.30	-0.69*	0.34	0.05
	(-1.8)	(0.6)	(1.5)	(-0.8)	(0.7)	(-1.7)	(1.0)	(1.2)
Region: % NfW households	-0.37	-0.21	-0.11	0.70***	2.34	-2.43	-0.34	0.42**
	(-1.5)	(-0.7)	(-0.4)	(2.9)	(1.1)	(-1.1)	(-0.2)	(2.0)
Region: specialization	-0.21	-0.48	0.32	0.37*	0.56	-0.24	-0.38	0.06
	(-0.8)	(-1.6)	(1.1)	(1.8)	(1.3)	(-0.6)	(-1.2)	(1.4)
Observations (AME)	4,682				5,256			
Observations (model)	8,439				9,699			
F (model)	22.76				16.76			

Notes: the table reports average marginal effects (AMEs), based on the multinomial regression estimates corresponding to equation (2.1), estimated separately for rural and urban areas and including regional and year dummies; for each jobs portfolio indicated (columns), only households included in the 2008/09 survey are employed to calculate the AMEs; selected coefficients shown; standard errors in parentheses account for survey design (e.g., clustering etc.).
significance: * 5% ** 1% *** 0.1%.

Source: authors' calculations from the Uwezo data.

References

Abowd, J. and Killingsworth, M. (1984). "Do minority/white unemployment differences really exist?" *Journal of Business & Economic Statistics*, 2(1):64–72.

African Development Bank (2012). *African Economic Outlook 2012: Promoting Youth Employment*. OECD Publishing. doi:10.1787/aeo-2012-en.

Ahlers, R., Güida, V., Rusca, M., and Schwartz, K. (2013). "Unleashing entrepreneurs or controlling unruly providers? The formalisation of small-scale water providers in Greater Maputo, Mozambique." *The Journal of Development Studies*, 49(4):470–82.

Allen, C., Johnsen, V., and Consult, M. (2010). Mozambique. Papers on Access to Housing Finance in Africa: Exploring the Issues 7. FinMark Trust.

Altenburg, T. and von Drachenfels, C. (2008). "Business environment reforms: Why it is necessary to rethink priorities and strategies." *Enterprise Development and Microfinance*, 19(3):191–203.

Alvarez, R. and López, R. (2008). "Is exporting a source of productivity spillovers?" *Review of World Economics*, 144(4):723–49.

Arndt, C., Garcia, A., Tarp, F., and Thurlow, J. (2012a). "Poverty reduction and economic structure: Comparative path analysis for Mozambique and Vietnam." *Review of Income and Wealth*, 58(4):742–63.

Arndt, C., Hussain, M.A., Jones, S., Nhate, V., Tarp, F., and Thurlow, J. (2012b). "Explaining the evolution of poverty: The case of Mozambique." *American Journal of Agricultural Economics*, 94(4):854–72. doi:10.1093/ajae/aas022.

Arndt, C., Jones, S., and Tarp, F. (2007). Aid and development: The Mozambican case. In: *Theory and Practice of Foreign Aid*, S. Lahiri (ed.), volume 1, pp. 235–88. Amsterdam: Elsevier B.V.

Arndt, C. and Tarp, F. (eds) (2009). *Taxation in a Low-income Economy: The Case of Mozambique*. New York: Routledge.

Barrett, C., Reardon, T., and Webb, P. (2001). "Nonfarm income diversification and household livelihood strategies in rural Africa: Concepts, dynamics, and policy implications." *Food Policy*, 26(4):315–31.

Bartus, T. (2005). "Estimation of marginal effects using margeff." *Stata Journal*, 5(3): 309–29.

Benfica, R. (2007). Income Poverty Effects of Expansion and Policies in Cash Cropping Economies in Rural Mozambique: An Economy-wide Approach. Food Security Collaborative Working Papers 64E, Michigan State University, Department of Agricultural, Food and Resource Economics.

Benfica, R., Tschirley, D., and Sambo, L. (2002). Agro-industry and Smallholder Agriculture: Institutional Arrangements and Rural Poverty Reduction in Mozambique. Flash Brief 33E, Directorate of Economics, Ministry of Agriculture and Rural Development, Government of Mozambique.

Benjamin, D. (1992). "Household composition, labor markets, and labor demand: Testing for separation in agricultural household models." *Econometrica*, 60(2):287–322.

Boughton, D., Mather, D., Barrett, C., Benfica, R., Abdula, D., et al. (2007). "Market participation by rural households in a low-income country: An asset-based approach applied to Mozambique." *Faith and Economics*, 50(1):64–101.

Bourguignon, F., Fournier, M., and Gurgand, M. (2007). "Selection bias corrections based on the multinomial logit model: Monte Carlo comparisons." *Journal of Economic Surveys*, 21(1):174–205.

Byiers, B., Rand, J., Tarp, F., and Bentzen, J. (2010). "Credit demand in Mozambican manufacturing." *Journal of International Development*, 22(1):37–55.

Clement, J. and Peiris, S. (2008). Post-stabilization Economics in Sub-Saharan Africa: Lessons from Mozambique. International Monetary Fund.

Cook, S. (1999). "Surplus labour and productivity in Chinese agriculture: Evidence from household survey data." *The Journal of Development Studies*, 35(3):16–44.

Cunguara, B., Fagilde, G., Garrett, J., Uaiene, R., and Heady, D. (2011). Growth without Change: The Elusiveness of Agricultural and Economic Transformation in Mozambique. Paper presented at Dialogue on Promoting Agricultural Growth in Mozambique July 21, 2011, Hotel VIP, Maputo, Dialogue on Promoting Agricultural Growth in Mozambique, June.

Cunguara, B. and Moder, K. (2011). "Is agricultural extension helping the poor? Evidence from Rural Mozambique." *Journal of African Economies*, 20(4): 562–95. doi:10.1093/jae/ejr015. URL: http://jae.oxfordjournals.org/content/20/4/562.abstract.

de Janvry, A., Fafchamps, M., and Sadoulet, E. (1991). "Peasant household behaviour with missing markets: Some paradoxes explained." *The Economic Journal*, 101(409):1400–17.

de Janvry, A. and Sadoulet, E. (2010). "Agricultural growth and poverty reduction: Additional evidence." *The World Bank Research Observer*, 25(1):1–20.

DNEAP (2010). Pobreza e bem-estar em Moçambique: Terceira avaliação nacional. Technical report, Ministry of Planning and Development, Government of Mozambique. URL: http://www.mpd.gov.mz/index.php/documentos/estudos/outros/551–45. [Accessed May 2016.]

Duranton, G. and Puga, D. (2004). "Micro-foundations of urban agglomeration economies." *Handbook of Regional and Urban Economics*, 4:2063–117.

Ellis, F. (2008). "The determinants of rural livelihood diversification in developing countries." *Journal of Agricultural Economics*, 51(2):289–302.

Feder, G. (1983). "On exports and economic growth." *Journal of Development Economics*, 12(1–2):59–73.

Fox, L., Bardasi, E., and Van den Broeck, K. (2005). *Poverty in Mozambique: Unraveling Changes and Determinants*. Washington, DC: World Bank.

Fox, L. and Kweka, J. (2011). The Household Enterprise Sector in Tanzania: Why It Matters and Who Cares. Policy Research Working Paper 5882, World Bank, Africa Region, Poverty Reduction and Economic Management Unit.

Fox, L. and Pimhidzai, O. (2011). Is Informality Welfare-Enhancing Structural Transformation? Evidence from Uganda. Policy Research Working Paper 5866, World Bank, Africa Region, Poverty Reduction and Economic Management Unit.

Fox, L. and Sohnesen, T. (2012). Household Enterprises in Sub-Saharan Africa: Why they Matter for Growth, Jobs, and Livelihoods. Policy Research Working Paper 6184, World Bank.

French, E. and Taber, C. (2011). "Identification of models of the labor market." *Handbook of Labor Economics*, 4:537–617.

Future Agricultures (2010). Future Farmers? Exploring Youth Aspirations for African Agriculture. Policy Brief 037. URL: http://www.future-agricultures.org/publications/research-and-analysis/945-future-farmers-exploring-youth-aspirations-for-african-agriculture/file. [Accessed May 2016.]

Grömping, U. (2006). "Relative importance for linear regression in R: The package relaimpo." *Journal of Statistical Software*, 17(1):1–27.

Gulyani, S. and Talukdar, D. (2010). "Inside informality: The links between poverty, microenterprises, and living conditions in Nairobi's slums." *World Development*, 38(12):1710–26.

Günther, I. and Launov, A. (2012). "Informal employment in developing countries: Opportunity or last resort?" *Journal of Development Economics*, 97(1):88–98.

Haggblade, S., Hazell, P., and Reardon, T. (2010). "The rural non-farm economy: Prospects for growth and poverty reduction." *World Development*, 38(10):1429–41.

Hanlon, J. (2009). "Mozambique: The panic and rage of the poor." *Review of African Political Economy*, 36(119):125–30.

ICT Africa (2012). Africa Prepaid Mobile Price Index 2012: South Africa. RIA Policy Brief SA 1, Research ICT Africa.

Inchauste, G., Azevedo, J.P., Olivieri, S., Saavedra, J., and Winkler, H. (2012). When Job Earnings Are Behind Poverty Reduction. Economic Premise 97, World Bank. URL: http://siteresources.worldbank.org/EXTPREMNET/Resources/EP97.pdf. [Accessed April 2016.]

Jones, S. and Tarp, F. (2012). Jobs and Welfare in Mozambique. Background Study for the 2013 World Development Report, UNU-WIDER. URL: https://www.wdronline.worldbank.org/handle/10986/12136. [Accessed April 2016.]

Krause, M., Ackermann, M., Gayoso, L., Hirtbach, C., Koppa, M., and Brêtas, L. (2010). Formalisation and Business Development in Mozambique: How Important Are Regulations? Technical report, German Development Institute/Deutsches Institut für Entwicklungspolitik.

Le, K. (2010). "Separation hypothesis tests in the agricultural household model." *American Journal of Agricultural Economics*, 92(5):1420–31.

McMillan, M.S. and Rodrik, D. (2012). Globalization, Structural Change and Productivity Growth. IFPRI Discussion Paper 01160, International Food Policy Research Institute.

Magnac, T. (1991). "Segmented or competitive labor markets." *Econometrica*, 59(1):165–87.

Mattes, R. (2008). The Material and Political Bases of Lived Poverty in Africa: Insights from the Afrobarometer. AfroBarometer Working Paper No. 98. URL: http://afrobarometer.org/publications/wp98-material-and-political-bases-lived-poverty-africa-insights-afrobarometer. [Accessed May 2016.]

Page, J. (2012a). "Can Africa Industrialise?" *Journal of African Economies*, 21(suppl 2): ii86–ii124.

Page, J. (2012b). Mozambique: Structural Change in an Evolving Natural Resources Economy. Unpublished report (based on a public lecture given at the Mozambique Growth Forum sponsored by the International Growth Centre, Maputo, March 9, 2012), Brookings Institution.

Paulo, M., Rosário, C., and Tvedten, I. (2008). Social Relations of Urban Poverty. CMI Brief: Monitoring and Evaluating Poverty Reduction Policies in Mozambique 2, Chr. Michelsen Institute.

Perry, D. (2009). "Fathers, sons, and the state: Discipline and punishment in a Wolof hinterland." *Cultural Anthropology*, 24(1):33–67.

Poulton, C. and Macartney, J. (2012). "Can public–private partnerships leverage private investment in agricultural value chains in Africa? A preliminary review." *World Development*, 40(1):96–109.

Rhoades, S.A. (1993). "The Herfindahl-Hirschman Index." *Federal Reserve Bulletin*, 79:188–9.

Rodrik, D. (2007). Industrial development: Some stylized facts and policy directions. In: *Industrial Development For The 21st Century: Sustainable Development Perspectives*, United Nations Department of Economic and Social Affairs (UNDESA) (ed.), chapter 1, pp. 7–28. Geneva: United National Publications.

Rosenfeld, D. (2012). The Coal Mining Sector in Mozambique: A Simple Model for Prediction of Government Revenue. Unpublished background paper; forthcoming as a DNEAP Working Paper, Direcção Nacional de Estudos e Análise de Políticas (DNEAP), Ministério de Planificação e Desenvolvimento, República de Moçambique.

Tarp, F., Arndt, C., Jensen, H.T., Robinson, S., and Heltberg, R. (2002). Facing the Development Challenge in Mozambique: An Economywide Perspective. Research Reports 126, International Food Policy Research Institute (IFPRI).

Verme, P. (2000). "The choice of the working sector in transition: Income and non-income determinants of sector participation in Kazakhstan." *Economics of Transition*, 8(3):691–731.

World Bank (2009). Mozambique—Investment Climate Assessment 2009: Sustaining and Broadening Growth. Washington, DC: World Bank. URL: http://hdl.handle.net/10986/3158. [Accessed April 2016.]

World Bank (2012). World Development Report 2013: Jobs. Washington, DC: World Bank. doi:10.1596/978-0-8213-9575-2.

3

Bangladesh

Jobs and Growth in an Urbanizing Economy

Mahabub Hossain, Binayak Sen, and Yasuyuki Sawada

3.1 The Ascent of the Poorest

In the 1974 World Atlas ranking of per capita income, Bangladesh came second lowest, slightly ahead of Rwanda. The development trajectory of Bangladesh has gone through phases of economic hardship and phases of economic renewal since then. So have the perceptions in the academic and policy community at large—often alternating between pessimism and hope—about the country's long-term development prospects. In the end, however, the reality turned out to be richer compared to the initial predictions: a country allegedly deemed as the international basket case and whose lifeline was seemingly hanging on foreign aid has made a silent transition since Independence. It has become a lead performer among the LDCs and aims at becoming a middle-income country by 2021.[1] Whether that target will be reached by that date may look less certain amid today's uncertainty in the global economic outlook, but very few in the West dispute that possibility in the near future. Bangladesh's ascent has received more attention in view of limited expectations about its development prospects against the backdrop of multiple and overlapping adverse initial conditions, such as frequent natural

[1] The epithet of "bottomless basket" is widely attributed to Henry Kissinger, though it is not fully certain that he actually uttered it. The skeptical assessment of Kissinger as regards the viability of Bangladesh as an independent state was well known in the early 1970s. It is remarkable that Kissinger has changed his negative perception quite dramatically since then. In his recent book, he noted that due to a shift to a consumption-driven growth strategy in China, low-wage, export-oriented jobs have started "started shifting from China to Vietnam and Bangladesh" (Kissinger 2011).

disasters, scarce natural resources, very high population density, and weak state institutions. No wonder pessimism prevailed—only a few could bet on its chances of rapid progress given these initial odds.

Bangladesh currently occupies third place in global exports of readymade garments (RMG) and is deemed the next hotspot for labor-intensive exports. The country's share in the global apparel market is less than 5 percent compared to 30 percent for China, indicating the potential for future growth for Bangladeshi garments exports, especially as wages are on the increase in China's apparel sector.[2] The country has also achieved decent progress in human development: some MDG targets have been achieved and it is on track for meeting most others soon. An additional striking feature is the remarkable stability of the growth itself—Bangladesh being one of the least volatile countries in terms of year-to-year fluctuations in the growth rate. The social part of the development story augurs well: (a) poverty nearly halved between 1991 and 2010; (b) girls' enrollment at the secondary level has outpaced that of boys and female labor force participation has increased considerably and plays an important role in activities ranging from RMG to microcredit; and (c) notwithstanding many challenges on the way, the country remains on the course of liberal democracy with a strong commitment against religious extremism. All these features indicate a certain social cohesiveness that comes with inclusive growth.

There is an embedded story of jobs as the accelerator of growth and as a source of social cohesion in the process of economic and social transformation, but that story is not readily available from the existing literature. It is about the role of jobs in accelerating growth and maintaining development, that is, not just any jobs, but good jobs, which may be seen as an integral part of "good life" (Dworkin 2011). This chapter is about that story.

The chapter is divided into eight sections. After outlining the three broad themes relating to jobs and economic transformation in Bangladesh, Section 3.2 provides the country context of development. Based on summary comparisons between what was expected and what eventually turned out, the section sets the tone for the remainder of the chapter. Section 3.3 briefly outlines the analytical framework that underlies the analysis of the role of jobs in Bangladesh's development.

Section 3.4 turns to the role of surplus-releasing agriculture under the influence of agricultural modernization, leading to the creation of new jobs in farm and non-farm sectors. Here we draw attention to the employment effects of new high-yielding variety (HYV) rice technology, as well as changes

---

[2] However, to achieve this goal, the country needs to address the challenge of worker safety and related compliance issues, as evidenced by the recent episodes of industrial accidents.

in agrarian institutions that have taken place over the past two decades—changes that generated jobs for the poor.

Section 3.5 discusses non-agricultural sectors as the new destination of jobs for the poor, especially in the last decade. Section 3.6 discusses the social effects of urban/industrial growth on rural/agricultural wellbeing, encouraging a virtuous cycle of labor mobility from rural areas.

Section 3.7 discusses the issue of social cohesion through the prism of three angles: (a) jobs that improved the wellbeing of the poor and even helped to maintain stable consumption inequality; (b) jobs that were economically empowering for women; and (c) jobs that met the expectations of the youth reasonably well irrespective of their education status. Concluding observations summarizing the main messages and the broader implications of the Bangladesh case study for other low-income agrarian and urbanizing economies are captured in Section 3.8.

3.2 The Country Context: Initial Pessimism and Subsequent Surprises

3.2.1 Initial Pessimism

In one of the very first appraisals of Bangladesh's development, Faaland and Parkinson (1976: 5) famously commented: "If the problem of Bangladesh can be solved, there can be reasonable confidence that less difficult problems of development can also be solved. It is in this sense that Bangladesh is to be regarded as the test case of development." This appraisal was equally shared by some of the leading economists of Bangladesh at the time. Alamgir (1978) saw Bangladesh being trapped in "Below Poverty Equilibrium," while Sobhan (1982) expressed the view that the country had fallen into a "crisis of external dependence."

Such negative perceptions were conditioned by the adverse initial conditions facing the country during the early years of independence, such as high population density, prevalence of malnutrition, a limited natural resource base, underdeveloped infrastructure worsened further by the War of Independence in 1971, and frequent natural disasters influencing the level as well as stability of investments.

This negative perception has been gradually replaced by cautious optimism in global development circles. There are countries that have done well on the social indicators front, and there are countries that have done well on the economic growth front. But Bangladesh belongs to a rather small group of countries that have done well on both fronts notwithstanding initial pessimism. This is the crux of the "surprise"!

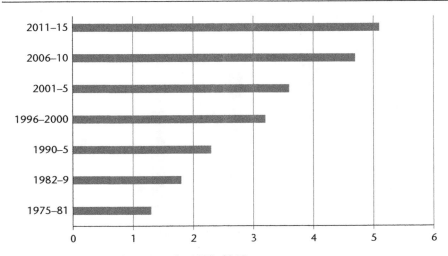

Figure 3.1. Per capita GDP growth, 1975–2015

Source: based on data given in *Bangladesh Economic Review* published by the Ministry of Finance, Government of Bangladesh (various issues).

3.2.2 Development Surprises: Improved "Wellbeing" Indicators

Several "development surprises" are noteworthy. The first is that the vicious cycle of low growth has been broken. Growth accelerated in successive decades and phases, which in itself merits recognition (Mujeri and Sen 2006; Government of Bangladesh (GoB) 2014; see also Figure 3.1).

Second, the wellbeing dimensions of development have improved significantly. Both rural and urban poverty have declined noticeably since 1991/92 (especially in the 2000s). The country is now on track to meet the poverty MDG (Figure 3.2). In fact, the recent poverty projections for 2015 carried out by the Planning Commission show that the country has met the MDG poverty target.[3] Consumption inequality has remained relatively stable since 1995/96 (which matters for poverty), though income inequality has increased.

Third, achievements on basic human development indicators have been impressive for a country with a relatively low level of income. Bangladesh has performed well on a range of social targets, that is, non-income MDGs (MDG2, MDG3, MDG4, and MDG5 covering education, gender equality, and health), though quality concerns in education and health persist and not all dimensions

[3] Poverty projections for the 2010s are based on past poverty elasticities observed between 2005 and 2010 (the last year for which household survey data are available). They are, by definition, not a substitute for the actual survey, which will be carried out in 2016. The results of the poverty projections show a substantial drop in the poverty headcount index from 60 percent in 1991/92 to 31 percent in 2010, down further to 24 percent in 2015 under a 6 percent growth scenario actually achieved during 2010–15. On these poverty projections, see Sen and Ali (2015).

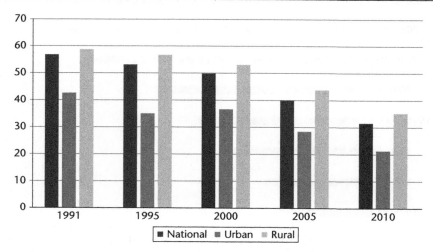

Figure 3.2. Trends in the poverty rate in Bangladesh by place of residence, 1991–2010
Source: based on poverty estimates in HIES reports of BBS (various years).

within these goals are adequately addressed. Fourth, there have been improvements in terms of security, resilience, and coping capacity against predictable and unpredictable income shocks such as frequent natural disasters.

Finally, with 45 percent of the population aged below 20, Bangladesh has been relatively successful in maintaining social cohesion by responding to the job aspirations of the majority of youth, educated and uneducated, female and the poorest, leading to relative social peace and cohesion.

3.2.3 Development Surprises: Improved "Structural Shift" Indicators

Several shifts in the composition of output have taken place since 1990: from farm to non-farm, from agriculture to industry, from low-value-added products and informal services to high-value-added products and formal services, from rural to urban, and from domestic markets to export markets.

Between 1990 and 2010, the rise of industrial sectors was the most prominent structural shift. Industry's share of GDP increased from about 20 to 30 percent, while the share of the service sector remained at around 50 percent. However, within the latter, the share of formal services (financial services, wholesale trade, ICT, etc.) has grown, raising the productivity of the service sector. Urbanization is now around 35 percent, up from a low of about 8 percent in 1974, indicating a significant transfer of population between rural and urban areas (Mujeri and Sen 2006; GoB 2014).

Export's share in GDP has increased from 7 percent (1977–82) to 18 percent (2006–10), with more than 90 percent originating in the manufacturing sector

(GoB 2014). This has been mainly driven by RMG, but the list also includes other items such as processed leather, frozen food, pharmaceuticals, even software. This forms a striking contrast to low-income countries, whose exports tend to be dominated by primary goods.

Remittances from abroad together with manufactured exports have been instrumental in supporting these structural shifts in national output. The remittances share had increased to around 10 percent of GDP in 2010/11, up from 5 percent in the late 1990s (Mujeri and Sen 2006; GoB 2014). In contrast, external concessional aid is now below 2 percent of GDP, compared to 10 percent in 1981/82. In this respect, too, Bangladesh contrasts with most least-developed countries, heavily dependent on external concessional aid. However, Bangladesh still needs aid for financing the budget deficit (in the order of 5 percent of GDP) and for financing public investment programs included in the annual development plan. The role of concessional foreign aid has been especially important in the financing of mega infrastructural projects such as the Jamuna Bridge, and would merit serious consideration for future mega-projects such as the Padma Bridge and the Metro Rail.

3.3 Jobs and Development: Outlining the Analytical Approach

What do all of these stylized facts mean for broader development outcomes, especially those seen from the perspective of labor: that is, creating jobs, access to poverty-reducing employment, and favorable changes in labor market arrangements? The reverse loop from jobs to development is also important. The story of how job creation and labor market changes have supported the development turnaround in Bangladesh needs more analytical attention.

The Jobs WDR argues that job creation can make a difference in the process of development in three dimensions: (a) it can help raise living standards (including improved economic security); (b) it can increase aggregate productivity; and (c) it can enhance social cohesion (World Bank 2012). Jobs that contribute to this process are called "good jobs for development." The main hypothesis of this chapter is that Bangladesh has been successful in generating good-enough jobs, that is "good-enough for development," by improving farm–non-farm, rural–urban, intersectoral labor mobility at a relatively low skill level with welfare-enhancing (poverty reducing and social cohesion-enhancing) effects.

3.3.1 *Three Emerging Themes*

We identify three broad themes that inform the nexus between the nature of job creation and developmental transformations of the Bangladesh economy and society. These are: (a) agricultural modernization through new agricultural technology, infrastructure, and access to finance; (b) non-agricultural orientation through urbanization, international migration, export-oriented industrialization, and the creation of small- and medium-sized enterprises (SMEs); and (c) supportive social policy through human development of children and youth, female advancement, and social protection.

3.4 Jobs and Agricultural Modernization

Employment effects of the green revolution and agricultural diversification aided by the spread of new high-yielding variety seed technology, rural infrastructure, and access to finance (especially microfinance) have been considerable.

3.4.1 Role of New Technology in Agriculture

Sequentially, the modernization process in agriculture started with faster technology adoption under severe population pressure—even under difficult production and institutional environments—mainly in the form of new HYV technology in rice agriculture. This possibility was already anticipated by Boserup (1981). Rice dominates crop production in Bangladesh, with an acreage and production share of about 75 and 70 percent respectively (Shahabuddin 2012). The trend annual growth rate in rice production in the post-Independence period (1973–2010) has been estimated to be 2.8 percent. This growth has been driven mainly by the dissemination of HYV rice, especially in *boro* (winter) and *aman* (rain-fed) seasons. The share of HYV rice in total acreage was only 15 percent in the 1970s, but doubled during the 1980s, rising to more than half of the acreage in the 1990s, and 68 percent in the 2000s. As a result, the contribution of HYV rice in total rice production has gone up from 30 percent during the 1970s to more than 80 percent in the 2000s (Shahabuddin 2012). Correspondingly, the share of non-HYV rice in total acreage and production has declined. This has implications for creating employment in rural areas, as HYV rice production is more labor intensive—it demands about 45 percent higher labor inputs compared to the local rice production.

Rising land and labor productivity growth in rice agriculture in the 2000s had beneficial effects on the agricultural wage rate and hence on rural poverty. First, the average wage income earned by agricultural wage laborers was much higher for HYV rice cultivation compared to traditional-variety-based rice cultivation. In 1988, at the early stage of the green revolution, the difference in wage income between the two groups of agricultural wage laborers was as high as 95 percent. The difference has come down over time—it was 60 percent in 2000—but the relative gains for wage labor are still considerable (Hossain and Bayes 2009). Second, wage growth also tends to be higher in villages experiencing high growth in land productivity. Thus, high growth rates for agricultural wages have been cited more frequently by households in villages experiencing high productivity growth compared with villages experiencing low productivity growth (38 percent vs 25 percent).[4] Gains in land productivity enabled agricultural wages to rise. This is not to deny the presence of some surplus labor still in agriculture. However, increases in agricultural wages in the presence of some surplus labor do not contradict the conclusion drawn by the Lewis model (see Lewis 1954) in the sense that productivity gains in Bangladesh agriculture have exceeded a threshold level, which has pushed wages up.

The spread of new technology in rice agriculture has created the scope for releasing workers for higher-productivity, non-agricultural work. As a result, there is a more pronounced shift towards non-agricultural occupations in villages with the highest land productivity compared to villages with the lowest land productivity. In villages with high land productivity, the proportion of household heads reporting farming as the main occupation was 39 percent in 2008, compared to 47 percent in villages with low land productivity. In contrast, those engaged in trade were more prominent in high land-productivity villages (17 percent as opposed to 10 percent).

Part of this shift is caused by consumption demand-induced linkage effects of the green revolution for non-farm products and services, but other factors such as investment in rural infrastructure have also been in play here. We do not have time-series data on villages with differing infrastructures, but the comparisons for the same year are available. In villages with developed infrastructure, total days of employment per household deployed in the non-agricultural sector were higher by 34 percent compared to villages with underdeveloped infrastructure (Ahmed and Hossain 1990). In contrast, total days of agricultural employment per household in infrastructurally-developed villages remained the same as in villages with underdeveloped infrastructure (or even lower slightly by 2 percent). This pattern of non-farm orientation in

---

[4] Estimated from primary data from the 62-village panel survey for 2000 and 2008. The survey was conducted by Mahabub Hossain and his team initially in BIDS and later in IFPRI. Data were also collected in 1988 and 2004. The surveys had nationally representative rural samples. For details on the surveys, see Hossain and Bayes (2009). Comparing the 2000 and 2008 data, we can estimate the growth in real wages and relate them to economic drivers of interest, such as land productivity growth as well as growth in overseas remittances that were received by the rural households during 2000–08, to examine the effects of farm productivity and international migration. Real agricultural wages are expressed in rice equivalents and have been computed by dividing the nominal wages by the coarse rice prices prevailing in the village.

the sectoral composition of employment has become more pronounced in recent comparisons (Hossain and Bayes 2009).

In the 2000s, with ongoing adoption of new technology, the process of moving out of crop agriculture has extended more visibly beyond the boundaries of the village economy leading to accelerated growth in export-led manufacturing.

3.4.2 Pro-Poor Shifts in the Tenancy Market

Agricultural modernization of the crop sector has led to pro-poor shifts in rural factor markets such as the land tenancy market. This was not initially expected, however. With the advent of the green revolution, the initial prediction was that farming would become a more lucrative area of investment, making owner-operated farms more profitable. Consequently, the share of tenant-operated farms among all farms would decline over time (Osmani and Sen 2011). This did not happen in Bangladesh. To the contrary, there is some evidence that land under tenancy has actually increased, with a pronounced shift from share tenancy to fixed rent/leasehold tenancy, and (rather surprisingly) a rise in the share of leased-in land held by the landless households (the so-called "pure tenancy"). These changes in rural institutions generated pro-poor effects. Several pieces of evidence support this conclusion (see Sen et al. 2007).

First, the share of leased-in land in total operating land held by rural households increased impressively, from 23 percent in 1988 to 33 percent in 2000, rising further to 40 percent in 2004 (Hossain and Bayes 2009).[5] This has also benefited landless groups (those owning up to 0.20 ha). The share of leased-in land in total land cultivated by the landless group increased from 31 percent to 50 percent during 1988–2004.

Second, the proportion of households renting or leasing land from others also increased from 44 percent in 1988 to 54 percent in 2000, rising to 58 percent in 2004. Remarkably, the class of "pure tenants" did not vanish: the share of landless tenants in fact went up from 34 percent in 1988 to 54 percent in 2004.

Third, the form of tenancy has also changed: inefficient forms of sharecropping have declined gradually over time. Thus, sharecropping represented no more than 60 percent of total leased-in land in 2004. This is a marked change, as share-rent was the predominant form historically, with cash-rent virtually missing as a form of leasing in the early 1980s (Hossain and Bayes 2009).

---

[5] The Agricultural Census data (1983/84, 1996, 2008) also tend to support this broad conclusion.

These changes in the tenancy market have had favorable employment and welfare implications for the land-poor groups. Cash-rent allows a greater return to farm labor than share-rent (cash-rent is equivalent to one-fourth of the produce to be paid to landowners while the typical share-rent claim is about one-half of the produce). Favorable changes in land tenure as a source of additional remunerative employment for the landless—and, consequently, as an exit route out of poverty—may come as surprise, as many observers in the 1980s and 1990s believed that the only way out from land-scarce conditions was movement towards rural non-farm labor.[6]

What explains the unexpected rise in the share of land under tenancy, especially the emergence of pure tenancy and the rise of cash-rent as a form of rental payment? This warrants attention to factors that acted on the supply and demand for leased-in land that had implications for the land-poorest farmers.

What increased the supply of land through the tenancy market? The old tenancy literature conceptualizing tenancy as a form of labor contract under-estimated the role of rapid urbanization and international migration. Increasing permanent relocation of middle-income and richer rural households in urban areas as well as abroad has meant that the family labor-based owner-operated farming option became unattractive over time; the same applies to the option of wage labor-based farming which demands supervision. As a result, an increasing amount of land became available through the tenancy market during the period of rapid urbanization and international migration in the decade of the 2000s.[7]

Increased supply of land through the tenancy market does not explain why landless or near-landless tenants became major players in the land rental market. Where did they get capital needed to pay for the cash rent (not to mention capital to cover the costs of land cultivation)? Normally, the credit market option would be ruled out as the land-poor are not seen as bankable borrowers. It is here that the role of microfinance becomes a relevant consideration.

---

[6] All these pro-poor changes could happen without land reform measures—the neighboring Indian state of West Bengal, where land reform was vigorously pursued, is a case in point—but arguably yielding similar results in terms of job creation in agriculture and poverty reduction. Bangladesh and West Bengal have similar agro-ecological, land availability, and population density conditions. While the literature agrees on the early positive results of land-reform measures on farm productivity in West Bengal in the 1980s and, consequently, on the pace of rural poverty reduction (Bardhan and Mookherjee 2006), the subsequent analysis has been less enthusiastic on this point (Deininger et al. 2009).

[7] The urbanization rate was only 12 percent in 1983/84, but increased to 30 percent by 2011 (current estimate is around 35 percent); two major cities—Dhaka and Chittagong—account for about 40 percent of the country's consumption expenditure and hence act as a pool for attracting economic migrants from the rest of the country. Remittances were only 5 percent of GDP in 2004, but increased to 10 percent by 2010, and have stayed at that level notwithstanding global uncertainties.

The evidence suggests that the landless/near-landless group accounts for the bulk of the institutional (government plus microfinance institution (MFI)) credit in Bangladesh. The share of the landless group in total rural institutional credit flows increased from 21 percent in 1988 to 43 percent in 2008 (Hossain and Bayes 2009). Although MFI loans are usually given for rural non-farm sectors, the funds are often rechanneled to farm operations (and vice versa). Again, since clients of MFIs are mainly rural women, the above-mentioned transformation of the tenancy market also coincided with the "feminization" of agriculture: 66 percent of economically active women participated in agricultural activities in 2008, an increase from 58 percent in 2000 (Jaim and Hossain 2011).

3.4.3 Bridging the East–West Divide: The Jamuna Bridge Effect

The Jamuna Multipurpose Bridge (JMB) was inaugurated on June 23, 1998, as the largest physical infrastructure in Bangladeshi history. The Jamuna Bridge has been a major channel for integrating the lagging western region of the country with its leading eastern region. This has manifested in several ways. First, transportation of natural gas, electricity, and telecommunication is now faster, cheaper, and more reliable. Second, transport costs have been reduced and access to key consumption centers like Dhaka has improved. Third, traffic over the bridge increased by 11.5 percent per year after its opening in 1999 (Bayes 2007). Fourth, the bridge paved the way for faster marketing of perishable goods: distribution of non-leafy vegetables from the northwestern region to the eastern part of the country has increased by at least 50 percent, according to truckers. Fifth, household surveys through simple project-control village comparisons show that there has been a significant reduction in income and non-income dimensions of poverty (Bayes 2007).

Analysis indicates considerable effects of the Jamuna Bridge on the integration of labor markets between the eastern and western sides of the Padma River, enhancing labor mobility and the wellbeing of workers in the western region. An econometric exercise based on primary data (Sawada 2012) has led to three key observations. First, subjective poverty data confirm significant livelihood improvement effects in the lagging areas after connectivity.[8] Second, the JMB induces the transition of male (though not female) labor from farming/fishing occupations to casual-wage labor, business, and services. The switch to casual labor can be found among uneducated males, while the shift to business and services can be found among educated males. Unemployment

---

[8] The lagging region was defined as areas falling into Sirajganj district on the western side of the bridge and it is also considered as the "treatment group" in this analysis. Tangail areas on the eastern side of the bridge were considered as the "control group."

has been significantly reduced among uneducated males and females in the middle-age group (31–50 years old). Third, the aforementioned job transitions are more prominent for the younger age groups. There is also evidence that the JMB motivates some youth to leave traditional occupations for further schooling, thus having human capital effects as well (Mahmud and Sawada 2015).

3.4.4 Pro-Poor Shifts in the Agricultural Labor Market

There has been significant tightening of the agricultural labor market over the past three decades. Long-term trends indicate a substantial increase in real wages in agriculture from a level equivalent to less than 2.5 kg rice per day in 1983 to over 9 kg currently. Several points are noteworthy. First, the context for such changes had been set up initially by the spread of the green revolution that progressed rapidly in the 1980s and 1990s. However, real wages in agriculture did not increase much during this period. Benefits to agricultural workers were derived more from increases in wage employment opportunities. The new HYV rice technology increased demand for both family and wage labor, but the demand for wage labor under HYV tends to be higher than under the traditional rice variety. Thus, in the transition from traditional to HYV technology, the proportionate increase in demand for hired labor was 82 percent compared with only a 15 percent increase in demand for family labor (Hossain 1988b).

Second, this period also saw a rapid expansion of rural non-farm (RNF) self-employment, but such expansion was mainly taking place at a very low level of productivity. A strong view in the literature that reviewed the evidence of the 1980s concluded that the average earnings in RNF self-employment were even lower than earnings for agricultural wage labor and hence highlighted the residual nature of such employment (Osmani 1990). A subsequent view drew attention to the new evidence for the 1990s and argued for the greater differentiation within the RNF sector between the residual and dynamic segments. Those who participated in the latter reported self-employment earnings that exceeded the level of agricultural wage earnings and hence offered improved prospects for unskilled labor mobility from the farm to non-farm sector within rural areas (Rahman and Hossain 1995; Sen 1996).

Third, if we focus on the specific segment of the RNF sector that was directly financed by the MFIs, a large number of non-panel and panel studies carried out from the 1980s through to the 2000s confirmed the poverty-reducing effects as well as empowering effects of microfinance on its poor borrowers (Hossain 1988a; Khandker 2000; Khandker 2005; Bandiera et al. 2009; Armendariz and Morduch 2010; Osmani 2012). Rural women have been the main economic agents (accounting for over 90 percent of MFI members) of the microcredit expansion. Most of the female members were employed as unpaid workers or were not part of the labor force at all prior to their enrollment in MFIs. Hence, even though the return to women's labor in MFI activities was low, the poor and the poorest households—the so-called target group of MFIs having less than 0.5 acres of land—benefited as household incomes increased due to inclusion in the MFIs. MFI members have had better social indicators—lower fertility, lower child mortality, better sanitation, improved schooling for children, improved nutrition, and improved access to maternal and child health care—than their non-MFI counterparts from the same land-ownership group.[9] Even in cases where women acted as mere conduits for financing business, service, and transport investments of their male partners, their status within the household and the community rose over time, and eventually the female workers in such households also entered into those economic activities (for a range of relevant readings, see Khalily and Osmani 2011). However, the expansion of such a pronounced economic role for women became prominent only in the 2000s.

Fourth, the transition of farm labor to rural non-farm self-employment contributed to the tightening of the rural wage-labor market and thereby indirectly benefited those who remained as agricultural wage workers. This transition was facilitated by the expansion of rural road infrastructure: investment in rural connectivity took off significantly in the 1990s, spearheaded by the newly established institutional initiative of the Local Government Engineering Department.

Fifth, a breakthrough in the form of a significant rise in real agricultural wages came later, only in the 2000s, and was possibly more to do with urbanization, domestic and international migration, and with the changing pattern of economic growth in general that was fueled by the expansion of industry and services.[10]

Sixth, the period of the 2000s also witnessed sharp rises in rice prices, especially since 2007–08, which continue today. The higher rice-price regime coincided with the faster poverty reduction in the second half of the 2000s. Analysis based on Household Income and Expenditure Survey (HIES) data shows that there was poverty stagnation in the 1980s, only a 0.5 percentage point per year drop in rural poverty during the low rice-price regime in the 1990s, then a one percentage point per year decline in rural poverty in the first half of the 2000s, which progressed to an even faster 2 percentage point annual drop in the

---

[9] For example, see Pitt and Khandker (1998) and the debate on the social impact of microfinance programs (Roodman and Morduch 2009; Pitt 2011). For a randomized control trial case study, see Banerjee et al. (2010), which investigated only short-run impacts of an MFI program in India. Based on a panel dataset from Pakistan, Lee and Sawada (2010) show that binding credit constraints inhibit poor households' intertemporal consumption smoothing significantly.

[10] This is also argued elsewhere by, for example, Otsuka (2007) and Otsuka et al. (2008).

second half of the 2000s (Ravallion and Sen 1996; Narayan and Zaman 2009; BBS 2010). The argument is that while rice farmers benefited from the changing rice-price regime, the benefits also trickled down to the agricultural wage workers. If in the 1980s and 1990s there was a significant lag between rice-price increases and nominal agricultural wage increases in the order of two to three years (Ravallion 1990), the lag period became even narrower in the 2000s (Rashid 2002; IFPRI 2012).

Seventh, the shortage of farm labor and increasing real agricultural wages have, in turn, encouraged labor-saving techniques during the peak agricultural seasons. Faced with acute shortages of labor and attendant high labor costs in times of tillage/plantation and harvest, farmers are now routinely making recourse to labor-saving techniques, so much so that over 80 percent of tillage operations are currently carried out by power tillers (Hossain and Bayes 2009).

All these changes in the production conditions of agriculture and consequent tightening of the agricultural labor market cannot be understood without appreciating the part played by domestic and international migration. With the increasing urbanization, the rural–urban relocation of labor has been an important factor behind rural poverty reduction through the channel of the labor market. The significance of international migration is equally noteworthy in this regard, as evidenced by the rising share of overseas remittances in the country's GDP, as noted earlier.

3.5 Jobs and Non-agricultural Growth

The main focus in this section is the direct employment effects of domestic and international migration, export-led manufacturing, construction, and urbanization. The other important issue examined is the indirect employment effects of these developments in rural areas.

3.5.1 *Role of Migration*

The proportion of households reporting domestic migration increased from 13 percent to 16 percent between 2000 and 2008, according to the 62-village panel survey. A majority of the domestic migrants belong to landless and functionally landless households: the combined share of these groups in the pool of domestic migrants increased from 51 to 57 percent during 2000–08.[11]

[11] This share of the landless and functionally landless in the overall pool of domestic migrants would be even higher if seasonal migration to urban construction activities were taken into account, which seems to have been missed by the 62-village panel survey.

Education is positively correlated with mobility: only 10 percent of households with heads with no formal schooling report domestic migrants, compared to 12 percent for households with heads with primary education, and rising to 20 percent for those with secondary school certificate (SSC) level education.

If domestic migrants are mainly from landless and functionally landless households, the same cannot be said of international migration that occurred from rural areas. Here the share of small landowner households (those who own land up to 0.40 ha) in the pool of rural households with international migrants increased considerably during 2000–08, from 39 percent to 54 percent. In short, even though the poorest could not participate as much as the less poor groups, the overall effect of international migration has been pro-poor during the 2000s. The education status of the overseas migrants confirms this pro-poor trend. The share of those with no formal schooling in the pool of households with overseas migrants increased from 29 percent to 40 percent during the period.

A recent analysis of remittance and income inequality in rural areas shows that international migration explains 70 percent of the increase in rural inequality over the period between 2000 and 2010 (Osmani and Sen 2011). The share of overseas remittances in total income was only 11 percent for the landless, but rose to 16 and 19 percent for marginal and small farmers. The share was only 3 percent for casual agricultural laborers as opposed to 14 percent for the self-employed in agriculture. Remittances accounted for 12–13 percent of total income for the less-than-primary education group, compared to 16–17 percent for the primary-plus and secondary-plus education categories (Osmani and Sen 2011).

However, while casual agricultural laborers have limited resources for financing international migration, indirect effects of international migration through the labor market are of greater significance for this group. Wage growth tends to be higher in villages experiencing high growth in overseas remittances.[12]

Migrant households have higher per capita consumption, non-farm physical assets, and greater accumulation of financial assets than non-migrant ones, but the same cannot be claimed unambiguously for human capital accumulation. Sharma and Zaman (2009), for instance, show that per capita education and health spending does not differ statistically between migrant and non-migrant households.

---

[12] This is evidenced from 62-village panel survey data cited earlier (see footnote 4).

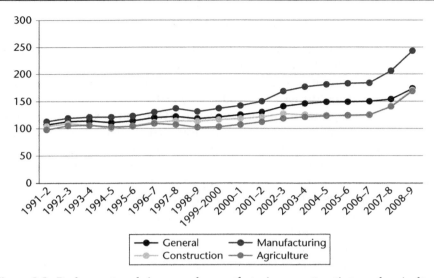

Figure 3.3. Real wage trends in general, manufacturing, construction, and agriculture sectors, 1991–2009
Source: estimated from BBS data using sector-specific real wage indices (1991/92=100).

Rural-to-urban and international migration have had other indirect effects. For instance, they seem to have been important in reshaping agrarian institutions over the past decade. The relocation of households or main earners has meant very high supervision costs involved in owner-operated farming. This is applicable even for those households who may nominally reside in villages but spend most of their time in non-agricultural activities. In all such cases, households with relatively high supervision costs may opt for leasing out land to others.

Finally, incentives for migration have been created by persistent intersectoral wage differentials. Time-series data on service sector wages are not available, but a comparison of real wages can be made for the manufacturing, construction, and agricultural sectors from 1991/92 to 2009/10. Throughout this period, wages have been highest in manufacturing, followed by construction and agriculture (Figure 3.3). While the real wages of agricultural workers rose over the period, they increased faster in manufacturing and construction. The rising wage trends in all three sectors are especially prominent in the second half of the 2000s, coinciding with high growth in export-led manufacturing and international remittances.[13]

---

[13] Both channels have particularly favorable implications for rapid development of the real estate sector, in turn leading to sustained growth in construction sector wages.

3.5.2 The Transformative Role of Export-Led Manufacturing

The first thing to note is the employment-intensive nature of the manufacturing sector itself. Manufacturing employment went up from 3.5 million in 1995/96 to 5.2 million in 2005/06, implying an annual growth rate of 4 percent, increasing further to 6.7 million by 2010. Value added in manufacturing grew 6.6 percent annually between 1995 and 2005, indicating an employment elasticity of 0.61. This suggests that the recent manufacturing growth has been moderately employment intensive. This is in contrast to India, where the employment elasticity to value added in organized manufacturing was assessed at only 0.33 during 1986–96 and was even depressed at −1.42 during 1996–2002 (Mazumdar and Sarkar 2008).

From the comparison of aggregate value added and employment growth during 1995–2005, it follows that there has been only a modest growth in labor productivity (about 2.6 percent per year). Manufacturing growth was mainly due to more labor input rather than higher productivity; as a result, it is difficult to attain or sustain a high level of wage growth in the manufacturing sector.[14] Further analysis suggests that about 27–30 percent of these productivity gains have been transferred to workers in the form of higher wages (Ahmed et al. 2011).

This pattern of employment expansion at a relatively low-skill, low-wage level could be sustained for three reasons. First, even though the wage rate in the manufacturing (or, for that matter, construction) sector was low, as we have already noted, the level was still considerably higher than that prevailing in the agricultural sector, thereby providing incentives for moving out of agriculture (Figure 3.3). Second, the largest part of the manufacturing employment growth came from the RMG sector; its woven and knitwear segments together constituted only 16.7 percent of manufacturing employment in 1990/91, but went up to 53 percent by 2005/06. The RMG sector could register phenomenal growth in Bangladesh mainly based on low-wage competitiveness. In the woven subsector (the mainstay of RMG), a regular supply of female labor at a relatively low wage was possible due to low opportunity costs of female labor. But even here the wage situation of garment workers has improved.[15] Third, the relatively low inflation rate (3–5 percent annually) prevailing from the 1990s up to the mid 2000s also helped to maintain the low wage level during the period. Nevertheless, it is important to note that the

---

[14] The discussion on growth in manufacturing employment, as presented in Sections 3.5.2 and 3.5.3, draws on the evidence presented in Ahmed et al. (2011).

[15] However, this argument does not hold true to the same extent in the case of the knitwear subsector, which employed mostly men (though here too 33 percent of the workforce was female in 2011). This subsector was absent in the early 1990s, but its contribution was already visible by the mid 2000s.

growth of the RMG industry had a beneficial effect on women workers, as 90 percent of them were migrants from rural areas and three-quarters of them hailed from landless and/or poorer strata (Afsar 2000). Another export sector where female workers were important was footwear. For example, in case of Apex Group—the leading footwear firm in the country—almost 90 percent of the employed workers are women.[16]

Several manufacturing subsectors with high employment intensity grew either in response to the rapid growth of the RMG industry or as a result of the expansion of the construction sector that indirectly benefited from the increased flow of international remittances. The former led to the growth of backward-linkage industries such as cotton textiles, while the latter led to the growth of cement, bricks and tiles, iron, and steel re-rolling mills.

Other export-oriented sectors also played a role in creating jobs, though their successes were much more modest. To illustrate this, we focus on units employing ten or more workers based on the 2005/06 Census of Manufacturing Industries (CMI) data. These data suggest that processed fish and seafood export units constituted only 1.7 percent of manufacturing value added, and they provided an even lower (0.4 percent) share of total manufacturing employment. The same goes for the partially export-oriented pharmaceutical sector.[17] This sector accounted for 5 percent of total manufacturing value added, but only 2 percent of manufacturing employment. The only exception to this pattern of modest job creation is the export-oriented footwear industry, which tends to have medium-sized (between ten and ninety-nine workers) firms and registered strong employment growth of 8 percent annually during 1986–2001/03, according to the Economic Census Reports. While the potential contribution of non-RMG export sectors to manufacturing growth and employment remains considerable, the actual realization of that potential would require addressing the bottlenecks relating to development of industrial capability in specific sectors, removing uncertainty with FDI inflows, and fostering flexible skills (similar to China).

3.5.3 Declining "Duality": Changes in the Size Distribution of Manufacturing Firms

Duality in manufacturing employment refers to a persistent polarization between traditional units engaged in subsistence types of activities (the cottage

---

[16] This is based on discussions by the authors with the Apex Group.

[17] The pharmaceutical industry is termed "partially export-oriented" because only four out of about fifty units surveyed were engaged in export activities. However, this sector holds considerable promise in the future, as demand for pharmaceutical products from Bangladesh continues to grow. Pharmaceutical products currently are exported from Bangladesh to more than seventy countries.

industry is one example), and modern units based on power, hired labor, and moving towards more market-oriented production. Although there is still a familiar U-shaped distribution of firms, with two distinct concentration points around small firms (less than ten workers) and large firms (with one hundred or more workers) along with a thin middle (between ten and ninety-nine workers), the traditional segment is fast losing ground. There have been important changes in the size distribution of manufacturing units according to Economic Census data for 1986 and 2001/03.[18] The share of the smallest units (less than ten workers) in total manufacturing employment declined from about 61 percent to 40 percent over this period.[19] In contrast, the employment share of large enterprises (with 100 or more workers) increased from 27 percent to 42 percent in the same period.[20]

What explains the strong growth in employment in large enterprises? The answer lies mainly in the growth of the RMG sector, which dominates the large-firm groups, that is, those with 200–499 workers and 500 workers and more. To establish this, we need to go beyond economic censuses and focus on the results of the sample surveys, such as the Census of Manufacturing Industries. According to CMI data, the share of manufacturing employment accounted for by very large enterprises (employing 500 workers or more) increased from 30 percent in 1995/96 to 37 percent in 2001/02, driven mainly by the RMG growth. The share of employment in very large firms accounted for by RMG firms increased from 23 percent in 1991/92 to 63 percent in 2001/02, with the trend becoming even more pronounced in the decade of the 2000s. Employment in the RMG sector grew at an impressive rate of 11 percent annually over the 2001–14 period. Thus, as of 2013/14, the RMG sector employed about 4.2 million workers, up from 1.8 million in 2001/02, 2.2 million in 2005/06, and 3.6 million in 2009/10.[21]

At this point, it is worth noting that the remarkable growth of RMG enterprises in Bangladesh is attributable to several factors. Institutional innovations

---

[18] The first Economic Census of non-farm economic activities was carried out by BBS in 1986 and was repeated again in 2001, but it was at first done only in urban areas. In 2003, the Census was extended to rural areas. In what follows we also use other sources of data, such as the Census of Manufacturing Industries, where applicable. The CMI is actually not a census, but a large-scale sample survey.

[19] The decline in subsistence manufacturing is also evident from the Annual Establishment and Institution Surveys (AEIS), which show that employment in household-based manufacturing dropped in absolute terms between 1992/93 and 2002/03. In comparison, non-household-based manufacturing units with less than ten workers registered a modest growth in employment of 2.5 percent over this period.

[20] Note that the Economic Censuses of 1986 and 2001/03 do not provide employment data on very large (500 or more employees) enterprises, and hence the comparison of firms with less than ten workers is made only with firms having 100 or more workers.

[21] This is based on the data provided by the Bangladesh Garment Manufacturers and Exporters Association (BGMEA) in 2014.

such as bonded warehouses (allowing duty-free imports of fabrics from abroad as well as reducing the risks of leakages of such imports for the local market) and back-to-back Letters of Credit (reducing the upfront capital requirement for opening a Letter of Credit) supported the sector. But other factors also mattered. While Easterly (2001) emphasizes the importance of initial technology transfers from Korea, such a one-time infusion of knowledge alone may be insufficient to explain the sustained growth. Mottaleb and Sonobe (2011) find that the high profitability of garment manufacturing due to the initial infusion of specific human capital attracted a number of highly educated entrepreneurs to the industry. But sustained growth in the sector was due to the continuous learning from abroad by these entrepreneurs. Most of these entrepreneurs originally came from a middle-class background with no prior exposure to running modern industry. The success of RMG—and the example it set of "learning by doing and seeing"—thus fostered the development of a broad-based industrial entrepreneurship in Bangladesh within a span of two decades.

As regards the medium-sized manufacturing firms, the following may be noted. The units falling into the middle (i.e., those with between ten and ninety-nine workers) registered a modest increase from 13 percent to 17 percent of manufacturing employment between 1986 and 2001/03 according to the Economic Censuses, but even here significant interindustry variation is noticeable. Of the top twenty-five manufacturing subsectors in terms of employment in the ten to ninety-nine worker category, at least fourteen of them registered fast growth in employment exceeding 5 percent per year (Ahmed et al. 2011). These include paper products, plastic products, footwear, non-metallic mineral products, wearing apparel, knitted wear and fabrics, furniture products, metal tanks and reservoirs, printing, and processing. These products cater to domestic markets.

3.5.4 *Shifting Pattern of Employment in the Service Sector*

Mapping of the employment dynamics in the service sector is limited by data availability, with only two Economic Censuses carried out, for 1986 and 2001/03. The share of the service sector in total non-farm employment increased from 57.1 to 68.9 percent over this period (Rahman and Hossain 1995; Mahmud 1996; Sen 1996). A further breakdown within the service sector shows very little increase in employment in wholesale and retail trade, with the bulk of the increase in "other services," which includes the transport sector and community services (Sen 2012). Available evidence for the 2000s suggests that there has been a distinct shift within the service sector towards more dynamic "modern" subsectors, such as professional and financial services, as well as the emergence of modern establishments within trade, transport, and a range of other personal services.[22] There is a huge potential for this rising modern service sector to employ skilled workers in urban areas in the coming decade. Most of these workers have been educated in private higher-secondary and higher-education establishments and now seek entry into modern domestic and export-oriented service firms, including electronic media, IT, real estate, health, and financial services. However, the contribution of the modern service subsectors to employment warrants greater empirical scrutiny.

3.6 Urban Growth and Rural Wellbeing

Apart from the direct job-creating effects of migration, export-led manufacturing, and service sectors, there are also important indirect effects of urbanization and export sectors on the wellbeing of rural labor, especially on the sending households. Here we focus on three examples: (a) effects of urban proximity on the rural non-farm sector by providing enhanced market access to the latter; (b) the impact of seasonal migration to the urban construction sector on the economic lives of the sending rural households; and (c) social (human development) effects of the RMG sector on the villages that send garment workers.

3.6.1 Urban Proximity and Rural Non-farm Development

Access to markets matters for rural growth and proximity to urban centers provides this access. Thus, large urban centers not only have had favorable effects on the migrants themselves, but close urban proximity may also have supported productivity growth for laborers engaged in rural non-farm sectors through spatial linkage effects. Deichman et al. (2009), in the only study that analyzes such effects for Bangladesh, identifies three noteworthy features. First, proximity (as measured by arched distance) to major urban centers increases the concentration of high-return non-farm activities. Second, while urban demand is an important explanatory factor underlying such high returns, farm productivity also matters, as urban linkages are stronger in areas with higher agricultural potential. The results of the study seem to indicate that the green revolution combined with urban access is what is needed for boosting non-farm productivity in rural areas. However, low-return

---

[22] Thus, simple van-carts and boats have been increasingly being replaced by more mechanized transports even in rural areas. A range of new personal and community service establishments have emerged in urban areas catering to the new consumer needs and tastes of the growing urban middle class.

non-farm jobs (defined as paying equal to or less than the median agricultural wage of a village) are driven by local demand and, hence, are distributed much more evenly across geographic space. Third, not all urban access matters though, as there is a threshold effect here. Access to smaller rural towns (about 5,000 in the Bangladesh case) exerts little influence on non-farm activities. The empirical results of Deichman et al. (2009) emphasize the role of improved connectivity of regions with higher agricultural potential (north-west region), especially through the Jamuna Bridge, to urban centers for stimulating rural non-farm growth.

3.6.2 *Impact of Seasonal Migration to the Construction Sector on Sending Households*

Rapid growth in the real estate sector played an important role in the creation of non-agricultural jobs for rural as well as urban laborers. Here we focus on the high-growth real estate construction activities in urban areas. The number of real estate construction companies rose from just 10 in 1994 to 100 in 2004, and then rose dramatically to 1,200 by 2012.[23] The subsector now employs about 2 million construction workers, who are mainly recruited from the countryside through a contracting system led by labor-hiring middlemen on behalf of real estate companies.[24] The price of land in Dhaka city has increased quite dramatically.[25] The housing industry has experienced massive growth, further boosting domestic demand for labor in related industries.

A case study of seasonal migration to the urban construction sector (specifically the brick-making industry) illustrates how this migration can lead to a reduction in seasonal-related distress, perhaps more effectively than social protection programs.[26] The study of brickfield workers in the areas adjacent to Dhaka city shows that they come from the disaster-prone areas of both the southern (coastal belt) and northern (river erosion belt) parts of the country. Several observations are noteworthy.

First, most of these migrant workers are in the 30–45 age group, and 57 percent have no education with only a quarter having completed primary education. So this is rural–urban mobility at a very low skill level. Most of the respondents were engaged in agriculture (both self-employed and laborers)

[23] In Dhaka city alone, as per the information of just one large real estate firm Sheltech, the number of housing apartments was only 147 in 1982, increasing to 900 in 1996, then rising dramatically to 13,309 in 2010.

[24] This is based on communication with Tanvirul Haque Probal, ex-President of the Real Estate Association and the co-owner of a leading real estate company, Building for Future Ltd.

[25] See Seraj (2012), based on Sheltech data. This has made Dhaka one of the most expensive cities in the world in terms of housing costs.

[26] The results of the case study are based on primary analysis of a small field survey carried out by Hossain and Sen (2011).

and non-agricultural wage labor as their main occupations prior to their migration.[27]

Second, the average monthly income of the brickfield respondents before migration was Taka 1,280 in contrast to an after-migration monthly income of Taka 5,385 with just one cycle of seasonal work. However, this underestimates the total income gain, since the brickfield workers do at least two cycles of seasonal migration in a year (spending in total about six months in cities).

Third, these workers send, on average, Taka 16,000 in annual remittances to their families back in the village (termed the "sending community"). In comparison, a social protection beneficiary in rural areas would receive at most Taka 6,000 per year, including conditional cash transfers. As a result, the subjective poverty data show that 70 percent of migrant households were in the extreme food deficit category before migration but that figure fell to 3 percent after migration. Seasonal rickshaw pullers who migrate to cities for work during the lean seasons provide a similar example.

If the benefits are so evident, why don't all poor households from sending communities avail themselves of this migration opportunity? Differential access to funding for migration can provide one explanation: 70 percent of the workers surveyed reported being members of microfinance institutions in the sending villages and used MFI resources for migration financing. This is an option not always available to many extreme poor.

3.6.3 *Impact of Export-led Manufacturing on Human Development in the Village Economy*

The growth of export-led manufacturing has had sizable effects on human capital accumulation in the sending villages. Evidence of demand in the job market conveys positive signals to households remaining in these villages about the potential returns to education, thus changing their incentives for human capital accumulation.

The continuous growth of the RMG sector has typically attracted low-skilled—but not illiterate—young female workers. This has certainly provided a boost to literacy among girls in the villages. The parents of young women in rural areas seem to have responded to the employment opportunities in the RMG sector by sending daughters to schools (to attend or complete at least

[27] Brick-making has a seasonal character, being usually discontinued in the monsoon season due to regular flooding. Seasonality allows the brick-making workers to remain in their village for parts of the year while taking advantage of employment opportunities in the construction sector in other times of the year. The peak season for brick-making is usually November to May. This is somewhat coincident with the aman cycle, the summer crop rice harvesting season in November–December, and with the boro cycle, the winter crop rice sowing season in January and harvesting in May. This may suggest the possibility of further tightening of the rural labor market in areas from where the construction workers are recruited.

primary education) in order to grasp these opportunities later on (Paul-Majumder and Begum 2006). One study actually quantifies the difference in female secondary enrollment between the RMG-proximate villages and control villages, and estimates the matched gap to be 27 percent (Heath and Mobarak 2012). This study attributes this to the RMG proximity/association alone after controlling for the effects of incentives that come with secondary stipend schemes.[28]

3.7 Jobs and Social Policy for Improved Social Cohesion

Good jobs may generate positive externalities in the workplace, community, and society, building up social cohesion. These are the World Development Report's "good jobs for development" (World Bank 2012). Social cohesion can be defined in various ways; for example, relating to the "nature and extent of social and economic divisions within society." A cohesive society is also one that is "richly endowed with stocks of social capital" or, alternatively, described with "a sufficiently high 'aggregated' level of 'social capital' which is accumulated at micro-level," that is, individuals, communities, and workplaces (see Easterly et al. 2006 on various definitions). The effects of jobs on social cohesion will depend on the nature of job creation, the level of trust, and the presence of social policy that encourages human development. The last of these encompasses investments in female education and participation, child and youth education measures, and social protection policies for the extreme poor.

In the Bangladesh case, this nexus between jobs and social cohesion has been aided by pre-existing social and cultural institutions as well as geography, that is, by faith and by the habitat. Socio-ethnic fragmentation can adversely affect long-term economic growth (Easterly 2001). One channel through which such growth effects percolate is social cohesion. Socio-ethnic fragmentation negatively influences the degree of social cohesion, giving rise to heterogeneous social preferences regarding the choice of public goods in the society (Alesina et al. 1997). As a result, both public and private investments suffer, with implications for long-term growth and sustainable job creation. From this perspective, the Bangladeshi society has remained more homogenous culturally, that is, less susceptible to the risks of ethnic/caste divide that are present in most other countries of South Asia.

[28] The female secondary stipend scheme was introduced in rural areas in the 1990s and is widely considered to have had a positive effect on girls' schooling even though the magnitude of stipend was minimal—only Taka 300 (or about $4US) per female student per month. The study by Heath and Mobarak (2012) revealed the additional effect of the RMG proximity on school enrollment over and above the cross-cutting effect of the female stipend scheme across the villages.

The social and religious institutions also seem to be less conservative given the influence of the *Hannafi* tradition of Islam, which is more open than other extreme interpretations of custom, creed, and culture such as the *Waahabi* orthodoxy (Ahmed 2010). In the Bangladesh example, the creation of jobs has minimized the conflicts between the social segments adhering to different religious and secular views. Even religious leaders have followed a pro-development growth path by allowing room for practicing population control and women's education more vigorously since the early 1980s. In the recent period, though the conflict between the two views has at times become acute, women's economic empowerment situation can still be negotiated within a national development framework. Here, the role of civil society (including the media) has come out very strongly as a vigilant actor in the political process. Some have even argued that the relatively open village setting (in the geographic sense with no distinct village boundary) has been an expression of social inclusiveness with respect to the excluded and ostracized (Eaton 1993; Khan 1996).

The country's habitat (geography) also has had long-term psychological effects on social cohesion. Much of rural Asia is based on the need for large-scale surface-water-based irrigation schemes, which made the Asiatic villages dependent on state investments, resulting in more allegiance to centralized rule in the first place. Such compulsions were missing in the agrarian society of Bangladesh historically. This has conditioned a certain social skepticism towards large-scale, state-led social mobilization and has shaped a certain preference for more small-scale cooperation (as in the case of Grameen Bank and BRAC small-group interventions).

The peasant agriculture could not be atomistic based on exclusive individualism either under the agro-ecological constraints. Being located in a hyperactive delta that gave farms access to several mighty rivers (which made the land extremely fertile), the agriculturalists were highly susceptible to periodic natural disasters, ecological risks, and crop failures. All these led to a social formation that was pre-inclined to become more open to new ideas and practices, and also to avoid extreme paths, that is, blind loyalty to centralized rule and purely opportunity-driven atomistic individualism. The social fabric of rural Bangladesh seems to have preferred a "middle path" between the two aforementioned extreme paths and hence left more room for social cohesion than (arguably) could be accommodated in some other more settled parts of South Asia. Because of negative shocks arising from unforeseen contingencies such as natural disasters, both informal mutual insurance and formal arrangements play important roles in Bangladesh villages (Sawada 2007).

In addition, Bangladesh has produced NGOs on a much larger scale than any other countries in the region. This was also shaped by a favorable initial condition. Most of the initial founding members of the NGOs in the 1970s were active middle-class participants of the secular political and social movements of the 1960s; in addition, a large segment of them had taken part directly in the national liberation movement of 1971.[29] After Independence, with the backdrop of a war-ravaged economy, NGOs fostered social cohesion in Bangladeshi villages through strong disaster-management activities, thereby helping the government to maintain overall economic stability. Later, the government allowed the NGOs to grow by accepting partnerships with these organizations in the development process, which has led to a win–win situation for both. From the 1990s onward, NGOs can be seen to be changing their roles through greater professionalization. NGO professionals have become involved in diverse areas of development beyond microcredit while maintaining the complementary social cohesion-enhancing role throughout this period.

On the other hand, social inequality in terms of landownership—especially the dominance of large landholders—is considered to have negative effects on the schooling of lower classes, non-farm development, and labor mobility.[30] The phenomenon of large-scale landownership had been relatively absent in Bangladesh before the introduction of the Zamindari Settlement in 1793 by the colonial rule. As the population density increased over time, drawn by the availability of fertile land, the peasantry became differentiated, but did not see the emergence of large landholders comparable to what was witnessed in some other parts of South Asia during the postcolonial period (Sindh, Punjab, Bihar, Uttar Pradesh). In short, the initial social inequality revolving around land ownership—especially the conflict between large non-cultivating and small cultivating holdings over land rights—was much less acute in Bangladesh and hence provided favorable initial historical conditions for faster social mobility of peasantry and succeeding generations during the years after Independence.[31]

Social policy also mattered for social cohesion by putting a human face on democracy. Successive democratic regimes have pursued social policy in rural areas over the past two decades. The need for such policy was apparent after the 1974 famine, which was followed by frequent flood episodes in the 1970s and 1980s. Social policy has been instrumental in reducing population growth, thus encouraging better (private) investments in the education and health of children, better skill formation in rural areas, and much broader access to social

---

[29] This has been ascertained by interviewing selected leaders of the NGO sector.

[30] This argument was theoretically elaborated in Ray (1998), and empirically validated by Alesina and Rodrik (1994), Acemoglu et al. (2001), and Banerjee and Iyer (2005) with different sets of data and historical contexts.

[31] Social inequality around land ownership between cultivating and non-cultivating landholders possibly became less acute after the Partition of 1947 with the exit of Hindu absentee *zamindars* by and large.

protection.[32] Pro-poor, pro-female, and pro-youth social policies (through both government and NGO interventions) have led to greater aspirations for work-force participation among youth and females (those with some education), feminization of agriculture in the face of male outmigration, and in general has played a supportive, socially transformative role in a traditional context as carriers of "modernization values."

However, social cohesion in a developing society cannot be influenced only by social policy. Recent attitudes in Bangladeshi villages or towns may have been shaped (arguably) more by the complex interplay of globalization, marketization, and individualism, blended with a certain distrust for electoral politics and the state actors. The rise of individualism may affect trust and vitiate the atmosphere for social cohesion both in rural and urban areas. When everyone has a job, social peace can reign. When some have access to good jobs, and others do not, it can breed distrust, even signal brewing social conflict. Insights from experimental economics based on empirical trust game trials in Bangladesh—testing the level of trust among participants of various social groups—can provide insights in this regard.

3.7.1 *Job Satisfaction and Social Cohesion: Results from "Trust Games"*

Social capital is an important subset of social cohesion. Trust is a key measure of social capital and, through that channel, represents an important dimension of social cohesion. Johansson-Stenman et al. (2005, 2009) conducted "trust games" in the Netrokona, Mymensingh, Manikganj, Gazipur, and Narayanganj districts of the Dhaka Division of Bangladesh.[33] Based on their data, Sawada (2012) carried out further analysis exploring job status and job happiness as possible explanatory factors of trust and, hence, social cohesion. The results lead to several observations. First, for the entire sample, job status does not have any statistically significant impact on trust or social capital.[34] Second, restricting the sample to the relatively younger age group (below 37 years), however, renders the job-status variable a significant correlate of trust and social capital. The results suggest that educated but jobless youth will feel less trusting towards others. For example, unemployment among the edu-cated decreases their (fraction-based) trust and trustworthiness measures by

---

[32] The budgetary allocations for social protection increased from 5 percent of total public expenditure in 1991 to 16 percent in 2010. However, for inexplicable reasons, the urban poor are still largely bypassed by social policy.

[33] Trust games refer to the experimental games involving monetary transfers—with provisions for explicit rewards and penalties—between individuals and social groups belonging to diverse social networks. Subjects were selected randomly from randomly selected villages.

[34] The job status is proxied in alternative specifications by unemployment status, a dummy variable for not currently working, and an ordered job-happiness variable (scaled from 1 to 10), all of which turned out to be statistically insignificant.

80.2 percent and 106 percent on average, respectively. Third, the study also finds that unemployment decreases the level of job-related happiness and overall happiness by 30.6 percent and 18.3 percent, respectively.[35]

The main result of the experimental game is to point out the importance of job status (unemployment, job satisfaction) as a correlate of trust and trust-worthiness in society and, by implication acting through the trust channel, as a correlate of social cohesion in that society. The results suggest declining unemployment and underemployment rates among youth are likely to be correlated favorably with enhanced trust and social cohesion in the Bangladeshi villages.

3.7.2 Jobs and Inclusion of the Poor in Growth and Development

Given the nature of job creation in Bangladesh—intersectoral mobility of labor from lower-earning jobs to higher-earning jobs at a relatively low level of skills—it is not surprising that such jobs would be poverty reducing, especially for the poorest. This is seen in four dimensions. First, there has been a drop in overall poverty incidence. Second, consumption inequality remained stable in the decade of the 2000s, meaning that poorer groups experienced the same rate of consumption expenditure growth as richer groups (Osmani and Sen 2011). This has somewhat reduced the socially disruptive effects of rising income inequality in the same period, and contributed to social cohesiveness. Third, there was evidence of regional convergence in the level of rural poverty by 2010, thanks to faster progress against poverty in the lagging regions between 2005 and 2010. Fourth, while there is still considerable presence of specific chronic (long-duration) poverty groups, the incidence of extreme income poverty is decreasing over time, though at a slower pace than that of moderate income poverty.

3.7.3 Jobs and Inclusion of Women in Growth and Development

Inclusion of women in growth and development has been one of the most celebrated aspects of the country's ascent. But it was thought that female labor force participation—an important ingredient of growth acceleration in the initial stages of development—would be restricted in Bangladesh due to the oppressive nature of patriarchy, with conservative social norms such as Purdah constraining female labor mobility outside the sphere of household work.

---

[35] To the extent that a happy society creates a conducive psychological environment for the functioning of a cohesive society, job-related happiness may be an important determinant of social cohesion.

One view strongly expressed the disempowerment of women in the Bangladesh countryside in the following terms: "The picture that emerges from our analysis of patriarchy and women's work in rural Bangladesh is bleak. Powerful norms of female seclusion extend to labor markets, severely limiting women's opportunities for independent income generation. At the same time evidence suggests that under the pressure of increasing poverty, male bonds of obligation to support women are weakening, thus creating increasing numbers of women who must fend for themselves" (Cain et al. 1979).

Such a pessimistic appraisal of the female role in the labor market in the 1970s could not anticipate that women would provide the secret ingredients of success that was achieved in Bangladesh from exports to schooling to microcredit use. These stories have been described already in this chapter. Why was such pessimism about female empowerment overstated? There are several possible explanations. First, many failed to assess the progressive potential of moderate Muslim society already existing in many parts of rural Eastern Bengal. Second, the rich legacy of female empowerment literature was overlooked. Such literature ranged from the urban feminist writings in *Totto-bodhini* to *Begum* (the latter inspired by Begum Rokeya—the preeminent feminist Muslim thinker in early twentieth-century Bengal). It was also inspired by a rich tradition of urban women's and civil rights movements in Bangladesh in the 1950s and 1960s. The moot point is to recognize the beneficial initial intellectual condition in terms of the presence of liberal attitudes among the rising vernacular elite, who later adopted gender-friendly and pro-female social policies after Independence.

Third, incentives for female participation mattered. Pessimistic appraisals did not anticipate that resources would come from outside (microcredit, RMG work opportunities, and conditional food/cash for female education) into traditional village societies, which would strengthen the voice and agency of rural women. Pessimistic views on women's potential roles also did not antici-pate that some women would be willing to take risks even in the face of social exclusion to take advantage of any opportunities that came by. Socially nega-tive images of the RMG workers as "fallen women" prevailing in the early 1990s are a case in point. Most female workers defied or redefined the terms of engagement in modern factory jobs to their favor, often by wearing *hijab* in the public place, but with increasing assertiveness for gender rights. Public policy also supported the formation of favorable gender norms via conditional food/cash transfers, female work programs/safety nets, and women's health and nutrition programs.

Finally, the strong future role of NGOs was not foreseen by many in the 1970s and 1980s. Yet such a role was not a novelty; it was anticipated already by the "Comilla model" to some extent, which emphasized the social role of women cooperatives.[36] As a result of all these factors, female workforce participation rose from a very low level of 12 percent in 1983/84 to over 30 percent at present.

3.7.4 *Jobs and Inclusion of Youth in Growth and Development*

The country also managed well the job market expectations of the growing youth population. This is not just a social issue in a country dominated by youth (the below 20 age group constitutes about 45 percent of the population and the below 30 age group about 60 percent). Recent migration to cities—as indicated by the construction sector case study—is mainly dominated by youth. Young workers with some education are now visible in urban transport, manufacturing (large and small), and the trade/service sectors. This suggests that the country's labor market dynamics have been able to manage the social equation between the supply and demand for jobs reasonably well. This applies also to tertiary-educated youth—a formidable voice in social and political movements in Bangladesh historically. These young people mostly (70 percent) were educated in private educational establishments and got jobs mostly (90 percent) in the modern sector, ranging from NGOs, banking, insurance, leasing companies, export firms, and in overseas employment. The role of overseas employment for youth has been particularly important in maintaining social cohesion in the country.[37]

Compared to the private sector, the public sector has played a very limited role in generating jobs for the educated youth in Bangladesh. Public-sector job opportunities are constrained by the fiscal situation, skills mismatches are more pronounced than in the private sector, and the problem of queuing is more acute.[38] Bangladesh was more fortunate in this regard compared to economies that continued to have dominant public sectors, with the gradually declining share of public-sector enterprises (which now constitute only 20–30 percent of total employment, assets, and investments in the formal sector).

[36] The "Comilla model" was started by Akhter Hamid Khan—a civil servant with deep commitment to rural development—in the 1960s within then East Pakistan. It focused on organizing small and medium farmers into cooperatives built around input use and marketing of output. The cooperatives were formed separately for male and female farmer groups.

[37] This issue merits separate scrutiny, however. While no precise data are available on the stock of migrants working abroad, estimates based on HIES 2010 data suggest that about 9 percent of households in urban areas and 11 percent of households in rural areas have at least one migrant worker abroad. Most of the workers are in the category of "skilled workers" (accounting for 70 percent of total migrant workers according to the official data provided by the Bureau of Manpower, Employment, and Training), suggesting a positive correlation between education and overseas employment.

[38] This has been observed almost universally in developing countries, irrespective of level of income and human development, with a high share of public employment in total employment. For an empirical application to Sri Lanka (having similarity to the Bangladesh situation prevailing in the 1970s and 1980s), see Rama (2003).

3.8 Conclusions

Notwithstanding the initial pessimism about Bangladesh's long-term development prospects and sporadic skepticism about sustaining development success
in the face of weak governance, the country has achieved decent progress in
raising per capita income, which more than doubled between 1991 and 2011.
Bangladesh belongs to a rather small group of countries that has maintained
reasonably high growth without too much volatility, accompanied by an
impressive poverty reduction and human development record. It has become
the lead performer among the LDCs and, according to recent World Bank data,
has already joined the club of "lower middle-income country" in 2013/14.
A recent HSBC (2012) report included Bangladesh in the list of the top thirty
countries that would have a very high growth rate in the decades up to 2050.
Standard and Poor's rating of Bangladesh has shown consistent improvements
in the past five years at a time of global financial turmoil.

There is an embedded story of jobs as an accelerator of growth and as a
source of social cohesion in this turnaround. Bangladesh has been successful in
generating "good jobs" by improving farm–non-farm, rural–urban, intersectoral labor mobility at a relatively low skill level that has had welfare-enhancing
(poverty reducing and social cohesion-enhancing) effects. There were several
sectoral drivers in this process, some acting sequentially and others simultaneously, over the course of the last two decades. The chapter's main findings are
summarized in ten key moments.

First, the "green revolution" in the form of a new HYV seed–irrigation–
fertilizer package provided the required technological breakthrough in the
rice sector. This not only increased the productivity of self-employed workers
but also increased wage employment opportunities in crop agriculture, bene-
fiting the poorest. Even in the presence of surplus labor, a rise in agricultural
wages occurred through the channel of productivity gains.

Second, farm–non-farm linkages were important. Increases in farm productivity released surplus farm labor for non-agricultural jobs. During the
1990s, such jobs were mostly created in the rural non-farm self-employment
sector, where productivity growth was slow but the level of RNF income
still provided incentives to move in. Later, during the 2000s, migration
became more common, as farm labor started shifting to urban areas in a
more pronounced way.

Third, this process was aided first by improved connectivity within rural
areas—spearheaded by the Local Government Engineering Department—
and, later, between rural and urban areas through the Roads and Highways
Department. Construction of mega-projects such as the Jamuna Bridge helped
to integrate the product and labor markets, connecting lagging western
regions with the leading eastern regions.

Fourth, this transformation of surplus-releasing agriculture was supported by simultaneous broad-based public investments in human development in the 1990s leading to intergenerational occupational mobility in the subsequent period. These human development programs and MFIs also led to another significant socially desirable result, namely the social and economic empowerment of women. As a result, population growth came down impressively along with the reduction in child mortality, leading to improved education and health of children, and more savings/investment potential at the household level. This tendency became stronger in the decade of the 2000s when the demand for female labor was further stimulated by growth in manufacturing.

Fifth, the incentives for rural–urban, agricultural–non-agricultural labor mobility were provided by two main factors operating at the macro level—export-led manufacturing growth and rapid expansion of international migration opportunities. This tendency became stronger in the decade of the 2000s, when the demand for female labor was particularly pronounced. The bulk of the jobs created came from readymade garments. The success of RMG was due to a mix of policies, incentives, and changing gender norms. Persistent risk-taking behavior amid liberalized market opportunities fostered the development of private entrepreneurship. There has been a remarkable transformation literally in one generation from a trader and a loan-defaulter class to a successful industrial entrepreneur and a dynamic exporter class. Here learning by doing and seeing played a pivotal role. The relatively low inflation rate prevailing in the 1990s up to the mid 2000s also helped to maintain export competitiveness during the period. The growth of the RMG industry had a beneficial effect on rural women workers. But the success in exports was not limited to RMG alone. Other non-traditional export industries—from frozen food, to ceramics, to footwear, to food-processing, to pharmaceuticals—also developed during the period, as did the domestic linkage industries associated with RMG and other export industries.

Sixth, with rising per capita GDP, domestic demand-driven industries became more viable. Some industries that started as export activities catered increasingly to domestic demand (as in the case of tea). In contrast, others such as pharmaceuticals, ceramics, and food-processing, which initially operated only in the domestic market, started producing for export markets. As a result the duality of the manufacturing sector—marked by the extreme polarities between very small (less than 10 workers) and very large (500 and more workers) enterprises—declined. The gradual disappearance of the traditional cottage industries was counteracted by an emerging segment of middle-sized enterprises and by an increasingly higher share of large enterprises. The net outcome of these changes in the size-class distribution of employment in the manufacturing sector was pro-poor in nature and forms a contrast to instances of "jobless growth" found in some other countries.

Seventh, for casual agricultural laborers with limited resources for financing international migration, indirect effects of international migration through the channel of the labor market had greater significance. The main point to note is that wage growth tends to be higher in villages experiencing high growth in overseas remittances. Overseas remittances indirectly supported the growth of the construction sector in general and the real estate sector in particular (besides contributing to an improved current account balance).

Eighth, as the pace of urbanization increased, sustained and remunerative economic migration of farm labor to gainful non-agricultural sectors in urban areas became a pattern. In many cases, construction and transport workers such as those engaged in brickfields and rickshaw-pulling could be seasonally combined with agricultural and non-agricultural work, thus reducing the burden of underemployment in agriculture. There was a persistent gap between wages in non-agricultural sectors and agriculture throughout this period, but the gap increased more prominently in the second half of the 2000s encouraging further migration.

Ninth, increased relocation of farm labor to non-agricultural jobs in urban areas also had beneficial effects on the place of origin of migration. This can be seen in several aspects. The size of the rural land tenancy market increased sharply in a way that was not anticipated. So did the contractual forms of tenancy: sharecropping declined, while cash-rent became increasingly prominent. This happened due to increased relocation of landowners in more remunerative non-agricultural activities, especially with faster urbanization. All these changes worked to the favor of tenant farmers. The benefits of such agrarian changes also reached the landless tenants, whose total leased-in land rose due to the relaxation of liquidity constraints provided by rapidly expanding microcredit. As a result of all these changes, the agricultural labor market further tightened with pronounced increases in real wages. In the face of rising agricultural wages and a shortage of seasonal agricultural labor in the 2000s, farmers gradually started using labor-saving techniques in the peak seasons, thereby accelerating the growth in farm-sector productivity. Urbanization also had positive indirect effects on rural productivity.

Finally, the success of Bangladesh in triggering and sustaining the movement of labor from farming to non-agricultural sectors was attributable to several factors. Success would not have been achieved without policies to support agricultural modernization, basic human development, improved connectivity, and policies that supported export-oriented production and explicit female orientation in human development and employment. Transition to democracy and staying firmly on that course over the past two decades also helped. Access to global markets made a difference, as is evident in the case of RMG exports and overseas remittances. Institutional innovations also played an important role, such as encouraging alternative service delivery for human development and self-employment.

A lack of ethnic heterogeneity and relative absence of social inequality based on large landownership helped in maintaining social cohesion by setting the initial tone, but the main impetus came from the nature of job creation itself. The poor, women, and youth benefited from job creation. Growth was not jobless. The broad-based nature of employment also provided social stability which was important to maintain growth acceleration and social cohesion at the same time even amid rising incomes. The creation of jobs also has minimized the conflict between religious and secular views, which has not constrained and destabilized the development process of the country as it has elsewhere. The challenge for the Bangladesh economy—from the jobs perspective—lies, however, in maintaining this momentum.

The readymade garments industry does not face the risk of decline in the next twenty to thirty years. Even though considerable compliance challenges persist in the RMG sector, they are being addressed sequentially through the combined efforts of the government, private sector, and global buyers. This is being done by addressing the workers' safety concerns in the first place through relocation of at-risk sites and/or closure of such premises. As a result of these initiatives, RMG exports continue to show robust growth. By diversifying textile products in the future, the sector can still grow and has enormous potential to respond to the new apparel export opportunities provided by the rise of minimum wages in the apparel export sector of China. The main reason is the competitiveness of the RMG sector, based on relatively low labor costs as well as the presence of dynamic entrepreneurship in the modern sector. The female labor force participation rate is still very low and only a small fraction of these female workers currently participates in the RMG sector. Footwear and leather exports also hold out considerable future promise. However, the pharmaceutical industry may face constraints in accessing the export market (currently it is exporting to over 70 countries) if the country loses its LDC status and open access to patent technology that it is enjoying now. In such a situation, cheap raw materials for pharmaceuticals may not be available to Bangladesh, which would reduce its competitive edge in this product line.

Given the market access, Bangladesh still has room for growth acceleration. Having said that, policy attention should be drawn to two relatively neglected dimensions of jobs in Bangladesh. One is gradually overcoming the informality of the job market, which will be a relevant consideration in the next two decades. A large layer of informal workers may have acted as a buffer for the less-skilled or surplus agricultural workers shifting to the non-agricultural labor market. While not much evidence has been available on this segment of the labor market, overcoming informal–formal sector dualism may emerge as an important policy challenge in creating "good jobs" as Bangladesh aims to maintain its current status as a lower middle-income country and move up further.

Second, while the number of jobs has grown and the sectoral shift has occurred, education and skills may be a limitation for higher-skill employment. International migrant workers are taking relatively low-skilled and low-paid jobs when compared to the migrant workers from neighboring countries like India and Nepal. While manufacturing and especially the garments sector are attracting foreign investments to Bangladesh, high-skill industries, such as IT, have not, despite the internationally competitive wage rates. This is due partly, if not largely, to the low skill levels of Bangladeshi workers. In all likelihood, the demand for skilled labor especially in the tertiary sector will increase over the next decade, even if skilled jobs constitute a very small fraction of value added currently.

What comes next, then? Bangladesh needs to adopt a two-pronged approach to job creation. For one, it still needs to prioritize unskilled labor-based growth. But it also needs to address the education limitations and harness skills to foster human capital-based growth in selected sectors where such opportunities arise.

Bangladesh's success in creating jobs also helps to explain another puzzle relating to the so-called Bangladesh "governance conundrum" (World Bank 2003). It is true that poor governance quality, which is apparent in Bangladesh, dampens the growth rate especially through the investment channel. However, it can be argued that sustained and remunerative job creation for the poor, women, and youth has largely compensated for the socially adverse effects of weak governance. In this context, it is important to distinguish between "total governance" and "minimum governance," the former claiming the full range of rule-based institutions and norms, with the latter requiring only the bottom-line conditions such as law and order supplemented by a critical minimum functioning of public infrastructural and social services.[39] Qualitative leaps in governance improvements occur only after achieving a threshold-level per capita GDP. The challenge for low-income countries such as Bangladesh is to be able to sustain a decent long-term growth rate in per capita income based on minimum governance while striving towards total governance. The country has been able to reasonably maintain that scenario in the last two decades without lapsing into protracted periods of social chaos, class conflict, and political disorder that would have irreversibly harmed

---

[39] The distinction between "total" and "minimum" governance has been argued in the present study at the analytical level. The recent growth literature examining the nexus of governance and growth lends indirect support to this view where it has been shown that growth acceleration is possible even in the absence of compliance on all the dimensions of core governance. In particular, we derive insights from the works of Mushtaq Khan (see Khan 2007).

economic growth interests.[40] Weak governance may not turn out to be a binding constraint for growth as a whole, at least for the next ten to fifteen years. It can be expected, however, given the politically-aware electorate, that governance issues will be resolved mostly from the demand side where accountability will increase as the demand for quality goes up.

In sum, one of the most important lessons derived from the case study of Bangladesh's successful job transformation is that farm jobs and non-farm jobs evolve together in an integrated manner, and thus the welfare and livelihood of both poor farmers and workers improve simultaneously. Reinterpreting what Faaland and Parkinson (1976) said almost four decades ago (which we alluded to earlier), one could now venture to project why the Bangladesh experience could potentially transform from a mere "test case" with largely negative connotations into an "inspiring case" for the modernization of other low-income agrarian and urbanizing economies. If Bangladesh could make it under the most challenging of circumstances, others in the parallel universe of destitution and hopelessness can also make it. The implications of the Bangladesh case study should be seriously incorporated into pragmatic development strategies in other low-income emerging economies.

References

Banerjee, A. and Iyer, L. (2005). "History, institutions, and economic performance: The legacy of colonial land tenure systems in India." *The American Economic Review*, 95(4):1190–213.

Acemoglu, D., Johnson, S., and Robinson, J.A. (2001). "The colonial origins of comparative development: An empirical investigation." *The American Economic Review*, 91(5):1369–401.

Afsar, R. (2000). *Rural-Urban Migration in Bangladesh: Causes, Consequences, and Challenges.* Dhaka: The University Press Limited.

Ahmed, I. (2010). *Sufis & Sufism: A Closer Look at the Journey of Sufis to Bangladesh.* Singapore: Middle East Institute.

Ahmed, N., Bakht, Z., and Yunus, M. (2011). *Size Structure of Manufacturing Industry and Implications for Growth and Poverty: Bangladesh Country Paper.* Dhaka: Bangladesh Institute of Development Studies.

Ahmed, R. and Hossain, M. (1990). Developmental Impact of Rural Infrastructure in Bangladesh. Research Reports 83. International Food Policy Research Institute, Washington, DC.

---

[40] This rather optimistic appraisal has been put to the test by real turns of events every now and then. In the very recent period, there have been disquieting signs of widespread political unease because of the non-participation of the major opposition party in the 2014 (January) Parliamentary election. There was political turbulence at the beginning of 2015 (January–February) as well. However, the political situation has stabilized since then.

Alamgir, M. (1978). *Bangladesh: A Case of Below Poverty Level Equilibrium Trap*. Dhaka: Bangladesh Institute of Development Studies.

Alberto Alesina, A., Baqir, R., and Easterly, W. (1997). Public Goods and Ethnic Divisions, NBER Working Paper No. 6009. NBER.

Alesina, A. and Rodrik, D. (1994). "Distributive politics and economic growth." *The Quarterly Journal of Economics*, 109(2):465–90.

Armendariz, B. and Morduch, J. (2010). *The Economics of Microfinance*. Second Edition. Cambridge, MA: MIT Press.

Bandiera, O., Burgess, R., Gulesci, S., and Rasul, I. (2009). Community Networks and Poverty Reduction Programmes: Evidence from Bangladesh. EOPP/STICERD Working paper No. 15. London: London School of Economics, RED, BRAC: Dhaka.

Banerjee, A., Duflo, E., Glennerster, R., and Kinnan, C. (2010). The Miracle of Microfinance: Evidence from a Randomized Evaluation. MIT (mimeographed).

Bardhan, P. and Mookherjee, D. (2006). "Pro-poor targeting and accountability of local governments in West Bengal." *Journal of Development Economics*, 79(2):303–27.

Bayes, A. (2007). Impact Assessment of Jamuna Multipurpose Bridge project (JMBP) on Poverty Reduction. Japan Bank for International Cooperation.

BBS (2010). Preliminary Report on Household Income Expenditure Survey 2010. Dhaka: Bangladesh Bureau of Statistics (BBS).

Boserup, E. (1981). *Population and Technology*. London: Basil Blackwell Publishers.

Cain, M., Khanam, S.R., and Nahar, S. (1979). Class, Patriarchy, and the Structure of Women's Work in Rural Bangladesh. Working Paper No. 43. The Population Council, Center for Policy Studies, New York.

Deichman, U., Shilpi, F., and Vakis, R. (2009). "Urban proximity, agricultural potential and rural nonfarm employment: Evidence for Bangladesh." *World Development*, 37(3):645–60.

Deininger, K., Narayan, D., and Sen, B. (2009). Politics of the middle path: Agrarian reform and poverty dynamics in West Bengal. In: *Moving out of Poverty: The Promise of Empowerment and Democracy in India*, Deepa Narayan (ed.), Palgrave Macmillan and World Bank.

Dev, M., James, K.S., and Sen, B. (2002). "Causes of fertility decline in India and Bangladesh: The role of community." *Economic and Political Weekly*, 37(43):4447–54.

Dworkin, R. (2011). "What is a Good Life?" *New York Review of Books*, February 10, p.3.

Easterly, W. (2001). *The Elusive Quest for Growth: Economists' Adventures and Misadventures in the Tropics*. Cambridge, MA: MIT Press.

Easterly, W., Ritzen, J., and Woolcock, M. (2006). "Social cohesion, institutions and growth." *Economics & Politics*, 18(2):103–20.

Eaton, R.M. (1993). *The Rise of Islam and the Bengal Frontier, 1204–1760*. Berkeley: University of California Press.

Faaland, J. and Parkinson, J.R. (1976). *Bangladesh: The Test Case of Development*. London: C. Hurst & Company.

GoB (2014). Bangladesh Economic Review 2014. Ministry of Finance, Government of Bangladesh (GoB), Dhaka.

Heath, R. and Mobarak, A.M. (2012). Does Demand or Supply Constrain Investments in Education? Evidence from Garment Sector Jobs in Bangladesh? Yale University (mimeographed).

Hossain, I. and Sen, B. (2011). Results of a Brickfield Survey in the Outskirt of Dhaka City. Dhaka: Bangladesh Institute of Development Studies (draft).

Hossain, M. (1988a). Credit for Alleviation of Rural Poverty: The Grameen Bank in Bangladesh. Research Report No. 65. Washington, DC: IFPRI.

Hossain, M. (1988b). Nature and Impact of the Green Revolution. Research Report No. 67. Washington, DC: IFPRI.

Hossain, M. and Bayes, A. (2009). *Rural Economy & Livelihoods: Insights from Bangladesh.* Dhaka: A. H. Development Publishing House.

HSBC (2012). The World in 2050. HSBC Global Research Report.

IFPRI (2012). Rising Wages and Poverty Reduction in Bangladesh, June 15, 2012 (draft).

Jaim, W.M.H. and Hossain, M. (2011). "Women's participation in agriculture in Bangladesh 1988–2008: Changes and determinants," paper presented in the pre-conference event on "Dynamics of Rural Livelihoods and Poverty in South Asia," 7th Asian Society of Agricultural Economists (ASAE) International Conference Hanoi, Vietnam, October 12, 2011.

Johansson-Stenman, O., Mahmud, M., and Martinsson, P. (2005). "Does stake size matter in trust games?" *Economics Letters*, 88(3):365–9.

Johansson-Stenman, O., Mahmud, M., and Martinsson, P. (2009). "Trust and religion: Experimental evidence from rural Bangladesh." *Economica*, 76(303):462–85.

Khalily, M., Baqui, A., and Osmani, S.R. (eds) (2011). *Readings in Microfinance: Reach and Impact.* Dhaka: University Press Ltd.

Khan, A.A. (1996). *Discovery of Bangladesh: Explorations into Dynamics of a Hidden Nation.* Dhaka: University Press Ltd.

Khan, M.H. (2007). Governance, Economic Growth and Development since the 1960s. Economic & Social Affairs, DESA Working Paper No. 54. United Nations.

Khandker, S.R. (2000). *Fighting Poverty with Microcredit: Experience in Bangladesh.* World Bank/Oxford University Press.

Khandker, S.R. (2005). "Microfinance and poverty: Evidence using panel data from Bangladesh." *World Bank Economic Review*, 19(2):263–86.

Kissinger, H. (2011). *On China.* The Penguin Press.

Lee, J.J. and Sawada, Y. (2010). "Precautionary saving under liquidity constraints: Evidence from rural Pakistan." *Journal of Development Economics*, 91(1):77–86.

Lewis, W.A. (1954). "Economic development with unlimited supplies of labor." *The Manchester School of Economic and Social Studies*, 22:139–91.

Mahmud, W. (1996). "Employment patterns and income formation in rural Bangladesh: The role of rural non-farm sector." *The Bangladesh Development Studies*, XXIV (3 & 4):1–28.

Mahmud, M. and Sawada, Y. (2015). Infrastructure and Well-being: Employment Effects of Jamuna Bridge in Bangladesh. CIRJE F-Series CIRJE-F-986. CIRJE, Faculty of Economics, University of Tokyo.

Mazumdar, D. and Sarkar, S. (2008). The Employment Problem in India and the Phenomenon of the Missing Middle. Working Paper No. 6. New Delhi: Institute of Human Development.

Mottaleb, A.M. and Sonobe, T. (2011). "An inquiry into the rapid growth of the garment industry in Bangladesh." *Economic Development and Cultural Change*, 60(1): 67–89.

Mujeri, M.K. and Sen, B. (2006). Economic Growth in Bangladesh, 1970–2000. In: *Explaining Economic Growth in South Asia*, Kirit Parikh (ed.), New Delhi: Oxford University Press.

Narayan, A. and Zaman, H. (2009). *Breaking Down Poverty in Bangladesh*. Dhaka: The University Press Limited.

Osmani, S.R. (1990). "Structural change and poverty in Bangladesh: The case of false turning point." *The Bangladesh Development Studies*, 18:55–74.

Osmani, S.R. (2012). Asset Accumulation and Poverty Dynamics in Rural Bangladesh: The Role of Microcredit. Working Paper No. 11. Institute of Microfinance: Dhaka.

Osmani, S. and Sen, B. (2011). "Inequality in rural Bangladesh in the 2000s: Trends and causes." *The Bangladesh Development Studies*, 34(4): 1–36.

Otsuka, K. (2007). The rural industrial transition in East Asia: Influences and implications. In: *Transforming the Rural Nonfarm Economy*, S. Haggblade, P. Hazell, and T. Reardon (eds), Baltimore: Johns Hopkins Press.

Otsuka, K., Estudillo, J.P., and Sawada, Y. (eds) (2008). *Rural Poverty and Income Dynamics in Asia and Africa*. Routledge.

Paul-Majumder, P. and Begum, A. (2006). *Engendering Garment Industry: The Bangladesh Context*. Dhaka: The University Press Limited.

Pitt, M. (2011). Overidentification Tests and Causality: A Second Response to Roodman and Morduch, April 8, 2011, Brown University (mimeographed).

Pitt, M. and Khandker, S. (1998). "The impact of group-based credit on poor households in Bangladesh: Does the gender of participants matter?" *Journal of Political Economy*: 106(5): 958–96.

Rahman, H.Z.R. and Hossain, M. (eds) (1995). *Rethinking Rural Poverty: Bangladesh as a Case Study*. New Delhi/Thousand Oaks/London: SAGE Publications.

Rama, M. (2003). "The Sri Lankan unemployment problem revisited." *Review of Development Economics*, 7(3):510–25.

Rashid, S. (2002). Dynamics of Agricultural Wage and Rice Price in Bangladesh. MTID Discussion Papers 44. International Food Policy Research Institute, Washington, DC.

Ravallion, M. (1990). "Rural welfare effects of food price changes under induced wage responses: Theory and evidence from Bangladesh." *Oxford Economic Papers*, 42:574–85.

Ravallion, M. and Sen, B. (1996). "When method matters: Monitoring poverty in Bangladesh." *Economic Development and Cultural Change*, 44(4):761–92.

Roodman, D. and Morduch, J. (2009). The Impact of Microcredit on the Poor in Bangladesh: Revisiting the Evidence. Working Paper No. 174. Center for Global Development.

Sawada, Y. (2007). "The impact of natural and manmade disasters on household welfare." *Agricultural Economics*, 37(s1):59–73.

Sawada, Y. (2012). Infrastructure, Social Cohesion, and Jobs in Development: A Note on the WDR Bangladesh Case Study, JICA Research Institute, Japan International Cooperation Agency (mimeographed).

Sen, B. (1996). "Rural non-farm sector in Bangladesh: Stagnating and residual, or dynamic and potential." *The Bangladesh Development Studies*, 24(3 & 4):143–80.

Sen, B. (2012). Breaking the Cycle of Urban Chronic Poverty? Insights from the DSK-Shiree Project, Shiree/DSK, March 8, Dhaka.

Sen, B. and Ali, Z. (2015). Ending Extreme Poverty in Bangladesh during the Seventh Five Year Plan: Trends, Drivers and Policies. Background Paper for the Preparation of the Seventh Five Year Plan, General Economics Division (GED) of the Planning Commission, Dhaka (mimeographed).

Sen, B., Mujeri, M.K., and Shahabuddin, Q. (2007). Explaining pro-poor growth in Bangladesh: Puzzles, evidence, and implications. In: *Delivering on the Promise of Pro-Poor Growth*, T. Besley and L.J. Cord (eds), pp. 79–118. Palgrave Macmillan and World Bank.

Seraj, T.M. (2012). *A Review of the Real Estate Sector of Bangladesh*. Dhaka: Sheltech.

Shahabuddin, Q. (2012). *Food Security Situation in Bangladesh: Achievements, Challenges and Prospects*. Dhaka: Bangladesh Institute of Development Studies.

Sharma, M.P. and Zaman, H. (2009). Who Migrates Overseas and is it Worth their While? An Assessment of Household Survey Data from Bangladesh. World Bank, Washington, DC.

Sobhan, R. (1982). *The Crisis of External Dependence: The Political Economy of Foreign Aid to Bangladesh*. Dhaka: University Press Limited.

World Bank (2003). Bangladesh Development Policy Review. Washington, DC: IBRD, December 14, 2003.

World Bank (2012). World Development Report 2013: Jobs. Washington, DC: World Bank.

4

Papua New Guinea

Jobs, Poverty, and Resources

Colin Filer, Marjorie Andrew, Benedict Y. Imbun,
Phillipa Jenkins, and Bill F. Sagir

4.1 Introduction

Papua New Guinea (PNG) is a "resource-rich" country with extreme levels of poverty and very poor human development indicators. Throughout its forty-year history as an independent nation, PNG has been heavily dependent on the resource sector—here defined as a combination of the mining and petroleum subsectors—for both export earnings and government revenues. However, like many other resource-dependent countries, PNG has been unable to convert its mineral wealth into development for the broad mass of the population.

Although PNG is treated as a resource-rich country in this volume, it also faces some of the challenges discussed in other chapters. It is still an agrarian country, in the sense that urban areas account for less than 20 percent of the population, and formal employment barely accounts for more than 10 percent of total employment. It is also a country with high youth unemployment, and could even be regarded as a conflict-affected country because of the rebellion that took place on the island of Bougainville and the widespread incidence of "tribal fighting" in parts of the central highland region.

Conventional wisdom says that PNG's resource sector is not the place where one would expect to find jobs that are good for development, let alone create more of them. First, it is thought to supply very little in the way of employment opportunities when compared with other sectors of the economy, especially the agricultural sector. Second, it is thought to consist of a set of economic enclaves that do not produce more business or more jobs in the rest of the economy by means of backward or forward linkages. Third, a large and booming resource sector may even destroy jobs in the rest of the economy by inflating the value of the national currency and raising the costs of doing business in other sectors—an affliction known as the "Dutch Disease." For these reasons, the sector has long been seen as a sort of cash cow whose role is to supply the national government with the revenues it needs to achieve development by means of public spending.

In this chapter, we aim to challenge this conventional wisdom in several ways. We argue that the number of jobs created by the resource sector, directly and indirectly, is much larger than is commonly assumed. We question the idea that the resource sector is any more isolated from the rest of the economy than some of the other export industries that employ large numbers of people. We concede that the Dutch Disease has been a real problem in periods when the resource sector has been booming, but the mismanagement and mis-appropriation of the government's mineral revenues has been an even bigger problem, even when the sector has been stagnant. We do not equate the social value of jobs with the social value of the economic sector in which they are located, but propose that jobs in the resource sector may have good qualities that are shared with jobs in other sectors. And instead of thinking of workers themselves as being locked up for life in one economic sector, we aim to focus on the social value of the career paths that take workers from one sector to another or one location to another.

The main problem we faced when embarking on this study was that PNG boasts very little in the way of statistical evidence that would enable us to compare the social value of jobs in different parts of the economy, or even to compare the levels of productivity, living standards, or social cohesion between different sections of the population. Given the limited resources available for the collection of new data, we therefore decided to interview a group of workers who were currently or formerly employed in the resource sector in order to assess the social values of their jobs and their careers. In reporting the findings of this survey, we shall focus attention on what the World Development Report describes as "positive spillovers" (World Bank 2012: 15). In particular, we consider the value of the remittances which workers provide to households other than their own and the additional job opportunities created by those who have taken new jobs overseas.

4.2 Plenty in the Midst of Poverty

To understand the apparent paradox in the failure of mineral wealth creation to alleviate the poverty of many, if not most, Papua New Guineans, we shall not simply invoke the well-worn concept of the "resource curse," but rather consider the relationship between the country's resource development policies and its poverty alleviation or broader national development policies.

4.2.1 A Resource-Rich Country . . .

Even at the time of Independence in 1975, when the Panguna copper mine was the only large-scale mining operation in the country, mineral exports accounted for 60 percent of the value of all PNG's exports. Since 1984, when the Ok Tedi mine came into operation, the proportion has rarely fallen below 60 percent, even after the Panguna mine was forcibly closed in 1989. Since 2002, the proportion has been fluctuating around 79 percent (Table 4.1). Over the same period, the production of these mineral exports has normally accounted for 20–30 percent of the country's GDP (Table 4.2), while payments by mining and petroleum companies have accounted for roughly 20 percent of PNG government revenues.

Insofar as PNG has experienced a resource boom in recent years, it has not been a boom in production, but a boom in exploration and construction. Although there was a steep rise in the world market prices of oil, copper, and

Table 4.1. Percentage of PNG export values by sector, 2002–14

Sector	2002	2003	2004	2005	2006	2007	2008	2009	2010	2011	2012	2013	2014
Resources	75.0	75.3	75.6	80.3	84.2	82.3	79.0	78.8	79.5	73.5	77.5	79.5	83.8
Agriculture	15.1	13.8	13.1	11.9	8.5	10.9	13.9	13.7	13.4	18.5	13.7	11.3	8.7
Forestry	6.5	5.3	5.6	4.7	4.1	4.5	3.4	3.9	4.8	4.7	4.8	5.5	4.4
Other	3.4	5.6	5.7	3.1	3.2	2.3	3.7	3.6	2.3	3.3	4.1	3.7	3.1

Source: Bank of Papua New Guinea.

Table 4.2. Percentage of PNG's gross domestic product by sector, 2002–13

Sector	2002	2003	2004	2005	2006	2007	2008	2009	2010	2011	2012	2013
Primary industry	38.6	37.4	34.9	34.0	32.1	32.2	32.8	33.1	31.5	31.2	28.5	27.1
Extractive industry	20.6	22.7	24.5	27.5	30.4	29.7	27.9	21.6	23.0	18.9	14.6	13.8
Manufacturing	6.3	6.4	6.5	6.3	5.9	5.8	5.9	6.1	5.8	6.6	7.3	7.3
Power & water	1.7	1.8	2.0	2.0	2.0	2.0	1.9	2.1	2.1	2.1	2.3	2.4
Construction	8.7	8.8	9.0	8.4	8.7	9.5	10.5	13.4	14.1	16.5	20.3	21.9
Wholesale & retail trade	6.5	6.6	6.8	6.4	6.3	6.4	6.6	7.4	7.6	8.3	9.8	10.0
Transport & communications	2.3	2.3	2.3	2.1	2.0	2.0	2.1	2.8	3.0	3.2	3.7	3.7
Financial services	3.5	3.3	3.2	3.3	3.5	3.5	3.6	4.3	4.2	4.7	5.1	5.2
Community & social services	11.8	10.9	10.7	9.8	8.9	8.9	8.6	9.2	8.6	8.4	8.5	8.6

Source: Asian Development Bank.

gold between 2002 and 2012, and the total value of PNG's exports doubled over that period in real terms, there was a parallel fall in the physical volume of resource exports. Recent spikes in net foreign direct investment are almost entirely due to spending on resource project construction. The huge spike that began in 2009 reflects the 19 billion US dollars that were spent on construction of the PNG LNG Project, but only 5 percent of this investment is thought to have entered the national economy when the construction phase ended in 2014.

Windfall revenues from the resource boom enabled the PNG government to reduce its debts from 70 percent of GDP in 2002 to 22 percent in 2011, but the ratio rose to 34 percent in 2013 and a likely 37 percent in 2014 (IMF 2014). This is largely because the resource sector's contribution to government revenues has been a lot more volatile than its contribution to GDP: it reached a peak of 40 percent in 2007, but fell below 10 percent in 2013 (ADB 2014a). Despite earlier predictions that the LNG Project would make a significant addition to government revenues once it became operational, it is now thought that it will simply replace the revenues that are no longer flowing from other resource projects, and much of the revenue that it does provide will have to be used to repay the debt which the government has incurred to buy its equity stake in the project (Bulman 2013; IMF 2014).

Although the LNG Project will certainly restore the extractive industry share of GDP to the levels recorded in the middle of the last decade, there is now less confidence in previous government predictions that it would make a net addition of 15–20 percent to GDP, and 10 percent to GNI, over its thirty-year life span. It is now clear that the government has raised spending and borrowing in anticipation of a net addition to its tax revenues that may not materialize, and has done so at a time when the weighted average price of its exports has been falling (Flanagan 2014). Much the same thing happened in the early 1990s when the country's GDP grew by more than half over a four-year period in which two major resource projects became operational. That episode ended in a fiscal crisis from which the government had to be rescued by a structural adjustment loan from the World Bank (Chand and Stewart 1997).

There are expectations in some quarters that one or two more LNG projects will prove to be feasible and will be granted development licenses within the next two or three years, and that one or two large-scale copper mines will follow suit. If these expectations are realized, then PNG's economy will be more resource dependent than ever before, despite the rapid decline in output from most of the major resource projects already in operation. If they are not realized, there will simply be a shift in the composition of outputs and benefit streams derived from the resource sector without any increase in its overall significance for the national economy.

4.2.2 . . . But Still a Poor Country

In 2014, PNG ranked 158th out of 187 countries listed in the United Nations Human Development Index. There has been some improvement since 1980, when it was ranked 110th out of 124 countries, but this is mainly due to the growth of GNI per capita from $1,564 to $2,463 (in 2011 PPP dollars). If cash incomes are left out of the equation, and human development is measured only by health and education indicators, the country fares worse—in 2013, occupying the 172nd place in the rankings (UNDP and Government of PNG 2014: 3).[1]

Preliminary data from the 2011 national census indicate that PNG had a population of almost 7.3 million in that year. In 2000, the last year for which detailed national census data are currently available, about four-fifths of the population (then less than 5 million) still lived in traditional rural village communities, while the rest was distributed between large and small urban centers, peri-urban settlements, and "rural non-villages," such as oil palm estates and resettlement schemes. Half of the total population was living in the densely settled valleys of the central highlands, while another third was living within 10 kilometers of the coastline. The most recent census data suggest that there has not been much change in this geographical distribution since 2000.

Evidence from various sources suggests that the rural village population can be divided between three zones of relative prosperity or poverty:

- About 40 percent inhabit an inner zone where there is reasonably good access to markets or urban centers, and villagers can therefore derive a reasonable income from the sale of cash crops or other commodities.

- Another 40 percent inhabit an intermediate zone, where income-earning opportunities are much more limited, but where schooling has enabled some people to get paid employment and hence to provide some support to their home villages by means of remittances.

- The final 20 percent inhabit an outer zone where contact with both the market economy and the formal education system has been very limited, and there are barely any social or economic links between village and town.

Household surveys indicate that the proportion of the population living below the basic needs poverty line actually rose from 34 percent in 1996 to 36 percent in 2010 (Gibson 2000; World Bank 2004; UNDP and Government

---

[1] Even these measures may be overly optimistic. The index shows a maternal mortality rate of 230 per 100,000 live births in 2010 and an adult literacy rate of 62.4 percent in 2011. There is compelling recent evidence to indicate that the former rate is much higher (Mola and Kirby 2013) while the latter is much lower (Asia South Pacific Association for Basic and Adult Education and PNG Education Advocacy Network 2011).

of PNG 2014). In 1996, about 5 percent of the people living below the poverty line were living in urban and peri-urban squatter settlements, but the vast majority were to be found in the intermediate and outer rural zones. Poverty levels were especially acute in the lowland interior and highland fringe areas that accounted for most of PNG's total land area but only one-sixth of its total population.

The only recent change in the spatial incidence of poverty is an apparent increase in the number of poor people living in the national capital, which now accounts for roughly 40 percent of the total urban population. The proportion of this segment of the urban population living below the poverty line apparently increased from 30 percent in 1996 to 44 percent in 2010 (Gibson 2013: 22). If urban and rural poverty rates have converged, this could help to explain why the rate of urbanization has been relatively slow. Although nominal earnings from both formal and informal sector employment have risen more rapidly in the national capital than in other urban areas, real earnings seem to have fallen because of an increase in the cost of living, which could be 70 percent or more since 2002 (Bulman 2012). If this increase is itself a symptom of the Dutch Disease, then the resource boom has so far done nothing to alleviate the incidence of urban poverty.

There is some political resistance to the very idea of poverty in PNG. This is due to an assumption that all native Papua New Guineans are customary landowners and therefore have a right to a life of "subsistence affluence" in the rural village communities to which they already belong or to which they could easily return (ADB 2002). In practice, it is not clear how many of the people who do not live in rural village communities could actually exercise this right of return, but more importantly it is not clear how many would even wish to do so, given the conditions in which most rural people actually live. For example, in the intermediate and outer rural zones, life expectancy at birth typically varies between thirty and fifty years, while the infant mortality rate varies between 10 and 40 percent (Bakker 1986; Bauze et al. 2012).

There has indeed been a steady flow of migrants from less-advantaged to more-advantaged areas, but the flow has been limited by the unwillingness of many customary landowners to accommodate migrants on their land, while migrants who squat on the relatively small areas of vacant state land in urban areas are often threatened with eviction. The ability of the poorest villagers in the intermediate and outer rural zones to move beyond the confines of their own customary land is constrained by the absence of close relatives who have already secured their own livelihoods in better locations and could therefore facilitate this type of movement. At the same time, the spatial extent of the intermediate and outer rural zones seems to have grown as the quality of economic and social infrastructure in rural areas has declined (Gibson et al. 2005; Howes et al. 2014).

All this helps to explain why most rural villagers welcome the prospect of a major resource project because they think it represents their best chance of development. But a substantial proportion of the benefit streams that ought to flow to the original residents of areas directly affected by the development of these projects has been captured by local elites, by relatives living in town, by new migrants to the affected area, or by politicians and public servants who have no local ties at all. As a result, many of the people living in the affected areas show little or no improvement in their standard of living, even after a project has been operating for ten or twenty years. And when a major resource project closes down, the only significant change in the situation of such people might be an increase in the number of their relatives who have managed to escape from what then ceases to be a directly affected area and reverts to simply being a more or less impoverished area.

4.2.3 Resource Development Policies

The development of major resource projects in PNG is framed by three main types of agreements that are normally negotiated in the following order:

1. *Compensation agreements* between the holder of an exploration license and the customary owners of the land covered by that license. These are subject to some degree of government regulation and are likely to be revised and expanded if exploration leads to a development proposal.

2. *Development agreements* between the national government and prospective investors are based on feasibility studies that the investors provide to the government and are primarily concerned with the distribution of economic costs and benefits between the two parties. These agreements are also conditional on a prior process of environmental and social impact assessment.

3. *Benefit-sharing agreements* between the national government, the provincial and local government(s) hosting the project, and the customary owners of the land required for development purposes are negotiated through an institution known as the Development Forum (Filer 2008). The developers are not formally involved in the negotiation of these agreements, but development licenses are not granted until the benefit-sharing agreements have been finalized.

Compensation agreements normally make no reference to project employment or other forms of national and local participation in project development. Development agreements have normally required that national participation be specified in training and localization plans and business development plans whose implementation is then reported to the national government at regular intervals. These plans are subject to the "preferred area policy" which has come to inform the negotiation of benefit-sharing agreements.

In effect, the preferred area policy creates concentric rings of entitlement to a range of benefit streams that are subject to such agreements, including entitlements to training, employment, and business development opportunities. The innermost ring is occupied by the customary owners of the land covered by development licenses, the next by "project area people" (however these might be defined), the next by the people or government of the host province, and the outermost ring by the population or government of the nation as a whole (Filer 2005). These zones of entitlement cut across the geographical zones of relative prosperity or poverty described in Section 4.2.2.

In the period since the Development Forum was invented in 1988, there has been a steady increase in the proportion of government revenues from each new resource project that is captured by organizations or individuals in the three inner circles of entitlement. In 1988, less than 5 percent of the money that the national government collected from the operation of the Panguna mine went back to the host province (Filer 1997). By 2002, with four large-scale mines in four different provinces producing revenues for the national government, the proportion had risen to more than 25 percent (Finlayson 2002). It is not so easy to calculate the distribution of wages and other benefits paid to workers on major resource projects, or the value of contracts to supply goods and services to these projects, but the available evidence indicates that the preferred area policy has also served to increase the proportion captured by workers and companies within the host provinces and more limited areas of preference. Since 1993, the economic privilege bestowed on preferred areas has been compounded by a tax credit scheme for developers who supply social and economic infrastructure to local communities (Filer 2008).

The share of resource project benefits captured by the different beneficiaries changes through the life of each major project. The national government has been inclined to postpone the revenue share that it collects on behalf of the country as a whole while providing more in the way of up-front payments to provincial and local stakeholders in order to secure their political support for the construction and initial operation of each new project. This temporal imbalance grows more acute with the scale of the project. When the LNG Project began to export gas in 2014, 4 percent of the value of production was instantly made available to the host provincial governments, local-level governments, and assorted landowner groups in the form of royalties and development levies.

The perceived failure of the national government to make wise use of its mineral revenues has stimulated the demand for these revenues to be redistributed under the preferred area policy. The implementation of this policy has created many new opportunities for mineral revenues to be misappropriated as they flow back from the national government to the host provinces. And even if benefits were properly distributed in accordance with the terms specified in benefit-sharing agreements, there would still be a greater problem of resource dependency at the provincial and local levels than already exists at the national level. The more that local organizations and individuals come to depend on a single resource project for their incomes and general welfare, the more they are likely to lose when that project comes to the end of its life (Filer and Imbun 2009). The purchase of provincial and local political support for major resource projects by means of benefit-sharing agreements appears to be a necessary condition for their development, but it has also created intractable problems of governance and sustainability.

4.2.4 Poverty Alleviation Policies

It is hard to disentangle the national government's poverty alleviation policies from its broader national or rural development policies because of the poverty denial syndrome. National policy-makers tend to associate the concept of poverty alleviation with the country's continued reliance on foreign aid. Since the contribution of foreign aid to government revenues fell from 9 percent in 2002 to 5.5 percent in 2013, they can point to this as evidence of growing national prosperity, even if the human development indicators tell a different story.

Aspirations for national prosperity are embodied in a national vision statement which says that PNG could be ranked among the top 50 countries in the Human Development Index by 2050 if its people undergo a sort of mental revolution that will enable the establishment of a set of new "economic growth centres" (Government of PNG 2009: 51). The shift from a "scarcity mentality" to an "abundance mentality" is explicitly linked to a program of land reform that will make it possible to establish new forms of economic enterprise on the customary land that is generally thought to account for 97 percent of PNG's total land area. In this way, a nation of customary landowners competing (or just hoping) to get a share of the rent generated by major resource projects can be turned into a nation in which half of the working-age population will be "self-employed entrepreneurs" (Government of PNG 2009: 7). The vision statement assumes that all districts should be treated equally when it says that one or two "impact projects" should be implemented in each of them (Government of PNG 2009: 4). This view is consistent with the current practice of dividing 20 percent of the development budget between members of parliament to spend as they see fit on the development of their own electorates, regardless of whether they host a major resource project, have an unusually large population, or suffer from extreme levels of poverty.

The long-term national development plan has a somewhat different vision of what it calls "economic corridors." It proposes that 50 percent of the development budget will be divided between ten of these entities and they "will be located in the poorest regions of PNG with the aim of extending the benefits of development to the most disadvantaged regions" (Government of PNG 2010: 18–19). However, there is no evidence that the ten "corridors" shown on the relevant map have in fact been defined by reference to any known indicators of poverty or human development. It also seems rather odd that the first such entity to be approved by the National Executive Council (in 2009) was the Petroleum Resource Area Economic Corridor, whose boundaries overlap those of the preferred area for the LNG Project.

4.3 Understanding the Jobs Challenge

We shall now consider the ways in which PNG's job configuration has evolved since Independence, the ways in which the recent "resource boom" has altered this configuration, and the ways in which the PNG government currently treats the problem of job creation (or unemployment). Since so little is known about the productivity of labor or the wages and other benefits secured by workers in different parts of the national economy, it is all but impossible to make a quantitative assessment of trade-offs between the contributions that different types of jobs make to productivity, living standards, and social cohesion.

4.3.1 *Changing Patterns of Employment*

The dearth of statistical information makes it quite hard to even establish employment trends in different parts of the economy. The last national census, which has been used to calculate the numbers of men and women holding jobs in the formal and informal sectors, was the one conducted in 1980. If we confine our attention to the citizen population aged 15 and over, which approximates the current definition of the working-age population, it appears that 12 percent had jobs in the formal sector and 60 percent had jobs in the informal sector (Table 4.3).

In 2002, it was estimated that there were roughly 187,000 people formally employed in PNG's urban centers, which was somewhere between 5 and 6 percent of the working-age population at the time (Booth et al. 2006). There is no comparable estimate of formal-sector employment in rural areas at that time. Wages accounted for 19 percent of GDP in 2002, but this proportion had fallen to 13 percent by 2006, and may have shrunk even further since then (ADB 2014b). This may be taken as evidence of a growth

Table 4.3. Economic activities of citizens aged 15 years and over, 1980

Activity	Number	Percent
Formally employed	198,029	11.7
Informally employed	1,012,967	59.8
Not in labor force	275,879	16.3
Apparently unemployed	201,941	11.9
Not stated	5,709	0.3
Total	1,694,525	100.0

Source: Government of PNG (1988), Tables IV.1 & IV.6.

Table 4.4. Distribution of working-age men and women (excluding students) by labor force activity, National Capital District, 1986 and 2010

Labor force activity	1986 (percent)		2010 (percent)	
	Males	Females	Males	Females
Wage employment	56.4	19.8	48.1	24.9
Household business	2.4	0.4	2.3	2.4
Informal sector	4.6	14.0	10.2	22.9
Looking for work	7.7	2.7	8.1	4.9
Not in labor force	32.2	64.0	37.6	49.5

Note: column distributions sum to more than 100 because some people were engaged in more than one economic activity.
Source: Gibson (2013), Tables 1 and 3.

of income inequality that constitutes a threat to social cohesion in its own right (Packard and Nguyen 2014: 52).

The most recent evidence on national employment comes from the Household Income and Expenditure Survey (HIES) undertaken by the National Statistical Office in 2009 and 2010. However, the published survey results appear to significantly overestimate formal employment, especially in rural areas.[2] In the national capital and other urban areas, some additional work has been done to compare the latest HIES data with data from the Urban Household Survey conducted in 1986, which is the only previous nationwide sample survey that contains comparable data (Gibson 2013). Over a twenty-five-year period, there had been a significant increase in the proportion of women, and a corresponding decline in the proportion of men, formally employed in urban areas, although men still outnumbered women by a ratio of 2 to 1 (see Tables 4.4 and 4.5). Both men and women were now more likely to have jobs in the informal sector, and 80 percent of them were engaged in

[2] The HIES data imply the existence of just over 200,000 wage earners in urban areas and almost 1.2 million in rural areas (Government of PNG 2012), but the number of wage earners in rural areas is unlikely to have been more than 250,000.

Table 4.5. Distribution of working-age men and women (excluding students) by labor force activity in other urban areas, 1986 and 2010

Labor force activity	1986 (percent)		2010 (percent)	
	Males	Females	Males	Females
Wage employment	61.9	18.2	45.5	22.7
Household business	8.1	3.8	4.6	2.9
Informal sector	9.4	27.7	11.7	32.7
Looking for work	8.5	1.6	5.8	4.2
Not in labor force	21.4	51.6	37.8	43.5

Note: column distributions sum to more than 100 because some people were engaged in more than one economic activity.

Source: Gibson (2013), Tables 1 and 3.

petty trading activities of one kind or another, but women still outnumbered men in this sector by a ratio of 2 to 1 in the national capital and 3 to 1 in other urban areas. There was no evidence of a reduction in the high rates of youth unemployment discovered in the earlier survey. More than two-thirds of urban respondents aged 15–24 (excluding students) were either looking for work or were not in the labor force.

Given the absence of any reliable data on the current size of the formal-sector workforce, it is hard to estimate the contribution of the resource sector to formal employment. The PNG Chamber of Mines and Petroleum estimated that the number of people formally employed in the work of exploration, construction, and extraction grew from 12,000 in 2004 to 30,000 in 2010. These numbers included expatriates as well as Papua New Guineans, and people employed by on-site contracting companies as well as those directly employed by mining and petroleum companies.

It is not clear how many of the estimated 30,000 workers in 2010 were part of the LNG Project construction workforce, given that construction started in that year. The number of people employed in construction of that project reached a peak of around 19,000 in the second half of 2012, but only half of them were Papua New Guineans, and the number of jobs available for national workers has fallen to less than 1,000 since the construction phase ended in 2014. The number employed in construction of the Hidden Valley gold mine reached a peak of around 3,000 in 2008, and the number employed in construction of the Ramu nickel–cobalt mine reached a peak of around 5,000 in 2011. Both of these large-scale mines have since started operating with a workforce that is roughly one-third the size of their peak construction workforce.

In a 2010 survey of employment in the three largest and oldest mining operations in PNG (Ok Tedi, Porgera, and Lihir), the Chamber of Mines found that the number of people employed by the mining companies themselves was roughly equal to the number employed by their on-site contractors—about

7,000 in each category altogether. About 90 percent of these workers were Papua New Guineans, and 90 percent were men. The proportion of national workers drawn from the "preferred area" (or directly affected area) varied from 35 to 70 percent.

The Chamber reckons that the extractive industry creates four or five additional jobs in the rest of the national economy for each job directly tied to the work of exploration, construction, and extraction. If jobs created by on-site contractors are included in the second of these categories, this would seem like a rather optimistic estimate of the multiplier, but all such estimates are hazardous in a country with so little in the way of reliable statistical evidence (Baxter 2001; Brooksbank 2002).

It is also hard to estimate the number of jobs that exist in that branch of the informal economy which consists of alluvial or artisanal mining. In 2000, there were thought to be as many as 60,000 artisanal gold miners in PNG, although many of them only worked on a part-time basis (Susapu and Crispin 2001). Given the subsequent increase in the gold price, the number of people involved in this activity is likely to have grown much larger. Evidence collected for this study shows that there are now large numbers of artisanal miners operating in areas where there were hardly any ten or fifteen years ago. The only scenario in which former artisanal miners are likely to gain formal employment on major resource projects is one in which a development license is granted over the area in which they have been working and they acquire the status of preferred area people as a result. Likewise, when a major mining operation reaches the point of closure, former employees from the preferred area may revert to artisanal mining as a livelihood, especially if they do not have the skills required to gain formal employment in another part of the country.

4.3.2 Impacts of the Recent Resource Boom

Evidence collected by the Bank of PNG from its own company surveys shows that the number of people formally employed in the resource sector grew by about 70 percent between 2002 and 2012 (Table 4.6). This is a lower growth rate than that estimated by the Chamber of Mines and Petroleum because many of the new jobs created by the resource boom are registered as jobs in the construction sector or other sectors of the national economy. This explanation is consistent with the evidence from job advertisements published in PNG's national newspapers (Table 4.7). Here it can be seen that the number of jobs advertised in the construction sector rose by a greater margin than the number advertised in the resource sector. But what is most notable is the overall trend: the number of jobs almost doubled between 2002 and 2007, and almost doubled again between 2007 and 2012. There is no obvious way to

Table 4.6. National employment index by sector, first quarters 2002, 2007, and 2012

Sector	2002	2007	2012
Wholesale trade	100.0	159.0	199.4
Manufacturing	100.0	136.8	181.5
Construction	100.0	130.9	180.6
Extractive industry	100.0	116.4	172.7
Primary industry	100.0	134.7	167.1
Transport	100.0	116.2	151.9
Financial & other services	100.0	111.1	142.2
Retail trade	100.0	111.3	138.0

Source: Bank of Papua New Guinea.

Table 4.7. Percentage distribution of job advertisements by industry, February–March 2002, 2007, and 2012

Industry	2002	2007	2012
Agriculture, hunting & forestry	2.9	2.8	2.2
Fishing	2.2	0.0	0.0
Mining & quarrying	6.3	11.0	8.1
Manufacturing	6.4	3.7	3.7
Electricity, gas & water	1.0	1.8	0.6
Construction	6.8	14.9	17.7
Wholesale & retail trade & repairs	16.0	12.3	13.6
Hotels & restaurants	2.1	2.0	2.4
Transport, storage & communications	4.9	7.3	6.4
Financial intermediation	2.1	2.2	4.0
Real estate, renting & business services	23.6	19.3	26.3
Public administration & defense	4.9	2.5	2.5
Education	7.5	6.0	1.4
Health & social work	3.0	0.6	2.3
Other community, social & personal services	4.7	4.7	3.1
Private household with employed persons	0.1	0.1	0.0
Extra-territorial organization & bodies	4.2	8.1	5.5
Unspecified	1.2	0.7	0.2
Total jobs advertised	730	1442	2828

Source: authors' calculations based on advertisements in national newspapers.

explain this increase except by reference to the impact of the resource boom and other aspects of recent economic growth.

Jobs advertised by mining and petroleum companies accounted for less than 10 percent of all jobs advertised during the six months covered by our survey, although many of the other jobs are likely to have been advertised by contractors and suppliers to the resource sector. Table 4.8 gives an indication of the differences between the occupational structure of the resource sector and the rest of the formal sector.

Table 4.8. Percentage distribution of jobs advertised by occupational category in the resource sector and in all sectors, February–March 2002, 2007, and 2012

Occupational category	Resource sector	All sectors
Senior executives, general managers & branch managers	0.0	1.7
Specialized (divisional/departmental) managers	3.2	3.8
Physical & engineering science professionals & associates	24.2	8.1
Life science & health professionals & associates	3.0	2.9
Education & training professionals & associates	3.2	3.4
Business & legal professionals & associates	6.7	13.5
Aid project staff, applied social scientists & associates	1.4	3.7
Media & sports professionals & associates	0.7	0.9
Clerical workers & junior sales staff	2.8	10.4
Providers of miscellaneous personal services	0.9	3.1
Security service providers & supervisors	4.8	12.6
Mineral extraction and processing workers	15.2	1.6
Building & construction workers & supervisors	0.9	6.6
Metal & machinery trades workers & supervisors	23.3	18.1
Drivers & mobile machine operators & supervisors	6.2	7.2
Miscellaneous manual workers & supervisors	3.5	2.5
Total jobs advertised	434	5000

Source: authors' calculations based on advertisements in national newspapers.

The workforce in an operational resource project can be divided into four main segments:

- Expatriates occupy the most senior management positions and most specialized technical positions: they may account for less than 10 percent of the total workforce but more than 50 percent of the operator's total labor costs (Johnson 2012). This in itself constitutes a strong economic incentive for companies to implement their training and localization plans if they can find suitably qualified citizens.

- At the other end of the scale, preferred area employees may account for more than 50 percent of the workforce but less than 20 percent of the total labor costs. These workers are likely to include the least qualified members of the workforce, and their opportunity to exchange one job for another is limited by the fact that they are only preferred for employment if they stay within a project's area of preference (Brooksbank 2002).

These two groups of workers are unlikely to be recruited by means of job advertisements in national newspapers, so their types of jobs are not reflected in Table 4.8. In between are two groups of national employees who are more likely to be recruited in this way, and who are recruited because of their qualifications rather than their place of origin:

- Some, like geologists, metallurgists, or specialized plant operators, are qualified for jobs that can hardly be found outside the resource sector, so their capacity to find better jobs is largely dependent on the fortunes of the sector as a whole.

- Others, like electricians, clerical workers, or community relations officers, are qualified for jobs that can be found in several sectors, and therefore find it easier to move between different parts of the national labor market.

Some of the more specialized workers have taken advantage of resource booms in other countries to emigrate from PNG, thus increasing the competition between resident mining and petroleum companies for the services of those who remain. Meanwhile, recruitment of less-specialized workers by mining and petroleum companies has created a shortage of skilled labor in other sectors of the national economy, which is one of the classic manifestations of the Dutch Disease. In both cases, employers are confronted with a limited supply of suitably qualified individuals graduating from PNG's tertiary education and training institutions, and must often invest additional resources in further training.

4.3.3 *Job Creation Policies*

Despite its central focus on business development, the PNG government's national vision statement also recognizes the need for a "well educated, healthy, appropriately skilled, and honest work force that is committed, proactive and innovative" (Government of PNG 2009: 12), and treats "relevant education and job creation" as a strategic and political priority (Government of PNG 2009: 22). The long-term national development plan proposes to add more than 2 million jobs to the national economy (Table 4.9). This plan anticipates that 680,000 (34 percent) of the new jobs will result from the creation of formal property rights over customary land in both urban and rural areas, and another 600,000 (30 percent) from the resolution of law and order problems, primarily in urban areas (Government of PNG 2010: 15).

It has long been recognized that high rates of youth unemployment are associated with a high incidence of criminal activity, that this problem is especially acute in urban areas, and that it constitutes one of the biggest costs of doing business and thus one of the main barriers to job creation

Table 4.9. Projected job growth anticipated in PNG's long-term national development plan (2010–30) compared to plan not implemented

Types of jobs	With plan	Without plan
Formal jobs in agricultural sector	592,900	44,800
Formal jobs in other sectors	1,128,300	167,500
Informal jobs in urban areas	48,800	5,400
Informal jobs in rural areas	266,300	144,800
Total	2,036,300	362,500

Source: Government of PNG (2010), Table 1H.

(Levantis 1997). Additional public investment in law enforcement agencies is currently seen as the main strategy for creating additional jobs through improvements in law and order (Government of PNG 2010: 46).

The job-creating potential of land reform is ascribed to the very high cost of securing access to the small amount of land (about 3 percent of the total land area) that was alienated from customary ownership during the colonial period. This is the most significant barrier to expansion of small- and medium-scale enterprise in urban areas, and also the biggest driver of the recent increase in the urban cost of living, especially in the national capital. Port Moresby now ranks among the top three developing country capital cities for the price of hotel and rental accommodation. The resource boom is widely blamed for the recent acceleration in urban land and housing prices, but has only served to compound a problem of scarcity that has been growing for decades.

Government policy-makers are aware that land availability and urban criminality are not the only major barriers to job creation. While PNG ranked 145th out of 174 countries listed in Transparency International's Corruption Perceptions Index in 2014, it also ranked 133rd out of 189 countries assessed in the World Bank's Ease of Doing Business Index. The government routinely undertakes to lower the costs of doing business, with a particular focus on the class of national entrepreneurs whose growth is central to the national vision statement. The government is also committed to additional investment in transport infrastructure and the electricity supply, which together constitute another major cost of doing business in both urban and rural areas. However, despite its recurrent undertakings to lower all such costs in various ways, the government has not articulated any new job creation strategies beyond those already contained in the long-term development plan.

4.4 The Quality of Jobs in the Resource Sector

The main body of new data collected for this study consists of interviews conducted between February and April 2012 with 285 PNG citizens currently or formerly employed in the resource sector. This survey was designed to elicit information about the employment history of the individuals who were interviewed, their reasons for changing jobs, their levels of job satisfaction, their social activities, and their contributions to development in the form of economic support to other people in the areas from which they originated. Here we shall focus on the findings that relate to labor mobility and spillovers in the form of remittances.

Of the 285 interviews, 180 were conducted with a "mainstream group" of people currently employed by private companies in the resource sector within

PNG; 60 were conducted with a "sidestream group" comprising 45 people formerly employed by such companies and 15 people employed in the government agency responsible for regulating the mining industry; and 45 were conducted with a group of "exiles" who had emigrated to take up jobs in the resource sector overseas.[3] Here we shall focus attention on responses provided by members of the mainstream group and the group of exiles.

4.4.1 Gender and Mobility

Thirty-nine of the workers in our mainstream group were women. This means that the group contained a higher proportion of female workers than is characteristic of the resource sector as a whole, but it also means that our interviews revealed some interesting and possibly significant differences in the careers of men and women in this sector.

The average age of the women was a good deal lower than the average age of the men: 85 percent of the women, but only 48 percent of the men, were under 40 years old, while 41 percent of the women, but only 19 percent of the men, were under 30 years old. There was a similar discrepancy in pay rates: 82 percent of the women, but only 68 percent of the men, said that they took home less than K2,000 (US$800) a fortnight, while 41 percent of the women, but only 17 percent of the men, said they took home less than K800 (US$320).[4]

These disparities are consistent with a hypothesis that women tend to drop out of jobs in the resource sector when they get married and have a certain number of children. The men in the group had an average of 3.8 children each, whereas the women had an average of 1.8 children; and 59 percent of the men, but less than 3 percent of the women, said they had a spouse who was not currently employed. We might imagine that women with young children would be inclined to drop out of the resource sector workforce rather than face the prospect of working on a fly-in-fly-out (or drive-in-drive-out) basis. However, our survey data show that the women who worked on a long rotation had a somewhat higher average number of children than those who traveled from home to work each day.

The women in the group had a narrower range of educational qualifications than the men. All the women had a minimum of ten years of formal schooling, but only one had postgraduate qualifications. Nevertheless, 44 percent of

---

[3] We call these groups rather than samples since there was no way to establish whether the people in each group were representative of a larger category of workers. While the distribution of jobs between workers in the mainstream group was similar to the pattern displayed in national job advertisements (Table 4.5), we know that preferred area employees and employees of on-site contractors were underrepresented in this group.

[4] The average value of the PNG kina over the period from 2010 to 2013 was approximately US $0.40 (or 40 Australian cents). This exchange rate has been applied to all currency conversions.

the women, as against 39 percent of the men, had university degrees. If female graduates were not earning as much as their male counterparts, the difference might be explained by their relative youth or inexperience, if not by some form of gender discrimination. It might also be explained in part by the concentration of men in more specialized technical jobs, and the greater likelihood that women will occupy clerical jobs of the sort found in many parts of the national economy. However, while 41 percent of the women in the sample did indeed have clerical jobs, 28 percent had more specialized technical jobs—the same proportion as the men.

One of the most interesting gender discrepancies in the mainstream group was the length of time spent in particular jobs. The women had been in their current and previous jobs for a shorter average period of time than their male counterparts. The most plausible explanation for this discrepancy is that workers tend to stay longer in the same job as they grow older, so the higher rate of turnover among the women may be due to their lower average age. However, the discrepancy disappears if attention is confined to their history of employment over the past decade instead of their whole career: both men and women had held an average of 2.6 jobs over that period. Male and female workers were equally likely to have held a job outside the resource sector before taking up a job inside it, but the evidence indicates that once they do have a job in the resource sector, their next job is likely to be in the resource sector as well. Experience of jobs outside the resource sector did not appear to vary significantly between workers in different age groups or at different rates of pay. However, the rate of movement between jobs did seem to reach a peak among workers in their thirties and those earning more than K2,000 a fortnight. Workers in these categories had held an average of more than three jobs over the course of the previous decade.

4.4.2 *Interhousehold Transfers*

Workers in the survey were asked to specify their contributions to development "at home" in the previous year (2011) under three main headings: goods supplied as gifts to relatives outside of the worker's own nuclear family; payments of cash to meet a variety of expenses on behalf of such relatives; and accommodation of rural relatives for various periods of time by workers resident in urban areas. Ninety-one percent of the 180 workers in the mainstream group claimed to make one or both of the first two types of remittance, while 55 percent of the 143 town-based workers claimed to have hosted rural relatives in their homes during the previous year.

Nearly all of the workers who said that they made one or both of the first two types of remittance went on to specify their purpose and their monetary value. The combined value of remittances in kind made by 115 workers in the mainstream group was just over K1 million (US$400,000). The combined value of remittances in cash made by 152 workers in this group was almost K1.2 million. The proportion of these remittances that could be counted as contributions to the formation of physical, human, or social capital, as opposed to personal consumption, was remarkably high. Almost 80 percent of the value of remittances in kind was said to consist of construction and building materials, working tools and equipment, or means of transport (including vehicles, motors, parts, and fuel). The rest was spread between household furniture and appliances, food, clothing and accessories, mobile phones and digital devices, and other miscellaneous items. The purchase of building materials and means of transport accounted for 12 percent of the value of reported cash transfers, while the payment of school fees for relatives accounted for 23 percent. The balance of the cash transfers was allocated between funeral expenses, compensation payments, brideprice payments, other customary activities, church activities, travel expenses, medical expenses, and other miscellaneous expenditures.

As might be expected, the value of both in-kind and cash remittances is related to the income level of the workers making them. For workers earning more than K4,000 (US$1,600) a fortnight (net of tax), the median annual value was K22,000; for those earning less than K800 a fortnight, it was K2,400. For most of the workers in the mainstream group, the value of reported remittances accounted for between 10 percent and 25 percent of their disposable income. In general, our findings are consistent with those of previous studies that have investigated the social and economic signifi-cance of remittances from town-based workers to rural villagers in PNG (Morauta 1984; Dalsgaard 2013).[5]

The proportion of town-based workers accommodating rural relatives for various periods of time was fairly constant across different income categories. This practice represents a hidden form of remittance to the extent that the hosts are normally liable to pay for the food consumed by their guests, sometimes for the cost of their attendance at educational institutions, and often for the cost of their travel back home at the end of their stay. On the other hand, guests often provide assistance with housework and childcare, and that could be counted as a reverse form of remittance or subsidy.

Sixty percent of the 408 guests accommodated by 79 workers in our main-stream group stayed for more than a month, and 33 percent stayed for more than six months; 25 percent were said to be mainly helping with childcare,

---

[5] We did not ask our town-based respondents for information about transfers to other urban households since this would have added too much complexity to our interview schedules, but there is published evidence that such transfers are also important as a mechanism for urban poverty alleviation (Monsell-Davis 1993; Gibson et al. 1998).

while 21 percent were apparently being educated at the expense of their hosts. It might be argued that the presence of relatives helping with childcare is one of the factors that explain why some of the married women in this group were able to remain in the formal-sector workforce, and even commute to work on a long rotation, despite having young children. However, our survey responses do not support this argument. Only 15 percent of the 110 guests reported by 19 female workers in the group were said to be mainly helping with childcare, as against 30 percent of the 298 guests reported by 60 male workers.

4.4.3 *International Migration*

There is no hard evidence on the number of Papua New Guineans who have left their country to take up jobs in the resource sector overseas, but anecdotal evidence suggests it is somewhere between 700 and 1,000. Most of these emigrants are likely to be highly skilled and specialized workers, since Papua New Guineans do not have easy access to any foreign labor market. Their departure would therefore be one of the key factors behind the occupational mobility of those workers with equivalent qualifications who have remained in PNG.

Thirty-nine of the forty-five workers in our group of "exiles" were living in Australia and six in other countries. Forty were men and five were women. All of them had grown up in PNG, 84 percent had university degrees, and 29 percent had additional postgraduate qualifications. Sixty percent would count as "physical and engineering science professionals and associates" in our occupational classification (Table 4.8), which is more than twice the proportion in our mainstream group. All but four had fortnightly take-home pay equivalent to at least 2,000 Australian (or American) dollars, and 22 (49 percent) earned more than $4,000 a fortnight. They were clearly a well-qualified and well-paid group of workers. All the workers in this group seem to have been employed in the PNG resource sector before migrating overseas, and had changed jobs more frequently than the workers in the mainstream group.

All of these migrant workers made remittances in cash or kind or both to relatives at home in PNG. Their pattern of spending on different items is quite similar to that of their counterparts in PNG. The median values of the remittances made by these workers also varied with their level of income, but not to the same extent. The median annual value of all remittances made by workers earning more than $4,000 a fortnight was $4,195, while the value for those earning less than $4,000 a fortnight was $3,500. These values are comparable to those of the remittances made by workers in the mainstream group, but since the migrant workers were earning two or three times more than their mainstream counterparts in comparable jobs, the proportion of their disposable incomes devoted to remittances was two or three times lower. Furthermore, the expatriate workers accommodated a much smaller number of visiting relatives, and the visitors stayed for much shorter periods of time, because of visa restrictions imposed by the countries where they were living.

Even if there are 1,000 migrants from PNG working in the resource sector overseas, this is a very small number by any standard measure of international labor migration. However, it seems more significant when we consider the very limited avenues for Papua New Guineans to gain any form of overseas employment. These limitations are even evident in Australia, despite its physical proximity to PNG and its status as the former colonial power. The Australian census counted 613 PNG-born workers in the resource sector in 2011. It seems safe to assume that 600 of these workers would claim Melanesian (as opposed to European) ancestry. To judge by the dependency ratios in the group we interviewed, it is likely that these individuals and their families account for more than 25 percent of the wholly indigenous Papua New Guineans now living in Australia.

The Australian government has recently been promoting a scheme through which Pacific Island economies can be strengthened by remittances from workers employed in the Australian agricultural sector on a seasonal basis (mainly as fruit-pickers). According to the Australian Department of Immigration and Citizenship, eighty-two Papua New Guineans entered Australia under the Pacific Seasonal Worker Pilot Scheme between mid 2010 and mid 2012. A study of the operation of this scheme suggests that they are unlikely to have taken home more than $400,000 between them if they remained for the standard period of six months (Hay and Howes 2012). If 600 Papua New Guinean workers were employed full time in the Australian resource sector over the same two-year period, then our survey data suggests that their combined net pay would have been in the order of $120 million and the value of their combined remittances to PNG would have been in the order of $5.5 million, which is almost fourteen times the value of the remittances attributed to the seasonal workers. That is before we even start to consider the present or future contribution of the partners and children of the 600 workers to PNG's social and economic development.

Our group of "exiles" regarded their expatriate status as a major achievement. They saw their "escape" from PNG as a reflection of their experience and skill, and an opportunity to become part of a globalized professional industry workforce. Many said that the opportunity of providing a better education for their children was one of the main reasons for their emigration. International evidence suggests that the emigration of highly skilled workers from developing countries should not necessarily be regarded as a brain drain because it can have a positive effect on human capital formation in their country of origin (Beine et al. 2011; Gibson and McKenzie 2011; Packard and Nguyen 2014). It is unlikely to have a negative effect in PNG, first because the number of highly skilled emigrants is such a small proportion of the working-age population, and second because a significant proportion of the migrants or their children may well go back to live and work in PNG at some point in their careers. Two of the men included in our mainstream group had already held jobs with mining companies overseas before returning to take up their present jobs in PNG, and one of the men in our migrant group was commuting to work in PNG from his home in Australia (Box 4.1).

The main disincentive for this type of circular migration is the dual salary system that operates in most branches of PNG's formal economy, including the resource sector (Imbun and Morris 2001). In this system, Papua New Guinean workers are generally paid less than half the amount paid to expatriate workers with the same formal qualifications. Employers justify this disparity by reference to the problem of recruiting expatriates with rare skills to work in a forbidding environment, or to the lower productivity of Papua New Guinean workers who may seem to possess these skills, or even to the perceived need to limit the income disparities within the national population in order to reduce the risk of social and political conflict between the rich and the poor. By creating new opportunities for skilled Papua New Guinean workers to migrate

---

Box 4.1 A HIGH-FLYING MIGRANT WORKER, GENERATING POSITIVE SPILLOVERS FOR HIS COUNTRY

Peter (not his real name) is a highly qualified petroleum engineer. He was among the last cohort of Papua New Guinean students to undertake the final two years of secondary education at a boarding school in Australia under a scheme supported by the Australian government's aid program. While still at school he watched news coverage of the 1991 Gulf War, and when told that it was basically a war about oil, he decided that he would try to make a career out of understanding this vital substance. At that time, it was not possible to get an undergraduate degree in petroleum engineering at any Australian university, let alone a PNG university, so he enrolled for a degree in medicine at the University of PNG. After completing his science foundation year, he was lucky enough to win a scholarship to an American university to study his preferred subject. Having obtained a postgraduate certificate from a Japanese institution, he worked in PNG's Department of Petroleum and Energy for a while and then completed his higher education with a Master's degree from a Scottish university. He got a job in the Australian gas industry, and on that basis secured permanent residence in Australia. He now lives in Sydney with his Papua New Guinean wife and six children, but has recently taken a job back in PNG on a fly-in-fly-out basis, with twenty-eight days working on site alternating with twenty-eight days of field break. During his field breaks, Peter normally spends a week doing development work in his home village in one of PNG's highland provinces. His main project for the past year has been to plant hundreds of trees to make up for a serious shortage of timber suitable for building houses. His next project is to build a guesthouse and other facilities that will attract tourists to the area.

to countries where they are paid on a par with all other workers, regardless of nationality or ethnicity, the resource boom has produced a paradox.

If we leave aside the 9,000 or 10,000 expatriate workers employed at the peak of the LNG Project's construction phase, the number of foreigners normally employed in the PNG resource sector, where they account for roughly half of the total wage bill, is now roughly equivalent to the number of Papua New Guineans who have taken jobs in the resource sector overseas (around 1,000). Employers in PNG have since found that the cost of training their national workforce continues to escalate as the best and brightest of the trainees escape to greener pastures. Anecdotal evidence indicates that the Papua New Guinean expatriates are generally unwilling to return unless they are paid as if they were foreigners in their own country. If our mainstream group is broadly representative of the national workforce in the resource sector, then it raises the interesting possibility that the proportion of women in that workforce—especially those with university degrees—has actually been increasing as employers seek to fill the gaps created by the emigration of highly qualified male workers with women—and especially married women—who are less likely to look for job opportunities overseas.

4.5 Jobs in the Resource Project Cycle

We now turn to an examination of the ways in which the creation or destruction of good jobs inside and outside the resource sector is related to the preferred area policy and the life-cycle of major resource projects. First we examine the capacity of "landowner companies" whose establishment has been subsidized under the terms of the preferred area policy to create jobs in other economic sectors that will outlast the life of the resource project with which they were initially associated. Then we consider the capacity of workers employed under the terms of that policy to find new jobs that are also good jobs when the policy no longer applies to them.

4.5.1 *Job Creation by Landowner Companies*

Landowner companies (LANCOs) have no clear legal definition in PNG, but have become a significant part of the institutional landscape in the resource sector because of the business development provisions of the preferred area policy. What distinguishes LANCOs from other nationally owned companies is that their shareholders are the customary owners of land within a particular area. LANCOs have proliferated around major resource projects as their directors and managers compete to benefit from the supply of goods and services to the developers and from the national government's provision of "seed

125

capital" under the terms of benefit-sharing agreements negotiated through the Development Forum. The bigger the project, the more intense the competition. There were thought to be hundreds of LANCOs competing for benefits from the construction phase of the LNG Project and for access to the K1.2 billion (US$480 million) allocated to provincial governments as infrastructure development grants under the project's benefit-sharing agreements.

The developers of major resource projects have tried to strengthen the capacity of local LANCOs, but these efforts have not been very successful, partly because the developers have tried to avoid the risk of alienating public opinion in their preferred areas by awarding contracts to a large number of small LANCOs, many of which have failed because of mismanagement or misappropriation. Among the few LANCOs that have survived and thrived are the so-called "umbrella companies" whose principals have somehow managed to persuade the directors of many smaller LANCOs to become shareholders in their operations. Even these larger LANCOs have sometimes run into major financial difficulties and have had to be bailed out by the developers who are normally their main customers (Brooksbank 2002).

One of the survival strategies adopted by the more successful LANCOs has been the formation of joint ventures with national or foreign companies that have already built a solid reputation in some particular line of business, such as catering or mechanical repairs. If the joint venture partner takes over the management of the business, the LANCO can easily lose popular support in the preferred area because its own directors and managers lose the ability to distribute jobs, dividends, and donations to members of their local community. At the same time, their business is still constrained by its narrow customer base and the prospect that this will disappear when the local resource project reaches the point of closure.

A few of the umbrella LANCOs have managed to escape these forms of dependency by finding new customers outside the preferred area from which they originate, and even outside the resource sector, while retaining overall control of specific lines of business operated by wholly-owned subsidiary companies. One notable example of such an entrepreneurial LANCO is Anitua, an umbrella company whose shareholders are six clan-based LANCOs and the business arm of the Nimamar (Lihir) local-level government. One of its subsidiaries, National Catering Services Ltd (NCS), originally catered for the workforce at the Lihir gold mine, but now supplies this service at other mine sites and to other organizations outside the resource sector (Packard and Nguyen 2014: 186). The business was originally expanded through a joint venture with a foreign catering company that has since been discontinued. In early 2012, NCS employed around 1,600 people, 96 percent of whom were Papua New Guineans, and most of whom were Lihirians. The directors of the umbrella company have ensured that their subsidiary company maintains its own training and localization program, with specific emphasis on the training of Lihirian employees, while protecting NCS from the social pressures that have undermined the viability of many other LANCOs.

A few of the LANCOs that have emerged to compete for benefits derived from the construction of the LNG Project could be counted as entrepreneurial companies, but it is still too early to say whether and how they will survive as the developer's demand for locally produced goods and services shrinks dramatically during the project's operational phase. If margins are compressed by weaker demand, the directors and managers of entrepreneurial LANCOs may struggle to maintain high levels of efficient investment if their local shareholders and employees seek a greater share of the profits, either through dividend payments or appointments to better-paid jobs.

While it is possible to argue that a few entrepreneurial LANCOs have made a positive contribution to the creation of good jobs, it is not clear that this outweighs the enormous subsidies that a very large number of LANCOs have received from both resource developers and the national government under the terms of the preferred area policy. Most of the LANCOs in the resource sector are little more than rent-collecting agencies (Bainton and Macintyre 2013). Even if there is a recipe for the success of the few entrepreneurial LANCOs, it is hard to see how it could be incorporated into public policy without creating an additional incentive or excuse for the government to subsidize the much larger number of LANCOs that will never match this record.

4.5.2 *Impacts of Resource Project Closure*

If the preferred area policy can create more jobs for local people when resource projects are initially developed, those jobs are liable to be lost when projects come to an end. A gold mine on the island of Misima in Milne Bay Province is the only major resource project in PNG to have closed down since 2000. The operator of the mine had been remarkably successful in its efforts to recruit most of its national workforce from Misima Island and the smaller neighboring islands that belong to the Louisiade local-level government (LLG) area. We were therefore interested to find out how many of the locally recruited workers had managed to find new jobs after the mine closed, and what contribution they were still making to the local economy.

The Misima mine closed in 2004 after fifteen years of gold production. The number of locally recruited employees rose from 488 at the start of production in 1989 to a peak of 642 in 1999, but had fallen to 307 by 2001, while the number of other Papua New Guinean employees rose from six in 1989 to a peak of seventy-two in 1998, but had fallen to 16 by 2001 (Finlayson 2002). At the peak of local employment in 1999, more than 15 percent of the men of working age in the Louisiade LLG area had jobs with the mine. There were never more than forty local women in the workforce.

The mine played a huge role in the local economy. At the peak of local employment, wages and related benefits from the mining operation contributed about K10 million (US$4 million) to the local economy in one year. Wages accounted for roughly three-quarters of the monetary benefits that local people obtained from the operation during the 1990s (Finlayson 2002: 23). The rest mainly consisted of royalties and other payments to customary landowners of the mine lease areas. The mining company also made significant improvements to the social and economic infrastructure on Misima Island (Finlayson 2002: 24), but this was associated with a decline in the government's contribution to the delivery of public goods and services.

The national government did at least begin to show concern about the likely impacts of the mine closure as soon as local workers began to be laid off. It was noted that some of the highly skilled local workers who had been trained by Misima Mines were already finding jobs with other mining companies (Jackson 2000: 40). However, the cash crops that had been the mainstay of the local economy before the mine was built had since been neglected. In the absence of any alternatives, and with the evident decline in public-sector employment on the island, it was predicted that per capita cash incomes from local economic activities could fall to half their pre-mine levels, in real terms, after the mine had closed (Jackson 2000: 5). The mining company did make some effort to revive the local agricultural economy in its last few years of operation, but not with any great success. The government eventually took action by promising to spend K20 million on the rehabilitation of the economic infrastructure that the company had left behind, and gave another K6 million to a local business group to conduct feasibility studies on new economic development projects.

It is difficult to determine the total number of workers who used to work on the Misima mine and are still employed in the resource sector. Prior to mine closure, it was thought that very few of the locally recruited female workers would be likely to take jobs elsewhere, either because of family commitments on the island or because of their low levels of skill (Jackson 2000: 40). Of the 600 local men employed in 1999, our best estimate would be that 200 or 300 of them now have jobs with other resource projects and, of these, perhaps half are commuting to work from their homes in the Louisiade LLG area.

We were able to learn more about the impacts of mine closure through interviews with thirty-seven islanders who had been employed at the mine and still had jobs in the formal economy, as well as a number of people involved in artisanal or alluvial mining, which now appears to be the most lucrative informal economic activity on the island. The thirty-seven workers still in the formal economy had typically been recruited in the early stages of the mining operation and their average tenure in the mine had been just under twelve years. Most of them had some difficulty finding new jobs after they ceased their employment with Misima Mines or its contractors.[6] At the time of our study, twenty-four were fly-in-fly-out workers (part of our mainstream group) who still had jobs in the resource sector and returned to the island on their field breaks, while the rest (who were part of our sidestream group) had jobs on the island itself. A notable feature of the group as a whole was its low level of formal education. Only three had completed twelve years of secondary education (of whom two had university degrees); most had finished school at Grade 10 or a lower grade and then obtained a trade-related certificate after being recruited to work on the mine. None had obtained any additional qualifications since the mine closed, and few are likely to have found a formal job in the absence of the mine.

All but three of the twenty-four fly-in-fly-out workers were earning between K800 and K1,990 a fortnight, while all but one of the thirteen still employed on the island were earning less than K800. The value of remittances supplied to other local households by the fly-in-fly-out workers was somewhat lower than the value of remittances from workers in the rest of our mainstream group with comparable fortnightly pay rates. The value of interhousehold transfers by workers still employed on the island was even lower. The difference may be due to the fact that these thirteen workers were all living in their home villages, or else to the possibility that some of them were earning little more than the minimum wage (K200 a fortnight). Nonetheless, four of these thirteen workers said that the wages and benefits were what they most liked about their current job, while another four said that what they most liked was the contribution they were making to community development.

If this group is representative of the larger group of former local mine workers who still have jobs in the formal sector of the economy, then the total value of their annual take-home pay would be somewhere between K5.5 million and K8.5 million, and the total value of their annual remittances to other households in the local economy would be somewhere between K1 million and K1.8 million. People on the island debate whether the earnings and remittances of the former Misima miners now formally employed represent more or less of a contribution to the local economy than the earnings of alluvial and artisanal miners, some of whom also worked on the large-scale mine when it was operating. While it is difficult to calculate the earnings of these informal miners, it seems unlikely that their economic contribution matches that of the workers in formal employment. With the passage of time, the current cohort of workers from Misima who are still employed in

---

[6] This is not surprising since PNG's resource boom did not pick up steam until 2007, three years after the mine had closed.

the resource sector will leave the workforce and are unlikely to be replaced by other workers from the island unless another large-scale mine is developed in the vicinity. The Misima case seems to support the argument that local employment under the terms of the preferred area policy can mitigate the negative impact of mine closure by enabling some local workers to find jobs in other parts of the country while still contributing to the local economy, but this effect may still be temporary.

4.6 Conclusion: The Possibilities of Policy

The recent resource boom in PNG has had a mixture of positive and negative impacts on the labor market, on productivity, on livelihoods, and on social cohesion. The number of Papua New Guineans directly and indirectly employed in the development of major resource projects grew significantly between 2002 and 2012. Most of those we interviewed seem to believe that they have better jobs than their fellow citizens employed in other parts of the national economy, but this does not prevent them from seeking better jobs for themselves in a context of increasing labor mobility. While this puts some upward pressure on wages and creates some headaches for many employers, it also means that jobs in the resource sector are less isolated from jobs in the rest of the economy. There has been considerable public debate about the negative effects of the resource boom on the quantity and quality of jobs available in other economic sectors, but this problem may be exaggerated in comparison with other symptoms of the Dutch Disease that are currently in evidence, especially the urban cost of living and the volatility of public finances.

The scale and content of remittances made by workers in the resource sector job stream to relatives at home represents a significant contribution to social and economic wellbeing beyond the limits of major resource project enclaves. Workers formally employed in other sectors, including the public service, no doubt make similar contributions, but the evidence collected for this study indicates that the amount of remittances grows with the size of a worker's pay packet, so if workers in the resource sector are especially well paid, their contributions will be larger. The evidence collected for this study also indicates that town-based workers make bigger remittances to their rural relatives than those who live in villages and commute to work in major resource projects on a fly-in-fly-out basis. Whatever the reason for this, remittances from town-based workers can partly be understood as investments in a sort of social and economic safety net that makes it easier and more attractive for such workers to retreat to their home villages when they retire or if they lose their jobs. Even workers now based overseas are motivated to make this type of investment, but their emigration has a more significant impact in creating new job opportunities in the domestic labor market and possibly contributing to an increase in the number of jobs available for women in the resource sector.

The government policies that apply to the domestic distribution of benefits (including jobs) that flow from large-scale investment in the resource sector now have wider national application because of the sector's prominence in PNG's national economy. The benefit-sharing agreements associated with the preferred area policy are thus regarded as an integral feature of the political landscape, despite their distorting effects on the labor market and business activity. The agreements associated with the LNG Project pose bigger questions about good governance than have previously been posed by any major resource project. However, national policy-makers have paid more attention to the question of who should get how much in the way of benefits from major resource projects than to the question of how these benefits might be translated into more and better jobs for the people of PNG. So, how might this second question be addressed?

Let us first consider what the Jobs WDR calls the "fundamentals" that constitute "a precondition for strong job creation by the private sector" (World Bank 2012: 257). As we have seen, PNG's policy-makers have recently assigned these to four main categories: land access, law and order, an enabling business environment, and public investment in economic infrastructure. Given the extent of the PNG government's dependence on mineral revenues, we might treat the need for transparency in the management of these revenues as a factor in its own right. The government has in fact declared an interest in signing up to the Extractive Industries Transparency Initiative, but this in itself would not entail a commitment to greater transparency in the redistribution of such revenues under the preferred area policy.

The PNG government is now struggling to maintain macroeconomic stability in the face of temptations to spend revenues from the LNG Project before it receives them (IMF 2014), but it has at least signaled an intention to moderate the future volatility of such revenues by establishing a Sovereign Wealth Fund (Duncan 2010; Basu et al. 2013). It has set remarkably ambitious targets for the number of new jobs that it expects to create by solving the country's law and order problems and formalizing rights over customary land, but its strategies for achieving these goals do not give adequate recognition to the difference between urban and rural areas. In particular, the government seems unwilling to recognize that a faster rate of urbanization could be good for productivity and living standards throughout the country if only it could focus on the urgent need to bring down the cost of urban land and housing. There is a parallel failure to deal with trade-offs between public investment in new economic infrastructure in urban as opposed to rural areas, with what appears to be an in-built preference for rural "economic corridors" and "impact projects" whose relative priority has not been established. Although the

131

government appears to recognize the need to maintain or upgrade existing economic infrastructure before embarking on the construction of new facilities, history suggests that local politicians much prefer to open things that will make a big public impression for a short period of time. So long as the PNG government allocates half of its spending to the development budget, lots of new things get built, or partly built, but there is not enough money to staff or maintain them (Howes et al. 2014). While this may mean more new jobs in the construction sector, those jobs may not be "good for development" in the long term.

There is a strong case to be made that the best way for the PNG government to apply its mineral revenues to the objective of creating "good jobs for development" is to spend them on the formation of human capital. Health and education are two of the four priority areas identified in recent budget papers, along with infrastructure and law and order. The amount allocated to these four areas has risen from 20 percent of the 2007 budget to 50 percent of the 2015 budget (ADB 2014a). Yet there are still doubts about the quality and effectiveness of this spending. Extra government funding has produced a measurable improvement in the performance of primary schools since 2002, even though this improvement has been concentrated in the urban areas and "inner rural zone" that together account for roughly half of the country's population. But there is no evidence of a comparable improvement in the delivery of health services in any part of the country (Howes et al. 2014).

When the Prime Minister announced that the government would use some of its extra revenues to import hundreds of foreign doctors, teachers, and nurses to fill vacancies in the public health and education systems, there followed a public debate about where these people might come from, why they were needed, and how much they would have to be paid by way of an incentive. The interesting point here is that the vacancies do not seem to have been created by the emigration of qualified personnel from PNG, as is known to occur in other developing countries, but by the unattractive terms and conditions of employment for national workers in both sectors, especially the health sector, and the difficulty of recruiting replacements for those workers who resign or retire. This raises important questions about the relationship between public-sector pay scales, the lack of enthusiasm for manpower planning, and the self-evident decline in the quality of professional, technical, and vocational education in PNG.

Although these questions are fundamental to an understanding of PNG's labor market, they also take us into the realm of more specific policies that governments may apply to the protection or creation of jobs once the economic fundamentals have been guaranteed. In the PNG case, the government's favored method of creating more jobs outside the resource sector has been to adopt a mixture of subsidies and regulations to promote "downstream processing" activities in other rural industries. However, these efforts have not proven to be very effective in achieving the economic diversification that resource-rich countries are meant to pursue. Indeed, these types of government intervention may simply add to the market distortions already being created by the preferred area policy.

It should be no surprise that there has recently been much debate in PNG about the tendency of a booming resource sector to suck highly qualified workers out of the public service, as well as other industries in the private sector. This is a trend that can certainly be detected in those government agencies responsible for regulating the resource sector itself. This raises the question whether public service salaries need to be increased in order to limit the scale of the brain drain. There is perhaps an argument for raising salaries in some critical branches of government, but this currently runs up against the provisions of the Public Finance Management Act, and these can only be avoided by turning line departments into statutory authorities that can offer better terms and conditions to their employees. However, such measures do not address the cost of housing, which is the main cost-of-living pressure currently confronting urban workers, including public servants. The government has not so far shown any enthusiasm for restoring the differential that used to exist between urban and rural minimum wages in order to cope with this problem, since a major increase in the urban minimum wage would be strongly opposed by employers whose business costs have already risen substantially as an effect of the Dutch Disease.

In the resource sector itself, the government clearly has no interest in persuading the major resource companies to abandon the dual salary system, since the companies already have sufficient incentives to limit the employment of expensive foreign workers, and any increase in wages for national workers would only aggravate the Dutch Disease. If anything, the government would do better to promote the emigration of highly skilled national workers from the resource sector in order to create more jobs for workers who remain behind. However, the workers in question have proven to be quite capable of organizing their own emigration, with or without the support of their former employers in PNG or the PNG government. Some employers might even prefer a system of incentives that would discourage the emigration of highly skilled national workers, since this would reduce the cost of training new employees who do not yet have the requisite skills, but that is even less likely to be adopted as a matter of government policy.

Another thing the government should probably not do is to provide additional support to landowner companies based in resource project enclaves, beyond the support which they already receive from the application of the preferred area policy. While the application of this policy may have created the space for entrepreneurial LANCOs to emerge in the first place, their emergence from a much larger group of LANCOs with defective business models owes nothing to government support, and there is no reason to give them further competitive advantages against other nationally owned companies. Foreign investors in the resource sector now have a better idea of how to foster the emergence of such companies in their fields of operation, and if there is a role for government here, it should mainly be concerned with policies to improve levels of corporate governance and accountability that would apply to all landowner companies.

Two measures are required to reduce the socio-economic costs of resource project closure: first, an industrial training program that succeeds in creating a cohort of preferred area employees who are sufficiently skilled to gain employment in other parts of the country where they no longer count as preferred area employees; and second, the formation of at least one entrepreneurial LANCO that can also compete in a national marketplace, even if some of its staff are still recruited from the preferred area. In some areas, it may be possible for mining and petroleum companies to subsidize small-scale commercial activities that will provide a reasonable living for local people after project closure, but the record to date has not been impressive, and there is no reason to think that government policy measures would improve it.

This leaves us with three policy priorities that are already recognized to some extent, though not clearly distinguished from the many other things that the government aims to do to manage the impacts and benefits of the resource boom. First, as we have already said, skyrocketing rental costs in PNG's major urban centers, and especially in the national capital, are not simply a symptom of the Dutch Disease. They are part of a longer-term trend for the urban population to expand much faster than land can be freed up for the construction of new housing, even if the size of the urban population is increasing no more rapidly than that of the national population as a whole. Since this problem has been recognized for a long time, there is also a long history of government failure to deal with it effectively. But like other priority areas for government action, the problem will not go away, so some solution must be found.

A second priority should be to strengthen the public institutions of professional and technical training, which currently have glaring weaknesses. This does not entail the reintroduction of centralized manpower planning of the kind attempted in the early years after Independence, nor does it entail a specific focus on the more specialized skills required by the resource sector. There is no point in having a surplus of qualified geologists at the end of a resource boom. On the other hand, it is unreasonable to expect that mining and petroleum companies should bear all the costs of making up for deficiencies in the public education of their national employees in a situation where workers trained at company expense are likely to find a new job with a new employer within a few years. There needs to be a concerted effort by relevant government agencies and organizations representing employers in different branches of industry to improve the overall quality of postsecondary education.

The third priority should be the development of human capital in those rural areas with the most acute levels of poverty, where the windfall benefits of a major resource project may never materialize, and where local people would struggle to take advantage of them even if they did. For the most part, these areas may get no benefit from an increase in the quantity and quality of jobs in the formal sector of the economy because anecdotal evidence suggests that children born and brought up in these villages have an ever-diminishing chance of getting the sort of technical or professional education that would qualify them for such jobs, while adults from these villages may not even have the opportunity of migrating to a major town, getting jobs as security guards, and receiving the minimum wage of K200 a fortnight. The question of what to do about these areas of extreme disadvantage has been recognized as a major policy problem for a long time. The present national government might claim that it has come up with its own solution in the form of the free education policy that is now meant to relieve parents of the financial burden of school fee payments. However, free access to primary schools does not have much value if the schools are unable to provide a realistic path to further education. If the preferred area policy is a political necessity, it still needs to be accompanied by a "less-developed areas" policy that puts less emphasis on impact projects and economic corridors, and more emphasis on measurable improvements in health and education outcomes.

Acknowledgments

The study whose findings are reported in this chapter was funded by the Australian Agency for International Development (AusAID). The data collection process was managed by the PNG Institute of National Affairs. We thank Rosemary Benjamin, Casper Damien, Jennifer Krimbu, and Deane Woruba for their assistance in the collection of the survey data, and acknowledge the cooperation of all 285 Papua New Guineans who responded to our questions. We are also grateful to the participants in the survey design workshop held in Port Moresby at the beginning of February 2012. Finally, the lead author acknowledges the support of The Cairns Institute at James Cook University for time and space taken up in drafting the penultimate version of this chapter.

References

ADB (Asian Development Bank) (2002). Priorities of the Poor in Papua New Guinea. Manila: ADB.

ADB (Asian Development Bank) (2014a). Pacific Economic Monitor: Papua New Guinea Budget 2015. Manila: ADB.

ADB (Asian Development Bank) (2014b). Key Indicators for Asia and the Pacific 2014: Papua New Guinea. Manila: ADB.

Asia South Pacific Association for Basic and Adult Education and PNG Education Advocacy Network (2011). PNG Education Experience Survey and Literacy Assessment: A Report on 5 Provinces. Canberra and Port Moresby.

Bainton, N.A. and Macintyre, M. (2013). "'My land, my work': Business development and large-scale mining in Papua New Guinea." *Research in Economic Anthropology*, 33:139–65.

Bakker, M.L. (1986). *The Mortality Situation in Papua New Guinea: Levels, Differentials, Patterns and Trends*. Port Moresby: PNG National Statistical Office (Research Monograph 4).

Basu, S., Gottschalk, J., Schule, W., Vellodiand, N., and Yang, S.S. (2013). The Macroeconomic Effects of Natural Resource Extraction: Applications to Papua New Guinea, Working Paper No. 13/138. Washington, DC: International Monetary Fund.

Bauze, A.E., Tran, L.N., Nguyen, K.H., Firth, S., Jimenez-Soto, E., et al. (2012). "Equity and geography: The case of child mortality in Papua New Guinea." *PLoS One*, 7:e37861.

Baxter, M. (2001). *Enclaves or Equity: The Rural Crisis and Development Choice in Papua New Guinea*. Canberra: AusAID (International Development Issues 54).

Beine, M., Docquier, F., and Rapoport, H. (2011). "Brain drain and human capital formation in developing countries: Winners and losers." *Economic Journal*, 118:631–52.

Booth, H., Zhang, G., Rao, M., Taomia, F., and Duncan, R. (2006). Population Pressures in Papua New Guinea, the Pacific Island Economies, and Timor Leste, Working Paper 102. Canberra: Australian National University, Research School of Social Sciences, Demography and Sociology Program.

Brooksbank, J. (2002). Sustainable Development Policy and Sustainability Planning Framework for the Mining Sector in Papua New Guinea, Working Paper 3: Business Development, Training and Employment. Port Moresby: PNG Mining Sector Institutional Strengthening Project.

Bulman, T. (2012). The Challenge of Transforming Today's Boom into Better Living Standards Tomorrow. Washington, DC: World Bank (PNG Economic Briefing 2012–1).

Bulman, T. (2013). Navigating Turbulent Waters: Addressing Looming Policy Challenges for Revived Growth and Improved Living Standards. Washington, DC: World Bank (PNG Economic Briefing 2013–2).

Chand, S. and Stewart, R. (1997). "Economic reforms and structural change in Papua New Guinea: Progress, performance and prospects." *Pacific Economic Bulletin*, 12:53–69.

Dalsgaard, S. (2013). "The politics of remittance and the role of returning migrants: Localizing Capitalism in Manus Province, Papua New Guinea." *Research in Economic Anthropology*, 33:277–302.

Duncan, R. (2010). "Managing natural resource revenues in Papua New Guinea." *Pacific Economic Bulletin*, 25:261–4.

Filer, C. (1997). Resource rents: Distribution and sustainability. In: Papua New Guinea: A 20/20 Vision, Pacific Policy Paper 20, Ila Temu (ed.), pp. 222–60. Canberra: Australian National University, National Centre for Development Studies.

Filer, C. (2005). The role of land-owning communities in Papua New Guinea's mineral policy framework. In: *International and Comparative Mineral Law and Policy: Trends and Prospects*, Elizabeth Bastida, Thomas Wälde, and Janeth Warden-Fernández (eds), pp. 903–32. The Hague: Kluwer Law International.

Filer, C. (2008). "Development forum in Papua New Guinea: Upsides and downsides." *Journal of Energy & Natural Resources Law*, 26:120–50.

Filer, C. and Imbun, B.Y. (2009). A short history of mineral development policies in Papua New Guinea, 1972–2002. In: *Policy Making and Implementation: Studies from Papua New Guinea*, R.J. May (ed.), pp. 75–116. Canberra: ANU E Press.

Finlayson, M. (2002). Sustainable Development Policy and Sustainability Planning Framework for the Mining Sector in Papua New Guinea, Working Paper 2: Benefit Stream Analysis. Port Moresby: PNG Mining Sector Institutional Strengthening Project.

Flanagan, P. (2014). Papua New Guinea's Vanishing LNG Export Boom. Policy Brief 10. Canberra: Australian National University, Development Policy Centre.

Gibson, J. (2000). "The Papua New Guinea Household Survey." *Australian Economic Review*, 33:377–80.

Gibson, J. (2013). The Labour Market in Papua New Guinea (with a Focus on the National Capital District). Unpublished technical report on the 2009/10 Household Income and Expenditure Survey.

Gibson, J., Boe-Gibson, G., and Scrimgeour, F. (1998). "Are voluntary transfers an effective safety net in urban Papua New Guinea?" *Pacific Economic Bulletin*, 13:40–53.

Gibson, J., Datt, G., Allen, B., Hwang, V., Bourke, R.M., and Parajuli, D. (2005). "Mapping poverty in rural Papua New Guinea." *Pacific Economic Bulletin*, 20:27–43.

Gibson, J. and McKenzie, D. (2011). "Eight questions about brain drain." *Journal of Economic Perspectives*, 25:107–28.

Government of PNG (1988). Social Indicators of Papua New Guinea 1980–1985. Port Moresby: National Statistical Office.

Government of PNG (2009). Papua New Guinea Vision 2050. Port Moresby: National Strategic Plan Taskforce.

Government of PNG (2010). Papua New Guinea Development Strategic Plan 2010–2030. Port Moresby: Department of National Planning and Monitoring.

Government of PNG (2012). 2009–2010 Papua New Guinea Household Income and Expenditure Survey: Summary Tables. Port Moresby: PNG National Statistical Office.

Hay, D. and Howes, S. (2012). Australia's Pacific Seasonal Worker Pilot Scheme: Why Has the Take-up Been So Low? Discussion Paper 17. Canberra: Australian National University, Development Policy Centre.

Howes, S., Mako, A.A., Swan, A., Walton, G., Webster, T., and Wiltshire, C. (2014). A Lost Decade? Service Delivery and Reforms in Papua New Guinea 2002–2012. Port Moresby and Canberra: PNG National Research Institute and Australian National University.

Imbun, B.Y. and Morris, R. (2001). Labour and mining in remote areas: Toward an assessment of benefits. In: *Mining in Papua New Guinea: Analysis and Policy Implications*, B.Y. Imbun and P.A. McGavin (eds), pp. 81–93. Waigani: University of Papua New Guinea Press.

IMF (International Monetary Fund) (2014). Papua New Guinea: 2014 Article IV Consultation. Country Report 14/325. Washington, DC: IMF.

Jackson, R.T. (2000). *Kekeisi Kekeisi*: A Long Term Economic Development Plan for the Misima Gold Mine's Impact Area. Unpublished report to the Government of PNG.

Johnson, P. (2012). Lode Shedding: A Case Study of the Economic Benefits to the Landowners, the Provincial Government, and the State from the Porgera Gold Mine. Discussion Paper 124. Boroko: PNG National Research Institute.

Levantis, T. (1997). "Urban unemployment in Papua New Guinea—it's criminal." *Pacific Economic Bulletin*, 12:73–84.

Mola, G. and Kirby, B. (2013). "Discrepancies between national maternal mortality data and international estimates: The experience of Papua New Guinea." *Reproductive Health Matters*, 21:191–202.

Monsell-Davis, M. (1993). "Urban exchange: Safety-net or disincentive?" *Canberra Anthropology*, 16:45–66.

Morauta, L. (1984). *Left Behind in the Village: Economic and Social Conditions in an Area of High Outmigration*. Monograph 25. Boroko: PNG Institute of Applied Social and Economic Research.

Packard, T. and Nguyen, T.V. (2014). *East Asia Pacific at Work: Employment, Enterprise, and Well-Being*. Washington, DC: World Bank.

Susapu, B. and Crispin, G. (2001). Report on Small-Scale Mining in Papua New Guinea. Working Paper No. 81. London: Mining, Minerals and Sustainable Development Project.

UNDP (United Nations Development Programme) and Government of PNG (2014). From Wealth to Wellbeing: Translating Resource Revenue into Sustainable Human Development. Port Moresby: UNDP and PNG Department of National Planning and Monitoring (2014 National Human Development Report).

World Bank (2004). Papua New Guinea: Poverty Assessment. Washington, DC: World Bank.

World Bank (2012). World Development Report 2013: Jobs. Washington, DC: World Bank.

5

St Lucia

Jobs and Integration of a Small-Island Nation

Andrew S. Downes, Edwin St Catherine, and Ezra Jn Baptiste

5.1 Introduction

This chapter examines job challenges in the context of a small-island nation, using the Caribbean island of St Lucia as a case study. A former British colony that gained independence in 1979, St Lucia epitomizes the small-island developing country with a resident population of about 180,000 in 2014 and a land area of just 237 square miles (616 square kilometers). St Lucia is located in the Windward Islands[1] group of the Lesser Antilles on the eastern side of the Caribbean Sea. It is a volcanic island with several hilly and forested areas, thus making it a densely populated country. Its capital, Castries, is the most densely populated area in the country and the main center of economic activity. According to the United Nations Human Development Index (HDI), St Lucia is classified in the "high human development" category with a rank of 89 out of 188 countries in 2014 (United Nations Development Program 2015). It is defined by the World Bank as an "upper middle-income" country, with a per capita gross national income (GNI) in 2013 of US$10,290 at constant purchasing power parity (World Development Indicators).

St Lucia reflects the characteristics of a typical small-island nation, namely a small population size, limited land area and natural resources, small domestic market coupled with the lack of economies of scale in production, limited range of manpower, high dependence on imported goods and services, and vulnerability to external economic and environmental shocks such as hurricanes,

---

[1] The Windward Islands consist of Dominica, Grenada, Martinique, St Lucia, and St Vincent and the Grenadines.

oil price increases, and recession in external markets. Like other small Caribbean countries, St Lucia has a highly concentrated production structure with the tourism and banana production sectors being significant contributors to output and foreign exchange. It is, however, well located to take advantage of its 200-mile exclusive economic zone beyond its coastline as an island state.

The ensuing analysis of St Lucia provides a basis for examining the relationship between jobs and living standards, productivity, and social cohesion in the context of a small-island developing nation. Section 5.2 reviews some generic features of small-island nations with respect to job creation and "good jobs for development" taking the case of St Lucia into consideration. Section 5.3 provides an overview of the St Lucian economy, paying particular attention to changes since 1995 as banana production became increasingly less central to the economy and the services sector, especially tourism, became more prominent. This section provides the backdrop for informing the relationships between jobs, living standards, productivity, and social cohesion which are empirically analyzed in Section 5.4. The barriers to the World Development Report's (World Bank 2012) three "transformations" (living standards, productivity, and social cohesion) are discussed in Section 5.5, while the final Section 5.6 examines policy measures for overcoming these barriers.

5.2 Job Challenges in a Small-Island Nation

By virtue of their size, small-island nations have small domestic markets for goods and services, which means that international trade plays a critical role in their economies. The units of analysis (for example, households and firms) are effectively globalized, in that they have to incorporate the impact of international trade and finance into their operations. In addition, there is a relatively high degree of production and export concentration in small nations, that is, one or two sectors dominate economic activity. In this context, "good jobs for development," defined as jobs which produce the greatest development payoff in terms of poverty reduction, enhancing productivity, and social cohesion (trust and civic engagement), would be closely connected with global markets and the global value chain. Jobs that reduce poverty would be those that provide incomes consistently above the poverty line, while those that involve teamwork, networking, and community engagement would build social cohesion. In small-island nations, it is likely that there will be more social contact among persons which can spill over into the labor market. For small-island economies, jobs in the export sector can be associated with greater productivity, which underlies the competitiveness of the goods and services produced by firms. Jobs that build social cohesion can lead, in turn, to higher levels of productivity and improved living standards.

The labor market reflects the nature of the production and trading structure of a small nation like St Lucia. The main export sectors—such as agricultural production (sugar, bananas, cocoa), tourism, mining, and financial services—tend to employ the bulk of the workforce in well-remunerated jobs, both directly and indirectly. In some cases, the seasonality of production (for example, tourism and agriculture) creates seasonal employment. Where the production cycle cannot keep persons employed on a sustainable basis, then they migrate to other countries (regional and international) in search of employment. For example, migration to the United Kingdom, Canada, and the US has been a common feature of the Caribbean, while in the Pacific small-island states, New Zealand and Australia have been the principal destinations for migrant workers. Remittances received from such migrant labor tend to support economic activity in small nations (Downes 2008).

An important aspect of the labor market in a small-island nation is the role of the "blue economy." The blue economy refers to economic activity that is dependent on the marine and coastal resources available to the country (Roberts n.d.). Countries are able to utilize the 200-mile economic zone beyond the coastline. For small-island nations, economic activities in such areas as tourism, fishing, aquaculture, offshore mining, boat building and repairs, and yachting/marina activities can offer job creation opportunities. In some cases, a shock (economic or environmental) to the traditional and longstanding sources of employment might mean that the economy would have to identify alternative sources of employment in some of these areas. The challenge is identifying the appropriate sector(s) and also developing the skills set to meet the labor demands of the sector(s). In the case of St Lucia, it will be seen that tourism and marina activities have offered "good jobs for development" with the decline of the banana industry. Other areas in the "blue economy" offer further prospects for job creation in St Lucia, as will be discussed later.

Since several small-island developing states (SIDS) lie in the tropics and have fragile ecosystems, there are also opportunities for job creation in the "green economy," namely renewable energy using solar and wind systems and waste management, which reduce the environmental impact of economic activity (Bowen 2012). St Lucia has been developing its renewable energy sector particularly through the use of solar water heating and geo-thermal energy systems. These systems have been used in residential houses and businesses (including hotels in the tourism sector).

The development of both "blue" and "green" economic activities not only offers opportunities for the creation of "good jobs" (those that offer good remuneration, employment protection, and a good quality of life), but also contribute to poverty reduction, productivity improvement, and social cohesion (i.e., good jobs for development) in small-island nations that are undergoing economic transformation. St Lucia offers a good example of a small-island nation that has been making the transition from a traditional agriculture- (banana-) based economy to a services-based economy. With high levels of unemployment, especially among the youth, and high levels of poverty, it is imperative for the country to find avenues for creating "good jobs for development" capitalizing on certain key elements that have not been fully explored—specifically, marine and coastal-based activities, renewable energy, and waste management.

In effect, good jobs in small-island nations are found in the "primary labor markets" of key production sectors that dominate the economy (e.g., tourism, agriculture, mining, financial services). These jobs are linked to the foreign exchange generation of these small nations. The public sector is also a source of good jobs, as the government has to be the "employer of first resort" when the private sector lacks dynamism or is embryonic. Although labor unions might exist, they capture a small (but sometimes strategically important) segment of the employed labor force.

The challenge for small-island nations is to identify opportunities that can expand the range of good jobs in the economy and that contribute to social cohesion, improved productivity, and higher standards of living; that is, the World Development Report's "good jobs for development." St Lucia, and other small-island nations, have a major task in creating jobs that are con- nected to global commodity and labor markets, are environmentally benign given the fragility of their ecosystems, can reduce poverty and the numbers of "working poor," empower women and offer a sense of fairness, provide social identity, and are linked to social networks. Invariably there will be trade-offs associated with these multiple objectives, such that careful planning and policy-making would be essential.

5.3 An Overview of the St Lucian Economy since 1995

In this section, an overview of the basic features of the St Lucian economy is provided as background to the analysis of the relationship between job cre- ation and the three transformations in the context of a small-island nation.

5.3.1 Economic Growth and Structural Change

The real GDP (at 2006 prices) increased from EC$1,872.5m (US$693.5) in 1995 to EC$2,626.2m (US$972.7) in 2010, representing an average annual growth rate of 2.3 percent (exchange rate of EC$2.70 to US$1). The economy, however, experienced declines in activity during the periods 2001–02 (associated with the September 11, 2001 shock), 2005 and subsequent years (associated with

Table 5.1. Level and growth of real GDP, 1995 to 2014

	Real GDP (EC$m) (2006 base year)	Growth of real GDP (%)
1995	1,872.5	1.59
1996	1,897.1	1.32
1997	1,915.6	0.98
1998	1,978.8	3.30
1999	2,055.8	3.89
2000	2,148.3	4.50
2001	2,089.7	−2.73
2002	2,055.0	−1.66
2003	2,147.6	4.50
2004	2,289.4	6.60
2005	2,264.6	−1.08
2006	2,431.7	7.38
2007	2,472.1	1.66
2008	2,590.1	4.77
2009	2,584.0	−0.23
2010	2,587.6	0.14
2011	2,626.2	1.49
2012	2,543.8	−0.8
2013	2,494.6	−1.9
2014	2,477.2	−0.7

Note: there is a break in the series at 2011.
Source: St Lucia Department of Statistics.

the decline in banana production occasioned by tropical storm damage in 2004), and 2009–10 (associated with the Great Recession and Hurricane Tomas). From 2012 to 2014 the country recorded three consecutive years of negative growth rates. These declines reflect the vulnerability of the small-island nation to external economic and environmental shocks (Table 5.1). Per capita real GDP increased from EC$12,875 in 1995 to EC$15,859 in 2010, that is, an average annual growth rate of 1.4 percent. This growth rate reflects a relatively low population average growth rate of 0.9 percent per annum over the period.

The production structure of St Lucia epitomizes the basic features of a small-island nation. Historically, the country has depended on the agricultural sector, namely, the production of bananas for the export market. In the 1950s and 1960s, over 80 percent of the island's income and foreign exchange was derived from the export of bananas to the United Kingdom under a preferential trading arrangement. During the 1970s and 1980s, the tourism sector emerged as the main secondary source of foreign exchange earnings after banana exports. With the formation of the European Economic Community in the early 1990s, the UK was forced to eliminate the preferential access arrangement for St Lucia and the other Windward Islands, which would obviously be expected to have adverse effects. Competition from banana producers in Latin America in the European market also hastened the decline of the industry in the Windward Islands.

Table 5.2. Percent distribution of banana production by country, main Windward Island banana producers, 1995–2014

Country	1995	2000	2005	2010	2014
St Lucia	54.4	50.0	51.7	77.0	94.0
St Vincent	26.2	30.1	30.0	13.0	0.0
Dominica	17.0	19.3	18.3	10.0	6.0
Grenada	2.4	0.5	0.0	0.0	0.0
Total	100.0	100.0	100.0	100.0	100.0

Source: Windward Islands Banana Producing and Exporting Company (WIBECO).

St Lucia has remained the main producer of bananas in the Windward Islands, since it has experienced a slower rate of decline as the Windward Islands export market shrunk. St Lucia's proportion of overall Windward Islands production increased by 40 percentage points in the 1995–2014 period (Table 5.2). The European Union has provided financial assistance to St Lucia and other Windward Islands to assist with the restructuring of the agricultural sector. The assistance received included support for increasing diversification away from banana exports, general private sector support and strengthening, and support to improve the resilience of the banana industry to international competition; for example, by developing fair-trade branded bananas among other measures.

The historical dependence on the agricultural sector as a source of production, employment, foreign exchange, and government revenue has waned over the years. The contribution of the sector to real gross domestic production declined from 13.3 percent in 1980 to 2.8 percent in 2014 (Table 5.3). Production diversification in the country has occurred through the promotion of the tourism and financial services sectors. The tourism sector as measured *directly*[2] by hotels and restaurants accounted for an average of 10 percent of GDP over the 1980 to 2014 period. The *indirect* effects of the tourism sector are, however, felt in the sectors (principally agriculture, distribution, transportation, etc.) that supply goods and services to the tourism sector or use goods and services produced by that sector. The employment in the hotels and restaurants sector has increased from being consistently under 10 percent of total employment in the 1990s to over 10 percent from 2010 onwards. However, the share of total GDP of the sector has not changed due to the introduction of "all-inclusive" hotels, increased competition from cruise ships lowering the profit margins of traditional "stay-over" hotels, increased productivity especially in hotel marketing, and the impact of the global economic crisis, which disproportionally affected the hotels and restaurants sector.

---

[2] The tourism sector is not identified clearly in UN System of National Accounts standard GDP tables; it can only be identified through the GDP of the hotels and restaurants sector.

Table 5.3. Percent distribution of real gross domestic product by sector, 1980–2014

Sector	1980	1985	1990	1995	2000	2005	2010	2014
Agriculture/fishing	13.3	14.3	14.6	11.6	6.4	3.6	3.3	2.8
Mining/quarrying	0.9	0.5	0.4	0.5	0.1	0.1	0.3	0.1
Manufacturing	6.7	8.1	8.2	7.9	4.9	5.2	5.1	4.7
Construction	6.9	6.2	6.4	9.6	11.1	8.8	9.5	7.3
Electricity, water, gas	2.4	2.6	2.9	4.2	3.8	4.1	4.2	4.4
Whole and retail trade	17.5	14.1	16.5	15.2	7.3	8.8	7.5	7.6
Hotels and restaurants	10.1	9.4	9.6	12.6	10.4	11.4	10.1	11.0
Transport, communications	12.1	14.3	16.8	21.3	18.4	20.9	20.6	19.1
Financial services	5.2	6.1	7.3	9.7	6.5	6.6	7.4	8.0
Real estate	10.9	9.5	7.2	7.7	15.8	16.5	17.4	18.9
Government	14.5	16.0	12.7	14.3	13.9	12.6	12.3	13.4
Other services	3.2	3.2	3.8	5.1	2.8	3.3	4.8	4.5
Imputed banking service charge	(3.7)	(4.2)	(6.4)	(8.1)	(1.2)	(1.6)	(2.4)	(2.0)
Total	100.0	100.0	100.0	100.0	100.0	100.0	100.0	100.0

Note: the imputed banking service charge is an implicit charge incurred by corporations for financial intermediation provided by the banks.
Source: St Lucia Department of Statistics.

The embryonic financial services sector accounted for 8 percent of GDP in 2014. While the country continued to record growth in imports of goods up to 2007, it experienced a precipitous decline due to the impact of the global financial crisis in 2008, which affected the construction and wholesale and retail sectors in particular.

By 2014, the main contributors to output were transportation and communication, real estate, government services, and tourism (hotels and restaurants). St Lucia has therefore made the transition from an agriculture-based economy in the 1950s and 1960s to a services economy in 2010—a shift from one form of production concentration to another.

Banana production declined significantly from 103,000 tons in 1995 to 12,000 tons in 2011, while exports declined by the same extent over this period. Tourist arrivals rose from 407,500 in 1995 to 1 million in 2014. There was, however, a shift in the type of tourist arrivals from stay-over to cruise (short-term) over the 1995 to 2014 period. While stay-over tourists, who occupy the hotels, rose by 32 percent from 1995 to 2010, cruise-ship tourists grew by 300 percent in these years. There has also been a corresponding increase in the nominal value of tourist expenditure, from EC$715m in 1995 to EC$2,015m in 2014 (Table 5.4). While the share of tourism (as measured by hotels and restaurants) in real GDP remained relatively constant over the years, the growth in tourist arrivals and expenditure suggests that the indirect effects of tourism are likely to be significant.[3]

---

[3] Over the period 1995 to 2014, nominal tourist expenditure increased by 81.9 percent while the retail price index rose by 60.8 percent, giving a real increase of 21.1 percent.

Table 5.4. Performance indicators for the banana and tourism industries, 1995–2014

Year	Banana production (000 tons)	Banana exports (000 tons)	Banana export earnings (EC$m)	Total tourist arrivals (000)	Tourist expenditure (EC$m)
1995	103.1	103.1		407.5	715.0
1996	105.6	104.8	125.8	421.7	725.0
1997	71.4	71.4	85.9	563.6	766.0
1998	73.2	73.0	92.4	629.6	765.0
1999	65.2	65.2	87.0	625.3	740.0
2000	70.0	70.3	86.0	742.2	752.3
2001	34.0	34	41.2	766.3	629.0
2002	48.2	48.2	58.6	673.9	567.0
2003	34.0	34.0	43.6	704.2	761.0
2004	43.4	42.3	53.8	813.7	879.0
2005	31.1	30.0	41.5	726.1	919.1
2006	35.1	34.0	48.1	695.3	768.4
2007	31.9	30.3	43.7	931.8	1,446.9
2008	40.5	38.4	58.9	946.7	1,233.0
2009	37.7	33.9	56.4	1,014.8	1,121.8
2010	26.1	21.7	41.9	1,015.6	1,517.0
2011	11.8	6.5	13.2	976.2	1,398.6
2012	n.a.	12.1	21.1	931.2	1,602.4
2013	n.a.	12.4	22.0	960.6	1,763.7
2014	n.a.	8.9	16.2	1,034.3	2,015.3

Sources: St Lucia Department of Statistics: Economic and Social Review.

The production of goods and services in St Lucia is dominated by micro, small, and medium-sized enterprises, employing less than 100 persons (Cato 2005; IFC 2010). This is typical of a small developing country, where export production takes place in a small number of large enterprises that can achieve economies of scale, while production for the small domestic market is undertaken by a large number of micro, small, and medium-sized firms. Enterprise surveys for St Lucia indicate that "small" enterprises (fewer than twenty employees) tend to be sole proprietorships, while "medium" (between twenty and ninety-nine employees) and to a great extent "large" enterprises (over 100 employees) tend to be partnerships and limited liability/shareholding companies. Small and medium-sized enterprises are largely owned by local entrepreneurs, while large enterprises are dominated by foreign investors (St Catherine 2013). Indicators point to a low level of innovation in St Lucian enterprises, although there is significant use of ICT (websites and email), especially by large enterprises (ECTEL 2010).

In terms of "ease of doing business" in the region, St Lucia has been a top performing country, although its global ranking has declined in recent years, from 45 (out of 183) in 2010 to 77 (out of 189) in 2016 (World Bank 2010, 2016). Since 2014, the government has responded to the private sector's call to address the decline in the business climate by setting up a committee to review processes that affect the ease of doing business. Specifically, reforms at the Customs Department have been introduced to reduce, among other things, the administrative burden of importation of investment-related goods, the setting up of a commercial court to allow the speedy resolution of business-related conflict, and raising the threshold for the payment of VAT (value-added tax) by businesses. In addition, the government has established a National Competitiveness and Productivity Council with the aim "to identify the key issues related to competitiveness and productivity in St. Lucia as well as provide timely and effective recommendations to policy makers, private sector and other stakeholders."

The main constraints to business activity identified in the World Bank surveys have been: access to finance, getting electricity, transportation, and the inadequately educated workforce—especially in large enterprises. Some of these constraints may be due to the size of the country and the topography, which is hilly.

Research on economic growth in the Organization of Eastern Caribbean States (OECS) points to the important role that exports (especially tourism), capital investment, and human resources development play in the growth process (Schipke et al. 2013). There is also evidence of declining total factor productivity (Schipke et al. 2013). It is therefore important that the constraints to business activity be removed in order to promote economic diversification, growth, and job creation in St Lucia.

5.3.2 Macroeconomic Performance

In small developing economies, the rate of inflation is influenced primarily by increases in the prices of imported goods and services. St Lucia is a member of the Eastern Caribbean Currency Union (ECCU), which maintains a fixed exchange rate of EC$2.70 with the $US, while it floats with all other currencies.[4] The US is St Lucia's main extra-regional trading partner; hence changes in export prices from the US influence the rate of inflation in St Lucia. The inflation rate for the period 1995–2014 was relatively low, due to low rates in the US with which it is highly correlated (correlation coefficient of 0.55). Inflation rates over 5 percent were recorded in 1995, 2001, and 2008 and reflect spikes in the US inflation rate (see Table 5.5).

As a small nation, St Lucia has a highly open economy. The average ratio of exports and imports of goods and services to GDP over the 1995 to 2010 period was 1.18 (Eastern Caribbean Central Bank Statistics). In terms of macroeconomic management, the fiscal and balance of payments (BOP) accounts need to be carefully managed in order to avoid serious economic

---

[4] The members of the ECCU are Antigua and Barbuda, Dominica, Grenada, St Kitts and Nevis, St Lucia, and St Vincent and the Grenadines.

Table 5.5. Inflation rates in St Lucia and the US, 1995 to 2014

Year	Inflation rate St Lucia (%)	Inflation rate US (%)
1995	5.6	2.8
1996	0.9	3.0
1997	−0.01	2.3
1998	3.2	1.6
1999	3.5	2.3
2000	3.6	3.4
2001	5.4	2.8
2002	−0.3	1.6
2003	1.0	2.3
2004	1.5	2.7
2005	3.9	3.4
2006	2.3	3.2
2007	2.8	2.8
2008	5.5	3.8
2009	−0.2	−0.4
2010	3.3	1.6
2011	2.8	3.2
2012	4.2	2.1
2013	1.5	1.5
2014	3.5	1.6

Sources: Eastern Caribbean Central Bank, Economic and Financial Review (various issues) and US Bureau of Labor Statistics.

dislocation and a lower standard of living. For example, increases in the fiscal deficit can result in pressure being placed on the BOP. Since many of these OECS countries, including St Lucia, have debt-to-GDP ratios in excess of 90 percent, many difficult policy choices between ensuring fiscal stability and sustaining social programs had to be made, particularly from 2010.

Typical of small developing countries, St Lucia is characterized by a "structural" current account deficit. The current account deficit increased from EC $89.4m in 1995 to EC$936.3m in 2008 (Table 5.6). St Lucia has had to rely on direct investment and capital inflows (especially for the hotel/tourism sector) to resolve the deficit on the current account. The country recorded a deficit on the overall BOP account in 1996, 2005, and 2008, partly as a result of declines in banana prices and tourism activity. The St Lucian government was able to achieve savings on the current fiscal account (current revenue being greater than current expenditure) over the period 1995–2011 (except in 2003) (Table 5.6). These savings have been used to fund capital works projects as the government sought to enhance the social infrastructure of the country. Such an approach allows the "crowding in" of public investment so that the private sector can increase its economic activity. The government's deficit financing approach reached high levels during the period 2003–06, partly related to the Cricket World Cup tournament, and in 2011 as the effects of

Table 5.6. Balance of payments (BOP) and fiscal accounts, 1995–2011 (EC$m)

Year	BOP current account balance	BOP capital and financial account balance	BOP overall balance	Government current account balance	Overall fiscal balance
1995	−89.4	110.2	14.1	57.7	−15.9
1996	−146.9	139.9	−18.7	54.3	−25.4
1997	−211.7	254.4	13.3	52.9	−19.3
1998	−162.4	224.5	25.5	108.6	63.0
1999	−261.5	246.7	10.6	120.6	60.7
2000	−212.8	229.7	13.2	117.5	−22.6
2001	−202.5	189.4	32.5	41.2	−62.9
2002	−286.2	306.8	15.6	41.7	−46.1
2003	−397.6	412.3	49.4	−1.3	−131.1
2004	−235.9	296.3	72.4	47.4	−100.5
2005	−405.4	345.6	−41.2	79.0	−151.0
2006	−834.3	866.2	36.3	90.5	−156.6
2007	−930.6	984.3	50.0	150.4	−56.7
2008	−936.3	914.6	−29.5	153.9	1.4
2009	−377.6	490.7	89.5	109.0	−65.2
2010	−471.5	495.0	85.7	53.1	−20.5
2011	−511.9	618.1	78.4	41.1	−238.4

Sources: Eastern Caribbean Central Bank, Economic and Financial Review (various issues).

the Great Recession persisted. The overall fiscal deficits were therefore due to high levels of capital expenditure, which exceeded surpluses on the current account.

Data on the real effective exchange rate (REER), which is a measure of the degree of export competitiveness, show that the index increased from 101.7 in 1995 to 113.5 in 2001, but declined to 94.5 in 2011, thus indicating some degree of improved competitiveness for the country in recent years. This might have given some impetus to the growth of the tourism sector. However, during the Great Recession, the hotel sector experienced a decline in the occupancy rate, the average length of stay, and profitability, thus resulting in layoffs and higher levels of underemployment. A number of planned major hotel developments were either postponed or cancelled. In effect, the "income effect" of the recession outweighed the "price effect" of the more competitive exchange rate.

The overview of the St Lucian economy over the past twenty years indicates a decline in the agricultural sector (dominated by the banana industry) and a move to a service economy with tourism and other related services playing a critical role in the transitional/diversification process. The economy has displayed some degree of volatility as different external shocks had adverse effects. The process of transformation has been gradual, with the services sector now accounting for over 70 percent of GDP. With the exception of a few large hotels and agricultural estates, production takes place largely in small and medium enterprises. Although there has been an attempt to promote light manufacturing—garments, furniture, agro-processing, and informatics—this sector has not grown significantly. Some production diversification has taken place with respect to financial services, information technology services, and vegetable and food crop production. These changes over the past two decades have transformed the socio-economic landscape of St Lucia as it moves from a rural agrarian economy and society to a services-oriented urban one.

5.4 Labor Market Effects of Economic Change

The movement of production from an agrarian economy to a services one has had a significant impact on the labor market in St Lucia. Although the external sector is still the driver of economic activity, the location of work, the sources of income, and the skill requirements have changed with this transition. In addition to the changes taking place in the economy, there have been demographic and social changes that have compounded the dynamics of the structural transition. This section examines these demographic and labor market changes along with the relationships between the labor market and the three transformations: poverty reduction, productivity, and social cohesion.

5.4.1 Demographic Change

Population growth slowed down over the last thirty years, declining from an average of 1.6 percent per year between 1984 and 1993 to an average of 1.2 percent per year between 2003 and 2013 (World Development Indicators). This has been due to a declining birth rate from 22.4 per 1,000 in 1995 to 11.9 per 1,000 in 2012 and a relatively constant death rate. In recent years, the population density has been relatively high in the capital (Castries) and other towns such as Gros Islet and Vieux Fort. In 2010, 40 percent of the population lived in Castries. In general, the population lives mainly on or near the coastal areas due to the hilly areas that extend throughout the country. Overall, population density has increased from 140 persons per square kilometer in 1960 to 270 persons per square kilometer in 2010.

The country has witnessed a fall in the number of young people over the 1990 to 2014 period, but a rise in the working-age population. The population under 15 years dropped in both absolute and relative terms: from 48,972 (37 percent) in 1990 to 39,877 (21 percent) in 2014. The working-age population (15 to 64 years), however, increased from 75,645 persons (57 percent) in 1990 to 111,445 persons (69 percent) in 2014. There has been a steady aging of the population over the years as the number and percentage of the population 65 years and older have increased: 8,691 persons (7 percent) in 1990 to 18,261 persons (11 percent) in 2014. The old-age dependency ratio has therefore increased over the period. Although there are more females than males in the population, there has been a gradual decline in the female to male ratio from 1.12 in 1990 to 1.02 in 2014.

An important feature of a small-island nation is the degree of emigration. In many cases, skilled persons who cannot find rewarding job opportunities migrate to either developed countries or growing developing countries. Mishra (2006) found that the share of the labor force with tertiary-level education that migrated from St Lucia to OECD countries during the 1965 to 2000 period was 71 percent, with 53 percent going to the US. It is estimated that 33 percent of the emigrants from St Lucia went to the US, while 27 percent went to the UK and 10 percent to Canada and a small percentage to Barbados (St Lucia Population and Housing Census 2010). Estimates from the Population and Housing Census 2010 for the inter-census period 2001–10 found that more females emigrated than males (54 percent versus 46 percent) and that 38 percent of those emigrating during the period had at least secondary-level education, while 28 percent had tertiary-level education. These figures compare with 27 percent with secondary-level education and 7 percent with tertiary-level education in the total population of St Lucia. While there are benefits associated with emigration (such as remittances, networking, market potential in the diaspora), the absence of a well-educated labor force can retard economic growth and development in critical areas of the economy. Work permits data suggest that there is a shortage of persons in the professional and managerial occupational categories. Remittances to St Lucia rose from US $26.4m in 2005 to US$30.1m in 2013. The average remittances-to-export ratio was 6 percent and the remittances-to-GDP ratio was 3.5 percent over the 2005 to 2013 period. The issue is whether these remittances can adequately compensate for the loss in human capital from the country, especially since those left behind are not as skilled and educated as those who have migrated to more developed countries.

Within the Caribbean Single Market and Economy (CSME) integration arrangement, certain categories of labor are able to move freely throughout member states.[5] These include university graduates, artists and musicians, media workers, sports personnel, nurses, non-graduate teachers (those without an undergraduate degree), persons with associate degrees, and artisans and domestics with Caribbean Vocational Qualifications (CVQs). Such persons

---

[5] This is the creation of a single large market and economic space among fifteen Caribbean nations. It allows for free movement of CARICOM goods, services, people, and capital throughout the Caribbean Community through the removal of fiscal, legal, physical, technical, and administrative barriers. It is expected to harmonize economic, monetary, and fiscal policies and measures across all CARICOM member states. To date, only the market segment has been implemented.

can obtain a Skilled National Certificate that exempts them from work permit requirements. In addition, the integration arrangement calls for the "right of establishment," whereby businesses and their senior personnel can establish operations in a member state with no restrictions. These provisions therefore create a regional labor market that can ease the constraints associated with demographic change and a small domestic labor force. Progress with intraregional migration under this regime has been slow. Mohammed (2012) indicates that between 2002 and 2012, an estimated 2,700 skills certificates were issued to CARICOM nationals, with movement taking place mainly from nationals of Guyana, Jamaica, and St Lucia. While persons obtaining regional skills certification are a small but growing group, the implementation of the process of accreditation has been slow.

5.4.2 Labor Force, Employment, and Unemployment

The St Lucia Statistical Office has conducted labor force surveys every year from 1992 to 2014 in conformity with the ILO's Labour Force Framework. In 2008 the survey was upgraded to include a module on the informal sector and decent work. Over the 1995 to 2014 period, the labor force grew at an average annual rate of 2.4 percent, increasing from 66,500 to 98,300, which represents a relatively low potential supply of labor (Table 5.7).

Table 5.7. Labor force, employment, and unemployment, 1995 to 2014

Year	Population 15 years and over	Total labor force (000)	Total labor force participation rate (%)	Employed labor force (000)	Unemployed labor force (000)	Average annual unemployment rate (%)
1995	98.1	66.5	67.8	55.9	10.6	16.2
1996	100.7	67.8	67.3	56.7	11.1	16.3
1997	103.4	70.3	68.0	55.9	14.4	20.4
1998	105.8	71.9	67.9	56.4	15.5	21.5
1999	105.5	73.1	69.3	59.8	13.3	17.9
2000	110.7	76	68.6	63.5	12.5	16.4
2001	112.1	75.1	67.0	62.1	13	17.3
2002	113.4	73.5	64.8	58.5	13.2	20
2003	118.8	82.1	69.1	63.9	18.2	22.3
2004	116.2	78.8	67.8	62.3	16.5	21
2005	117.0	80.9	69.1	65.8	15.1	18.7
2006	119.0	83	69.8	70	13	15.6
2007	121.1	82.7	68.3	71.2	11.5	14
2008	126.0	81.3	64.5	69.1	12.2	15
2009	129.7	84.4	65.1	69.1	15.3	18.1
2010	125.7	85.3	67.9	67.7	17.3	20.6
2011	131.3	90.7	69.1	71.4	19.3	21.2
2012	134.8	94.6	70.2	74.3	20.3	21.4
2013	137.5	97.6	71.0	74.8	22.8	23.3
2014	137.5	98.3	71.5	74.3	24	24.4

Sources: St Lucia Department of Statistics, Labor Force Reports, Population Census Reports.

The labor force participation rate increased from 68 percent in 1995 to 70 percent in 2006 (Table 5.7). There was a steady decline in the rate during the period 2007 to 2009, which can be attributed to the confluence of two events: the end of activities associated with the hosting of the Cricket World Cup (CWC) and the onset of the Great Recession. The CWC would have resulted in an increase in the number of persons interested in labor market activity, (i.e., *added worker effect*), while the Great Recession would have resulted in a withdrawal of such persons (i.e., *discouraged worker effect*). After 2009, the labor force participation rate increased steadily from 68 to 72 percent in 2014. Between 1995 and 2010, there was a decrease in the male labor force participation rate from 78 percent to 76 percent, while the female rate rose slightly from 58 percent to 63 percent. Nonetheless, men still account for the majority of the workforce—54 percent according to the 2010 Census data. As in many other developing countries, females are often assumed to undertake household (care) duties, while males engage in labor market activities.

Employment creation has been an important aspect of public policy in St Lucia, with the government pursuing different strategies to create jobs, as discussed earlier: agricultural diversification, light manufacturing, and services (especially tourism) promotion. Over the period 1995 to 2014, the number of persons employed increased from 55,900 to 74,300, that is, an average annual growth rate of 1.5 percent (Table 5.7). Compared with the increase in real GDP of 2.13 percent over the same period, the average employment elasticity of output has been 0.72. Policy efforts aside, this indicates the importance of economic growth to employment creation in St Lucia.

Data for 2008 indicate that 41.1 percent of the total employed workforce was in so-called "formal" jobs, while 58.9 percent were in "informal" jobs.[6] In terms of the status of the employed labor force, 20.6 percent were self-employed, while 74.3 percent were employees and 5.1 percent were classified as "unpaid family workers."

Given the changes in the structure of economic production (Table 5.3), it is not surprising that the structure of employment has also been changing. In 1997, the agriculture, fishing and forestry sector, the distribution sector, and the government were the main employers of labor. These three sectors accounted for approximately 53 percent of total employment in 1997, while in 2014 they accounted for 45 percent (Table 5.8). During the same period, services employment rose significantly, especially in hotels and restaurants and the "other services" category. There was also a decline in employment in the manufacturing sector.

---

[6] An informal job is one in which the employee does not have a contract for work, does not receive a pay slip, and is not registered with the National Insurance Cooperation.

Table 5.8. Percent distribution of employed persons by industry group, 1997–2014

Industry group	1997 (July–Dec.)	2000 (July–Dec.)	2005 (Oct.–Dec.)	2011 (Oct.–Dec.)	2014 (Annual)
Agriculture, fishing	20.8	19.5	13.1	10.9	10.1
Manufacturing	10.8	10.3	6.8	6.8	5.6
Electricity, gas, and water	1.4	0.8	0.7	1.0	0.7
Construction	7.2	10.0	10.9	7.4	6.7
Wholesale and retail trade	16.8	17.2	14.6	15.2	16.3
Hotel and restaurants	9.6	9.5	12.6	13.8	13.7
Transportation and communication	8.5	7.1	6.1	5.7	7.6
Financial services	2.2	1.4	2.3	1.1	2.0
Real estate	2.6	2.2	3.9	–	–
Public administration	14.0	12.7	14.6	10.6	9.9
Education and health	1.6	2.9	2.5	6.9	9.1
Other community services	1.6	1.8	3.9	–	4.0
Personal household services	2.8	2.2	2.4	3.9	3.1
Other	0.1	2.5	5.5	34.6	14.3
Total	100	100	100	100	100
(Number)	(55,700)	(64,370)	(68,930)	(73,349)	(73,351)

Note: a new classification was introduced in 2011 and since then "Other" includes Information and Communication Services, Cultural Services, Professional Services, and Administrative Services.

Source: St Lucia Department of Statistics: Labor Force Survey reports.

These sectoral trends are also reflected in the occupational distribution of employment. There has been a significant decline in the occupational categories of skilled agricultural and craft workers (Table 5.9). With the rise of the services sector, the share of service, shop, and sales workers has grown. There has been a noticeable decline in the percentage of "mid-skill" persons, namely, technicians and associate professionals and also those in elementary occupations. These trends point to some degree of job destruction in the agricultural and manufacturing sectors and job creation in the services sector over the 1997 to 2014 period.

A Labor Market Needs Assessment survey conducted in 2012 (St Catherine 2013) shows how these longer-term trends are reflected in hiring patterns. Most newly employed persons were found in the accommodation/food services, construction, and distribution sectors. The main occupational categories involved were: service managers, managing directors, teachers, waiters, shop assistants, security guards, and construction laborers. The bulk of the newly employed persons (84 percent) required only secondary school or lower education or specific technical/vocational skills, while 16 percent required a university degree with or without work experience.

There is a gender division of labor, with females being dominant in the clerical, services, and sales occupations (Table 5.9). An interesting observation, which has been made in other small Caribbean countries such as Barbados and Jamaica, is the relatively high percentage of females in the professional

Table 5.9. Percent distribution by sex of employed persons by occupation, 1997, 2011, and 2014

Occupational group	1997 (July–Dec.) Male	1997 (July–Dec.) Female	2011 (Oct.–Dec.) Male	2011 (Oct.–Dec.) Female	2014 (Annual) Male	2014 (Annual) Female
Senior officials and managers	51.9	48.1	53.1	46.9	46.8	53.2
Professionals	34.7	65.3	42.3	57.7	43.2	56.8
Technicians & associate professionals	59.4	40.6	60.1	39.9	48.8	51.2
Clerks	21.8	78.2	18.3	81.7	32.2	67.8
Service, shop and sales workers	34.2	65.8	34.1	65.9	44.1	55.9
Skilled agricultural workers	73.9	26.1	77.3	22.7	87.5	12.5
Craft and related trades workers	82.4	17.6	86.7	13.3	85.3	14.7
Plant & machine operators and assemblers	75.5	24.5	88.3	11.7	93.1	6.9
Elementary occupations	55.2	44.8	48.9	51.1	50.6	49.4
Other	52.4	47.6	58.2	41.8	51.8	48.2

Source: St Lucia Department of Labor Statistics, Labor Force Survey Reports.

occupational category and also an equal division in the senior managerial category. Although there has been some discussion relating to the existence of a "glass ceiling" facing the career progression of females, it seems that some breakthrough has been made in the St Lucian labor market (St Lucia Labor Force Surveys 1992–2014). One explanation for the rise of females in the "high-skill" occupational categories relates to the higher percentage of females gaining tertiary-level education and then entering the labor market. Between 1997 and 2011, the percentage of the female population 25 years and over with tertiary/university education increased from 8.8 percent to 10.1 percent, while for the male population, the share decreased from 8.2 percent to 6.5 percent. Over this period, more adult women had attained tertiary/ university education than men, with the female-to-male ratio increasing from 1.16 in 1997 to 1.68 in 2011. More females had diplomas and degrees than males in 2011 (a ratio of 1.78 to 1), while more adult males reported that they had no educational qualifications in 2011 (31 percent for males, 26 percent for females) (St Lucia Labor Force Survey Reports).

Data on enrolment in the University of the West Indies (UWI) indicate that in 1995/96 out of an enrolment of 245 St Lucians, 155 (63.3 percent) were female and 90 (36.7 percent) were male, while in 2013/14, out of 1,047 St Lucians, 826 (78.9 percent) were female and 221 (21.1 percent) were male. In terms of St Lucian graduates from the UWI, there were 116 in 1995/96—77 female and 39 male, while in 2009/10 there were 141 females and 35 males. Most of these St Lucians in the UWI pursue programs in the Social Sciences, Medicine, and Education. The establishment of the Open Campus in 2008 helped to boost the enrolment of St Lucians in the UWI. In 2013/14, 688 out of a total of 1,047 St Lucians were enrolled in the Open Campus (65.7 percent) with 84 percent being female. As indicated previously, the female labor force participation rate has increased over the past fifteen years.

Unemployment has been an endemic socio-economic problem in St Lucia. An unemployed person is defined as someone who was 15 years of age and over during the survey reference week and was

(i) without work (that is, not in paid employment or self-employment);

(ii) currently available for work and in a position to accept a job during the three-week period from the start of the reference survey week;

(iii) seeking work, that is, engaged in active job search four weeks prior to the reference survey week.[7]

The available data indicate that the number of unemployed rose from 10,600 or 16.2 percent of the labor force in 1995, falling to 14 percent in 2007, and rising to 24,000 or 24 percent in 2014 (Table 5.7). The lowest rate of unemployment over this period was in 2007 and was probably associated with activities related to the hosting of the Cricket World Cup. Unemployment declines with the level of educational attainment. Many of the unemployed have low levels of educational attainment and few marketable skills. For example, in 2011, 26 percent of the unemployed had no educational qualifications (that is, they had not attained passes in end of school examinations), while 44.4 percent had not gone beyond secondary (high) school.[8]

The rate of unemployment tends to be high among the youth. According to the Population Census of 2010, the unemployment rate was 63 percent for the 15–19 age cohort and 32 percent for the 20–24 age cohort. Young females tend to experience a much higher unemployment rate than males. For example, in 2007 the female youth (15–24 years) unemployment rate was 35.2 percent, while the male rate was 27.5 percent; in 2009, the rates were 41.4 percent and 36.3 percent, respectively. However, unemployment is not restricted to the young; unemployment does exist among heads of households (males and females), hence undermining the standard of living of the household. In the case of these heads, they depend on friends and relatives during the period of unemployment. In the case of unemployed youth, reliance is placed on parent/guardians and friends (Caribbean Development Bank/Kairi Consultants 2006). Since the onset of the global recession in 2008, unemployment has increased most rapidly among those 15 to 24 years old.

There have been several explanations for the high unemployment in St Lucia especially among the youth (Caribbean Development Bank 2015).

---

[7] Prior to 2011, this was two months, but with the change, St Lucia now conforms to the ILO recommendation.

[8] Compulsory education is up to the age of 15 years under the Education Act.

First, there is a mismatch between the level and type of education and training received and the needs of employers. This problem is exacerbated by the loss of better educated St Lucians through emigration (Blom and Hobbs 2008). Second, there is a demographic transition effect, demonstrated by an increase in the working age to total population ratio by an average of 3.5 percent in the period 2008 to 2013. Third, there is the limited availability of job opportunities, especially with the decline of the banana industry and inability of the tourism industry to absorb the additional supply of persons to the labor market. Fourth, low rates of economic growth recorded over the years have been insufficient to absorb the supply of labor. Fifth, there is the unwillingness of persons to accept certain jobs which are not well remunerated or have desirable characteristics. This reflects a form of voluntary unemployment and reflects a relatively high reservation wage. Finally, remittances from relatives who live abroad constitute non-labor income and tend to reduce the desire to actively engage in job searching, which also contributes to voluntary unemployment (Downes 2008).

5.4.3 Poverty and the Labor Market

Although St Lucia has been classified as a high human development, middle-income country by international agencies, it has experienced high levels of poverty. Two studies of poverty in St Lucia have been conducted over the past twenty years, in 1995 and 2005/06 (Caribbean Development Bank/Kairi Consultants 2006). In 1995, the share of individuals regarded as being "poor" was 25.1 percent, while in 2005/06, it was 28.8 percent. In the case of households, the corresponding percentages were 18.7 and 21.4 percent, respectively (Table 5.10).

Table 5.10. Poverty and inequality, 1995 and 2005/06

Indicator	1995	2005/06
Poverty line (EC$)	1,876.44	5,086.00
Population	144,000	164,842
Poor individuals (%)	25.1	28.8
Poor households (%)	18.7	21.4
Indigent individuals (%)	7.1	1.6
Indigent households (%)	5.3	1.2
Poverty gap	8.6	9.0
Poverty severity	4.4	4.1
Castries (poor households %)	15.2	13.1
Sub Castries (poor individuals %)	22.6	22.2
Gini coefficient	0.50	0.42

Sources: St Lucia Country Poverty Assessment Reports (Caribbean Development Bank and Kairi Consultants Limited)

While data from more recent poverty studies are not available, the evidence of rising levels and rates of joblessness and negative rates of growth of real GDP all indicate that the rate of poverty may have increased in the last ten years. The poverty studies point to important labor market elements, namely that the poor tend to have low levels of human capital and therefore tend to occupy low-paying jobs in both the formal and informal sectors. Poor persons tend to engage in "hustling" activities in order to make ends meet. These jobs are usually classified as "elementary occupations" in the labor market statistics. Furthermore, these jobs tend to be precarious, and hence the poor experience long and regular unemployment spells. Second, the decline in the banana industry resulted in an increase in the rural poor and also a drift to the urban areas, especially Castries, Gros Islet, and Vieux Fort. The poor tend to huddle in certain geographical areas (slums/ghettoes), which tends to result in stigmatization and victimization in the labor market. Persons who live in these areas and who have been able to enhance their human capital to a level to find good jobs in the formal sector tend to use alternative addresses in their job applications in order to secure at least an interview. Third, poor households tend to be female-headed with a large number of dependents (old and young). Such an arrangement has resulted in an intergenerational poverty phenomenon. Finally, the "working poor," that is, those persons who are working even in the formal labor market but receive incomes below the poverty line, tend to engage in multiple job-holding in order to provide support for themselves and their families. There is an inadequate social safety net in St Lucia to cover the adverse effects of poverty. While St Lucia introduced a Labor Code in 2012, which provides for redundancy and severance pay, there is no unemployment insurance scheme.

Several poverty reduction initiatives have been introduced over the years as part of the government's policy to reduce the incidence, depth, and severity of poverty. These have recognized that a critical element in reducing the high incidence of poverty and vulnerability to poverty is the creation of sustainable and rewarding jobs. As the country makes the transition to a post-banana economy, this necessarily involves identifying the areas of production for the new economy and the associated skill needs. The poverty reduction initiatives have focused primarily on employment creation and human capital/skill formation. Among these programs are: Single Mothers in Life Empowerment Project (SMILE), which provides beneficiaries with life skills training, technical and vocational training, and job placement support; The National Initiative to Create Employment (NICE), with the goal of assisting in the creation of sustainable employment opportunities for an estimated 4,500 people over a three-year period; and Holistic Opportunities for Personal Empowerment (HOPE), an EC$5 million program designed to provide short-term employment, training, personal development, and health care to unemployed St Lucians.

Some of the additional programs include the Poverty Reduction Fund (PRF) and the Basic Needs Trust Fund (BNTF), both with the assistance of the Caribbean Development Bank (CDB). These have now been amalgamated into the Social Development Fund as part of the country's poverty reduction strategy and policy framework; the short-term employment program (STEP) to provide temporary employment for displaced workers; the James Belgrave Fund (BELFund) for microenterprise development (such as cottage industries); and the Skills Training Program for Youth and the HOPE program for young persons. These programs, which focus on human capital development and short-term employment, have been supported by a School Support and School Feeding program and the SMILE project.

These programs have been targeted at small farmers, youth, females, microenterprises, and industrial zones to encourage employment growth and community infrastructural support. These form part of the social protection system available to persons living in poverty in St Lucia (Henry-Lee 2004; Foster 2013). They complement the traditional arrangements, such as social insurance for the employed, social assistance, social services, and health and education services for the poor and needy. There has been no comprehensive evaluation of this suite of initiatives in St Lucia, although there is a view that the costs of these programs could make them unsustainable. Furthermore, earlier evaluations of development assistance provided for reducing poverty in St Lucia show poor performance and a low level of implementation capacity for several projects (UNDP 2009).

5.4.4 *Skill Development and Training Needs*

As we have noted, the major challenge facing St Lucia is identifying and facilitating the nature of the post-banana economy. Although there have been discussions regarding the redevelopment of the banana industry within the context of agricultural diversification (UNCTAD n.d.), there has been a significant decline in the number of active banana farmers from an estimated 5,270 in 1998 to 501 in 2014. As indicated earlier, the thrust has been towards the development of a services economy with tourism, information technology, and other new exports supported by diversification in the agriculture sector. While jobs in these sectors can be regarded as "good jobs for development" as they are linked to the global economy, there is an adjustment issue. People who have worked in the banana industry would not have the prerequisite skills for working in the services sector; hence training and skill development is needed.

Few skill needs studies have been undertaken to identify the human capital needs of a post-banana economy for St Lucia. Gaible (2009) has identified the need for skill development in areas that could absorb the displaced workers in the banana industry who display a disposition for acquiring new knowledge and skills. Those areas are in keeping with the government's thrust to enhance national productivity and competitiveness as well as promoting access to a wider set of knowledge and skills which is required in today's knowledge and technology-based global environment. For example, in the areas of information and communications technology, priorities include hardware and software maintenance, network development and web design, and graphic design.

Peters and Whittington (2009) pointed to skill needs in hospitality and tourism as this sector has replaced the banana sector as the main generator of revenue for government and an alternative means of employment and income generation for citizens. The increasing expansion of the hotel sector and the diversification of tourism products through ecotourism, honeymoon destinations, and marine tourism call for a new skill set in order to sustain the sector. These include information communication and technology skills, skills in modern agriculture to meet the desires of visitors for local exotic food, technical and vocational skills that are essential in supporting maintenance of hotel plant and equipment, and skills in a wide variety of medical services and allied health services in order to ensure that the requisite primary and secondary care is available to address the various disease cultures that may exist or may invade the island and create a threat to the industry. These ideas are similar to those of Howe et al. (2011), who identified accounting, law, and policing as critical areas where knowledge and skills are required and should be seen as areas in which those displaced (farmers, farm workers and the their families, including children who complete secondary school) by the downturn in the banana sector could seek alternative livelihoods.

In recognition of the impact of the downturn of the banana sector, the government has also identified a set of training priorities that are in keeping with the knowledge and skill requirements of the new leading sectors of the economy. For example, during the period 2012–13, the government identified as priorities study areas in agriculture (extension, rural development, marine management, hydrology), science and technology (especially ICT, animation), finance and accounting (including forensic accounting), planning and surveying, law (including legislature drafting), education (special education, foreign languages, science, visual arts), health and wellness, tourism and hospitality, public sector management, trade policy, and consumer protection. These areas are required for the "new economy" in order to increase competitiveness, facilitate improvement in productivity at all levels of the economy, provide regulatory oversight, and increase negotiating expertise.

The available studies identify new-economy needs that include both high- and middle-level skills. The labor force data for St Lucia indicate a decline in the number of persons in the technicians and associate professionals occupations and represent the "missing middle" in the labor market (that is the unavailability of persons with middle-level technical and vocational skills). In effect, the country needs a Human Resource Development Plan to complement a National Economic Development Strategy. While the areas of production have been identified for future development, there has not been a corresponding plan to produce the trained persons to meet the needs of the emerging production areas.

A Labor Needs Assessment survey of 500 enterprises in 2012 reaffirmed the need for persons with skills in the "middle range," as the highest vacancy rate was in the technicians and associated professionals group followed by managers, craft and related trades, and plant and machine operators. The relatively high demand for such persons has been due to business expansion and reorganization. The survey also pointed to the need for persons with a strong work ethic, customer service skills, interpersonal skills, and adaptability, all of which are critical for the areas of future employment (services, accommodation, and distribution) (St Catherine 2013).

Over the years, the government and the private sector have responded to the skills and training gap via various initiatives. The private sector has concentrated on on-the-job training and limited apprenticeships. The government has established institutions to cater to the skill development and training needs of the country. Over the period 1995/96 to 2011/12, the government's educational expenditures increased from EC$84.5m to EC $156.9m, representing 6.6 percent and 4.8 percent respectively of GDP. Although the share of education expenditure in total government expenditure has declined from 25.8 percent in 1995/96 to 18.5 percent in 2010/11, education is still a major target in the national development thrust of the government.

The government has established a number of education and training institutions to assist with the supply of the human capital needed for the growth and development of the country. The Sir Arthur Lewis Community College (SALCC) is the major provider of post-secondary and tertiary education in the country. The SALCC was established in 1985 to offer education and training at the certificate, diploma, and associate degree level in such areas as agriculture, science, teacher education and administration, liberal arts, and technical education and management studies. It collaborates with the UWI in the delivery of selected degree programs in education and the social sciences. During the year 2011/12, the total enrollment in all programs (excluding continuing education development) was 1,929 (684 males and 1,245 females). Vieux Fort Comprehensive Post-Secondary department provides courses for "A" Level business students.

St Lucia also houses offshore universities that produce a small number of St Lucian graduates who add to the stock of human capital. For example, Monroe College offers undergraduate and graduate programs (especially in business management) and a certificate program in tourism and hospitality (a focus of the government's skill development program). In addition, the UWI also offers courses through its Open Campus facility. Students can access a wide range of UWI programs online. In the case of medical schools, there are four offshore private schools that offer programs in medicine and nursing, primarily to foreign students and a few selected St Lucians.

Over the years, a number of training programs targeted at lower- to medium-skill levels and also to vulnerable groups have been established by the government. Many of these have been noted earlier. Although these programs and institutions exist, there are still challenges associated with skill development and job creation in St Lucia, as highlighted in a recent Labor Needs Assessment survey (St Catherine 2013).

5.4.5 *Labor Productivity and Earnings*

Estimates of aggregate labor productivity (measured as the ratio of real GDP to number of persons employed) indicate some degree of volatility over the 1995–2010 period. Aggregate labor productivity increased between 1995 and 1998, then declined over the 1999–2003 period, and subsequently rose between 2005 and 2010 (Figure 5.1). It is noticeable that labor productivity peaked during significant declines in economic activity: 2002 after the September 11, 2001 shock and between 2008 and 2010 with the Great Recession. It seems that

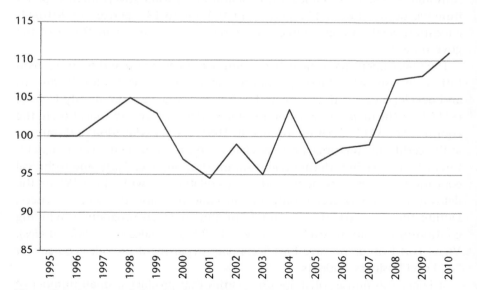

Figure 5.1. Aggregate Labor Productivity Index (1995=100), 1995–2010
Source: St Lucia Department of Statistics.

labor shedding was greater than the decline in output during these periods. It should be noted that the shift to a services-oriented economy makes the measurement of productivity in that sector difficult, so that the broader concept of performance is more appropriate. In an effort to enhance productivity and competitiveness, a commission has been established in the Ministry of Economic Affairs within the project sponsored by Compete Caribbean.

The World Bank (2005) calculated the private rates of return to education in St Lucia as 6 percent for secondary schooling, 34 percent for post-secondary, and 22 percent for university. These rates are higher than those in other Caribbean countries such as Barbados, Guyana, Trinidad and Tobago, and the Dominican Republic (World Bank 2005). In an analysis using data for 1996 and 2004, Bellony and Reilly (2009) found that the rate of return generally increases with educational attainment. They also found that both the average and marginal returns to educational qualifications were higher for females than males at all educational levels (especially in 1996 for the secondary level and in 2004 for the tertiary level). However, the shortage of males to fill low-skilled jobs (where demand exceeds supply) increases the rate of return for the small pool of primary-level educated men. Finally, they found that the labor market rewards qualifications at all educational levels as the skill requirements vary according to the job design, that is, the content and methods used to undertake a job.

Further econometric work we have undertaken for this study for 2004, 2008, and 2012 corroborates the results obtained by Bellony and Reilly, although the actual values of the rates of return are higher due to differences in estimation procedure and data used (Table 5.11). The estimates for the rates of return to post-secondary and university education suggest that investment in higher education is rewarded significantly in the labor market and that there is a high demand for educated persons. As indicated earlier, an increasing percentage of the adult population (especially females) is becoming more qualified for jobs that require a university education. The demand is partly driven by the labor demands of the new services sector and also to compensate for the skilled persons who have migrated.

Table 5.11. Annualized rates of return to education, 2004, 2008, and 2012

Level of education	2004 Male	2004 Female	2004 Overall	2008 Male	2008 Female	2008 Overall	2012 Male	2012 Female	2012 Overall
Primary	5.2%***	1.5%	4.1%***	2.2%	−0.3%	1.3%	−2.6%	−5.0%**	−2.9%**
Secondary	13.7%***	17.3%	15.1%***	11.2%***	17.6%**	13.6%***	9.1%*	18.0%***	12.6%***
Tertiary	25.5%***	51.9%***	42.9%***	30.3%***	47.7%***	39.7%***	30.6%***	39.2%***	33.5%***
University	39.0%***	49.5%***	45.2%***	35.5%***	61.8%***	49.0%***	45.8%***	44.3%***	43.7%***

Note: ***, **, and * denote statistical significance at the 0.01, 0.05, and 0.10 level respectively using two-tailed tests.
Source: authors' calculations.

Unfortunately, recent earnings data are not available and we have to rely on data for 1999 and 2003. Of course, significant changes could have occurred since that time, given the structural changes that have been taking place in the economy. These earlier data indicate that for salaried (i.e., white-collar) men, average normal gross earnings in 1999 were highest in the transportation/ communication sector followed by construction and financial services. The lowest paying sectors were health and social work, and distribution. The ratio of the highest to lowest earnings was 2.36. In the case of salaried women, the highest-paying sectors were transportation/communication, financial services, and then health and social work. The lowest-paying sectors were agriculture and community/social/personal (care) services. The ratio of the highest to lowest earnings was 2.78. Although the returns to education have been generally higher for females, they uniformly obtained lower average gross earnings (wage) than males. In the case of male wage earners (i.e., blue-collar), the highest-paying sectors were also construction and transportation/ communication, while the lowest paying were agriculture and education; while for female wage earners, the highest paying were transportation/com-munication and tourism and the lowest paid were in agriculture and health and social work.

These results help to determine the sources of "good jobs" in St Lucia requiring a post-secondary education; for men, such jobs would be in con-struction, financial services, and transportation; for women, such jobs would be in tourism and transportation and communication. With the growth of the services sector and the decline of the agricultural sector, improvements in the educational and training system over the years, and the skill needs of employers, it is likely that these conclusions are still valid (St Catherine 2013).

The qualitative aspect of this study involved the compilation of the views of a set of "key informants" who were non-randomly selected based on their know-ledge of the social and economic aspects of the St Lucian labor market.[9] Respondents were of the view that "good jobs for development" are associated with increased productivity and enhanced competitiveness, the use of modern technology, high demand for qualified workers, prospects for higher remuner-ation, the prestige associated with career and social mobility, and promoting "decent work" along with continuous improvement in living standards.

The respondents also indicated that jobs associated with increased productivity involve the use of modern technology; continuous research and development that would foster innovation and creativity among workers;

---

[9] These "key informants" included social development officials, agriculturalists, community workers, and economists who were non-randomly selected through a snowballing and convenience approach. They were interviewed to solicit their views and perceptions on the issue of jobs and social cohesion.

the establishment of guidelines and principles for quality control; access to continuous appropriate and relevant skills training; and the provision of adequate incentives to retain workers and promote loyalty among workers across all sectors. In effect, jobs that carry these features are "good jobs for development" as they enhance productivity and international competitiveness and result in a higher standard of living.

5.4.6 Social Cohesion and the Labor Market

Social cohesion generally relates to the capacity of a community or society to manage collective decision-making based on trust, participation, shared values, willingness to cooperate, and respect for diversity. An important aspect of "good jobs for development" is building such cohesion. In the context of the small-island nation state, Baldacchino (2005) has argued that "social capital," which is an important element of social cohesion, is important for understanding the development of "good governance" practices and the achievement of a commendable standard of living in "small, peripheral and network-driven island societies." Springer (2006) also makes a similar argument in the case of the Caribbean. He argues that social vulnerability impacts negatively on economic resilience and social cohesion and recommends the development of "integrated development planning" at the national and regional levels to build economic resilience and social cohesion. Prasad (2008) has also suggested that social cohesion is a major contributing factor to economic resilience building in small nations. He empirically shows that there is a higher level of social cohesion in small states than in other developing countries. Dimeglio et al. (2013) have observed "regimes" of social cohesion that reflect the values and behaviors of a country and hence the operation of the labor market, namely the degree of social networking associated with employment (getting a job), the degree to which there are labor disputes, and the degree to which teamwork can enhance productivity.

It has been observed by Springer (2004), Ramsaran (2003), and Payne (2006) that the decline of the banana industry disrupted the organization of rural communities, resulting in a general decrease in social cohesion. For example, Springer (2004) noted there has been a decline in "blockos," that is, community parties where persons gather to trade and socialize. Even though there might be a lack of jobs, resulting in income fragility for some households, there is still evidence of social cohesion when members of households receive various forms of assistance for basic needs from neighbors in the community (Springer 2004). It appears that those who participate in the labor market, whether on a regular or seasonal basis, are in a position to share resources with others.

In the post-banana era, a number of social protection programs have been implemented to restore a semblance of social cohesion. Formal means include

165

programs executed by the St Lucia Social Development Fund (SSDF), such as Koud Main Ste. Lucie. This program seeks to engage persons in the rural communities in collective activities that address community issues such as lack of access to homes by engaging in the construction of footpaths. As banana farmers went out of production, the demand for labor in rural areas fell. Additionally, the decline of manufacturing exports in the south of the island was caused by the flight of textile and electronic assembly plants that were a feature of the economy in the 1980s and early 1990s. This situation resulted in increased migration of labor to urban centers, especially in the north of the island, to find jobs. Internal migration has had a double impact. The sending community was stripped of able-bodied workers, and the receiving community was forced to accommodate new arrivals in search of fewer jobs. Both communities have had to undergo some level of adjustment as a result. It has been observed that the problems of conflict, crime, and violence in receiving urban areas are usually inflicted by young people who have just come to live in the community (Caribbean Development Bank/Kairi Consultants 2006). At the same time, the migration of persons from the rural areas to the urban areas in search of better paying and more rewarding jobs has disrupted rural family life and community building (Caribbean Development Bank/Kairi Consultants 2006).

People who are new members of a community tend not to participate in matters related to the welfare and improvement of the community. However, there seem to have been some attempts at promoting volunteerism in communities to involve all members, whether employed or unemployed. Such evidence was brought out by the impact evaluation of the Poverty Reduction Program (PRP) implemented during the period 1998 to 2003 by the Poverty Reduction Fund of St Lucia (ESA Consultores International 2004).

The interaction between youth and the elderly in many communities is perceived to be low, the so-called "generation gap." The mechanisms that bring these two together are not functioning as there is a greater concern for making a living first and foremost, which takes up a lot of time and leaves little or no time for interaction. This general reluctance is constantly fed by a desire to take care of basic needs no matter what (interview with Social Transformation Officer, Ministry of Social Transformation).

Lack of participation in the labor market drives people to use coping mechanisms that breed conflict. Social capital in the form of networks in the community is characteristic of gangs who use crime and violence as their survival strategy. This leads to the stigmatization of communities, which does not help social cohesion. It militates against employment opportunities, which effectively lock out entire communities from economic and social mobility (Caribbean Development Bank/Kairi Consultants 2006).

Where a particular institutional intervention—for example, increasing and improving access to potable water, or construction of footpaths and drainage in communities—may have a positive impact, inadequate resources prohibit a continuing positive trend. For example, the demand-driven approach (where communities play the lead role in identifying their needs and priorities) for community development of the PRP generated a bank of projects, but these could not be undertaken due to lack of funding. However, there is no doubt that the "coming together of the community" to deliberate promoted social inclusion to a large extent (ESA Consultores International 2004).

Social cohesion is affected when outside agencies and other institutional structures do not fulfill their operational mandates related to job creation. A number of community-based interventions (such as short-term public works programs) have seen basic jobs being taken up by persons who live outside of the beneficiary community. Promises of jobs for members in a community through basic infrastructure initiatives such as building of drains, installation of culverts and the like, do not materialize or, if they do, are absorbed by the workers of a contractor who resides outside the community with few beneficiaries inside the community. This situation breeds lack of trust in institutions and sometimes throughout the community (Caribbean Development Bank 2011).

The "cash nexus" character of the St Lucian society has almost eroded the age-old helping-hand approach (*coup-de-main*), which was a key instrument for cohesion at the community level. For example, people were given a free hand to build their homes, particularly in rural areas. The National Plan of 1997 called for a rekindling of this kind of cultural resource in the thrust toward integrated rural development. Although a few initiatives have been implemented since 1997, they have not been able to revive this barter approach to integrated community development and community spirit. Efforts have been made by several government agencies to revive the approach against a strong tide of unemployment and the demand for money to take care of basic needs.

Job creation fosters social cohesion in various ways. The views and perceptions generated from the key informants provide some points for consideration. The respondents generally agreed that job creation helps in deterring persons (especially young persons) from engaging in socially unacceptable behavior. According to one respondent, "... young people especially are easy to fall prey to doing things that are against the law when they are not gainfully employed. The drug business is an attractive option for them as they see it as a way to make quick money even though it is a risk they are taking..." (Interview with Social Transformation Officer). Apart from job creation by the formal sector, the government continues to encourage self-employment through enagagement in the informal sector and provides skills

167

training programs outside of the formal education sector in an effort to deter youth from engaging in various form of unacceptable behavior, including theft and other forms of crime and violence (UNDP 2012; St Lucia 2014).

There is a view among the respondents that the provision of resources by both government and private sectors can encourage community residents to volunteer their service to the community. "Many members of the community want to help out their communities, but the resources to get things done are most times not available. Before you had '*coup-de-main*' and people were coming forward. Now everything is couched in monetary gain. Some members do not mind giving free time and labor to see their communities improve but are not willing to put their hard earned money into collective community activities" (interview with Agricultural Extension Officer).

Interviews with key informants suggest that job creation fosters social cohesion by creating social acceptance and awareness; fostering household/ family stability and providing for basic household needs; deterring persons (especially young persons) from engaging in socially unacceptable behavior; and providing the resources to render service to the community.

At the enterprise level, social cohesion can promote employee engagement and increased productivity by providing a safe environment in which employees feel free to innovate, explore new ways of doing things, and socialize with each other.

Aspects of social cohesion are also important in job searching. Results from labor force surveys indicate that the main forms of job search by the unemployed (and some employed) are (in order of importance): direct application, seeking the assistance of friends and relatives, and checking at work sites (Downes and Gunderson 2003). Formal systems, such as public and private employment exchanges, are hardly used. The informal networks and the referral system (especially "who knows you" and "who you know") are important means of obtaining a job in St Lucia.

Hence the relationship between jobs and social cohesion is bi-directional: jobs lead to social cohesion, while social cohesion leads to people getting jobs or upgrading to jobs with higher productivity and income.

5.5 Constraints to Transformation

Job creation is important to the three transformations (living standards, productivity, and social cohesion) in small-island nations such as St Lucia, as indicated in Section 5.4. The relationship in some cases is bi-directional and can be either weak or strong. There are, however, barriers and constraints associated with the creation of jobs for development in a post-banana St Lucian economy. These barriers and constraints can be classified in different ways: those associated with the general business environment, those associated with the labor market, and those associated with the socio-political environment.

Job creation is driven by demand factors, hence an understanding of the barriers/constraints associated with the establishment and expansion of businesses in St Lucia needs to be taken into consideration. Springer (2004) and Compete Caribbean (2013) have undertaken analyses of the factors that adversely affect private sector development in the country. One of the main factors is associated with the small size of the domestic market, namely the inability of small and medium-sized enterprises to reap the benefits of economies of scale and scope. Most of the enterprises in St Lucia have less than 100 employees and are largely focused on meeting the needs of the domestic market rather than expanding to the regional or international markets. This inability to go beyond the domestic market may be due to the risk averse nature of the enterprises and the lack of appropriate international marketing skills. It has been noted that there has been little uptake by St Lucian businesses with respect to market access provisions in trading agreements with Canada, the US, and Europe (Economist Intelligence Unit 2015). A second major constraint that has been identified by the research is the limited access to finance/working capital. This issue has been a common one for several Caribbean states as highlighted in the World Bank's Doing Business and Enterprise Surveys. Small and medium-sized enterprises indicate that they have been unable to obtain finance from the commercial banking system to expand their operations. In the case of St Lucia, the government has established a development bank to "support entrepreneurship, economic and social development through business counseling services, technical assistance, and the provision of funding through loans, equity financing and other forms of assistance."

The third constraint identified in the research is the relatively high costs of doing business with respect to the costs of utilities (electricity, telecommunications, and transportation), registering a company, legal fees with respect to enforcing contracts, and port and shipping charges. These costs make enterprises uncompetitive in the regional and international markets given the fixed exchange regime which the country has with the US. Such high costs of operations limit business expansion and hence restrict the degree of job creation. A fourth constraint associated with business expansion is the threats from international organizations with respect to the tax concessions that the country offers to businesses in the international sector. St Lucia has been seeking to diversify its economy by providing facilities and incentives for international businesses (especially financial services) to operate in the country. But the tax benefits offered to these enterprises have been seen as tax evasion in developed countries, which have moved to bring sanctions against countries that provide tax havens. These responses have meant that small states, such as St Lucia, have to be much more circumspect in the provision of tax incentives. It should be noted that, in many respect, jobs in the international business sector—accountants, lawyers, corporate secretaries, and financial analysts—tend to be high-paying jobs.

While there are constraints to the establishment and expansion of business to create "good jobs for development," there are also constraints on the supply side of the labor market that need to be addressed. Research undertaken by Howe et al. (2011) and Compete Caribbean (2013) points to several issues. First, there is the mismatch between the output of the education and training system and the needs of employers (Blom and Hobbs 2008). Such a mismatch has been due to the asymmetric information problem existing in the two systems, whereby educators are not aware of labor market needs and employers are not involved in educational planning. The lack of a well-functioning labor market information system has been at the root of the problem. In recent times, the government has been seeking to strengthen the information system with assistance from the ILO. Second, there is a certain degree of stigmatization associated with certain jobs that educated people view as low paying and undesirable. Such a situation arises with jobs in the agricultural, fishing, and services sectors; many people prefer to wait in the "unemployment queue" for what they consider as better jobs. This view has been held by many young people with secondary education or more. Third, there has been the out-migration of skilled labor that has stymied the development process. Given the narrow range of post-secondary institutions in the country, many St Lucians attend foreign institutions to undertake specialized training. Many do not return or, if they do, it is only for a short period as employment opportunities are greater in other countries, especially Canada, the US, and the UK. Furthermore, the scarcity of skilled workers makes employers reluctant to pay for training for fear of poaching by other firms. In many cases, the high costs, location, and inflexibility of training programs are seen as barriers to skill development in the country.

In terms of the socio-political environment, there is a view that political patronage and "clientelism" create a culture of dependency and mendicancy so that people prefer to depend on handouts from the government rather than enhance their skills and improve their livelihoods. In addition, there has been a slow growth of civil society to give "voice" to the demands for social and economic developmental change. The lack of a long-term and credible development vision for the country has been cited as a constraint to skill development and job creation. The entrepreneurial class is seen as being weak in the country and hence there is an undue reliance on the government to create jobs for the new post-banana economy.

5.6 Policies to Address St Lucia's Jobs Challenges

In order to overcome the barriers/constraints associated with the creation of jobs in general, and "good jobs for development" in particular, St Lucia needs to develop a framework that includes the following elements:

- an integrated national development plan focusing on key areas of production and linked to regional initiatives within CARICOM;
- a human resources development plan to strengthen links between the education/training system and the labor market;
- a social partnership to foster greater social cohesion;
- a development finance plan to provide resources for key initiatives;
- the utilization of international/regional agreements (e.g., EU-CARIFORUM) and the St Lucian diaspora;
- strategic leadership and management at all levels to resolve the barriers to business formation and job creation.

This framework would allow St Lucia to successfully make the transition to a post-banana economy.

First, in order to identify and promote the creation of "good jobs for development" in the context of a small-island state such as St Lucia, there is a need for explicit coordination, specifically through a national development plan for the post-banana economy. The "revealed preference" of the policy-makers as indicated in speeches, budget presentations, and manifestos suggests that the future lies in the development of a diversified services economy based primarily on tourism and hospitality (linked to the cultural industries), international business, and financial services. The agricultural sector, including fisheries, should, however, be restructured to support the diversification effort. At present there is no national strategic development plan to guide the development of the private sector—which is expected to lead the process. The previous administration had developed a National Vision Plan 2008. When the current government assumed office in 2011, it did not follow through on the Plan but established a National Vision Commission in 2014 to develop a National Vision and Strategy for St Lucia. Consultations with several stakeholders (private sector, unions, youth, media, etc.) were still ongoing at the time of publication.

The OECS has prepared a regional growth and development strategy and action plan to guide development in member states as it seeks to develop an economic union in the Eastern Caribbean. This regional strategy and action plan involves the implementation of joint ventures to support sustainable development and enhanced resilience in the subregion. The key elements include a revitalization of exports, mainly tourism and agriculture, the forging of greater intersectoral linkages, the creation of opportunities for youth employment and entrepreneurship, the reduction in the "costs of doing business," the expansion of air and sea transportation, the enhanced use of ICT, and attention to the potential use of maritime resources (that is, the development of the "blue economy").

From this regional approach, St Lucia needs to situate its own development thrust while still being faithful to the broader initiative. Greater emphasis should be placed on developing "green" and "blue" economic activities as part of a long-term sustainable development plan. There is potential for the economy to provide job opportunities in the production of environmental goods and services (recycling, energy-efficient buildings) and renewable (e.g., solar) energy systems available in the country. In addition, as a small-island state, the maritime resources can be used for job creation in commercial fishing, yachting, boat repairing, aquaculture, offshore mining, and tourism as part of a "blue economy" thrust. Given the vulnerability of the economy to economic and environmental shocks, which is typical of small-island nations, more attention must be paid to sustainable consumption and production.

Second, the national development plan would provide the framework for a human resources development plan, which would link the education and training system to the labor market. Until now, St Lucia has adopted a "social demand" approach to education and training, with the government being the major financier of the system, and individuals and firms pursuing their own private interest, guided by market signals in some cases. This approach requires the education authorities to provide schools and facilities for all students who demand admission and who are qualified to enter the educational system. Hence there is universal primary- and secondary-level education. The system, though, has not produced the qualifications and skills demanded by the labor market, with the result that there has been a great degree of mismatch and human resource wastage. This mismatch is reflected in high levels of unemployment and underemployment, as discussed earlier. To get a better focus on the jobs that are good for development—through reducing poverty and enhancing productivity growth and social cohesion—and also to temper any possible trade-offs (such as initiatives to reduce poverty versus increasing productivity), a more strategic approach to job creation is needed using a combination of market signals and incentives (such as the provision of grants and national development scholarships).

Another important challenge for small states such as St Lucia is stemming the brain drain of people with critical skills needed for national development. It is important for the government working with the private sector to create a working environment to stem the degree of migration from the country, or at least find creative ways of using the skills of migrants to the advantage of the country (e.g., though joint appointments, liaison persons in adopted countries).

Third, national consensus among the key parties to development is an important starting point in a small state like St Lucia. These stakeholders include government, private sector organizations, the labor unions, and selected non-governmental organizations. Barbados, another small-island state in the Caribbean, has used such a consensus to good advantage since the mid 1990s (Fashoyin 2003; Downes and Nurse 2004). Such an institutional mechanism not only builds social cohesion in the country, especially during economic crises, but can also promote productivity and result in improved socio-economic welfare. The discussions and agreements at this level can also resolve issues associated with human security, which has been identified as a major barrier to business development in St Lucia. A broad-based approach to social partnership, dialogue, and action can result in the building of strong communities in the rural and urban areas of St Lucia via community-led projects and plans. Indeed, the approach taken to develop the planned National Vision and Strategy involves consultation with several stakeholders to ensure buy-in, commitment, and participation in the implementation process.

The Caribbean Human Development Report 2012 highlights the importance of institutions in helping to overcome the problems associated with youth unemployment and human security (UNDP 2012). For example, discussions with unemployed youth in the Caribbean point to the need to develop skills and provide the necessary opportunities to use these skills. Caribbean governments and non-governmental organizations have responded by establishing skills training and entrepreneurship programs. Although these initiatives have not been a panacea for the youth unemployment problem in the Caribbean, they have provided an avenue through which young people can get a second chance at skill development outside of the formal education system.

Fourth, access to finance, especially for small and medium-sized enterprises, has been identified as an ongoing barrier to business development in the Caribbean (Compete Caribbean 2013; World Bank 2015). Despite the creation of several special windows for financing, a need remains to improve development finance facilities with associated technical assistance at reasonable costs to assist with the growth and development of enterprises (Compete Caribbean 2013; Economist Intelligence Unit 2015). A more targeted approach is needed with due consideration to issues of risk management. St Lucia has recently passed the Citizenship by Investment Act No. 14 of 2015, which enables persons to acquire citizenship of St Lucia upon making a qualifying investment in the island. This approach to foreign direct investment has been adopted by other Caribbean countries, namely St Kitts and Nevis, Grenada, Antigua, and Barbuda and Dominica.

Fifth, the export market is critical to the growth and development of small states. With the erosion of preferences in traditional markets, especially the UK, small states in the Caribbean have had to find alternative markets, new production areas, and/or develop new trading relationships. In many respects, the business sector has not taken full advantage of access to markets provided by various trading agreements (for example, the Economic Partnership Agreement with the European Union). Small states like St Lucia need to resolve the supply constraints (that is, the ability to supply goods on a sustainable and timely basis) associated with entering new markets. In many cases, small states are unable to meet agreed quotas due to production and shipping problems in their countries. Small states need to use their diplomatic arrangements in various markets for economic gain by cooperating with each other to take advantage of the opportunities associated with market access. The establishment of the CARICOM Single Market and Economy in the Caribbean was premised on the development of production integration among member states in order to secure a meaningful and sustained integration into global markets. In the case of St Lucia, the formation of an economic union among the OECS countries would be an important platform to access a wider range of export niche markets.

The final requirement is for strategic management and leadership at all levels of the society and economy. Such leadership would provide the vision needed for small states to foster their development, and strategic management would ensure that the vision is kept at the forefront of actions on an ongoing basis. The identification of "good jobs for development" of small states such as St Lucia requires the integration of the elements outlined above, so that such jobs will lead to greater social cohesion, improved productivity, and a better standard of living.

Acknowledgments

The authors would like to thank Gordon Betcherman, Martin Rama, Polly Jones, Sonia Plaza, Francesca Lamanna, Dena Ringold, and the participants at a seminar to discuss the project for their comments on the first draft of this case study. The authors are solely responsible for any errors in the study.

References

Baldacchino, G. (2005). "The contribution of social capital to economic growth: Lessons from island jurisdictions." *The Round Table*, 94(1):31–46.

Bellony, A. and Reilly, B. (2009). "An analysis of labor market earnings in St. Lucia." *Social and Economic Studies*, 58(3 & 4):111–47.

Blom, A. and Hobbs, C. (2008). *School and Work in the Eastern Caribbean: Does the Education System Adequately Prepare Youth for the Global Economy?* Washington, DC: World Bank.

Bowen, A. (2012). Green Growth, Green Jobs and Labor Markets. Policy Research Working Paper No. 5990, World Bank.

Caribbean Development Bank (2011). *Basic Needs Trust Fund (BNTF) Completion Report.* Barbados: Wildey.

Caribbean Development Bank (2015). *Youth are the Future: The Imperative of Youth Employment for Sustainable Development in the Caribbean.* Barbados: Wildey.

Caribbean Development Bank/Kairi Consultants (2006). *Country Poverty Assessment Report 2005/2006.* Barbados: Wildey.

Cato, R. (2005). Production integration: Perspectives from the OECS. In: *Caribbean Imperatives: Regional Governance and Integrated Development*, D. Benn and K. Hall (eds), pp. 206–14. Jamaica: Ian Randle Press.

Compete Caribbean (2013). *Private Sector Assessment of Saint Lucia.* Barbados: Inter-American Development Bank.

Dimeglio, I., Germen Janmaat, J., and Mehaut, P. (2013). "Social cohesion and the labour market: Societal regimes of civic attitudes and labour market regimes." *Social Indicators Research*, 111(3):753–73.

Downes, A.S. (2008). *Labor Markets in Small Developing States.* London: Commonwealth Secretariat.

Downes, A.S. and Gunderson, M. (2003). Job search and labour market information in Latin America and the Caribbean. In: *Improving Labor Market Opportunities and Security for Workers in Developing Countries*, W. Kosanovich (ed.), pp. 107–36. Washington, DC: US Department of Labor.

Downes, A.S. and Nurse, L. (2004). "Macroeconomic management and building social consensus: An evaluation of the Barbados Protocols." *Journal of Easter Caribbean Studies*, 29(4):1–51.

Economist Intelligence Unit (2015). *Private Sector Development in the Caribbean: A Regional Overview.* London: Economist Intelligence Unit.

ECTEL (Eastern Caribbean Telecommunication Authority) (2010). Survey of Small and Medium Enterprises Survey 2010.

ESA Consultores International (2004). Poverty Reduction Fund St Lucia: 2003 Impact Evaluation Survey Final Report.

Fashoyin, T. (2003). *Fostering Economic Development through Social Partnership in Barbados.* Geneva: International Labour Office.

Foster, J.S. (2013). Poverty and Social Protection in a Time of Crisis: The Case of St Lucian Women and Opportunities for a Sustainable Recovery from the 2008 Global Financial Crisis. URL: http://www.open.uwi.edu/sites/default/files/bnccde/stlucia/conference/papers/foster2012.html. [Accessed April 2016.]

Gaible, E. (2009). *Survey of ICT and Education in the Caribbean: Volume 1: Regional Trends and Analysis.* Washington, DC: World Bank.

Henry-Lee, A. (2004). *Social Protection and Poverty Reduction in the Caribbean: Examining Policy and Practice in St Lucia Country Review.* Barbados: Caribbean Development Bank.

Howe, G., Thompson, B., Thomas, M., Jules, J., and Miller, J. (2011). *UWI Open Campus Needs Assessment Report*. Barbados: Open Campus University of the West Indies.

International Finance Corporation (2010). St. Lucia Country Profile 2010. Washington, DC.

Mishra, P. (2006). Emigration and brain drain from the Caribbean. In: *The Caribbean: From Vulnerability to Sustained Growth*, R. Sahary, D.O. Robinson, and P. Cashin (eds), pp. 225–57. Washington, DC: IMF.

Mohammed, L. (2012). Labor Migration in the Context of the CARICOM Single Market and Economy (CSME). CARICOM National Training Workshop, Data Collection and Management.

Payne, A. (2006). "The end of green gold? Comparative development options and strategies in the Eastern Caribbean banana-producing islands." *Studies in Comparative International Development*, 41(3):25–46.

Peters, B. and Whittington, L.A. (2009). *Human Resource Needs and the Tertiary Education Sector Response in the Caribbean*. Kingston, Jamaica: Ian Randle Publishers.

Prasad, N. (2008). Social cohesion, governance and social development in small states. In: *Small States and the Pillars of Economic Resilience*, L. Briguglio, G. Cordina, N. Farrugia, and C. Vigilance (eds), pp. 289–301. Malta/London: University of Malta/Commonwealth Secretariat.

Ramsaran, D. (2003). Understanding the socio-cultural dynamics of globalisation: The case of bananas in St. Lucia and St. Vincent and the Grenadines. In: *Living at the Borderlines: Issues in Caribbean Sovereignty and Development*, C. Barrow-Giles and D. Marshall (eds), pp. 95–117. Kingston, Jamaica: Ian Randle Publishers.

Roberts, J. (n.d.). *The Blue Economy: From Concept to Reality in the Caribbean Region*. London: Commonwealth Secretariat.

Schipke, A., Cebotari, A., and Thacker, N. (2013). *The Eastern Caribbean Economic and Currency Union: Macroeconomics and Financial Systems*. Washington, DC: IMF.

Springer, C. (2004). Overcoming economic vulnerability and building resilience in St. Lucia. In: *Economic Vulnerability and Resilience of Small States*, L. Briguglio and E. J. Kisanga (eds), pp. 269–88. Malta/London: University of Malta/Commonwealth Secretariat.

Springer, C. (2006). Economic resilience and social cohesion: The case of small island states in the Eastern Caribbean. In: *Building the Economic Resilience of Small States*, L. Briguglio, G. Cordina, and E.J. Kisanga (eds), pp. 196–211. Malta/London: University of Malta/Commonwealth Secretariat.

St Catherine, E. (2013). Analysis of the Saint Lucia Labor Market Needs Assessment Survey 2012. St. Lucia Central Statistical Office.

St Lucia (2010). Population and Housing Census 2010. St Lucia Central Statistics Office.

St Lucia (2014). Economic and Social Review 2013. Ministry of Finance.

UNCTAD. (n.d.). St Lucia: Country Strategy Paper for the Banana Industry, Agricultural Diversification and the Social Recovery of Rural Communities.

United Nations Development Programme (UNDP) (2009). Assessment of Development Results: Evaluation of UNDP Contribution-Countries of the Organisation of Eastern Caribbean States and Barbados, UNDP Evaluation Office, New York.

United Nations Development Programme (UNDP) (2012). Caribbean Human Development Report. New York: UNDP.

United Nations Development Programme (UNDP) (2014). Human Development Report. New York: UNDP.

World Bank (2005). A Time to Choose: Caribbean Development in the 21st Century. Washington, DC: World Bank.

World Bank (2010). Doing Business 2010. Washington, DC: World Bank.

World Bank (2012). World Development Report 2013: Jobs. Washington, DC: World Bank.

World Bank (2015). Doing Business 2015. Washington, DC: World Bank.

World Bank (2016). Doing Business 2016. Washington, DC: World Bank.

6

Mexico

Formalizing the Labor Market

Gabriel Martinez, Nelly Aguilera, and Martha Miranda

6.1 Introduction

This chapter considers the challenge of formalization in Mexico and, specifically, the challenge of increasing the share of jobs covered by social security. The discussion includes the role of the tax system, mandatory registration for social security—including for self-employed workers and employees in micro-firms—as well as issues of discrimination and structural adjustment. The 2012–18 Mexican federal administration defined formalization as a touch-stone of its mandate. Soon after taking office it proposed a bill for a constitutional amendment to define a model of universal social security (Presidencia de la Republica 2013a). Soon thereafter, the government started to promote tax and social security reforms. Yet, as we will see, the path towards an egalitarian society with universal social security faces significant hurdles.

Mexico is one of the emerging countries admitted as OECD members during the last decades. In comparison to two others, Chile and South Korea, the coverage of Mexico's social security system has stagnated. Productivity growth was low and even negative between the mid 1970s and the mid 1990s and in spite of high, NAFTA-generated expectations, wage growth has been modest since the mid 1990s, and has stagnated since the advent of the Great Recession. Social security coverage rates have stabilized at around half of the total population. The extent of extreme poverty was somewhat reduced during the 1990s, but in recent years it has reversed its direction. The national, state, and municipal governments have expanded noncontributory programs that provide families lacking in social security coverage with small pensions and limited health care services.

Mexico's paramount jobs challenge is to increase formalization. This means that "the coverage of social protection systems is large enough to envision extending it to the entire workforce, but how to do it without undermining productivity is a challenge" (World Bank 2012: Box 6.7). Mexico is one of a set of countries where a large share of the jobs remains outside the mainstream of the social protection system notwithstanding the growth of a large middle class, high productivity gains in some industries, significant improvements in the quantity and quality of education, and improved health status and other favorable developments. In these countries, social protection is usually legislated but compliance is much less than complete; informal micro-firms absorb a large share of the labor force and sustain very low productivity levels. In these formalizing countries, governments have usually resorted to complementary support programs that were originally thought of as anti-poverty programs, but have in fact become much larger and permanent due to the large proportion of families relying on informal jobs. These countries face major fiscal dilemmas in seeking to establish a universal welfare state, with the need to increase revenues to finance it, yet recognizing the "silent vote" of firms and workers in the labor market against increased regulation and taxation.

To set Mexico's challenge in context, we draw comparisons on the labor market and informality with the Republic of Korea and Chile in Table 6.1. Mexico has lower social protection coverage and a higher share of employees in micro-firms than the other two. The proportion of self-employment is also higher in Mexico than in South Korea, but is similar to Chile. Informal employment means different things in each country. For example, South Korea has a single-payer universal health insurance fund; yet, the share of out-of-pocket payments in its total health expenditure is among the largest in the OECD and not really lower than the levels observed in Chile. Mexico has the highest out-of-pocket health expenditures, although in the early 1990s, levels were similar to those in South Korea (OECD 2011a). Reforms to social health insurance systems in South Korea and Chile probably explain the shift towards lower shares of out-of-pocket payments for health services in those countries (Chun et al. 2009; Aguilera et al. 2013). While South Korea and Chile have been more successful than Mexico in socially insuring health expenses, they have not separated themselves fully from other emerging countries and still have shares of out-of-pocket payments above Malaysia and Brazil, for example (WHO 2015).

Similarly, the three countries operate pension systems that provide little or no coverage for a large share of the labor force. Consequently, the three have introduced reforms to support the earnings of those reaching pensionable ages without enough periods or value of contributions to accrue a pension. Chile and South Korea have had guaranteed minimum pensions for all during the last few years (OECD 2011b). Mexico has been expanding a form of welfare

Table 6.1. Selected labor and social statistics, Mexico, South Korea, and Chile

	Mexico	South Korea	Chile
Part-time employment as a percent of total employment, males a/	12.6	7.2	12
Part-time employment as a percent of total employment, females a/	28.8	15.5	25.7
Informal employment as a percent of total non-agricultural employment a/	50.1	29.9	35.8
Self-employment as a percent of total employment b/c/	20.1	26.5	20.8
Employment in micro-firms as a percent of total employment b/c/	63.4	36.5	44.7
Youth employment rate (percent of the 15–24 year age group) d/	42	23.1	31.7
Youth unemployment rate (percent of the 15–24 year age group labor force) d/	9.8	9.6	17.5
PISA mean score reading literacy scales 2011 e/	425	539	449
Gini coefficient (late 2000s) f/	0.476	0.314	0.494
Gini coefficient, working age population (late 2000s) f/	0.469	0.3	0.496
Value added per worker, total national in USD a/	20,837	39,749	23,977
Primary	6,269	14,515	7,742
Secondary	27,497	91,830	39,481
Tertiary	21,103	30,423	21,281
Value added per worker relative to total national			
Primary	0.3	0.4	0.3
Secondary	1.3	2.3	1.6
Tertiary	1	0.8	0.9
Out-of-pocket health expenditures as share of national health expenditures f/	49	32.1	33.3

Note: data are for 2011, except when indicated otherwise.

Sources: a/OECD (2011a); b/(World Bank (2012); c/Grubb, Lee, and Tergeist (2007); d/OECD (2012b); e/OECD (2011c); f/OECD (2012c).

pension with coverage that may result soon in a universal pension. Benefits under these noncontributory or first-tier pensions represent a relatively small fraction of the average earnings in each country. In Chile, the basic benefit is only 15 percent of average earnings, while in South Korea it is between 3 and 7 percent. In Mexico the program *Pensiones para adultos mayores* (previously called *70 y más*) offers a benefit valued at around 15 percent of average taxable labor earnings (the minimum social security pension is at around 28 percent, but requires having contributed for 1,250 weeks). Chile has advanced furthest in attending to the problem of financing age-related programs, holding funds equivalent to nearly 60 percent of GDP in pension funds by 2011, while the corresponding figure for Mexico is 12.9 percent and only 4.5 percent in South Korea (OECD 2012a).

While noting the challenge of extending social protection without affecting productivity, the Jobs WDR goes further to argue that ill-designed social protection has led to lower productivity in Latin America (World Bank 2012). However, the relationship between low social protection and productivity can be more complex. South Korea has been more successful than Mexico and Chile in increasing productivity in all sectors, especially in the secondary sector where value added per worker is between two and three times higher than Mexico

(Table 6.1); it has a lower share of informal employment, but has not reduced the problem to negligible levels. A speech by the President of Mexico underlined the impact of the productivity lag. "Had the productivity indexes been similar to the Korean, our GDP...would be four times bigger than today and...the share of the poor among the population would be 86 percent lower" (Peña Nieto 2013: author's translation). We will see that low productivity and informality in Mexico are linked to employment in very small firms.

6.1.1 *Why are Formal Jobs Good for Development?*

The Jobs WDR defines "good jobs for development" as those that contribute most to societal goals, combining the job's value to the worker and the spillovers on others (World Bank 2012). If social protection is good for development, it is because it generates collective benefits beyond the individual firms and workers. A good social protection solution is believed to have substantial spillovers due to the following:

- Private markets rarely develop without an adequate regulatory framework to cover demands by households in areas such as disability insurance, income maintenance in the case of unemployment, or catastrophic health insurance.

- Negative consequences are associated with "segmented" social protection systems that operate on the basis of program silos, linking individuals to specific social programs and imposing large costs of entry and exit from a job, and after change in family conditions or another status (Perry et al. 2007). This segmentation inflicts substantial damage on the operation of major social processes and markets for health services, financial savings, childcare, long-term care, work injury insurance, and several others. The damage comes from increased moral hazard, higher administrative costs, and fragmentation of financial flows originating in the family.

- A segmented social protection system correlates with higher transaction costs in the labor market, distorting decisions by workers on taking protected or informal, unprotected jobs. Small firms face the highest relative costs of dealing with a segmented system, and face the highest marginal tax rates on growth. Segmented social protection systems are perceived as less valuable due to the probability of future reductions in benefits. The lack of trust leads to higher incentives for tax evasion and defensive actions (such as having alternative health plans or inefficient forms of savings).

- A segmented social protection system leaves out of the mainstream of society a large share of citizens, mainly in rural areas and among the

Indian pueblos in the case of Mexico. Among the largest groups affected by a segmented social protection system are youth with low human capital who face major barriers to break into the labor market. A segmented social protection system is less effective in incorporating women with children and with low human capital who face high costs in changing jobs due to childcare and retraining.

- Lack of social protection can lead to permanent damage from events that should have only temporary effects: unemployed workers incur negative health impacts and the losses become very large when unemployment is permanent; single mothers, inherently facing a challenge in combining household responsibilities with work, may not be able to pay adequate attention to children, which can permanently harm their human development; inefficient health and safety regulation and insurance favors harmful and dangerous locales over clean and healthy ones; and a segmented health system induces opportunistic behavior by consumers and providers, both public and private.

In Mexico's context, it is hard to overstate the case of social protection as necessary to a "good jobs for development" framework.

Section 6.2 describes Mexico's institutional framework for social protection and the levels of public expenditure, and discusses four issues that challenge policy-making in a formalizing country: social cohesion and coverage, taxation, organization of programs, and labor market policies. Section 6.3 reviews the main developments on employment, unemployment, wages, returns to education, the relative position of women, trade and international migration, and regional disparities. In Section 6.4 we discuss the hypotheses related to the debate on how to meet the formalization challenge. Section 6.5 offers conclusions on policy alternatives to deal with the challenge of formalization in Mexico.

6.2 The Framework for Social Protection

The cost of the lack of a comprehensive and high-coverage social security system can be illustrated through excessive consumption variability, precisely what an effective social protection framework should preclude. Figures 6.1 and 6.2 show the large effect that the Great Recession had on consumption and investment in the United States and in Mexico. Considering the absolute size of each economy, a back of the envelope calculation indicates that the decline in investment was approximately of the same relative size in the two countries. However, the relative decrease in consumption in Mexico was almost triple the decrease in the United States.

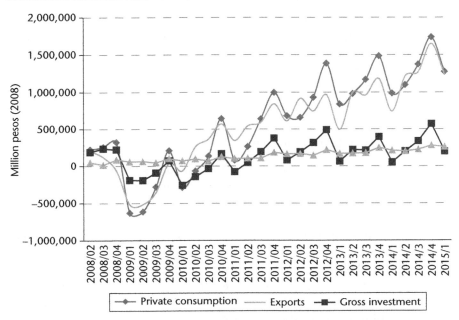

Figure 6.1. Changes in the components of GDP, Mexico, 2008Q2 to 2015Q1
Source: authors' calculations using data from INEGI. Sistema de Cuentas Nacionales de México.

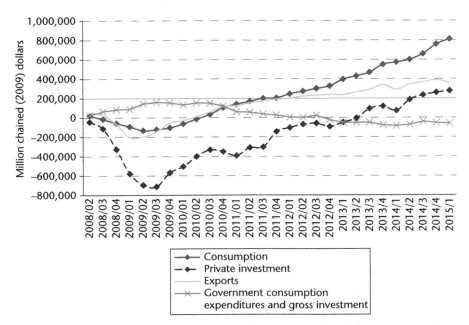

Figure 6.2. Changes in the components of GDP, United States, 2008Q2 to 2015Q1
Source: authors' calculations using data from US Bureau of Economic Analysis. http://www.bea.
gov/national/txt/dpga.txt.

183

During 2009, at the height of the crisis, the average Mexican cut consumption by an amount equivalent to more than one month's wages. This excessive variation in consumption reflects the uncertainty Mexican families face in their conditions of employment, access to health services, and liquidity to deal with emergencies.

6.2.1 *Overview of Social Protection*

Broadly speaking, social protection in Mexico comes from registration with social security or from accessing the noncontributory programs that are predominantly funded by the federal government. Additional sources of social protection are employment protection legislation (EPL), based on the Federal Labor Law, and active labor market policies (ALMPs), though these are very modest in Mexico.

Mexican social security offers benefits for health, maternity, illness, general disability, retirement, work injuries and illness, childcare, and housing. In comparison to the schemes in developed countries, the two major gaps are the absence of unemployment and long-term care benefits.

In principle, income earners must pay income and social security taxes. In practice, many do not pay either, some contribute to social security and do not pay taxes, and others pay taxes but do not contribute to social security.

Social security is provided by two sets of agencies. One is dedicated to public employees and includes separate agencies for federal public sector workers (ISSSTE), for the armed forces (ISSFAM), and for state and municipal workers. The other, and much larger one, is the Mexican Social Security Institute (IMSS), which covers workers in the private sector and in state enterprises. IMSS is the largest organization in the country in terms of employment, and the second largest in terms of revenues after the state oil corporation. These are all vertically integrated agencies in that they collect contributions, do all the necessary administration internally, and provide final services, but there is little horizontal integration or vertical contracting for the exchange of services or money across agencies or with other public or private programs. It is a "silo structure."

Noncontributory programs are regulated or directly managed by a variety of agencies. The two main ones are the Secretariat of Social Development (Sedesol) and the Health Ministry (MoH). Sedesol regulates and operates the *Prospera* (before, *Progresa* and *Oportunidades*) program to reduce income poverty and build human capabilities. The MoH operates *Seguro Popular*, which finances health services for those without social security. Noncontributory pensions are mainly provided through the federal program, *Pensión para adultos mayores* (recently reformed to reduce the age of eligibility to 65 and

Table 6.2. Federal government social expenditures in cash and health benefits, 2007–15 (2015 pesos)

	Monetary benefits				Health
	Total	Pensions	Family	Employment	
2007	362	297	62	3	413
2008	371	300	67	4	441
2009	388	316	69	4	462
2010	457	371	83	3	490
2011	469	381	84	4	511
2012	538	443	90	5	553
2013	568	477	86	5	568
2014	636	542	89	5	573
2015	642	549	88	5	578

Source: for Pensions, total pension expenditure in Federal Budget, SHCP (several years); for Health, state expenditures are included, SSA (2012) for 2007–11, and author's calculations for 2013–15; Family programs includes Temporary Employment Program (PET), Food Allowances (PAL), Life Insurance for Female Family Heads Federal Budget, SHCP (several years), and disability, marriage and funeral subsidies paid by social security (IMSS Memoria Estadística, several years). Exchange rate used is daily average for the year, up to July 2015, from Banco de Mexico.

to include non-rural populations). There are thousands of other federal, state, and municipal programs that we cannot try to list in this space.[1]

The Labor Law defines the general framework for employment contracts. By defining the employer–employee relationship, including protecting workers from various job-related risks, employment protection legislation can be seen as a form of social protection for wage and salary workers. However, this protection is limited due to noncompliance and ineligible workers, such as the self-employed.

Table 6.2 shows federal expenditures for social protection. Pension programs are the largest among those providing monetary benefits, and this item will grow faster than GDP for decades due to aging and indexation rules that define consumer price index variations as the floor to increase the value of pensions. Even the more optimistic estimates of future revenues possible after a fiscal reform yield financial resources that will be absorbed over the coming years by the already committed pension expenditures (Vasquez Colmenares 2012). Family programs are comprised mainly of the anti-poverty programs, of which *Prospera* is the largest. Public health expenditures include social security and MoH programs, including *Seguro Popular*. Since the early 1990s, public expenditures (mostly federal) have hovered around 2.7–2.9 percent of GDP. The composition has changed though, with

---

[1] The National Evaluation Council (Coneval 2015) has listed, for 2012, 3,788 state programs and 1,883 municipal programs. The measurement of the budget and services provided remain research tasks for the future.

IMSS expenditures declining by around a half of a percentage point and the MoH programs increasing by the same amount.[2] Finally, we see that employment programs are very small (active programs are small and passive programs are virtually non-existent). On a per capita basis, we estimate that by 2015, federal social expenditures were equivalent to $300 for pension programs, $48 for family programs, $3 for employment programs (this comprises active labor market policies), and $316 for health.[3] Over the 2007–15 period, expenditure per capita on pensions programs grew almost 68 percent, more than double the rate for any other item. Considering only the population age 65 and over, per capita federal expenditures on pensions reached $4,547 in 2015.

6.2.2 Coverage

Social security is inherently expected to cover all, and the inability of a society to succeed in bringing everyone into the system reflects a lack of trust and social cohesion. It signals the unwillingness of insiders to recognize the well-being needs of outsiders, and that outsiders cannot find traversable pathways out of a marginal condition. From this perspective, the welfare state is more than public spending and its administration: it contains the ideological, moral, and political justification for providing families with a framework of economic safety, and implies that the institutions of the state must continuously take actions to guide the focus, priorities, and the effect of expenditures on welfare.

Understanding who is covered by social security and who is not is necessary to understand the problem of formalization. However, the measurement of the coverage of social security and other social programs is a topic that has not found a satisfactory solution. The problem is illustrated in Table 6.3, showing the official measurement of health insurance by social security and *Seguro Popular* with respect to the total population. According to these figures, by 2010 the problem of universality in health insurance had been solved. However, the column indicating the overall coverage rate is the sum of diverse programs that offer different sets of benefits, with different funding mechanisms, representing a variety of relations between the citizen and the state: some are mandatory, others are voluntary, some require contributions from citizens while others do not, and in general they provide heterogeneous services.

---

[2] There has also been an increase in state expenditures. Between 1993 and 2011 the share of state expenditures on total public non-social security increased slowly from 17 to 23 percent. Still, this is equivalent to only 8 percent of the federal figure for public expenditures in 2011, and less than 4 percent of national expenditures, so the qualitative message is not affected by state expenditures.

[3] These calculations are made using the average annual exchange rate of 15.15 pesos/dollar, and 120.8 million inhabitants. Money figures in this chapter are in US dollars, unless we indicate they are in Mexican pesos.

Table 6.3. Social security and *Seguro Popular*, number of insured and percentage of population covered, 2004–14

	IMSS		ISSSTE		Other social security beneficiaries (Armed Forces, Pemex, States)	Total insured by social security divided by total population	Total insured population (social security plus *Seguro Popular*) divided by total population
	Insured	Beneficiaries	Insured	Beneficiaries			
	(millions of people)					(ratio)	
2004	16.4	43.0	2.9	10.5	3.0	0.53	0.58
2005	17.2	43.7	2.9	10.6	3.0	0.53	0.64
2006	18.1	45.7	3.0	10.8	3.1	0.55	0.69
2007	18.7	47.8	3.1	11.0	3.0	0.56	0.76
2008	18.4	49.3	3.2	11.3	3.0	0.57	0.82
2009	19.3	48.2	3.3	11.6	2.8	0.55	0.83
2010	20.7	50.3	3.5	12.0	4.0	0.58	0.96
2011	21.8	53.4	3.5	12.2	3.8	0.60	1.05
2012	22.9	55.9	2.7	12.4	3.5	0.61	1.07
2013	23.8	58.4	3.6	12.6	3.6	0.63	1.10
2014 a/	25.0	57.8	3.7	12.8	3.6	0.62	1.09

Sources: IMSS Memoria estadistica (several years); ISSSTE Anuario Estadístico, (several years); Other social security and Seguro Popular, INEGI Derechohabiencia y uso de servicios de salud.

a/ For 2014, author's estimates for ISSSTE and other social security.

Our best estimate is that social security coverage has been 50–52 percent of the population in recent years, while the noncontributory program, *Seguro Popular*, claims health insurance coverage that brings the total above 100 percent. However, there is overlap in the populations, with some individuals counted twice while others have no insurance. Similarly, simply adding the figures on pensions paid by social security and by the noncontributory programs would indicate nearly universal coverage levels. In 2011, the pension program, *Pensiones para adultos mayores*, made payments to more than 4.9 million individuals, mostly rural elderly (CONEVAL 2013; by 2014 the program was expanding its coverage of urban populations). Adding this to benefits received through social security, our best estimate of the share of the 65-and-over population receiving a pension is around two-thirds.[4]

In measuring the coverage of pension or health insurance in Mexico and in making cross-country comparisons, two caveats are in order. First, household surveys underestimate coverage of social security in Mexico, with administrative data estimates 14 percentage points higher in 2010 (51 vs. 37 percent, which includes both pension and health coverage), according to Rofman and

---

[4] Social security pensions are granted to former workers and can be inherited by dependent spouses or children. We count spouses of social security retirees as covered.

Oliveri (2011). One possible explanation is that many insured families are not regular users of social security's health services, which may result in an under-reporting of insured status. Second, countries label similar programs differently. Some define noncontributory programs as social security and classify them as such to international organizations that report coverage, while Mexico has considered those programs under other labels.

6.2.3 Taxation

A major issue in current debates is whether the social security system should move toward increasing funding through higher federal sales taxes and thus lower social security taxes. The motivation would be to reduce the cost of creating formal jobs, while increasing the share of new jobs protected with social security. Under these proposals, all workers would be covered since coverage would not be tied to social security contributions. According to current rules, average total tax and contribution rates are between 20 and 40 percent of gross earnings for the vast majority of workers, although around half of them do not pay social security contributions or participate in the income tax system.

To frame the issue, Table 6.4 shows the contribution rates and average taxes for workers with taxable earnings equivalent to one, three, ten, and

Table 6.4. Average tax rates and ratio of taxes to gross labor earnings (non-government employees), 2011

		Taxable earnings as multiple of minimum wage			
	Rate	1	3	10	25
Fixed health and maternity, government	0.14	0.14	0.05	0.01	0.01
Fixed health and maternity, employer	0.14	0.14	0.05	0.01	0.01
Variable for health and maternity	0.02	0.00	0.00	0.01	0.01
Health and maternity subsidies	0.01	0.01	0.01	0.01	0.01
General disability	0.03	0.03	0.03	0.03	0.03
Retirement	0.07	0.07	0.07	0.07	0.07
Social contribution for retirement, government	0.06	0.06	0.02	0.01	0.00
Work injuries	0.02	0.02	0.02	0.02	0.02
Day care	0.01	0.01	0.01	0.01	0.01
Housing	0.05	0.05	0.05	0.05	0.05
Total social contributions					
Including state contribution (sum all items)		0.51	0.29	0.22	0.21
Employer–employee (exclude government items)		0.32	0.23	0.20	0.20
Local payroll tax	0.02	0.02	0.02	0.02	0.02
Federal income tax		−0.17	0.02	0.10	0.15
Total contributions and income tax		0.17	0.26	0.32	0.37

Source: authors' calculations from various tax laws, mainly federal income tax and social security. (a) Rate applies to earnings above the equivalent of three minimum wages. (b) Local payroll taxes vary by state; we use the modal value for 2011 (a local tax of 2 percent on the payroll).

twenty-five minimum wages (based on the tax schedules applicable to those insured by IMSS). As shown in the last line of the table, the total tax rate that applies to labor progresses from 17 to 37 percent; for example, for a worker earning the equivalent of three minimum wages, 26 percent of the cash outlays by the employer go to social contributions and taxes. This number is largely due to the 23 percent rate for social contributions paid by employers and employees. The combined contribution and tax rate reaches its highest point at the level of twenty-five minimum wages, when it is 37 percent. In Table 6.4 we also see the progressive role of federal transfers to social security. The difference between "Including state contributions" and "Employer–employee" measures the federal subsidy paid for a worker at each wage level; for example, for workers earning the minimum wage the subsidy represents 19 percent of earnings, while at the level of three minimum wages it represents only 6 percent.

The current situation results from an evolution that began approximately twenty-five years ago. Between the end of the 1980s and the mid 1990s, the federal government substantially decreased marginal income tax rates, while it raised the social security contribution rates. Towards the second half of the 1990s, policies were aligned for the income tax and social security contributions, and both were reduced. More recently, and in particular after the crisis of 2008–09, taxes on labor began climbing again. The last point is shown in Figure 6.3, where we see the 2007 schedule of tax rates by earnings level below the 1990 level, and the rebound taking place since 2008 and until 2014.

Should Mexico move to a higher level of taxation with respect to GDP? This is a precondition for an expansion of the welfare state, in particular if

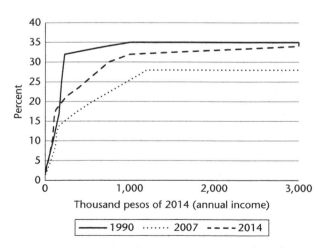

Figure 6.3. Personal marginal income tax rates by earnings levels, 1997, 2007, and 2014
Source: authors' calculations from federal income tax law.

Table 6.5. Total tax revenue as percentage of GDP, selected OECD and Latin American countries, 1975–2013

	1975	1995	2000	2009	2013
Argentina		20.3	21.5	31.4	31.2
Brazil		26.8	30.0	32.6	35.7
Canada	32.0	35.6	35.6	31.1	30.6
Chile		19.0	19.4	18.4	20.2
Colombia		13.2	14.1	17.4	20.1
South Korea	14.9	20.0	22.6	25.6	24.3
Costa Rica		16.3	18.2	20.9	22.4
El Salvador		13.0	12.2	14.4	15.8
Spain	18.4	32.1	34.2	30.7	32.6
United States	25.6	27.8	29.5	24.0	25.4
Guatemala		10.4	12.4	12.2	13.0
Mexico		15.2	16.9	17.4	19.7
Peru		15.4	13.9	15.9	18.3
Dominican Republic		10.6	12.4	13.1	14.0
Uruguay		19.7	20.0	22.5	27.1
Venezuela		13.3	13.6	14.4	14.2

Source: OECD (2014) and OECD/ECLAC/CIAT (2015).

centralized solutions are adopted (such as a National Health Plan). Table 6.5 shows tax revenues as a share of GDP for a group of OECD countries and non-member countries in Latin America. Only Brazil, Argentina, and Uruguay among the Latin American countries in this sample have collected significantly more tax revenues as a share of GDP than Mexico during the last two decades. Chile and Costa Rica also have higher tax revenues, but the difference with Mexico is small, and Chile does not show any increase. South Korea is the one OECD country included in Table 6.5 where contributions have increased substantially; other OECD countries collected more than Mexico by 2010 but not more proportionally than in the 1990s.

When and if higher tax collections are achieved, a second question relates to the structure of taxation: Should higher revenues be obtained through income, consumption, or social security taxes? Brazil, Argentina, and Uruguay collect more than double in social security contributions than Mexico. Overall, within the OECD, social security collections are more than one-quarter of total tax revenues (Table 6.6). In both Latin America and the OECD, there is greater use of general consumption taxation than specific consumption taxes. Yet, in Latin America, there is no trend towards lower overall consumption or social security taxation; there may be a trend toward a higher share of income taxation at the expense of all other forms of taxation, although changes in structure are not large and may have been affected by the Great Recession.

Specifically, we can say that Mexico could increase tax revenues if the structure moves towards higher social security contributions and if long-term

Table 6.6. Source of taxation as a percentage of total tax revenues, OECD and Latin American averages, 1995–2013

	1965	1975	1985	1995	2000	2005	2008	2009	2012 for OECD, 2013 for LA
OECD									
Personal income tax	26	30	30	26	25	24	25	25	25
Corporate income tax	9	8	8	8	10	10	10	8	9
Social security contributions	18	22	22	25	24	25	25	27	26
Payroll taxes	1	1	1	1	1	1	1	1	1
Property taxes	8	6	5	5	6	6	5	5	5
General consumption taxes	12	13	16	19	19	20	20	20	20
Specific consumption taxes	24	18	16	13	12	11	10	11	11
Other taxes	2	2	2	3	3	3	3	3	3
Latin America									
Taxes on income and profits				22	22	25	28	28	27
Social security contributions				17	16	14	13	15	17
Payroll tax				1	1	1	1	1	1
Property taxes				2	3	5	4	4	4
General consumption taxes				32	34	35	35	35	32
Specific taxes on consumption				24	21	19	17	15	17
Other taxes				2	2	2	2	2	2
Ratio (OECD/LatAm)									
Taxes on income and profits				1.55	1.59	1.36	1.25	1.18	1.26
Social security contributions				1.47	1.50	1.79	1.92	1.80	1.53
Payroll tax				1.00	1.00	1.00	1.00	1.00	1.00
Property taxes				2.50	2.00	1.20	1.25	1.25	1.25
General consumption taxes				0.59	0.56	0.57	0.57	0.57	0.63
Specific taxes on consumption				0.54	0.57	0.58	0.59	0.73	0.65
Other taxes				1.50	1.50	1.50	1.50	1.50	1.50

Note: the figures for OECD countries separate between corporate and personal income taxes. For Latin America, figures show only the total.
Source: OECD (2014) and OECD/ECLAC/CIAT (2015).

improvements in VAT and income tax collections can be sustained. If international comparisons are relevant, then gradual and sustained improvements in collections are feasible, but very large increases can come only if social security contributions increase. To move towards the levels of taxation in Brazil, Argentina, or Europe, social security contributions would need to be increased. But achieving a better functioning social protection system requires improved design and regulation of the programs, regardless of the changes in tax collections.

6.2.4 Issues in the Design of Public Programs

Parallel to the fiscal developments, noncontributory social programs have been expanding, sometimes in explicit competition with social security. Program size is important for determining the response of individuals to subsidized programs. When subsidized programs are small and essentially exist to serve the poor, particularly the rural poor, they likely do not affect urban labor markets. However, when they become very large, they begin to attract workers who otherwise would be willing to make social security contributions. When the state operates very large subsidized programs, distortions can also become large. This not only affects tax collections, but also accentuates the adverse selection process, in terms of decisions to participate in programs such as those for health and disability.

Levy (2008) argues that the expansion of subsidized programs increases incentives for informality. On the other hand, a body of literature disputes the existence of this negative effect (Knaul et al. 2012). To discuss this problem we must consider that the elasticity of labor supply is too low to generate significant changes in labor supply after the adoption of a policy such as the *Seguro Popular* or the conditional cash transfer programs of the Social Development Ministry. Thus, the results showing the low impact of *Seguro Popular* on labor supply in the studies cited by Knaul et al. (2012) are expected because of the low elasticity of labor supply (Martinez 2012a, 2012b). There is not any evidence of an elastic labor supply either at the intensive (participation decision) or at the extensive margins (i.e., between the formal and the informal sectors). Thus, the argument of Levy, writing with colleagues (Anton et al. 2013), which focuses on the effect of social security contributions on informality and criticizes *Seguro Popular* for its impact on informality, is also unlikely to find empirical support. Few would argue that informality is due to taxation for health insurance, since this is only a small part of the marginal tax rate on labor income (Table 6.4).

Juarez (2008) authored one of the few investigations directly relevant to this issue. She finds that for low-income females, the introduction of a free health program reduced affiliation to social security by 4 percent; she also found a wage gap of 23 percent between the insured and the uninsured, which is roughly similar to the social security contribution rates (Table 6.4). This is a large effect, but it is found only for low-income females in a large city; the results for other females show no effect. For low-income women, a new in-kind subsidy for health represents a large share of disposable income, and they are also likely to attach high relative value to alternative uses of time. For them, the Levy hypothesis is more likely to hold. For other workers, labor supply is very inelastic, and they are unlikely to change jobs due to a relatively small health benefit. High-income workers have high rates of compliance with social security but opt to make low use of services, so reducing their taxes would only reduce collections without reducing the demand for final services provided by public institutions.

Also, existing noncontributory programs are too small to affect the equilibrium in the labor or health-services markets. Consider the example of *Seguro Popular*, the main initiative to eliminate the segmentation of the health-services

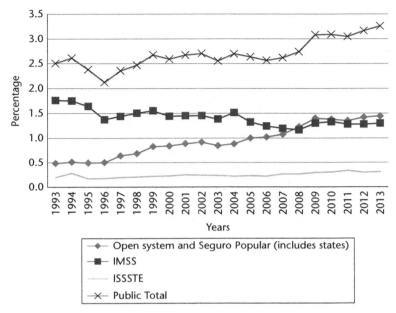

Figure 6.4. Public health expenditure as a percentage of GDP, 1993–2013

Source: Health Ministry. General Directorate of Health Information. System of Accounts at the Federal and State Level (SICUENTAS), México 2015.

market. This program represented just 8 percent of total expenditures for health services by 2011. Its impact on the residual demand for health services is likely to be smaller, due to crowding out of other public and private expenses (when new public expenditures pay for services with an inelastic demand, expenditures by social security and private parties are displaced). Overall public expenditures in health services have not increased much (Figure 6.4), and the growth in *Seguro Popular* expenditures came after decreases in social security. It is unlikely that even a program of this size (possibly the largest among all the new social programs) can alter the structure of either the health-insurance or the health-services markets, except at the local level (because poor localities receive a relatively large share of the expenditure flow). Summarizing the point, the increase in the size of *Seguro Popular* is an unlikely candidate to have a significant effect on labor formality, only because the program is small in relation to the size of the health-services and the labor market, and it has had little impact on total expenditures. On the other hand, the proliferation of agencies deepens the segmentation and the potential moral hazard problems, which are known to be acute in health services and insurance and in general disability insurance.

6.2.5 Labor Policies

The two main strands of labor policy in Mexico are employment protection legislation and active labor market policies. EPL in Latin America is strict relative to OECD standards (Heckman and Pages 2004). In some labor markets, EPL can be a partial substitute for social security because it aims to guarantee stable employment and benefits in case of dismissal. As we have noted, active labor market policies are quite small in Mexico.

EPL presumes that workers are better off when their labor contract is permanent and includes a battery of mandated benefits, including prohibitions on firing without a cause, high levels of severance payments, paid vacations, and profit sharing. In this chapter, we define informality as a deviation from that standard. Based on this, we find no trend towards formality, with the fraction of workers with permanent contracts for each age group and each gender quite stationary for nearly thirty years. These shares are never above 40 percent for men and 50 percent for women; for workers under 20 years of age and over 50, they are usually below 20 percent.[5] This stationary condition mimics the time-series behavior of social security coverage.

Active labor market policies were initiated in the late 1980s and early 1990s with the Program to Support Employment (*Programa de Apoyo al Empleo PAE*) (Samaniego 2002). Since the 1990s, *Probecat*—renamed *Bécate* in 2003—has been the main program and the most consistently evaluated one. ALMPs in Mexico cover training, promotion of employment, and public employment programs. Excluding passive programs (mainly unemployment insurance), the main types of ALMP disbursements in the OECD are programs for the disabled, and youth training and employment programs. Mexico has a very low level of expenditures on ALMPs even compared with Chile and South Korea (0.01, 0.09, and 0.29 percent of GDP in 2013, respectively) (OECD 2015). The resources dedicated to ALMPs in Mexico peaked in the recessionary, high-unemployment year of 2009 when expenditures reached 1.5 billion pesos, or $110 million. This is a little more than $2 per worker and less than $20 per unemployed worker (Secretaria del Trabajo y Prevision Social 2015).

South Korea and Chile introduced unemployment insurance several years ago. In 2014, Mexico's Executive sent a bill to Congress proposing the adoption of an unemployment insurance program. If approved, public expenditure levels for employment programs (active and passive) probably could move to the Chilean levels (0.31 percent of GDP in 2011). The reason is that the model adopted is based on individual savings accounts (as opposed to a collectively funded program) with contribution rates similar to the Chilean program. This

---

[5] These shares are based on calculations by the authors using data from the National Income Expenditure Survey (INEGI-ENIGH, several years).

means that Mexican UI will be a mandatory individual savings program, with a solidarity component paid collectively and with federal funds. Fiscal restrictions will make it hard to move to the levels of expenditure on employment programs provided by other OECD nations. In any case, the new legislation had not been passed by Congress by May 2016, and in a best case scenario the new program cannot operate before 2018.

Another item in the federal budget aimed at creating jobs is the Temporary Employment Program (*PET*), which is part of the battery of anti-poverty programs. It pays a salary to enrolled workers but does not involve training or other learning components, and there are individual limits on the number of days of enrollment. The PET has grown in recent years, from 343 to 790 million pesos between 2009 and 2011 (approximately $26 to $60 million; SHCP several years). The program is concentrated in low-income, rural municipalities. Given its small size and regional targets, the PET has no effect on formality because beneficiaries are in general too far from being able to get a formal job, and few formal workers would abandon their job to get this subsidy.

6.3 The Labor Market

The key developments in the evolution of the labor market since the 1990s have been the Tequila crisis (1994–95), which generated a large fall in wages, and the Great Recession, which resulted in increasing unemployment followed by wage stagnation. While some improvements in the general position of women have occurred, male–female earnings gaps are not closing. Over this period, a major regional restructuring has been taking place, with important implications for employment.

6.3.1 *Employment and Unemployment*

Employment growth has been significant and open unemployment has been low, but with a large number of discouraged workers. Between 1990 and 2015, total employment increased from 23 to 49 million (INEGI ENOE, National Employment and Occupation Survey data).[6] The male labor force participation rate continued a slow secular decline (from nearly 80 percent to around 77 percent) over this period, while the rate for women rose after the 2001

---

[6] ENE is the National Employment Survey; it was applied until 2004. ENOE is the National Occupation and Employment Survey and has applied since 2005. These data are the primary source for this discussion.

recession but has been virtually stagnant until 2015 at around 42.5 percent. Mexicans work long hours. Men between 20–50 years of age with only one job work on average nearly 48 hours per week, and women work between 35 and 40 hours. In recent years, this has been above almost all OECD countries; hours have decreased in Chile and South Korea since 2000, but not in Mexico (OECD 2012c).

Between 1990 and 2010, the decrease in the labor force in agriculture, the manufacturing boom of the 1990s, and the continuous growth of employment in retail trade and other services were important employment developments. During the first half of the liberalization period (from the end of the 1980s through the 1990s), the growth of employment in manufacturing was remarkable, but during the last decade the global trend towards the expansion of services has been replicated in Mexico. Service industries have accounted for most of the employment growth through these two decades. Retail trade employment went from 5 million to 8.5 million, accounting for one of every five new jobs. More than half of the new jobs were in other services and, within these, hospitality and food preparation services and professional services together accounted for 23 percent of new jobs, similar to retail trade. Agriculture is the only industry with a decline in absolute number of workers; it had nearly 8 million in the middle of the 1990s and ten years later it had around 6 million.

The rate of open unemployment has hovered around 5 percent since the start of the Great Recession, having been as low as 2 percent towards the end of the 1990s. This is a low rate by international standards, but there is a relatively large response in participation to the business cycle (Martinez 2010). In particular, the category of "available" workers—individuals who declare an intention to work but who were not seeking employment at the time of being interviewed—comprises a larger share of the working-age population in Mexico than in the United States (where the comparable term is "marginally attached") or other countries in the OECD.

6.3.2 Wages and Salaries

Real wages increased in the late 1980s, fell during the 1994–95 crisis, and, after recovering post-crisis, they have been virtually stationary since the onset of the Great Recession (Figure 6.5).

6.3.2.1 RETURNS TO EDUCATION

Figures 6.6 and 6.7 compare the relative earnings for males and females, respectively, for the following education levels: less than elementary; elementary complete; less than secondary (middle); middle school complete; less than preparatory (high school); and high school complete; some college or

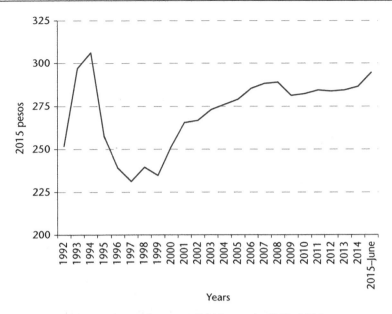

Figure 6.5. Average real taxable wages (2015 pesos), 1992–2015
Source: authors' calculations based on data from IMSS Memoria Estadística (several years).

higher.[7] These figures, as well as Figure 6.8, show these comparisons for earnings over the 1995–2011 period for different birth cohorts. The observations on earnings by cohort were summarized in a calculation of present value of lifetime earnings, following the methodology in Heckman et al. (2008).

We see that the earnings gap between the college educated and those with only high school education reached a peak for the cohort born between 1966 and 1975. The gap is lower for younger cohorts. Thus, it seems that there was an increase in the college earnings premium during the 1990s, and an equalizing trend during the 2000s.[8]

6.3.2.2 RELATIVE POSITION OF WOMEN

In Figure 6.8, we show male–female earnings differentials for each educational level, again by birth cohort. The gap between men and women is much larger among the less educated than among the better educated for all cohorts. For those with less than secondary schooling, the advantage for men was 60 percent for those born before 1975. The gap has been 20–30 percent for

[7] Elementary, secondary, and preparatory schooling take six, three, and three years, respectively; we use the term high school for preparatory and middle school for secondary.
[8] Campos et al. (2012) also found a decrease in the relative returns for more educated workers, using a different data source.

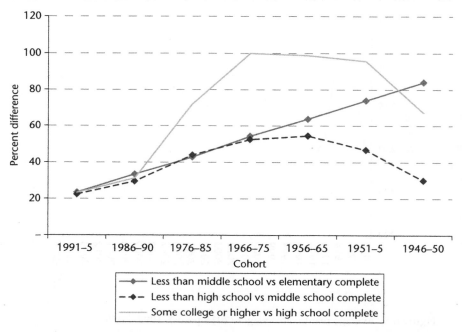

Figure 6.6. Comparisons of male earnings between 1995 and 2011 for different education levels, by birth cohort (five-year birth period)

Note: this figure shows ratios of net present values of lifetime earnings.

Source: authors' calculations based on data from INEGI (ENE and ENOE surveys), several years. www.inegi.org.mx.

those with at least some post-secondary education, and 30–50 percent for those with middle school completion. While Figure 6.8 shows smaller gender differences for the youngest cohorts, this may eventually be affected by experience, so it is too early to confirm any trend toward lower gender inequality.

Garcia-Cuellar (2000) suggested that trade liberalization would diminish the wage gap between women and men by increasing demand for low-skilled labor and the decline in discrimination associated with increased competitiveness. Her research, as well as Aguayo et al. (2010) and Juhn et al. (2012), confirms that trade favorably affects the earnings of women, at least in manufacturing export industries.

6.3.3 *Trade, International Migration, and Wages*

Can NAFTA lead to convergence in wages between Canada, the United States, and Mexico? With a level of integration and legal freedom of labor mobility higher than the NAFTA zone, Europe has achieved some convergence in levels

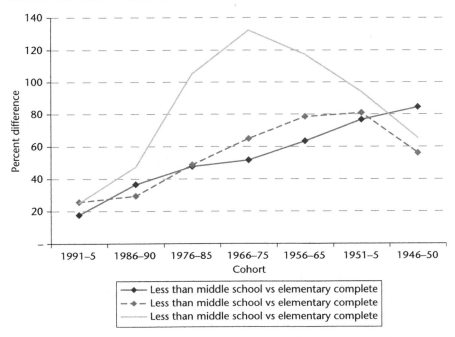

Figure 6.7. Comparisons of female earnings between 1995 and 2011 for different education levels, by birth cohort (five-year birth period)

Note: this figure shows ratios of net present values of lifetime earnings.

Source: authors' calculations based on data from INEGI (ENE and ENOE surveys), several years. www.inegi.org.mx.

and growth rates of wages. However, it is a slow process, which seems to have a "core" and "periphery," and the recent crisis may have long-term effects on the economic reorganization of that region with effects on the structure of wages.[9]

In the North American context, the convergence of wages can be affected by American immigration and international social security policies. With respect to the former, the US accepts relatively few Mexican legal non-immigrant workers. In 2013, 1.8 million non-immigrant workers were admitted (from all countries, not only NAFTA countries), 33 percent of which were professional workers entering through NAFTA and 39 percent were transfers (i.e., employees of multinational corporations); just 11 percent were seasonal agriculture workers. In 2011, only 70,000 of 865,000 professional workers (TN visa) covered by NAFTA were Mexican.[10] The social security agreement

---

[9] Slander and Ogorevc (2010) documented wage convergence in the EU. See Ramskogler (2010) for a study of the process of adjustment of wages in time in Europe

[10] Homeland Security (various years).

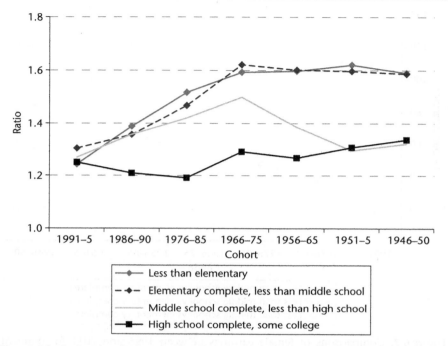

Figure 6.8. Ratio of male–female earnings, 1995–2011 for different educational levels, by birth cohort (five-year birth period)

Note: this figure shows ratios of net present values of lifetime earnings.

Source: authors' calculations based on data from INEGI (ENE and ENOE surveys), several years. www.inegi.org.mx.

between Mexico and the United States, which would contribute towards formalizing migrants, was signed in 2004, but has not been reviewed by the United States Congress or approved by the Mexican Senate.[11] Thus, neither immigration nor social security policies are favorable to wage convergence.

6.3.4 *Regional Disparities in Employment Structure and Formalization*

A large restructuring of economic activity across industries and states[12] has been taking place during the last two decades, favoring those more oriented to globalization, which also have higher social security coverage.[13] Export-oriented

---

[11] See Nuschler and Siskin (2006).

[12] When referring to states in Mexico, we mean the thirty-one states plus the Federal District.

[13] Martinez et al. (2012b) detail the methodology of calculation of the indices of participation in industry internal demand (PDI) for each entity for each industry, as well as the indices of concentration used to stratify by tradability.

Table 6.7. Social security coverage of the working-age population by state, 1990–2010

	Percentage of working-age population registered with IMSS			Change in percentage points		
	2010	2000	1990	2010–2000	2000–1990	2010–1990
Aguascalientes	45	52	49	–7	3	–4
Baja California	45	64	53	–19	11	–8
Baja California Sur	38	45	38	–7	7	0
Campeche	37	31	30	6	1	7
Chiapas	12	10	9	2	1	3
Chihuahua	47	61	50	–14	11	–3
Coahuila	49	60	53	–11	7	–4
Colima	33	35	35	–2	0	–2
Federal District	29	29	70	0	–41	–41
Durango	33	40	32	–7	8	1
Guanajuato	30	32	28	–2	4	2
Guerrero	12	13	14	–1	–1	–2
Hidalgo	16	19	18	–3	1	–2
Jalisco	40	41	43	–1	–2	–3
Mexico	11	12	25	–1	–13	–14
Michoacan	20	19	17	1	2	3
Morelos	23	26	29	–3	–3	–6
Nayarit	26	24	24	2	0	2
Nuevo Leon	60	61	62	–1	–1	–2
Oaxaca	12	11	10	1	1	2
Puebla	20	24	23	–4	1	–3
Queretaro	43	48	46	–5	2	–3
Quintana Roo	45	44	47	1	–3	–2
San Luis Potosi	30	30	28	0	2	2
Sinaloa	37	33	31	4	2	6
Sonora	40	43	44	–3	–1	–4
Tabasco	19	16	17	3	–1	2
Tamaulipas	43	48	40	–5	8	3
Tlaxcala	14	22	22	–8	0	–8
Veracruz	15	13	21	2	–8	–6
Yucatan	34	36	40	–2	–4	–6
Zacatecas	26	25	17	1	8	9
National	33	35	35	–2	0	–2

Note: Southern states shown in italics.

Source: INEGI, Censos de Población y Vivienda (several years); and IMSS Memoria Estadistica.

states had significant relative growth during the 1990s,[14] and their social security coverage increased accordingly. After 2000, the rest of the country has been catching up in terms of growth, except for the Federal District and other "old-economy" states.

Table 6.7 shows the large dispersion in social security coverage across states. In northern and more urbanized states, between one-half and two-thirds of the working-age population tends to be covered by social security, while in southern, more rural, and Indian pueblo states, barely one-fifth is covered.

[14] It has been shown empirically that trade liberalization shifted the demand for labor toward states more exposed to globalization (Hanson 2007).

The *level* of coverage is clearly related to urbanization, manufacturing and public sector employment, and orientation towards globalization, but the *growth* of coverage can be high in low-coverage states due to the convergence of the economic environments across states. We see that northern, NAFTA-oriented states were the leaders in improving coverage during the 1990s, with Zacatecas and Baja California having the best results (Table 6.7). Also during the 1990s, the Federal District showed a major decline coinciding with the fall in its participation in national employment in all industries, and other "old-economy" states also lost coverage. In the 2000s, there has been interstate convergence. The northern states (except the relatively small state of Zacatecas) had lost their advantage by 2010. The figures in Table 6.7 are the result of changes in location of large firms, state demographics, actual incidence of informality, changes in labor force participation, and other events that we have not discussed. Yet, we can see that growth in coverage was modest in any state, and in fact had declined by two percentage points nationally between 2000 and 2010.

6.4 Why Has Social Security Coverage Remained So Low?

There is no silver bullet to solve the problem of informality, and a host of issues needs be considered. Families may face long-term hurdles to increase their human capital, making it difficult for them to enter formal sector jobs; too many workers are employed by low-productivity/low-growth micro-firms; the business cycle has a large impact on formality; the cost of accessing credit can constrain productivity enhancing investments for families and small firms that could encourage formalization; and low-quality services and moral hazard can reduce incentives to formalize.

6.4.1 *The Family and Coverage*

Families of workers in the formal sector are different from those in the informal sector in important ways: they have fewer children, are more educated, and have longer life expectancy.[15] To study the effect of these differences on formalization, we can contrast the results of two alternative assumptions on the relationship between the behavior of the family and social security coverage. The first proposes that the differences between the two types of families are caused by their labor status and from having social security and access to other public goods (such as education), so that once universal protection and

---

[15] It is meaningful to draw this distinction since labor mobility across formal and informal sectors is very low, and it becomes lower with the age of workers (Rodriguez Oreggia 2007).

access are achieved, the differences will disappear. An alternative hypothesis is that there are factors that induce the segregation of populations: for example, there may be ethnic, racial, or human capital differences that have accumulated through the generations that have an impact on the probability a person has to gain access to a job with social security.[16]

We present a set of projections of social security coverage that test the hypothesis that there is a degree of social segregation that will be eliminated only gradually over time. This assumes there are "formal" and "informal" families rather than a continuum between the two. Thus, if there are large groups of the population segregated from access to formal-sector jobs due to causes that cannot be changed through interventions such as fiscal policies or subsidies, convergence in terms of behavior of the two populations can be very slow.[17]

An implication of the segregation hypothesis is that fertility depends on the overall social environment in which the family lives because women face a lower valuation for their time in the labor market when they are in the informal sector for the long run (and there is only slow gradual migration of families from the informal sector to the formal). The basic argument is that people are born and grow up in a social environment that in part determines their long-term labor behavior, and that the slow evolution of this environment makes it difficult to affect change through policy interventions: in particular, human capital and fertility decisions are based upon long-term constraints that change only slowly across generations. So, although presented calculations are not based on a complete specification of behavior, they provide an estimate of the quantitative importance of the intergenerational decisions by families (including decisions on fertility and human capital investments). This framework is consistent with a main prediction in the model of Becker et al. (1994)—that rates of return to human capital investments are increasing, leading to multiple education–fertility solutions. That is, low-human capital families can become trapped in a high-fertility, low education state across generations, while others move to a low-fertility, high-human capital state.

The reference scenario that is presented here starts from separating the entire population into two groups, according to whether the head of

---

[16] To illustrate the challenge of barriers that may not respond to economic growth or fiscal reforms, note that almost 7 percent of Mexicans speak an indigenous language, and less than 1 percent do not speak Spanish, but only a native tongue. However, in Chiapas, 26 percent of the population is bilingual and 6 percent are only indigenous-language speakers. In Chiapas, only 12 percent of the working-age population is registered with social security.

[17] Related evidence has been found by Vogl (2012). He evaluates the relationship between height and wages: in Mexico, taller people earn more money, and this has to do with the educational and occupational decisions of ancestors. These patterns are more pronounced for rural and indigenous populations.

Table 6.8. Data and assumptions for demographic growth model with formal and informal sector

	2010	2050	2110
Fertility rate			
Formal	1.92	1.6	1.12
Informal	2.5	2.18	1.17
Births			
Formal	885,852	791,733	398,988
Informal	1,249,321	1,134,066	528,453
Life expectancy male			
Formal	75.8	83.8	89.8
Informal	75.6	83.6	89.7
Life expectancy female			
Formal	84.7	89.2	92
Informal	84.5	89	91.8
Internal migration: informal to formal			
Total	269,126	269,126	269,126
Male	129,569	129,569	129,569
Female	139,557	139,557	139,557
Net international migration			
Total	−346,400	−346,400	−346,400
Formal	−69,280	−69,280	−69,280
Informal	−277,120	−277,120	−277,120
Social security coverage (% of economically active population)	51.9	53.37	57.08

Source: Authors' calculations based on data sources and assumptions for individual variables, as described in the text.

household has social security or not. Each group begins with the sample fertility rates obtained from the 2010 Census of Population and Housing, and social security membership shares come from administrative figures on coverage of social security for the same year. In Table 6.8, we see the values and assumptions to develop projections of the key variables, and the main results of the analysis.[18] The insured population has a much lower fertility rate (1.92 against 2.5 in 2010). The assumption on international migration is based on the average annual number of Mexicans migrating to the US between 2002 and 2011 (United States Census Bureau 2011). The assumption of internal migration of families between the formal and the informal sectors is ad hoc—that 1 percent of families in the informal sector migrates to the formal sector each year.

Figure 6.9 summarizes the projection of social security coverage. We can see that despite the assumption of a continued (yet relatively low) migration of families into the formal sector, the informal sector remains sizeable in the long term. The reason is the higher fertility rate of families in the informal sector.

[18] We used the RUP program to develop the projections. The program is available at: https://www.census.gov/population/international/software/rup/rupdocs.html.

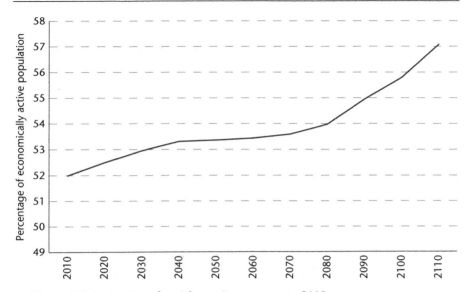

Figure 6.9. Projection of social security coverage to 2110

Source: authors' calculations based on assumptions described in Table 6.8 and in the text.

In the absence of this differential in fertility, social security coverage would approach levels above 90 percent by mid century. We ran scenarios varying the assumption on internal migration between the formal and the informal sectors, but the impact of that variation is small with respect to the effect of variations in fertility.

6.4.2 *The Firm and Coverage*

Any explanation of the causes of the lack of coverage of the social protection system has to deal with a plain fact: in large firms (100 employees or more) around 90 percent of workers are insured, while in micro-firms (less than ten employees) the figure oscillates around 7 percent (Figure 6.10). Further, since 2005 social protection coverage for workers in micro-firms has declined, while it has remained approximately constant or increased only slightly for firms with more than ten workers (Figure 6.11).

We have already noted that extending social protection without affecting productivity is a challenge posed by the Jobs WDR. Thus, increasing social protection may be a target in competition with increasing productivity. On the other hand, estimates of productivity trends show a story of stagnation between the end of the 1970s and the beginning of the 1990s, an event correlated with low wage growth (Guillermo and Tanka 2007). By the late

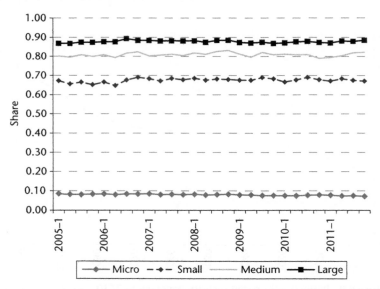

Figure 6.10. Share of formal employment in total employment by firm size, 2005–11
Note: micro-firms have 1–10 employees; small, 11–50; medium, 51–100; and large, more than 100.
Source: authors' calculations based on data from INEGI and ENOE, several years. www.inegi.org.mx.

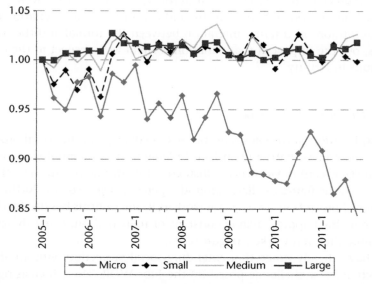

Figure 6.11. Change in the share of formal employment in total employment by firm size: 2005–11 (2005=1)
Note: micro-firms have 1–10 employees; small, 11–50; medium, 51–100; and large, more than 100.
Source: authors' calculations based on data from INEGI and ENOE, several years. www.inegi.org.mx.

1990s, productivity was finally recovering, but there remains a large share of low-productivity small firms. A hypothesis advanced by Anton et al. (2012) is that social security taxes explain the high share of micro-firms; these authors also argue that the tax for health insurance is the main obstacle to productivity growth. Yet, there is little evidence to support such an argument.

Nevertheless, low social security coverage in urban Mexico is predominantly a small and micro-firm issue. Thus, if there is something that thwarts firms from growing, low coverage is a result. Some relevant insights come from Hsieh and Klenow (2014), comparing the firm-size distribution in Mexico with India and United States. In the US, manufacturing plants "grow or die," which means that in the absence of continuous growth a plant ends up closing. On the other hand, in India companies stabilize at a smaller size. Mexico is in between. What are the possible explanations? These authors propose the following list: larger firms face greater risk of being audited by tax authorities; there are explicit regulations that limit size (in India); the marginal cost of increasing employment in a firm is greater in Mexico and India than in the United States (for example, for reasons of confidence or labor regulation, or because of an inadequate supply of human capital managers for large companies); or the marginal cost of growth can be higher in India and Mexico due to higher transport costs or regulatory differences between markets. An additional selection effect arises when the profitability of old plants favors new low-productivity plants, which further reduces average productivity. Thus, Hsieh and Klenow (2014), as well as a vast literature on informality, suggest that the set of determinants of firm-size distribution is wider than payroll taxes. For example, Lora and Fajardo (2012), using macrodata, find little evidence of social security taxes as the cause of informality for a sample of Latin American countries. LaPorta and Shleifer (2014) argue that human capital limitations are at the core of the informality problem.

It seems probable that many factors cause the very high level of informality among small firms, including not only regulation and tax issues, but also the intergenerational human capital issues we introduced in Section 6.4.1. While a general explanation of how productivity and social security interact may be complicated, research points out that small and micro-firms should be a main policy concern, because they share both very low productivity and very low social coverage.

6.4.3 *The Business Cycle*

During the past twenty years there have been three major downturns: the Tequila crisis, the dot.com crisis, and the Great Recession. In Mexico, the business cycle is associated with variations in formal employment that are larger than the variations in total employment. In the first two recessions,

Table 6.9. Distribution of households according to changes in labor income, health access, and employment by household income quintile, 2006–10

Variable	Change and direction	Quintiles				
		I	II	III	IV	V
Labor income	Amelioration	30.2	34.8	36.4	36.3	38.8
	Deterioration	51.3	50.2	50.3	50.8	49.9
	Unchanged	18.5	15.0	13.3	12.9	11.3
Health access	Amelioration	9.3	13.7	15.0	16.4	17.4
	Deterioration	17.3	19.5	20.9	21.4	19.6
	Unchanged	73.4	66.7	64.1	62.3	62.9
Employment	More	29.2	30.6	29.5	29.7	24.2
	Less	31.1	29.5	29.8	28.5	29.1
	Equal	39.7	39.9	40.6	41.8	46.7

Note: Quintile I comprises the lowest income households and Quintile V comprises the highest.
Source: Cantu et al. (2012).

total employment only returned to pre-downturn peaks two years after the bottom of the recession.

The Great Recession had different effects on different types of households. Of particular importance is how the downturn affected the most vulnerable workers: those of lower income and who do not have access to social security. Cantu et al. (2012) show how changes in labor income, health care, and employment differed along the income distribution between 2006 and 2010 (Table 6.9).

Around one-half of households in each income quintile experienced a worsening of their labor income, 20 percent a deteriorating access to health services, and 30 percent less access to employment. Thus, while the business cycle may not be a useful explanation for the permanently low levels of coverage of social security in low-income households, it correlates with the fall in coverage when some families need protection the most. Our own analysis (using the INEGI-ENOE survey) confirms that social security coverage falls during recessions: we estimate that formal employment as a share of the population fell from 19 to 17.6 percent (from the last quarter of 2000 to the third quarter of 2003, related to the dot.com recession), and in the 2008–09 recession it fell from 20 to 18.7 percent (from the first quarter of 2007 to the first quarter of 2011).

6.4.4 Financing

A lack of access to credit can limit families in investing in education and limit firms in making investments that increase productivity. The credit volume available to households is low and the interest cost is high. This situation was exacerbated during and after the 2008 crisis that resulted in tighter credit constraints. We estimate that the average financial credit per worker is very low: in 2012, mortgage credit was slightly below $500 (6,000 pesos), and credit for consumption has fluctuated at levels only slightly above that amount. In the more favorable periods during the past seventeen years, credit per worker was less than $1,000 (12,000 pesos) or roughly equivalent to three months of the average taxable earnings. The high cost of credit has induced a boom industry in pawnshops. In January 2013, legislation was enacted; although there is no statistical information in this regard, the analysis by Congress indicated that usual interest rates are 10 to 14 percent monthly in formal-sector pawnshops and that there are approximately 6,500 formal providers (Presidencia de la República 2013b). In summary, the financing cost is high for the consumer and for micro-firms, and credit constraints are especially restrictive in recessions.

Urrutia and Pratap (2012) argue that financial constraints facing companies in their working capital explains more than one-half of the fall in the total factor productivity and 74 percent of the drop in the labor productivity during the 1995 crisis. Thus, high financial costs make it more difficult for firms to invest in human capital and for small firms to invest, become more productive, and grow.

6.4.5 *Valuation of Services*

Benefits provided through formal social protection may be low quality when pensions pay low implicit rates of return, when administrative costs are high, or through uncertainty in the value of the health, pension, and other benefits. Also, programs such as health care or childcare may provide low-quality services. When quality is low, it increases the deadweight loss of taxation by increasing the elasticity of the supply of labor towards the formal sector, and thus increases the likelihood of individual workers opting for informal jobs.

Yet, measuring the effect of low-quality services on social security registration is a thorny issue because of moral hazard running in multiple directions. Health, general disability, and social insurance in general are always less than actuarially fair due to administrative costs. Imperfect information in key processes—such as the decision to grant a general disability benefit—reduces actuarial fairness even more. On the other hand, moral hazard also runs from the user to the social security agency in a system where individuals can register with ease as they near retirement age or become ill, not having paid most of their previous working life. This means that agencies have to balance their decision-making process between incurring type I or type II errors (granting benefits to the not disabled or not granting benefits to a truly disabled person; or providing access to health care to a non tax-payer, or denying access to a tax payer).

Whatever the policy, errors in granting benefits reduce the value of the benefit in relation to contributions. Even more, entitlement to social security benefits in Mexico means that individuals can stay out of the system while healthy and become contributors after becoming sick, and individuals can move within the rules to optimize their yield in the pension system. For example, given historical levels of inflation, for a worker who contributed for forty-five years and retired in 2012, payments made into the pension fund have had a negative rate of return; on the other hand, a worker who paid taxes only during the minimum number of periods required to obtain a pension (500 weeks for most of the current labor force) in a discontinuous career would be receiving several times the value of contributions. In summary, administrative costs and moral hazard reduce the quality of the benefits and services of social security, and thus increase the relative cost of formal jobs.

6.5 Summary and Conclusions

Formalization, measured by social security registration, has been stagnant over nearly two decades, remaining at around 50 percent of employment, with no discernible long-term upward trend. Many jobs are not linked to social benefits, and one-half of the population or more does not have health insurance or a pension provided by social security. Widening social programs is dependent upon fiscal revenues, and Mexico has lower levels of revenues and coverage when compared with Brazil, Argentina, Uruguay, and Costa Rica. Employment has grown substantially and unemployment has remained low, but real wages have not increased much in two decades and large disparities remain in the coverage of social security across states.

We explored the role that social segmentation can have in the long-term evolution of social security coverage; to the extent that such segmentation exists, the increase in coverage of social security can take a very long time. It is also evident that the problem of low coverage is concentrated in micro-firms, where only 7 percent of workers have social security. High costs of finance for households and small firms can limit their ability to invest in human capital and in other forms of capital to raise productivity and escape from informality. Reforms to taxes and benefits can have only a limited impact on reducing informality if social segmentation keeps many families under economic constraints that limit investment and access to opportunities. Our projections show that the process of bringing all of the population into social security could be slow due to segregation whereby many households have no real access to the formal sector due to long-term constraints in human capital accumulation or to discrimination. Moreover, these households have higher-than-average fertility rates, which could have significant implications on the future size of the formal and informal sectors given the limited mobility between them.

Any discussion about formalization in Mexico has to start with this reality of social segmentation, as well as the large gap in social protection and productivity between workers in small and large companies. The low social security coverage for employees in micro-firms is quantitatively the largest policy problem. The tax system and social security have in effect specialized in serving medium-sized and large enterprises, and it is difficult to imagine that a simple change in the tax laws can make a dent in the fundamental problem of serving micro-firms and the self-employed. Labor supply in Mexico—as almost anywhere else—has very low elasticity with respect to wages or taxes, so any small change in taxation on labor is unlikely to generate any significant change in registration to social security, and a large decrease in payroll taxes will mean a large loss in revenue (without major gains in formalization).

A significant development in Mexican labor and social protection policy has been the enactment of unemployment insurance. With a low open unemployment rate, formal employment accounts for the largest share of the variation in employment over the business cycle. Relatively few countries in Latin America have unemployment insurance, and the existing programs tend to rely on individual savings to finance unemployment spells (Conferencia Interamericana de Seguridad Social 2006). The Mexican program (if approved by Congress) will be a mix of a mandatory UI savings account and a contributory plan. This is an important development for labor policy, but its effect on informality will be small.

The federal government strategy to expand social protection has been based on noncontributory programs. By 2012, more adults received pension benefits from noncontributory programs than from social security, and in the area of health care, the strategy has been to expand noncontributory services in explicit competition with social security. The government that took office in 2012 set the integration of a universal social security system as a general policy target. Congress enacted a universal pension program that takes some steps to unify the pension system. IMSS will be in charge of administering the social security and the noncontributory pensions; however, no rules have been issued to explain how both types of pension can be integrated from the tax-benefit stance. Thus, we expect an active debate in the coming years on the ways the tax and benefit system has to evolve (see Martinez et al. 2013).

Returning to our initial comparison with Chile and the Republic of Korea, two of the more successful economies in terms of productivity growth and expansion of social protection—but still with a substantial informal share in the labor market, it is not hard to reflect on the complex road ahead for Mexico. Those countries have acted decisively in creating regimes for pensions and health insurance to support universal coverage. Mexican reforms in these areas have fallen short in expanding social protection provided through contributory social insurance, and Mexico has fallen behind those countries in terms of reducing the informal economy (see Miranda et al. 2013). True, Mexico may have larger internal social differences than South Korea or Chile due to its greater size and ethnic diversity. Yet, it seems that eliminating the segmentation of the pension and health systems is an area of opportunity for policy reform to reduce the hurdles to formalization of jobs in the long run. The Peña Nieto government vowed to press on with a "universal social security" agenda. This seems to be the best way to proceed to meet Mexico's formalization challenge. However, the expansion of noncontributory plans in this country with a deeply uneven distribution of income will remain as a major challenge for social and fiscal policies.

Acknowledgments

This chapter was prepared with the support of the International Development Research Centre (IDRC) and the Inter-American Conference of Social Security (CISS). The content does not represent the views of these organizations.

References

Aguayo-Tellez, E., Airola, J., and Juhn, C. (2010). Did Trade Liberalization Help Women? The Case of Mexico in the 1990s. Working Paper No. 16195. National Bureau of Economic Research.

Aguilera, N., Martinez, G., and Miranda, M. (2013). "Social health insurance." *Well-Being and Social Policy*, 9(1):43–64. URL: http://ssrn.com/abstract=2358669. [Accessed May 2016.]

Anton, A., Hernandez, F., and Levy, S. (2012). *The End of Informality in Mexico? Fiscal Reform for Universal Social Insurance*. Washington, DC: Inter-American Development Bank.

Becker, G.S., Murphy, K.M., and Tamura, R. (1994). Human capital, fertility, and economic growth. In: *Human Capital: A Theoretical and Empirical Analysis with Special Reference to Education* (3rd Edition), Gary S. Becker (ed.), Chicago: The University of Chicago Press.

Campos Vásquez, R.M., Esquivel, G., and Lustig, N. (2012). The Rise and Fall of Income Inequality in Mexico: 1989–2010. El Colegio de México, Centro de Estudios Económicos. Serie Documento de Trabajo IV.

Cantu, R., Gomez, A., Lopez-Videla, B., Rodriguez-Oreggia, E., and Villarreal, H.J. (2012). The Worsening of the Labor Market and Its Effects in the Poverty of Mexico. CISS-IDRC/World Bank. URL: http://www.ciss.net/special-studies/. [Accessed May 2016.]

Chun, C.B., Kim, S.Y., Lee, J.Y., and Lee, S.Y. (2009). *Health Systems in Transition. Republic of Korea Health System Review.* Copenhagen: World Health Organization Regional Office for Europe.

Conferencia Interamericana de Seguridad Social (Inter-American Conference on Social Security (CISS)). (2006). *The Americas Social Security Report 2007. Globalization and Social Protection.* Mexico: CISS.

Consejo Nacional de Evaluación (CONEVAL) (2013). Pensión para adultos mayores. Ficha de monitoreo. México: CONEVAL.

Consejo Nacional de Evaluación (CONEVAL) (2015). Inventario CONEVAL de Programas y Acciones de Desarrollo Social. Federal, estatal y municipal. México: CONEVAL. URL: http://www.coneval.gob.mx/. [Accessed May 2016.]

Garcia-Cuéllar, R. (2000). "Is Trade Good for Women? Evidence for the Lower-Skilled in Pre- and Post-NAFTA Mexico." PhD dissertation, chapter 1. Cambridge, MA: Economics Department, Harvard University.

Grubb, D., Lee, J.-K., and Tergeist, P. (2007). Addressing Labour Market Duality in Korea. OECD Social, Employment and Migration Working Papers No. 61. Paris: DELSA/ELSA/WD/SEM(2007)16.

Guillermo, S. and Tanka, B. (2007). "Measuring total factor productivity growth in Mexican manufacturing: The story before and after trade liberalization." *Ensayos sobre Política Económica*, 25(53):168–219.

Hanson, G.H. (2007). Globalization, labor income, and poverty in Mexico. In: *Globalization and Poverty*, Ann Harrison (ed.), Chicago: University of Chicago Press.

Heckman, J., Lochner, L.J., and Todd, P.E. (2008). Earnings Functions, Rates of Return and Treatment Effects: The Mincer Equation and Beyond. National Bureau of Economic Research Working Paper Series 13780.

Heckman, J. and Pagés, C. (eds). (2004). *Regulación y empleo: Lecciones de América Latina y el Caribe.* Santiago: CIEDESS and CISS.

Homeland Security. Yearbook of Immigration Statistics. (Various years). Washington, DC. URL: https://www.dhs.gov/yearbook-immigration-statistics. [Accessed May 2016.]

Hsieh, C.-T. and Klenow, P.J. (2014). "The life cycle of plants in India and Mexico." *Quarterly Journal of Economics*, 129(3):1035–84.

Instituto de Seguridad y Servicios Sociales de los Trabajadores del Estado (ISSSTE). *Anuario Estadístico.* (Several years). URL: http://www2.issste.gob.mx:8080/index. php/mder-int-finanzas-anuarios. [Accessed May 2016.]

Instituto Mexicano del Seguro Social (IMSS). *Memoria Estadística.* (Several years). URL: http://www.imss.gob.mx/conoce-al-imss. [Accessed May 2016.]

Instituto Nacional de Estadística y Geografía (INEGI). Censo de población y vivienda 2010. URL: http://www.inegi.org.mx/est/contenidos/proyectos/ccpv/cpv2010/Default. aspx.

Instituto Nacional de Estadística y Geografía (INEGI). Derechohabiencia y Servicios de Salud. URL: http://www3.inegi.org.mx/sistemas/sisept/default.aspx?t=msoc01& s=est&c=22594.[Accessed May 2016.]

Instituto Nacional de Estadística y Geografía (INEGI). Encuesta Nacional de Empleo (ENE). URL: http://www.inegi.org.mx/sistemas/microdatos2/encuestas.aspx?c=14649& s=est.[Accessed May 2016.]

Instituto Nacional de Estadística y Geografía (INEGI). Encuesta Nacional de Ingresos y Gastos de los Hogares (ENIGH). URL: http://www.inegi.org.mx/est/contenidos/Proyectos/Encuestas/Hogares/regulares/Enigh/default.aspx. [Accessed May 2016.]

Instituto Nacional de Estadística y Geografía (INEGI). Encuesta Nacional de Ocupación y Empleo (ENOE). URL: http://www.inegi.org.mx/sistemas/microdatos2/encuestas.aspx?c=14439&s=est. [Accessed May 2016.]

Juarez, L. (2008). Are Informal Workers Compensated for the Lack of Fringe Benefits? Free Health Care as an Instrument for Formality. Discussion Paper 08-04. Instituto Tecnológico Autónomo de Mexico, Centro de Investigación Economica.

Juhn, C., Ujhelyi, G., and Villegas Sánchez, C. (2012). Men, Women, and Machines: How Trade Impacts Gender Inequality. Working Paper No. 18106. National Bureau of Economic Research.

Knaul, F.M., González-Pier, E., Gómez-Dantés, O., García-Junco, D., Arreola-Ornelas, H. et al. (2012). "The quest for universal health coverage: Achieving social protection for all in Mexico." *Lancet*, 380(9849):1259–79. Published online August 16, 2012. doi: http://dx.doi.org/10.1016/S0140-6736(12)61068-X.

LaPorta, R. and Shleifer, A (2014). "Informality and development." *Journal of Economic Perspectives*, 28(3):109–26.

Levy, S. (2008). *Good Intentions, Bad Outcomes: Social Policy, Informality and Economic Growth in Mexico*. Washington, DC: Brookings Institution Press.

Lora, E. and Fajardo, J. (2012). Employment and Taxes in Latin America: An Empirical Study of the Effects of Payroll, Corporate Income and Value-added Taxes on Labor Outcomes. IDB Working Paper Series No. 334.

Martinez, G. (2010). Unemployment in Mexico: Policy options, unemployment insurance and a comparison with EPL rules. Inter-American Conference on Social Security.URL: http://ssrn.com/abstract=1619309. [Accessed May 2016.]

Martinez, G. (2012a). Comments on: The end of informality in Mexico? Fiscal reform for universal social insurance, by Arturo Anton, Fausto Hernandez and Santiago Levy. Inter-American Conference on Social Security. URL: http://papers.ssrn.com/sol3/papers.cfm?abstract_id=2066141. [Accessed May 2016.]

Martinez, G. (2012b). An estimation of labor supply elasticities for Mexico. Inter-American Conference on Social Security. URL: http://ssrn.com/abstract=2109933. [Accessed May 2016.]

Martinez, G., Aguilera, N., and Miranda, M. (2013). "Citizen-centered universal social security." *Well-Being and Social Policy* 9(1):3–21. URL: http://ssrn.com/abstract=2364605. [Accessed May 2016.]

Miranda, M., Aguilera, N., and Martinez, G. (2013). "Pensions, employment and family programs." *Well-Being and Social Policy* 9(1):23–43. URL: http://ssrn.com/abstract=2358645. [Accessed May 2016.]

Nuschler, D. and Siskin, A. (2010). Social Security Benefits for Noncitizens: Current Policy and Legislation. Domestic Social Policy Division. Congressional Research Service.

OECD/ECLAC/CIAT (2015). *Revenue Statistics in Latin America*. Paris: OECD Publishing. doi: http://dx.doi.org/10.1787/rev_lat-2015-en-fr.

OECD/OCDE (Organization for Economic Cooperation and Development) (2011a). *OECD Employment Outlook 2011*. Paris: OECD Publishing. OECD/OCDE. *Pensions at a Glance 2011: Retirement-income Systems in OECD and G20 Countries.* Paris: OECD Publishing.

OECD/OCDE (2012a). *Pension Markets in Focus.* URL: http://www.oecd.org/daf/fin/privatepensions/PensionMarketsInFocus2012.pdf. [Accessed May 2016.]

OECD/OCDE (2012b). *Project on Jobs for Youth.* URL: www.oecd.org/employment/youth. [Consulted November 2012.]

OECD/OCDE (2014) . *Revenue Statistics 2014.* Paris: OECD Publishing. URL: http://dx.doi.org/10.1787/rev_stats-2014-en-fr. [Accessed May 2016.]

Peña Nieto, E. (2013). Speech to the National Productivity Committee (Comité Nacional de Productividad). Mexico. URL: http://www.presidencia.gob.mx/articulos-prensa/instalacion-del-comite-nacional-de-productividad/. [Accessed May 2016.]

Perry, G., Maloney, W., Arias, O., Fajnzylber, P., Mason, A., and Saavedra-Chanduvi, J. (2007). *Informality-Exit and Exclusion.* World Bank Latin American and Caribbean Studies. Washington, DC: World Bank.

Presidencia de la República (2013a). Decreto por el que se reforman y adicionan los artículos 4o., 73 y 123 de la Constitución Política de los Estados Unidos Mexicanos, en materia de seguridad social universal. Mexico. URL: http://www.apartados.hacienda.gob.mx/presupuesto/temas/ppef/2014/ingresos/08_4_123_cpeum.pdf. [Accessed May 2016.]

Presidencia de la Republica (2013b). Decreto por el que se reforman los artículos 65 Bis y 128; y se adicionan los artículos 65 Bis 1, 65 Bis 2, 65 Bis 3, 65 Bis 4, 65 Bis 5, 65 Bis 6 y 65 Bis 7 a la Ley Federal de Protección al Consumidor. Diario Oficial de la Federación, 16-01-2013.

Ramskogler, P. (2010). The State of Wage Convergence in the European Monetary Union. Department of Economics Working Paper Series No. 130. WU Vienna. URL: http://epub.wu.ac.at/864/. [Accessed May 2016.]

Rodríguez-Oreggia, E. (2007). "The informal sector in Mexico: Characteristics and dynamics." *Social Perspectives,* 9(1):89–175.

Rofman, R. and Oliveri, M. L. (2011). La cobertura de los sistemas previsionales en América Latina: conceptos e indicadores. Banco Mundial. Serie de Documentos de Trabajo sobre Políticas Sociales N° 7.

Samaniego, N. (2002). "Las politicas de mercado de trabajo en Mexico y su evaluación." Serie Macroeconomia del Desarrollo. Division de Desarrollo Economico (CEPAL, 2002).

Secretaria de Desarrollo Social (Sedesol). (2011). "Quinto Informe de Labores." (Mexico: Sedesol, September 2011). URL: 2012.sedesol.gob.mx/work/models/SEDESOL/Resource/2140/V_InformeLabores2012SEDESOL.pdf. [Accessed May 2016.]

Secretaria de Salud (SSA) (2012). *Sistema de Cuentas en Salud a Nivel Federal y Estatal (SICUENTAS) Mexico.*

Secretaria del Trabajo y Previsión Social (STPS) (2015). "Servicio Nacional de Empleo." URL: http://www.stps.gob.mx/. [Consulted July 2015.]

Slander, S. and Ogorevc, M. (2010). "Labour cost convergence in the EU: Spatial econometrics approach." *Privredna kretanja i ekonomska politika,* 122:27–51.

United States Census Bureau. (2011). Current Population Survey. URL: http://www.census.gov/population/foreign/files/cps2010/T4.1.xls. [Consulted November 2011.]

Urrutia, C. and Pratap, S. (2012). "Financial frictions and total factor productivity: Accounting for the real effects of financial frictions." *Review of Economic Dynamics*, 15(3):336–58.

Vasquez Colmenares, G. P. (2012). *Pensiones en México: La próxima crisis*. Mexico: Siglo XXI Editores.

Vogl, T. (2012). Height, Skills, and Labor Market outcomes in Mexico. Working Paper 18318. National Bureau of Economic Research.

World Bank (2012). World Development Report 2013: Jobs. Washington, DC: World Bank.

World Health Organization (2015). Global Health Expenditure Database. Table of key indicators for all member states. 2015. URL: http://apps.who.int/nha/database/Key_Indicators/Index/en. [Accessed May 2016.]

7

Tunisia

Jobs to Combat High Youth Unemployment

Abdel-Rahmen El Lahga, Mohamed Ali Marouani,
and Rim Ben Ayed Mouelhi

7.1 Introduction

No one expected that the political upheavals triggered in late 2010, following a desperate act by street vendor Mohamed Bouazizi, would lead to the spectacular and rapid downfall of the longstanding Ben-Ali regime in Tunisia. Tunisia had been hailed as a model in the MENA region for its political stability, economic competitiveness, and social achievements. The country has managed fairly sustained economic growth of around 5 percent over the past few decades, while diversifying its production base and stabilizing its macroeconomy by bringing down inflation and government deficits. The 2016 Doing Business report ranked Tunisia 74th, one of best performers in the MENA region. On the social front, the country has experienced significant improvements in living standards, educational attainment, social protection, and gender equality, compared to regional norms. According to the latest poverty profile published by the National Institute of Statistics (INS 2012), the poverty rate dropped dramatically from 35.5 percent in 2000 to 15.5 percent in 2010. In terms of human development, the country is ranked in the high Human Development Index (HDI) group, according to UNDP statistics.

However, this portrait of Tunisia as a success story masks widening socioeconomic disparities and high unemployment rates, especially among the growing cohort of educated youth, which reflect structural weaknesses at both economic and political levels. Economically, while macro fundamentals may be sound, the fruits of economic growth have not been distributed fairly across the regions of Tunisia. Living standards, including access to quality social services and basic infrastructure, are unevenly distributed between the poor inland regions and the rich coastal regions that benefit from preferential treatment by the government. Western regions have the lowest per capita government expenditures, whereas almost all regions in the east have been above the national average (INS 2012). Bibi (2011) shows that growth over 2000–05 appears to have been inequitably distributed and to have exacerbated social exclusion, in that the living standards of the poor have grown less rapidly than those of the rest of the population. When we look at governance, it is important to note that the last decade saw a significant increase in corruption and clientelism, whereby ruling families close to the regime systematically benefited from preferential contracts with the government (e.g., privatization deals, protection against competing imports). Investment, which never fully recovered after a significant slowdown in the mid 1980s, has trended over the last two decades at around a rate of 25 percent of GDP, which is low compared with similar countries such as Morocco and Jordan.

Politically, the authoritarian Ben Ali regime generated public support through a virtual monopoly over communications networks, generous welfare provisions (subsidies on foods, fuel, housing, free health cards, etc.), and public-sector employment guarantees. However, the government faced increasing challenges sustaining these benefits, and a vast gap emerged between the large groups receiving benefits and growing segments of the population excluded from such forms of social welfare. This eroded the legitimacy of the Ben Ali regime. As a result, the political system faced, and continues to face, serious challenges in simultaneously responding to the democratic aspirations of the Tunisian people while effectively addressing pressing economic and social concerns.

Three years after the revolution, Tunisia managed its democratic transition by adopting a new constitution and holding free elections in 2014. However, economic challenges remain, including the persistence of high unemployment rates, especially among youth, and sluggish growth overall.

For the foreseeable future, the main challenge is thus to help youth satisfy their aspirations in terms of employment and improved wellbeing by ensuring more and better employment opportunities by removing barriers to job creation. This means that the focus needs to also be on the quality, not only the quantity, of jobs created. Good jobs are central to various forms of social and economic development. The Jobs WDR clearly established the transformational nature of employment, which affects living conditions and overall productivity, and improves social cohesion (World Bank 2012). Thus, creating good jobs with a maximum benefit for development is the real challenge. The success of the democratic transition absolutely depends on resolving this issue. Indeed, mitigating temptations of illegal migration to Europe or rallying behind terrorist groups depends closely on the availability of good economic opportunities for young Tunisians in their own country.

A natural starting point to achieve this goal is therefore to identify the main job-related challenges, especially those facing youth, as a way to identify which reforms are needed. This chapter aims to contribute to the current debate around this key concern by addressing the following central questions: What are good jobs in Tunisia? What are the obstacles to the creation of more good jobs? How can policies overcome these obstacles? These questions are addressed through an empirical analysis of the three-way relationship between jobs, living standards, and productivity.

The layout of the chapter is as follows. Section 7.2 describes the labor market and the structure of unemployment in Tunisia. Section 7.3 analyzes the link between employment status and various aspects of individual wellbeing. Section 7.4 investigates the dynamics of productivity growth, employment, and job reallocation. The main conclusions and policy recommendations are presented in Section 7.5.

7.2 Labor Market Characteristics

We begin this section with a presentation of the basic demographic characteristics of the population. We then describe the structure of the labor force and the nature of unemployment, especially between 2005 and 2014. While a more thorough analysis of the evolution of the Tunisian labor market would benefit from a longer period of data coverage, we could not obtain microdata for earlier years. Our analysis largely relies on data from a series of annual labor force surveys (LFS) undertaken by the Institut National de la Statistique (INS) covering about 130,000 households per year.[1]

7.2.1 Demographic trends

The rural–urban distribution of Tunisia's inhabitants has changed profoundly over the past half century. The rural share of the population declined from 60 percent in 1966 to 33 percent in 2014. The age structure of the population has also changed radically over the last five decades. Indeed, a declining birth rate reduced the share of the population under the age of 15 from 46 percent in 1966 to 24 percent in 2014. The size of youth population (defined henceforth as 15–29 years) has remained relatively important. It rose as a share of the population by about 3 percentage points over the same period (Table 7.1).

---

[1] Unless stated otherwise, all numerical data presented in Sections 7.2 and 7.3 are drawn from the LFS (various years), and the 2014 population census.

Table 7.1. Distribution of population by age group, 1966–2014

Age	1966	1975	1984	1994	2004	2009	2014
0–4	18.6	16.0	14.6	11.0	8.1	8.1	8.9
5–14	27.9	27.8	25.1	23.8	18.6	15.6	14.9
15–19	8.4	11.3	11.4	10.7	10.7	9.4	7.5
20–24	6.5	8.7	9.7	9.3	10.1	10.1	8.4
25–29	6.5	5.7	7.7	8.5	8.7	9.5	8.5
30–59	26.8	24.8	24.9	28.5	34.2	37.3	40.0
60 or older	5.5	5.8	6.7	8.3	9.3	9.9	11.8
Total	100	100	100	100	100	100	100

Source: INS, Census and population surveys various years.

Table 7.2. Migration flows between 2009 and 2014 and unemployment rates in 2014 by region

Region	Outgoing migration 2009–14	Incoming migration 2009–14	Outgoing/ incoming migration ratio	2014 unemployment rate
District of Tunis	154.9	201.2	0.77	13.4
North east	35.3	40.0	0.88	12.5
North west	53.5	18.7	2.86	20.3
Center east	57.8	86.7	0.67	11.1
Center west	60.1	20.6	2.92	18.4
South east	32.7	32.9	0.99	17.7
South west	20.4	14.6	1.40	22.9
TOTAL	414.7	414.7	1.00	14.8

Source: authors' compilation using 2014 INS data

The INS expects this "youth bulge" to last until 2020. Tunisia's age structure is creating demographic pressures in the labor market, with a 2 percent annual labor force growth rate.

The share of the population living in inland areas (north west, center west, and south west) declined from around 35 percent in 1994 to around 29 percent in 2014. More detailed INS statistics on internal migration for 2009–14 indicate that about half a million individuals (around 5 percent of the whole population) migrated in these years, largely from the more deprived western areas to the more prosperous coast. The location of employment opportunities is partially responsible for internal migration. Indeed, in Table 7.2, we show that, at the regional level, the outgoing-to-incoming migration ratio is closely related to the unemployment rate. More detailed statistics for 2012 show that the most commonly reported primary reason for internal migration is looking for jobs (60 percent), well above studying (20 percent), marriage (10 percent), and other reasons (10 percent). Most migrants look for work in tourism and in the labor-intensive manufacturing sector, both of which are concentrated in coastal regions. While migration from the west and/or rural areas of the country has helped many Tunisians improve their standard of living, it has also increased pressure on labor markets in the east, especially in urban areas.

7.2.2 Labor Force Characteristics

The labor force participation rate was estimated at 47 percent in 2014, representing a total of about 3.9 million individuals in the labor market. This aggregate rate, however, masks significant differences between population groups. The recently released 2014 census results show that the labor force participation rate is about 65 percent among men, similar to the rate in many other countries in the MENA region, but only 40 percent for the 15–29 year age group and just 28 percent for women. Table 7.3 shows that the composition of the labor force by age group and gender has remained stable in recent years; there are about 1 million women and about 1.8 million youth, aged 15–29. The youth share has been rising slowly over the last few decades and has now peaked. As noted above, the population forecast of the INS shows that the share of youth would start to decrease in 2020. Consequently, the pressure of a large youth cohort in the labor market should decrease at that time.

The low youth participation rate is essentially due to the high secondary school enrollment rate,[2] which delays youth transitions into the labor force, and the lack of employment opportunities, which we will discuss in detail later in this chapter.

Table 7.3. Labor force composition by age group and gender, 2005–14

	2005	2007	2009	2011	2014
Labor force composition by age*					
15–19	6.2	5.5	4.5	4.4	3.3
20–24	13.1	12.9	11.8	12.1	9.3
25–29	16.5	17.1	17.3	17.6	15.6
30–34	14.5	14.3	15.4	15.1	16.7
35–39	13.1	12.7	12.6	12.3	13.8
40–44	11.7	11.8	11.8	11.4	11.9
45–49	9.8	10.0	10.4	10.1	10.4
50–59	10.8	11.7	12.8	13.1	15.0
60+	4.1	4.0	3.4	3.9	4.0
Labor force composition by gender*					
Male	73.8	73.0	73.1	73.3	70.0
Female	26.2	27.0	26.9	26.7	30.0

Note: * Columns in each panel add up to 100.

Source: authors' compilation using 2014 LFS data.

---

[2] According to the Ministry of Education statistics, the enrollment rate is estimated at around 92 percent, which is among the highest rates in the MENA region.

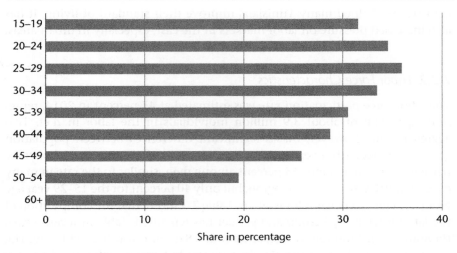

Figure 7.1. Share of women in the labor force by age group, 2013
Source: authors' calculations using 2014 Census data.

When we look at the situation of women, it should first be noted that while their participation rate is low relative to European countries, it remains close to the regional (MENA) average. Women's low participation rate could hide other forms of unpaid work, such as domestic work, care giving, and so forth. It is worth noting that despite important progress in terms of legislation to promote gender equity, social norms and the role assigned to women within the family continue to be serious obstacles for women's participation in the labor market. After marriage and/or childbirth, women tend to stop looking for work and exit the labor market. A more careful look at labor force participation among women shows that their share of the labor force declines significantly with age (Figure 7.1). Finally, it should be noted that female participation is strongly shaped by educational attainment. According to the 2013 LFS, the participation rate among women ranges from 44 percent for those with secondary education to 92 percent for those with a university degree.

Another important feature of Tunisia's labor force is the significant change in educational attainment due to the country's progress in this area. The high concentration of tertiary education is a notable feature of the "youth bulge" in the country. As shown in Table 7.4, the proportion of the labor force with higher education increased rapidly from 13 percent in 2005 to about 24 percent in 2014, while the share of those with primary education or less fell from about 52 percent to 38 percent over the same time frame. But at the same time, the largest group in the labor force is composed of 1.5 million (38.6 percent) individuals with just secondary education. This group is often forgotten in discussions of labor market issues, which tend to focus on the less

Table 7.4. Labor force by level of education, 2005–14

Education	2005		2007		2009		2011		2014	
	Size (000s)	Percent	Size (000s)	Percent	Size (000s)	Percent	Size (000s)	percent	Size (000s)	Percent
Illiterate	427.2	12.7	410.7	11.7	391.7	10.6	364.0	9.5	366.5	9.5
Primary	1,272.7	37.9	1,284.7	36.5	1,268.2	34.4	1,271.5	33.1	1,090.6	28.2
Secondary	1,211.9	36.1	1,288.0	36.6	1,386.3	37.8	1,457.7	37.9	1,493.2	38.6
Higher	443.9	13.3	533.8	15.2	636.2	17.2	746.9	19.5	908.4	23.5
Unknown	3.4	–	4.5	–	6.8	–	4.5	–	7.0	–
Total	3,359.1	100	3,521.7	100	3,689.2	100	3,844.6	100	3,866.5	100

Source: INS, LFS various years and 2014 Census data.

educated and those with higher education. This distribution of education levels in the labor force does not match well with the labor demanded by firms. While Tunisian firms continue to primarily demand and employ low- and medium-skilled workers, young people who leave school with a secondary diploma or a university degree have neither the right level of education nor the specific qualifications required.

7.2.3 Unemployment

Despite maintaining a fairly high growth rate, at an average of 5 percent annually during the last three decades, the unemployment rate has increased steadily in Tunisia, reaching an historical high of 18.9 percent, or 740,000 individuals, in 2011 (Figure 7.2).[3] This pattern of growth with persistently high unemployment was exacerbated by the political upheavals in early 2011 that led to massive job losses in the range of 200,000 positions and consequently to a striking increase in the unemployment rate over the last couple of years. The recent 2014 population census estimates the unemployment rate at 15 percent (572,000 individuals).

Unemployment is much higher among women than men (Figure 7.2): 22 percent of women in the labor force were unemployed in 2014 compared to 11 percent for men. Women were particularly affected by the job losses between 2009 and 2011, a period in which the female unemployment rate increased from 18.8 percent to 24 percent. Firms tend to hire more men than women, most particularly in the private sector. Moreover, the lack of women's geographical mobility and their preference to queue for public-sector positions or a family-friendly job could also explain the observed difference in the unemployment rates between men and women.

---

[3] According to Stampini and Verdier-Chouchane (2011), Tunisia has a low employment growth elasticity of about 0.4, reflecting a low propensity to create jobs.

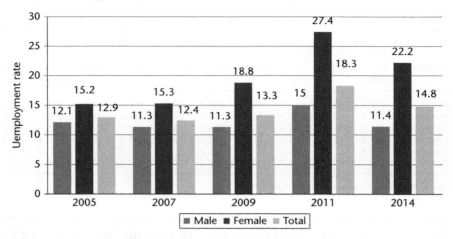

Figure 7.2. Unemployment rates, overall and by gender, 2005–14
Source: INS, LFS various years.

Table 7.5. Unemployment rates by age group, 2005–14

Age group	2005	2007	2009	2011	2014
15–19	27.7	29.3	33.6	43.6	33.3
20–24	28.4	27.3	29.9	41.8	33.7
25–29	21.6	21.8	25.7	34.5	28.3
30–34	11.6	11.6	11.4	19.0	17.0
35–39	6.3	5.8	5.6	8.8	9.8
40–44	4.8	3.9	4.3	4.3	6.0
45–49	3.8	3.0	3.9	2.8	4.6
50–59	3.2	2.5	3.2	2.5	3.9
60 or older	1.2	2.4	1.2	1.4	4.0

Source: INS, 2014 Census.

7.2.4 Youth Unemployment

We now turn our attention to the alarming problem of youth unemployment that represents the predominant challenge in the Tunisian labor market. Unemployment rates by detailed age group are shown in Table 7.5. The unemployment rate is about 33 percent for youth under the age of 25 and is 28.3 percent for the 25–29 year age group. These rates are considerably higher than the national rate of 14.8 percent in 2014 and are more than twice the rate among the population aged 30 and over. While their share in the labor force is only 28.2 percent, youth (15–29 years old) account for about 60 percent of overall unemployment. Data from Silatech-Gallup (2009) suggest that the majority of young people are resigned to unemployment. In 2009, less than 38 percent of youth in Tunisia "said it was a good time to find a job in the city or area where they live" (Silatech-Gallup 2009). Moreover, not only may young people not easily find a job, they also face barriers in creating their own through self-employment. About six in ten youths consider that it is not easy to obtain a loan to start a business (Silatech-Gallup 2009).

In addition to the negative effects of a lack of employment on mental health, delinquency, wage scarring, and so on, there are significant social costs faced by a society with such a waste of human capital. Persistently high youth unemployment may also curtail hopes for a better future among the Tunisian young, increase frustration and create uncertainty regarding the transition to marriage and the formation of their own families, and potentially lead to greater instability. According to the 2009 Silatech-Gallup data on young Arabs' attitudes, 59 percent of Tunisian youth say that "starting a family is essential and something they cannot live without."

The lack of job opportunities also contributes to weakening the collective identity. After January 2011, the Tunisian society recognized "unemployed young" as a social status in itself. The unemployed young claim publicly such status and they have even organized their activity under the auspices of the "National Union of Unemployed." The creation of such an organization in fact reflects increasingly radical attitudes toward a society that can no longer meet the aspirations of young people. This suggests that the issue of job creation has to be moved to the top of the policy agenda.

While it is commonplace to consider the phenomenon of high youth unemployment as a direct consequence of the growing numbers of new entrants in the "youth bulge" generation, a number of other factors are important as well. These factors originate from both labor demand and labor supply. The most convincing explanations relate to skill mismatches, a slow and inefficient transition from school to work, and a segmented labor market that impedes the mobility of young people. We will also argue later in this chapter that a significant factor for Tunisia's inability to create jobs stems from stagnant firm growth and the limited transition of firms from lower to higher value-added activities.

7.2.4.1 SKILLS MISMATCH

Table 7.4 shows the rising share of the labor force with university schooling. This has led to a mismatch of skills between the number and quality of jobs created and the average level of education in the labor force. This is reflected in the significant difference in unemployment rates by education level. Youth with the lowest levels of education (illiterate and primary) have lower unemployment rates than those with secondary and especially higher education (Table 7.6). The unemployment rate for young university graduates was estimated at 41.9 percent in 2014. Overall, people with university degrees accounted for about 31 percent of total unemployment in 2014. There is a particularly acute gender gap in the unemployment rate for young university

Table 7.6 Unemployment rates by education for youth, 15–29 years old, 2014

	Female	Male	Total
Illiterate	26.1	23.3	24.3
Primary	26.9	22.1	23.5
Secondary	31.8	27	28.5
University	47.9	33.2	41.9
Total	36.9	26.7	30.7

Source: INS, 2014 census.

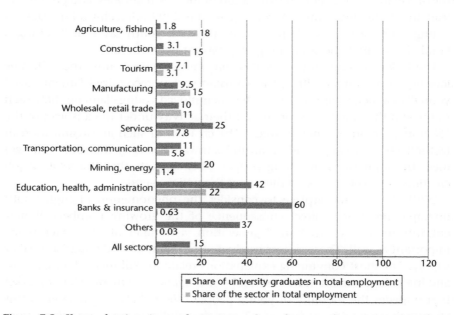

Figure 7.3. Share of university graduates in total employment by sector and share of sector in total employment in 2013
Source: INS, LFS 2013.

graduates. Young female university graduates had an unemployment rate about 15 percentage points higher than male graduates in 2014, 48 percent among women compared to 33 percent for men.

The inability of the Tunisian economy to absorb the growing number of university graduates is illustrated by looking at the share of university graduates in employment by sector, as shown in Figure 7.3. Major economic sectors, such as agriculture and fisheries, manufacturing, and wholesaling, have a rather limited capacity to absorb university graduates (10 percent or less of their total labor force) compared both to their respective contribution to GDP and employment. On the other hand, sectors that do have significant shares of university graduates, such as public administration, education, health

(42 percent), and finance and insurance (60 percent), are not as important in the country's overall employment.

High unemployment rates among young people with secondary or higher education could also be explained by their preference for public-sector jobs, which come with significant wage premiums and are accompanied by various non-wage benefits such as paid leave, generous social insurance coverage, and, often most importantly, job security. The unconditional wage premium in the public sector is highest among workers with secondary education and university graduates (Angel-Urdinola and Helel 2012). This leads many educated job-seekers to queue for a public-sector job rather than look for work in the private sector. This applies to female graduates who are most affected by unemployment and are less likely to be employed in the private sector, which is perceived to be inhospitable to women (Stampini and Verdier-Chouchane 2011). Despite an increasing scarcity, public-sector jobs remain highly valued because of the private returns. Indeed, data from Gallup show that Tunisian youth are more likely to prefer working in the public sector (56 percent) over any other sector, assuming similar wage and work conditions.

However, the issue of skills mismatches is complicated and only offers a partial explanation for the youth unemployment problem. The private sector continues to send weak and unclear signals for the type of skills it needs. On the other hand, there is a good match between education system outcome and students' perception of their preferred future employers (i.e., government), even if their actual hiring rates are not high.

The higher-education system continues to prepare people for jobs in public administration, education, and health. According to 2011 statistics from the Ministry of Higher Education, about half of university students were enrolled in the social sciences and humanities fields that constitute the main specializations required by the public administration. Despite the high unemployment rates, "69 percent of Tunisian youth say they are satisfied with the educational system in the city or area where they live" (Silatech-Gallup 2009). At the same time, despite signals from the government that recruiting will be vastly reduced, the reality is that a sufficient number of new hires take place to encourage young graduates to hope that, even if it's a long wait, they could one day find a job in the public sector. For example, after the 2011 political upheavals, the government recruited a large number of university graduates and converted fixed-term contract employees to permanent contracts, which reinforced individuals' preferences for public-sector jobs, even if they must endure a waiting period.

7.2.4.2 SLOW AND INEQUITABLE TRANSITION TO WORK

High youth unemployment can also be interpreted as a consequence of a slow and increasingly difficult transition from school to work. First-time job-seekers

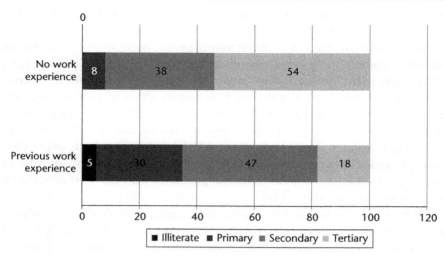

Figure 7.4. Distribution of job-seekers by education level and previous work experience, 2011

Source: authors' calculations based on INS, LFS 2011.

as a share of total unemployment increased from 38 percent in 2005 to 46 percent in 2011. The problem of labor market entry seems particularly serious for women, with first-time job-seekers accounting for almost 60 percent of the unemployed. Figure 7.4 shows that individuals with a secondary diploma or a university degree presently constitute nearly all first-time job-seekers.

In addition to skills mismatches, difficult transitions from school to work can be explained by information asymmetry and the limited capacity of labor inter-mediation systems to correct this. Data from Silatech-Gallup indicate that 83 percent of Tunisian youth say knowing people in high positions is critical to getting a job. In other words, using informal networks is a culturally acceptable practice. However, relying on informal networks may be an important source of inequality of opportunity among job-seekers, since individuals from poor families or disadvantaged regions are less likely to have the networks that will help them find a job. The public intermediation services have low institutional capacity and inefficient mechanisms that would support better integration of job-seekers.

Another symptom of the difficult school-to-work transition is that educated youth experience longer spells of unemployment than workers with primary education or less. Figure 7.5 shows that about half of university graduates and one-third of those with secondary education were unemployed for more than twelve months at the time of the 2011 LFS, as opposed to just 13 percent among the illiterate. Long spells of unemployment may lead to a loss of skills, thus significantly reducing employment prospects. The lack of job opportun-ities may also result in a larger number of discouraged workers, particularly

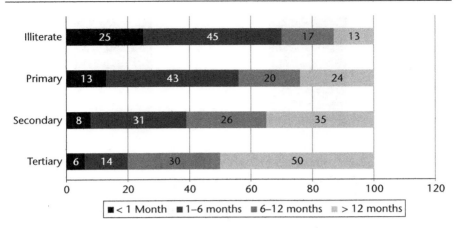

Figure 7.5. Duration of unemployment by education level, 2011
Source: authors' calculations based on INS, LFS 2011.

since many educated young people can rely on family support when they exit the labor force.

7.2.4.3 SEGMENTATION OF THE LABOR MARKET

Weak labor market institutions are another important factor contributing to the employability problem. A business climate characterized by labor market rigidities can discourage hiring, especially on a formal basis. Since young workers begin on the "outside" and do not have a track record to signal to employers, they tend to be more affected than other workers.

We can distinguish between three types of employment contracts: (i) formal open-ended contracts, (ii) formal fixed-term contracts, and (iii) no contract or informal work. Both formal types of employment are covered by the social insurance system, but as mentioned earlier, non-wage benefits tend to be less generous in private formal employment than in public administration. About 45 percent of employed persons in 2011 worked in the informal sector and 12 percent had a short-term contract. Workers with primary education or less are most involved in precarious work, with slightly over half employed in the informal sector. As shown in Figure 7.6, the picture is more difficult in rural areas, where 64 percent work in the informal sector. This pattern is due to certain characteristics of the rural labor market, such as demand for unskilled workers and low wages, both of which lead to jobs being precarious or being in informal segments of the labor market.

Segmented labor markets that create barriers for young people to enter the formal sector can have negative consequences on not only their initial earnings but also their longer-term employment trajectories. Some young people, especially the better educated, may choose to stay out of the labor

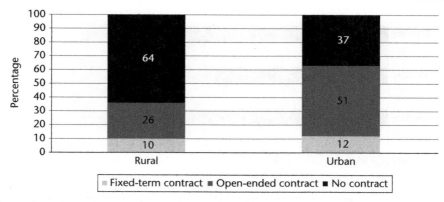

Figure 7.6. Employment by type of contract, rural vs. urban residence, 2011
Source: authors' calculations based on INS, LFS 2011.

market or queue for scarce formal-sector jobs rather than accept something in the informal sector. Other young people will accept an informal job if they consider it to be the best way to enter the labor market. However, workers in the informal sector may then face difficulties exiting that sector and often cycle between unemployment and informal work, especially in the absence of appropriate policies to reduce job precariousness.

The minimum wage is often not enforced in Tunisia, especially in the informal sector and among workers with fixed-term contracts. More than 60 percent of workers in these categories earn less than the minimum wage (Rutkowski 2012). Low-wage workers in these categories have limited training opportunities, poor working conditions, and a lack of health insurance and social security. This finding is reflected in Silatech-Gallup data which indicate that "81 percent of youth say that addressing the issue of quality jobs would have the greatest impact" on their transition to adulthood.

7.3 Jobs and Living Standards

As discussed earlier, the Tunisian workforce is increasingly young and educated, but the economy is not generating enough high-quality jobs in terms of pay and protection. As a result, unemployment is increasing, especially for the well-educated youth, and new entrants have limited options beyond jobs in informal and/or low-productivity sectors with meager earnings. This has important impacts on living standards and quality of life given that employment income is the primary source of household income in Tunisia. As will be argued below, beyond their direct contribution to income and thus monetary poverty, jobs affect other dimensions of wellbeing, such as living conditions, nutritional status, and the educational achievement of children.

In this section, we analyze the disparities in wellbeing across labor force statuses. More specifically, we investigate the links between unemployment and the nature of jobs on the one hand, and various monetary and non-monetary dimensions of household wellbeing on the other. The analysis of monetary poverty is based on per capita expenditures from the 2005 Household Consumption and Budget Survey—the most recent available data.[4] In order to assess links between employment status and non-monetary poverty, we use 2004 Census data to construct a wealth index as a proxy for household living conditions, including housing, access to public facilities, and asset ownership. Child nutritional status is calculated from the well-known MICS (Multiple Indicators Cluster Survey) survey sponsored by UNICEF and conducted in 2006 by the Office National de la Famille et de la Population (ONFP). Data on child educational achievements are derived from the 2009 Program for International Student Assessment (PISA) survey.

7.3.1 Overview of Poverty Trends

The poverty headcount index declined dramatically from 29.9 percent in 1980 to 11.4 percent in 2005 (Table 7.7).[5] This is a remarkable performance, even

Table 7.7 Poverty headcount rate and GDP growth overall and by sector, 1980–2005

Poverty rate	1980	1985	1990	1995	2000	2005
Total	29.9	19.9	14.1	17.1	9.9	11.4
Urban	18.7	12.0	8.9	10.1	6.2	7.5
Rural	38.9	29.2	21.6	28.1	16.1	18.6

GDP growth rate (percent)	1980–85	1985–90	1990–95	1995–2000	2000–05
Total GDP	3.7	3.0	3.9	5.6	4.2
Agriculture	7.1	3.8	−1.1	8.3	4.5
Manufacturing	7.9	5.2	5.7	5.3	2.8
Textiles, clothing	9.2	7.1	7.7	4.6	−0.02
Services	3.9	5.7	5.3	5.5	6.4

Source: World Bank (2003) and authors' compilation using 2005 Household Budget and Consumption Survey data and national accounts.

[4] The poverty line is set by the INS, at 740 Tunisian dinars (TND) for large cities, 626 TND for urban areas, and 518 TND for rural areas (2005 prices).
[5] More recent poverty rates are available for 2010 but the methodology used was different from earlier estimates. The poverty headcount rate in 2010 was 15.5 percent. The conclusions in this subsection would not change even if the more recent poverty rates were included.

though progress was uneven over this period. Poverty trended upwards over 1990–95, and more recently between 2000 and 2005. It should be noted that, while it has been reduced across the board, poverty remains a primarily rural phenomenon, with more than twice the incidence in rural areas than in urban areas.

Table 7.7 illustrates how poverty reduction occurred in a period of relatively high economic growth. Rural poverty was more sensitive to growth in the agricultural sector than to total GDP growth. Redistributive policies, via several social protection programs, did not play a significant role in reducing poverty. The Gini coefficient remained stable or nearly unchanged throughout the 1980–2005 period, at around 0.4.

The effect of economic growth on poverty reduction occurs primarily through the process of job creation. Regional-level data illustrate how access to the labor market plays an important role in improving living standards. As can be seen in Figures 7.7 and 7.8, there is a strong correlation between the unemployment rate and living standards. The eastern coastal region, where the manufacturing and tourism sectors are mostly located, has lower unemployment rates and poverty rates than inland regions. The coastal regions accounted for 85 percent of Tunisia's GDP and 84 percent of total employment in 2005. The western regions are essentially rural, are the most income deprived, and have the highest unemployment rates in the country. Most people in these regions are farm workers or smallholder farmers. Given the high volatility of farm production and consequently of labor demand due to highly unstable rainfall, many people supplement their income by working in the construction sector or engaging in retail activities.

7.3.2 Poverty and Employment

In this subsection, we analyze whether poverty status is correlated with the household head's labor force status and sector of employment. Table 7.8 shows these relationships using two poverty measures: the headcount (poverty incidence) and the poverty gap.[6]

Unsurprisingly, the group with the highest risk of poverty is comprised of households headed by an unemployed person. Nearly 38 percent of such households were poor in 2005, compared to 11.4 percent nationally. However, it should be noted that this group is relatively small in size, and thus only accounted for 7 percent of overall poverty. Among households where the head was employed, the incidence of poverty was much higher where the head was working in construction (26 percent) and agriculture (19 percent) than in

---

[6] The poverty gap measures the depth of poverty and is calculated as the mean shortfall from the poverty line expressed as a percentage of the poverty line.

Distribution of the unemployment rate (%)

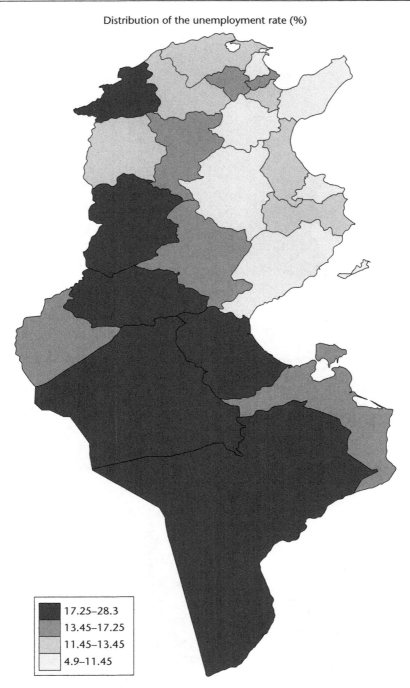

■	17.25–28.3
▨	13.45–17.25
▧	11.45–13.45
□	4.9–11.45

Figure 7.7. Unemployment rates by region, 2010
Source: authors' calculations based on INS 2010.

Distribution of the headcount (%)

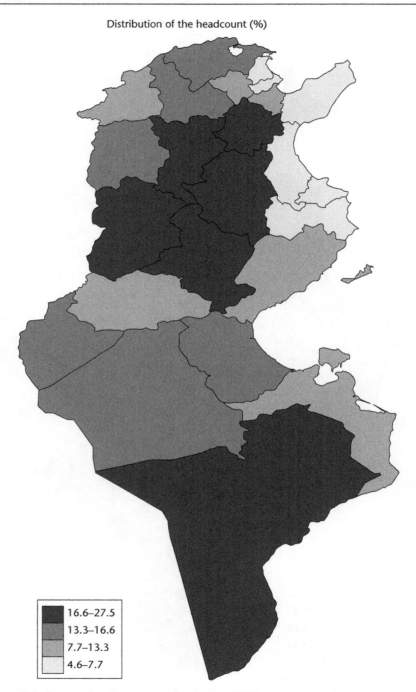

■	16.6–27.5
▨	13.3–16.6
▨	7.7–13.3
□	4.6–7.7

Figure 7.8. Poverty headcount rates by region, 2005
Source: authors' calculations based on 2005 HBCS.

Table 7.8. Poverty headcount and poverty gap by household head's labor force status and sector of employment, 2005

Labor force status	Poverty headcount (percent)	Distribution (percent)	Poverty gap (percent)	Distribution (percent)
Agriculture	19	29	5	29
Manufacturing	5	4	1	4
Mining, energy	7	1	1	1
Construction	26	22	6	22
Services	7	12	1	11
Administration, education, health	5	7	1	6
Unemployed	38	7	11	9
Retired	3	3	1	3
Undeclared activities	12	15	3	15
Total	11.4	100	3	100

Source: authors' compilation using 2005 Household Budget and Consumption Survey.

other sectors. Households headed by an individual working in these two very large sectors accounted for 51 percent of all poverty in 2005. The incidence of poverty was relatively low (less than 6 percent) among households headed by a worker in the manufacturing and public administration, education, and health sectors, and, to a lesser extent, the services sector. The picture remains essentially the same when looking at the poverty gap. The gap was highest among workers in the agricultural and construction sectors, as well as among households with an unemployed head (Table 7.8). As Figure 7.9 shows, these findings are not sensitive to the poverty line chosen.

A similar story emerges when we consider the household head's type of occupation. As Figure 7.10 shows, the incidence of poverty is highest among the unskilled, farm workers, and artisans and this is not sensitive to the level of the poverty line.

Although the expansion of the construction sector has helped many unskilled workers improve their living conditions, job instability and a lack of social protection in this sector make construction employees a vulnerable group. These problems are prevalent in the agricultural sector as well, which led the government to launch a large program to lease state-owned farms to the private sector in the 1990s for the purpose of growth and job creation in the agricultural sector. More than 200,000 ha were leased to agricultural engineers on a long-term basis with the expectation that they would create jobs for the poor. Under these landholding conditions, and given that agricultural output is highly dependent on rainfall, households' ability to effectively use their land to generate income remained fairly limited. Insecure land titles are also a major problem limiting farmers' ability to sell, rent, or mortgage land; this is also an important obstacle to the modernization of agriculture and expansion of irrigation because it implicitly constrains credit.

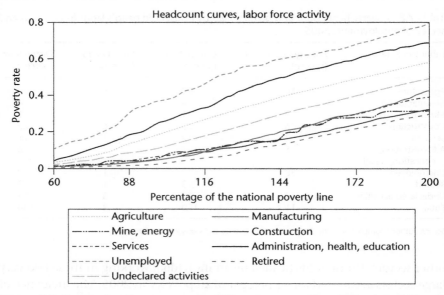

Figure 7.9. Poverty headcount rates for different poverty lines by household head's labor force activity, 2005

Source: authors' calculations based on 2005 HBCS.

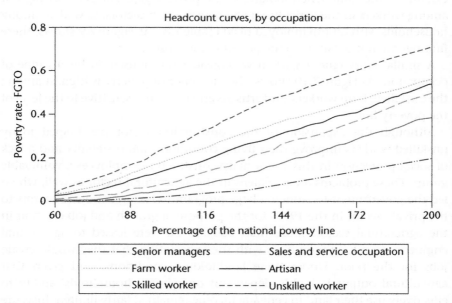

Figure 7.10. Poverty headcount rates for different poverty lines by household head's occupation, 2005

Source: authors' calculations based on 2005 HBCS

While from a social standpoint, the development of the agricultural sector is a key factor to reduce poverty, work in agriculture is not seen as providing stable and high remuneration. Thus, many, particularly unskilled, workers have migrated to coastal areas, looking for jobs in the manufacturing sector.

Tunisian manufacturing is mostly comprised of light industry, especially textiles, and has helped create large numbers of jobs for poor, low-skilled workers, allowing them to improve their wellbeing. However, given the profound changes in the size and quality of the labor force, the present capacity of the manufacturing sector to absorb new entrants into the labor market seems rather limited. Moreover, the manufacturing sector currently tends to hire workers with no more than a secondary education, and existing firms in the sector are unlikely to be able to meet Tunisia's challenge of absorbing the growing numbers of university graduates.

7.3.3 Employment and the Multidimensional Nature of Poverty

Given the often weak relationship between income and other dimensions of poverty, often including access to and the quality of social services and housing conditions, it is appropriate to look at the connection between employment type and wellbeing from a non-monetary perspective. In this subsection we analyze non-monetary deprivation and employment using a composite welfare index based on household living conditions, ownership of durable goods, and the nutritional status of household members.

The results presented in Table 7.9 confirm the findings of the monetary analysis. They show that the incidence of deprivation, as measured by the

Table 7.9. Distribution of households by wealth index quintile and household head's labor force activity, 2004

Sector	Wealth index quintile (percent distribution)					
	Poorest	Poorer	Middle	Richer	Richest	Total
Agriculture	59.8	19.5	9.6	6.7	4.5	100
Industry	15.9	23.0	24.9	21.4	14.8	100
Construction	30.6	29.0	20.3	13.3	6.7	100
Retail	9.6	16.1	22.5	27.1	24.8	100
Other services	9.7	14.7	18.5	21.5	35.6	100
Admin., health and education	4.6	8.8	16.8	28.9	40.9	100
Undeclared activities	15.1	20.3	22.9	21.9	19.8	100
Unemployed	20.9	27.7	26.3	17.4	7.7	100

Source: authors' compilation using data from the 2004 Census.

237

wealth index,[7] is greatest for households with heads who are unemployed or working in the agricultural or construction sectors. About 60 percent of people in households headed by a worker in the agricultural sector are in the first quintile, as opposed to less than 5 percent in the public administration, education, and health sector. Workers in the construction sector and the unemployed are also over-represented in the poorest quintile.

Having a job not only improves economic security and family wellbeing but also provides an opportunity to break the vicious circle of intergenerational transmission of poverty and exclusion by promoting children's outcomes. There is a widespread agreement that health, nutrition, and educational achievements early in life are crucial to individual cognitive and physical development. Children's living conditions in their early years may permanently impact the course of their entire life. An individual's inability to develop skills or to pursue higher education is rooted in living conditions early in life and primary school performance. In this respect, the father's working status and occupation, which is beyond children's control, may be an important source of inequality of opportunity among children. In a previous analysis based on data from the PISA survey and Tunisian health surveys, El Lahga et al. (2012) show that children of the unemployed, part-time, and/or "lower" occupation workers have worse educational outcomes and nutritional status than other children. The observed disparities suggest that employment can be a source of inequality of opportunity for children.

7.4 Productivity and Jobs

The labor market challenges facing Tunisia's young people are not related exclusively to a lack of skills and ineffective transition from school to work. As shown in Figure 7.11, the gap between job vacancies and labor supply in the formal sector has been increasing since 2000. The constraint for youth is above all a lack of labor demand for formal and high-quality jobs rather than a labor supply problem.

Hence, relying exclusively on supply-side reforms would only partially impact labor market performance and would not offer a satisfactory solution to the job-creation problem, including the lack of opportunities available to youth. Parallel demand-side reforms are clearly needed which enhance the

---

[7] This index is a composite measure of a household's living condition approximated by the ownership of selected assets: (e.g., television, bicycles; housing characteristics such as type of dwelling and access to water and electricity). The index is obtained by factor analysis of its different components.

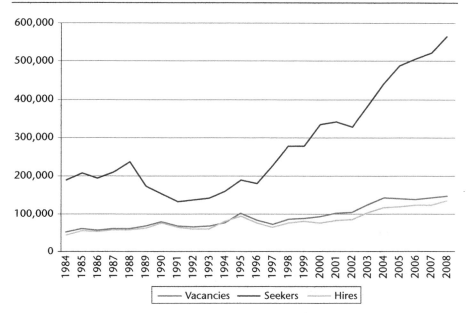

Figure 7.11. Job vacancies, job-seekers, and hires, 1984–2008
Source: ANETI, Ministry of Vocational Training and Employment, 2011.

dynamism of firms, the primary engines in the creation of viable and more productive jobs. This section uses firm-level data to analyze job reallocation and productivity patterns and discusses possible sources for improving job creation in the private sector.[8]

7.4.1 *Firm Size and Employment Growth*

We start by documenting patterns of employment and firm size, and then turn to job creation during the last two decades. Tunisian firms tend to be small, compared to international standards. As shown in Figure 7.12, one-person (self-employed) and micro- (1–5 employees) firms account for 97 percent of all firms. However, employment is disproportionally concentrated

[8] The data used in this section are drawn from the National Annual Firm Survey (NAFS) for the period 1997–2007. The survey contains information on employment and value added at the firm level and therefore provides information on productivity. We rely also on recent results on job creation compiled by Rijkers et al. (2013) from the INS registry of firms, the Repertoire National des Entreprises (RNE), for the 1996–2010 period. The RNE tracks all private-sector firms and provides better information on firm labor dynamics than the NAFS, but does not contain reliable information on value added.

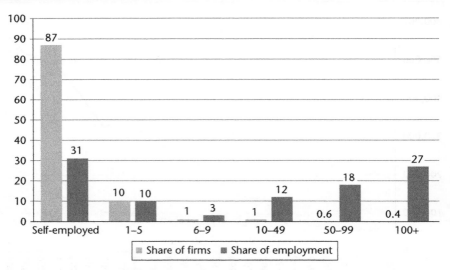

Figure 7.12. Distribution (% of firms and) employment by firm size, 2010
Source: INS, National Annual Firm Survey

in medium and large firms (ten employees and more), which accounted for only 2 percent of all firms but 57 percent of total employment in 2010.

Such patterns cannot be explained by the sectoral composition of the economy or production technology as the distribution of firms by size changed negligibly during the last two decades while the economic structure and technology changed considerably. We conjecture that Tunisia's financing constraints and institutional context may account to a considerable degree for these patterns. First, if access to credit is limited and start-up costs are high, one would expect more entry of micro- and small firms, which have small credit requirements. Second, under a corrupt regime, large firms attract rent-seeking activities from the government and influential families while small firms do not. Thus, many firms are kept small to operate outside the realm of corrupt activities.

Another significant fact is that, even over a relatively long period, very few formal-sector firms grow. Table 7.10 shows that less than 2 percent of one-person firms in 1996 were larger in 2010. Small and medium-sized firms (ten to forty-nine employees) are more likely to die than grow, and less than 2 percent of them became large firms (100 employees or more) by 2010. The overall picture that emerges is the clear lack of dynamism of Tunisian firms.

This stagnant private sector is also illustrated by Tunisia's disappointing job creation performance. As shown in Figure 7.13, the net job creation of continuing firms was negative over the 1996–2010 period. Job creation has been disproportionately driven by the entry of new, (mostly one-person) firms.

240

Table 7.10. Distribution of firms by number of employees in 2010 by size category in 1996

Firm size 1996 (number of employees)	Firm size in 2010 (number of employees)*							
	Exit	1	2–5	6–9	10–49	50–99	100–999	1,000+
1	66.9	30.9	1.8	0.2	0.1	0.0	0.0	0.0
2– 5	39.0	31.1	24.5	4.1	1.2	0.0	0.1	0.0
6–9	38.7	19.0	14.3	17.4	9.9	0.5	0.3	0.0
10–49	28.7	21.1	5.9	9.3	28.2	4.8	2.0	0.0
50–99	24.9	20.9	3.1	1.8	18.6	18.7	12.0	0.0
100–999	20.1	19.7	2.2	1.1	7.3	10.1	38.0	1.5
1,000+	12.1	9.1	0.0	0.0	3.0	0.0	36.4	39.4

Note: * Rows add up to 100.
Source: Rijkers et al. (2013).

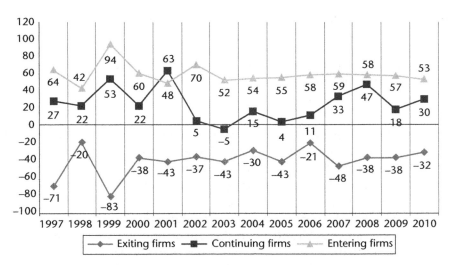

Figure 7.13. Net job creation (in 000s) by firm status, 1996–2010
Source: INS, National Annual Firm Survey.

Moreover, almost all jobs created between 1996 and 2010 were created by young firms, aged five years or less (Figure 7.14).

To further investigate the relationship between job growth dynamics and firm size, we use a panel of individual firm data drawn from the NASF. The percentage increase of employment for a firm i at time t is defined as:

$$g_{it} = \frac{L_{it} - L_{it-1}}{n_{it}}$$

Job creation (in 000s)

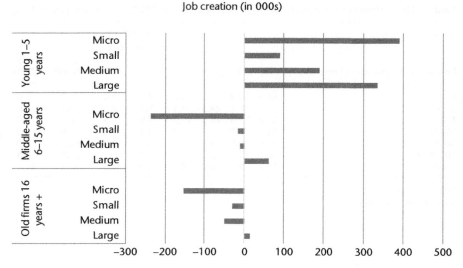

Figure 7.14. Job creation by firm size and age, 1996–2010

Source: National Annual Firm Survey

where employment at firm i in year t is given by L and average employment at firm i over time t is given by:

$$n_{it} = \frac{L_{it} + L_{it-1}}{2}$$

We use a simple regression model in which employment changes by firm and year are regressed on firm-size dummies,[9] industry fixed effects to control for industry heterogeneity, and year effects to control for macroeconomic shocks. A firm's size is defined by the average employment over the observation period. Table 7.11 presents the regression results.

Larger firms have higher growth rates than smaller ones and the magnitude of this effect increases significantly with size. These estimates are consistent with the hypothesis that big firms create more jobs than smaller ones. Meanwhile, the year dummy coefficients are negative and often significant, which is consistent with the fact that the job growth rate declined over the analyzed period.

7.4.2 Job Reallocation

To investigate how patterns of job creation and destruction compare across periods, sectors, and firm size, we follow Davis and Haltiwanger

[9] Dummy variable are used to distinguish four firm-size categories: small firms employing between six and nine persons; medium firms employing between ten and forty-nine persons; large firms employing between 50 and 199; and extra-large firms employing 200 or more.

Table 7.11. Regression results on firm employment growth, 1997–2007

	Coefficient	Coefficient
Firm-size dummies		
Medium	0.086***	0.09***
Large	0.17***	0.19***
Extra-large	0.26***	0.29***
Year dummies		
1999	−0.009	−0.009
2000	−0.014	−0.015
2001	−0.0038	−0.003
2002	−0.06***	−0.058***
2003	−0.031***	−0.031***
2004	−0.055***	−0.055***
2005	−0.044***	−0.044***
2006	−0.096***	−0.096***
2007	−0.063***	−0.064***
Sectors dummies	No	Yes

Note: Dependent variable is firm employment growth. 1998 is the excluded year and small firms are the excluded size group.

*** p value <.01.

(1992) and define gross job creation and destruction rates in sector s at time t as following:

$$JC_{st} = \sum_{g>0} \frac{n_{it}}{N_{st}} * g_{it} \quad \text{and} \quad JD_{st} = \sum_{g<0} \frac{n_{it}}{N_{st}} * |g_{it}|$$

N_{st} is a measure of the size of sector s at time t. $N_{st} = \sum n_{it}$

The index of job creation (JC) is defined as the weighted sum of the new jobs available through the expansion of existing firms and the creation of new establishments within the sector. The index of job destruction (JD) is defined as the weighted sum of employment losses in shrinking and dying establishments within a sector. Adding up job creation and job destruction produces a measure of the gross job reallocation rate (JR) in the sector. Subtraction of job destruction from job creation produces the net job creation ($JNet$).

$$JR_{st} = JC_{st} + JD_{st} \quad \text{and} \quad JNet_{st} = JC_{st} - JD_{st}$$

As shown in Table 7.12, the net job growth rates indicate losses in the extractive, transport, chemicals, building materials, finance, education, and hotels sectors and gains in agriculture, commerce, textile and clothing, housing, public utilities, electrical and mechanical engineering, health, construction, telecom, and other services. Over the period studied, there is little evidence of a pronounced change to a service-based economy that accompanies the development process. A number of services have negative average annual net employment change and agriculture and many manufacturing industries have positive rates.

Table 7.12. Rates of job creation, job destruction, and job reallocation, and net employment change by sector, 1997–2007

Sector	Job creation (%)	Job destruction (%)	Job reallocation (%)	Net employment change (%)
Agriculture	21.9	13.4	35.3	8.5
Commerce	8.2	6.1	14.3	2.1
Construction	17.3	15.6	32.9	1.7
Extractive	1.6	5.0	6.6	−3.4
Finance	1.3	2.2	3.5	−0.9
Hotels	8.2	10.2	18.4	−2.0
Agro-food	8.3	8.3	16.6	0.0
Chemicals	12.8	15.2	28.0	−2.4
Other industries	10.7	9.2	19.9	1.5
Building material	6.5	6.8	13.3	−0.3
Mechanical and electrical	11.0	7.2	18.2	3.8
Textile and clothing	9.1	7.7	16.8	1.4
Housing	11.9	7.7	19.6	4.2
Public utilities	2.9	2.0	4.9	0.9
Health	5.7	3.4	9.1	2.3
Other services	4.4	3.2	7.6	1.2
Transport	4.3	5.0	9.3	−0.7
Telecoms	3.5	0.6	4.1	2.9
Education	6.5	7.3	13.8	−0.8

Source: author's calculation based on National Annual Firm Survey.

Table 7.13. Mean rates of job creation, job destruction, and job reallocation and net employment change by size, 1997–2007

Size	Job creation (%)	Job destruction (%)	Job reallocation (%)	Net employment change (%)
Small	3.0	30.5	33.5	−27.5
Medium	6.1	19.0	25.1	−12.9
Large	7.6	11.0	18.6	−3.4
XLarge	9.5	5.9	15.4	3.6

Source: author's calculation based on National Annual Firm Survey.

As shown in Table 7.13, the dynamics of job creation and destruction vary significantly across size classifications. The net job growth rates indicate very significant losses in medium and small firms (12.9 percent and 27.5 percent, respectively) over the 1997–2007 period. These firms account for the bulk of job destruction. Only the extra-large firms (200 employees or more) experienced positive net job creation (3.6 percent) over the period. In fact, as firm size increases, job destruction rates decrease, while job creation rates increase. As noted by Haltiwanger et al. (2010), "Firms that have the most jobs create

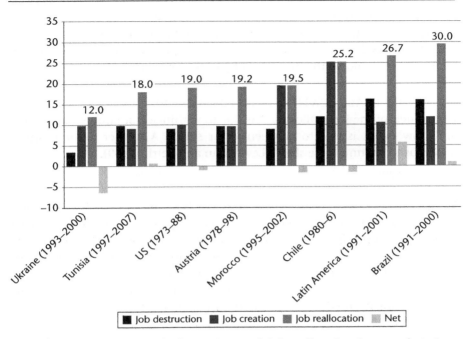

Figure 7.15. Job creation, job destruction, and job reallocation in manufacturing, selected countries

Source: authors' compilation based on various studies.

the most jobs."[10] From a policy perspective, our results suggest that if employment growth is the main objective, concentrating job-creation incentives on the largest firms where most of the jobs are being created is probably most efficient.

To compare our results with evidence from other countries, we focus on the manufacturing sector. Annual job reallocation (i.e., the sum of job creation and destruction) was, on average, 18 percent from 1997 to 2007 in Tunisia's manufacturing industries, slightly above the average for all sectors (16 percent). The net job growth indicates very little employment gain in Tunisian manufacturing (0.7 percent) in these years. Figure 7.15 compares these results with estimates of job reallocation in manufacturing in some developed and developing countries.[11] These results suggest that there is generally more reallocation in developing countries than in developed countries, as would be expected since developing countries are often growing faster and changing

[10] Job reallocation is more important in small firms because they are more volatile. Informality probably plays a role in this higher reallocation rate.
[11] It should be noted that this comparison is limited by sample coverage differences, including time period.

their specialization pattern (Bottini and Gasiorek 2009). However, this does not seem to be the case for the Tunisian manufacturing sector, where job reallocation is low compared to other developing countries. One of the explanations could be the low flexibility of the labor market.

7.4.2.1 JOB REALLOCATION BETWEEN AND WITHIN SECTORS

How much of the job reallocation is due to within-sector employment shifts and how much is due to between-sector shifts? A further decomposition allows us to capture these shifts (Levinsohn and Petrin 1999):

$$Between_t = \sum_s |net_s| - |\sum_s net_s| within_t = \sum_s JR_s - \sum_s |net_s|$$

From Table 7.14, we can see that a vast majority of the excess job reallocation is within sectors (about 71 percent). About 29 percent is accounted for by employment shifts between sectors. On the other hand, when we compare the between component in the Tunisian manufacturing sector with the available evidence, our results reveal that the between component is about 15 percent in Tunisian manufacturing over the studied period. It is higher than the results found by Davis and Haltiwanger (1992) for the US (between 1972 and 1986).

7.4.3 *Productivity*

Sectoral productivity trends, based on National Annual Firm Survey (NAFS) data for the period 1997–2007, are shown in Table 7.15. Almost all of the sectors with the highest average productivity are in services: finance, telecoms, transport, public utilities, commerce, and other services. The sectors with the lowest productivity are outside services: textiles and clothing, construction,

Table 7.14. Job reallocation between and within sectors, 1998–2007

	Between (B)	Within (W)	Between as a percentage of total reallocation (B/(B+W) in %)
1998	0.2	1.6	11.7
1999	0.9	2.0	29.9
2000	1.0	1.5	40.8
2001	0.8	1.7	32.3
2002	0.5	1.4	25.7
2003	0.3	1.5	16.4
2004	0.7	1.1	37.4
2005	0.9	1.2	43.0
2006	0.7	1.5	32.3
2007	0.5	2.2	20.0
1998–2007	0.7	1.6	28.9

Source: author's calculation based on National Annual Firm Survey.

Table 7.15. Average productivity trends by sector, 1997–2007

	Mean	Standard deviation	Minimum	Maximum
Finance	12.4	1.3	9.1	13.9
Extractive	11.9	0.9	10.3	13.2
Telecoms	11.0	0.4	10.3	11.7
Transport	10.5	0.1	10.3	10.7
Public utilities	10.3	0.3	9.9	10.7
Commerce	10.1	0.1	9.8	10.2
Other services	9.9	0.6	9.1	11.0
Chemicals	9.8	0.3	9.5	10.6
Education	9.8	0.6	8.9	10.8
Housing	9.8	0.3	9.5	10.3
Agro-food	9.7	0.1	9.6	10.0
Construction materials	9.7	0.2	9.4	10.0
Health	9.7	0.5	8.8	10.5
Other manufacturing	9.6	0.2	9.4	10.2
Mechanical and electrical	9.2	0.1	9.0	9.4
Hotels	8.8	0.2	8.6	9.2
Agriculture	8.7	0.3	8.1	9.2
Construction	8.6	0.2	8.3	8.9
Textile and clothing	8.5	0.1	8.3	8.8

Note: productivity measured as log value added per worker. Minimum and maximum values are the lowest and highest annual productivity measures during the period.

Source: National Annual Firm Survey.

agriculture, mechanical and electrical manufacturing, and other manufacturing. Productivity levels are comparable across all firm-size categories.

Productivity increased between 1997 and 2007 in some tertiary sectors including telecoms, education, health, and other services. The finance sector experienced significant productivity growth until 2002 and then declined.[12] Over the same period (1997–2007), sectoral productivity stagnated or grew at only a very slow rate.

7.4.3.1 DECOMPOSING PRODUCTIVITY CHANGES BY SECTOR

Changes in productivity depend partly on the change in any given firm's productivity ("within" effect) and partly on changes in aggregate productivity arising from the entry and the exit of firms ("between" or turnover effect). This latter component represents the contribution to productivity growth resulting from the reallocation of resources toward more productive firms. To quantify these two effects, we decompose industry productivity measures over the 1997–2007 period using the Olley and Pakes (1996) methodology.[13]

[12] See El Lahga et al. (2012) for a detailed sectoral analysis.

[13] In a given year the aggregate industry productivity measure (P_t) is the sum of the unweighted average of firm productivity and a weighted average of the firms' individual productivities (TFP_{it}) with an individual firm's weight (pm_{it}) corresponding to its output's share in total industry output in a particular year.

$$P_t = T\bar{F}P_{it} + \sum_i \triangle pm_{it} \triangle TFP_{it} = \text{within effect} + \text{between effect}$$

The decomposition shows that the within component, driven by internal restructuring and organizational change, was the most important source of productivity growth in all cases. The between (reallocation) component was insignificant in all sectors, except for the extractive and finance industries (only until 2002).[14] These results indicate that the reallocation of output from less-productive firms to more-productive firms has not been very important. Obstacles to free entry and exit, among other factors, have slowed the reallocation process and it is likely they have slowed productivity growth.

7.4.4 Job flows and Productivity

Table 7.16 shows how net job creation and job reallocation relate to productivity levels at the industry level. In general, high-productivity service sectors, such as finance, transport, and other services, experienced small and even negative net job creation over the 1997–2007 period. On the other hand, several low-productivity industries, typically in the goods-producing sector,

Table 7.16. Job reallocation, net job creation, and productivity by sector, 1997–2007

Sector	Job reallocation (%)	Net Job creation (%)	Productivity level (log of the value added per worker)
Finance	3.5	−0.9	12.3
Extractive industries	6.6	−3.4	11.9
Telecoms	4.1	2.9	11.0
Transport	9.3	−0.7	10.6
Public utilities	4.9	0.9	10.4
Commerce	14.3	2.1	10.4
Other services	7.6	1.2	10.1
Chemicals	28.0	−2.4	10.0
Education	13.8	−0.8	10.0
Housing	19.6	4.2	9.9
Agro-food	16.6	0.0	9.9
Building material	13.3	−0.3	9.9
Health	9.1	2.3	9.8
Other manufacturing	19.9	1.5	9.6
Mechanical and electrical	18.2	3.8	9.4
Hotels	18.4	−2.0	8.9
Agriculture	35.3	8.5	8.8
Construction	32.9	1.7	8.8
Textile and clothing	16.8	1.4	8.7

Source: author's calculation based on National Annual Firm Survey.

$T\bar{F}P_{it}$ is the unweighted average of firm-level productivity,
pm_{it} is the share of firm i in the given sector at time t,
TFP_{it} is the total factor productivity measure of an individual firm i at time t.

[14] One possible explanation for this result is that the finance sector was saturated; it did not grow after 2002 in terms of size. There were no new entrants.

such as agriculture, mechanical industries, construction, and textiles, experienced positive net job creation.

Table 7.16 also shows the inverse relationship between job reallocation rates and productivity. In general, the least productive industries had relatively high job reallocation rates. The two sectors where the job reallocation rate was the highest were construction and agriculture, both with low levels of productivity. At the same time, the most productive sectors, such as finance, telecoms, and other services, experienced low levels of job reallocation.

These patterns are confirmed by the results of econometric regressions (not reported here for the sake of brevity). We regress job flows (job creation and job destruction separately) on sectoral productivity, sectoral effects (to control for heterogeneity), and year effects (to control for macroeconomic shocks). The results suggest that productivity has negative and significant effects on job creation and on job destruction, that is, the most productive sectors create fewer jobs than the least productive but they destroy fewer jobs as well. In sum, there is a compensation for the effects of productivity on job creation and job destruction. The most productive sectors are not very dynamic. All in all, the regression analysis confirms our previous finding that the most productive sectors are not the ones that create most jobs.

7.5 Summary and Policy Diagnosis

While highlighted and aggravated by the recent political upheavals, high unemployment is a long-term feature of the Tunisian economy. The problem is particularly acute among young people and women. It has a strong regional dimension with huge disparities in unemployment rates between the coastal and more disadvantaged inland areas.

There is a strong link between employment and job quality, on the one hand, and wellbeing, on the other. Unsurprisingly, access to a job is the strongest determinant of escaping poverty, whether measured by household expenditures or non-monetary indicators such as access to public services, housing conditions, nutritional status, and so on. Being unemployed, or working in agriculture or construction—especially in rural areas—are the most common characteristics of households that are poor. Furthermore, employment status is a source of inequality of opportunity. Our diagnostics show the important role played by the father's occupation in determining his children's future prospects. Children with fathers who are unemployed or have low-quality jobs are more likely to suffer from malnutrition and have lower educational achievement. This result suggests that Tunisia's labor market problems create risks for the intergenerational transmission of poverty.

There are a number of determinants of Tunisia's high youth unemployment in particular. One is the difficult school-to-work transition exacerbated by skills mismatches. Firm surveys show that employers consider that new workforce entrants lack skills such as communication skills, team work, and critical thinking to succeed in the workplace.

A further problem is the limited capacity of labor market intermediation, in particular of the Agence Nationale de l'Emploi et du Travail Indépendant, to fill workers' and employers' needs, shorten search times, and reduce job search costs. A large majority of first-job-seekers find their jobs through social networks. The inadequate institutions interceding between job-seekers and employers negatively impact the school-to-work transition and explain, at least in part, longer unemployment spells experienced by youth. This situation leads to underutilization of the workforce, as reflected by the persistence of high unemployment and underemployment of university graduates.

While the supply side and intermediation are important problems, the demand side is an even more serious barrier for young people. The main message from this chapter is that Tunisia's high-productivity sectors do not create jobs and therefore are not absorbing the country's increasingly well-educated youth cohort. High-productivity sectors, such as finance and transport, have experienced small or even negative net job creation while other sectors with low productivity, such as agriculture, mechanical industries, construction, and textiles, are among the most dynamic sectors in terms of net job creation.

Job reallocation in Tunisia, specifically in manufacturing, is low, compared to other developing countries. Moreover, job reallocation is more important in sectors with low productivity than high productivity. These latter sectors, with little dynamism in terms of job creation, offer little opportunity for the young people who are queuing for jobs. The limited reallocation also hinders productivity growth since very little efficiency gain can be attributed to the process of job creation and job destruction.

Moreover, there is an important firm-size aspect to the story. Employment growth in large firms has been significantly higher than in small firms. However, they are not more productive. For reasons largely linked to non-competitive rules and practices (formal and informal), small firms do not grow, even though they are as productive as large firms.

Knowing the main causes, which measures might help to ease the problem of unemployment and improve employment opportunities, particularly for young people, in Tunisia? Many previous studies (e.g., Subrahmanyam 2012) have discussed reforms of the education system, aiming to narrow the skills gap and adjust the labor supply to firms' needs (even though these needs may not have been clearly expressed). The effectiveness of active labor market policies has also been questioned, mainly the narrow coverage, poor targeting to those in need, and the lack of creation of genuine jobs. However, as mentioned earlier, our analysis reveals that unemployment is largely a demand-side problem. The following discussion focuses on obstacles to job creation.

The low level of structural change and job creation appears to be due to various obstacles to the growth of firms, to barriers to entry in some specific sectors, and to labor market inefficiencies and bad governance. Should Tunisia focus more on the growth of firms than on their creation? If this is the case, the significant resources put in programs such as the microcredit funds for microenterprise creation may not be used in an optimal way.

7.5.1 Removing Obstacles to Firm Growth and Firm Creation

The survey conducted by Institut Tunisien de la Compétitivité et des Etudes Quantitatives (ITCEQ 2010) points out problems of anti-competitive behavior by firms that do not pay taxes or social security (their owners being protected by the government or informal firms) (World Bank 2010). Given the non-independence of the judiciary system, protection of property rights is not guaranteed. Thus, it is rational that some firms' owners prefer keeping their business small to avoid having to lose control in favor of the ruling families (most big businesses in Tunisia end up being controlled directly or indirectly by these families). Moreover, corruption, arbitrariness, and discretion in interactions with the public administration create a climate of uncertainty that does not favor investment.

There are also obstacles to free entry in some regulated sectors such as transport, telecom, and financial services (World Bank 2007). These barriers impede firm start-ups and job creation in these sectors and also have a negative impact on the rest of the economy as they induce higher production costs. For example, the monopoly of Tunisie Telecom on landlines had a negative impact on internet providers' development and thus on backbone services development.

The lack of access to credit and its high cost are also severe constraints for investment. Informal firms have almost no access, but also formal firms suffer from favoritism in access to credit (ITCEQ 2010, cited by World Bank 2010). Due to the high rate of non-performing loans in Tunisia, the Central Bank has imposed strict provisions on Tunisian banks which increased the credit rationing on firms seeking financing.

7.5.2 Reforming and Extending the Upgrading Program for Firms

The *"Programme de mise à niveau"* (PMN) was intended to help Tunisian firms compete with European firms after the implementation of the Free Trade Agreement with the EU in 1996. The sectoral distribution of program activities is dominated by three sectors: textiles and clothing, the food industry, and the mechanical and electrical industry. Textiles and clothing alone represented 48 percent of the accepted applications in 2008 and 27 percent of the volume of investments in 2008 (ITCEQ 2010). This high level of support granted to a sector suffering from increased competition at the global level may contribute to explaining the low level of structural change in the country. Services have been excluded from this program, which has been limited to manufacturing industries.

To our knowledge there is no independent evaluation of the PMN program impacts, based on a careful selection of a control group to avoid selection (or auto-selection) biases. The positive impact of the PMN seems to be the increase of intangible investment (mainly in technology) and the development of the export potential.[15] However, a risk of the program is that some firms may engage in "grant hunting" given that these grants are not linked to productivity improvements but to investments (Bougault and Filipiak 2005).

7.5.3 Reconsidering an Employment Strategy Based on Developing Micro-Firms

One of the main axes of the Tunisian employment strategy has been the development of small businesses through a microcredit fund. This strategy has never been seriously assessed. Moreover, since our results show that large firms create more jobs, a better employment strategy should focus on the development of existing small and medium-sized firms. To further this aim, the main obstacles to the growth of SMEs should be identified and employment funds could be (at least partly) reallocated to relieve the most binding constraints.

In the regions where unemployment is the highest and where economic activity is very limited, the government might think about promoting the development of large firms which may not only hire people, but also enhance the creation of SMEs (suppliers, subcontractors, etc.).

7.5.4 Activating Social Dialogue Between Citizens

In October 2015, the Nobel Peace Prize was attributed to the Tunisian National Dialogue Quartet[16] for their contribution to "building pluralistic democracy." Tunisians have demonstrated their capacity to resolve conflicts

---

[15] Sixty percent of PMN firms which had never exported before exported in 2002, according to Bougault and Filipiak (2005).

[16] The Quartet consists of the Tunisian General Labor Union (UGTT), the Tunisian Confederation of Industry, Trade and Handicrafts (UTICA), the Tunisian Human Rights League (LTDH), and the Tunisian Order of Lawyers (ONAT).

when their political institutions have failed during the democratic transition period. In January 2013, the social partners (UGTT, UTICA, and the government) were able to sign a new social contract that aims to change the rules of social and economic engagement and offers new opportunities to create a more cohesive society. Cohesion implies equitable access to education and health systems, good jobs, gender equality, and accountability.

This requires a national consensus via an inclusive social dialogue to establish policy reforms that can support firms to increase their productivity and create more and good jobs necessary for improving population wellbeing. The current effort to establish a council of social dialogue offers a real opportunity to activate discussion and achieve these goals. However, the Tunisian people must be aware that change will not be easy. The lobbies enjoying privileges from the current system pose a risk to reforms and will oppose any changes that remove these.

We can stress also the need to devise a comprehensive macroeconomic policy aiming to improve youth employability, protect vulnerable groups, and promote civic participation and an active role for women in society. Since the wellbeing of the population depends closely on the interaction of various government interventions, each component of such a policy should be designed with regard to the others. In the long run, more cohesive societies and greater fiscal legitimacy reinforce each other in a virtuous cycle.

References

Angel-Urdinola, D. and Helel, Y. (2012). Earnings in the Tunisian Labor market. Manuscript INS.

Bibi, S. (2011). La pauvreté et l'inégalité en Tunisie, au Maroc et en Mauritanie. Note économique, Banque Africaine de Développement.

Bottini, N. and Gasiorek, M. (2009). Trade and Job Reallocation: Evidence for Morocco. Working Paper No. 492. Economic Research Forum.

Bougault, H. and Filipiak, E. (2005). *Les programmes de mise à niveau des entreprises Tunisie*. Maroc, Sénégal: French Development Agency, Research Department, pp. 1–173.

Davis, S.J. and Haltiwanger, J. (1992). "Gross job creation, gross job destruction, and employment reallocation." *The Quarterly Journal of Economics*, 107(3):819–63.

El Lahga, A., Marouani, M., and Mouelhi, R. (2012). Employment, Living Standards and Productivity in Tunisia. Background paper for the World Development Report 2013.

Haltiwanger, J., Jarmin, R., and Miranda, J. (2010). Who Creates Jobs? Small vs. Large vs. Young. Working Paper No. 16300. NBER, Cambridge, MA.

Institut National de la Statistique: INS (2012). Mesure de la Pauvreté, des Inégalités et de la polarisation en Tunisie 2000–2010. Report.

Institut National de la Statistique: INS (2014). The 2014 Census result. URL: www.ins. nat.tn. [Accessed May 2016.]

ITCEQ (2010). Evaluation du programme de mise à niveau, Résultats de la septième enquête sur le Programme de Mise à Niveau. Annual report.

Levinsohn, J. and Petrin, A. (1999). When Industries Become More Productive, Do Firms? Working Paper No. 6893. National Bureau of Economic Research.

Olley, S. and Pakes, A. (1996). "The dynamics of productivity in the telecommunications equipment industry." *Econometrica*, 64(6):1263–97.

Rijkers, B., Baghdadi, L., and Raballand, G. (2013). Political Connections and Tariff Evasion: Evidence from Tunisia (mimeographed).

Rutkowski, J. (2012). Tunisian Labor Market Profile. Manuscript prepared for Development Policy review for Tunisia.

Silatech-Gallup (2009). The Silatech Index: Voices of Young Arabs. Report.

Stampini, S. and Verdier-Chouchane, A. (2011). Labor Market Dynamics in Tunisia: The Issue of Youth Unemployment. Working Paper No. 123. Tunis: African Development Bank.

Subrahmanyam, G. (2012). Tackling Youth Unemployment in the Maghreb. Tunis: African Development Bank.

World Bank (2003). Republic of Tunisia, "Poverty Update." Volumes I, IIA and IIB, MENA. World Bank.

World Bank (2007). Tunisia Global Integration: Second Generation of Reforms to Boost Growth and Employment. Report No. 40129. MNSED.

World Bank (2010). Development Policies Review: Towards an Innovative Growth. Report No. 50487. Economic and Social Development Group, MENA Region, pp. 5–98.

World Bank (2012). World Development Report 2013: Jobs. Washington, DC: World Bank.

World Bank (2013). Jobs for Shared Prosperity: Time for Action in the Middle East and North Africa. Washington, DC: World Bank.

8

Jobs for an Aging Society

Olga Kupets

8.1 Introduction

Ukraine is experiencing dramatic population changes, including its rapid aging and decline. The population decreased from 51.4 million in 1990 to 44.8 million in 2015 and is expected to fall to 32.5 million by 2060.[1] The proportion of those 65 years and older in the total population grew from 12.2 percent in 1990 to 15.3 percent in 2015 and will increase to 24.8 percent in 2060. At the same time, the share of the working-age population is expected to decline from 64.6 percent in 2015 to 58.8 percent in 2060. If gender- and age-specific labor force participation rates remain at current levels, the labor force in Ukraine is projected to shrink by almost 40 percent by 2060.

Population aging is already seriously affecting many developed countries and it is expected to be a growing concern in a number of others, including developing countries, in the near future. But the multiple challenges faced by aging countries in improving living standards, productivity, and social cohesion are especially formidable in Ukraine. First, aging is taking place against the backdrop of weak institutions, structural economic weaknesses, political instability, and a low level of trust within the population as the country continues to struggle with the economic, political, and social transformations triggered by the Soviet Union's collapse.

Second, aging in Ukraine is taking place from "below" and not from "above," that is, mainly due to a decline in fertility and continuous outmigration of the working-age population rather than due to a major increase in life expectancy as in developed countries. This constrains options in Ukraine

---

[1] Unless noted otherwise, the source of the population data cited in this chapter is United Nations World Population Prospects: The 2015 Revision. See United Nations (2015).

because significantly raising the retirement age, especially for men who have relatively short life expectancy, might shorten considerably their work-free time in old age.

Third, compared with higher-income aging countries, Ukraine has fewer financial resources for mitigating the negative impacts of population aging on the labor market and on the social protection and health systems. At the same time, slow progress in the development of the financial markets that are needed to introduce a mandatory funded second-pillar pension scheme aggravates the difficulties of dealing with population aging.

Fourth, the jobs challenge driven by a shrinking and aging population is amplified by relatively low levels of labor force participation and labor mobility, poor productivity performance, and the ineffective use of available human capital. Skills of the more abundant older cohorts who completed their education before the transition are not well rewarded in the new market environment, while decreasing young cohorts and the ineffective use of their skills reduce the innovative capacity of firms. This seriously undermines Ukraine's competitiveness and attractiveness to investors looking for knowledge-based and innovation-led opportunities. At the same time, the growing elderly population is creating enormous fiscal pressures on those who participate in the formal economy. This will ultimately lead to higher labor costs and a double burden on formally employed working-age individuals and formal firms that could create incentives to exit into the shadow economy and become a source of social strain. In the end, the country may fall into a fiscal trap with a lack of economic opportunities for youth. Aging can also make the population less mobile, both professionally and geographically. Such negative developments may hinder further economic growth, worsen living standards, and adversely impact intergenerational relationships and social cohesion.

On the other hand, Ukraine has more opportunities than many other aging societies to adjust to the challenges of an aging and shrinking population. There is potential to increase labor force participation and productivity levels by bringing hitherto inactive youth and adults into the workplace, by encouraging more internal migration and professional mobility of workers, and by improving and better utilizing their knowledge and skills. There is also scope for increasing productivity through technological and organizational innovations and the reallocation of firms and workers from less to more productive activities.

Yet these opportunities may only be realized if Ukrainian policy-makers effectively implement a multifaceted approach to the problems being created by the aging population. A prerequisite is to create a policy environment that is conducive to sustained job creation and productivity growth. The fundamentals, including macroeconomic stability, an enabling business environment, human capital, the rule of law, and modern infrastructure, need to offer a solid foundation for Ukraine's job policies. Labor policies, including measures that improve skills matching, promote labor mobility, and effectively protect the most vulnerable workers, are important not only for supporting efficiently functioning labor markets but also for confronting the aging issue. Finally, policy-makers need to support the creation of more "good jobs for development," that is, those that bring positive spillovers with respect to living standards, productivity gains, and social cohesion (World Bank 2012b). In Ukraine, jobs that maximize the years of economic activity and encourage a healthy population are likely to have large development payoffs. Improving fairness in the labor market is another priority task for rebuilding social cohesion in Ukraine's society and increasing the development payoff from jobs.

This chapter begins with an overview of the current and future demographic trends in Ukraine and their implications for the labor market. It directly addresses the potential impact of population aging on labor supply and labor productivity leaving aside the implications of aging on public finance and social protection of the elderly, health care and long-term care, savings, and financial markets. Section 8.3 examines the main employment trends and possible tensions between the three transformations, namely living standards, productivity, and social cohesion. It draws extensively on a quantitative analysis of available job-related data and existing empirical studies as well as qualitative research based on focus group discussions and in-depth interviews.[2] Sections 8.4, 8.5, and 8.6 offer examples of good jobs for development in Ukraine's particular context and discuss the main constraints to the creation of more of these jobs. The chapter concludes with a discussion of policy options for addressing these constraints and aging-related concerns.

8.2 Demographic Change and its Implications for the Ukrainian Labor Market

8.2.1 Demographic Trends in Ukraine

Ukraine's population decline is among the most rapid in the world. According to the UN World Population data, its population has been shrinking by about 0.55 percent every year since 1990. Ukraine's population decreased from 51.4 million in 1990 to 44.8 million in 2015, representing a loss of more than 12 percent. It is expected to fall to 32.5 million by 2060 under the UN's medium-fertility variant and to 27.2 million under the low-fertility variant (Figure 8.1).

Dramatic changes in population size have been accompanied by a sharp increase in the proportion of the population aged 65 years and older. Between

---

[2] These were conducted in March–April 2012 and are analyzed in detail in Kupets et al. (2012).

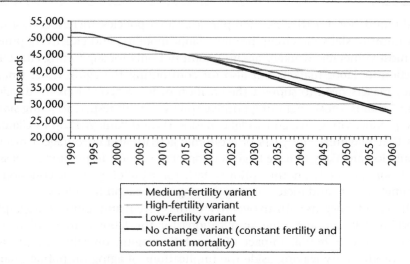

Figure 8.1. Total population by variant of projections, 1990–2060

Note: de facto population as of July 1 of the year indicated. Historical data for the 1990–2014 period. For 2015–2060, data refer to projections with four variants depending on the assumption about fertility trends. Figures include population of Crimea.

Source: UN (2015).

1990 and 2015, the working-age population (aged 15 to 64 years) declined by 3 million people (Table 8.1). In the same period, the elderly population increased by about 700,000. In the period to 2060, the working-age population is expected to decline further by over 12 million, whereas the elderly population is expected to grow by over 1.2 million people. As a result, the proportion of the elderly in the total population, which increased from 12 percent in 1990 to 15.3 percent in 2015, will increase to 24.8 percent in 2060 (under the medium-fertility variant). The natural consequence of aging is an increase in the old-age dependency ratio, that is, the number of people older than 65 years relative to those of working age (15–64 years). By 2060, this ratio is expected to increase to 42.1 percent, about double what it was in 2015 (Table 8.1).

Ukraine is aging differently from Western European countries or Japan. Those countries are aging both from "below" and "above," that is, because of both reduced fertility and longer life expectancies (Table 8.2). In Ukraine, aging is occurring primarily from below, with rapid declines in fertility but a shorter life expectancy which, according to the UN, was almost three years lower in 2005–10 than it was in 1970–75.

At less than 71 years, life expectancy in Ukraine lags far behind the level in developed European and Asian countries. Not only are Ukrainians dying younger than people in higher-income countries but they also have fewer years lived in full health, as documented by a fairly low level of

Table 8.1. Population dynamics by age group and old-age dependency ratio, 1990–2060

Indicator	Period	Age group			Total
		0–14 years	15–64 years	65+ years	
Population (thousands)	1990	10,829.9	34,370.3	6,169.8	51,370.0
	2015	6,691.1	31,271.8	6,860.8	44,823.8
	2030	6,336.6	26,426.0	8,129.9	40,892.4
	2060	5,334.1	19,140.5	8,067.4	32,542.0
Proportion of age group in	1990	21.1	66.9	12.0	100.0
total population (%)	2015	14.9	69.8	15.3	100.0
	2030	15.5	64.6	19.9	100.0
	2060	16.4	58.8	24.8	100.0
Old-age dependency ratio (%)	1990				18.0
	2015				21.9
	2030				30.8
	2060				42.1

Note: population projections for 2015–60 are based on medium-fertility variant. The old-age dependency ratio is the ratio of the number of elderly people (aged 65 and over), compared to the number of people of working age (i.e., 15–64 years old).
Source: author's calculations based on data from UN (2015).

Table 8.2. Life expectancy and fertility trends in Ukraine and selected developed countries, 1950–2015

Country	Life expectancy at birth for both sexes combined (years)						Total fertility (children per woman)					
	1970–5	1990–5	1995–2000	2000–5	2005–10	2010–15	1970–5	1990–5	1995–2000	2000–5	2005–10	2010–15
Japan	73.1	79.4	80.5	81.8	82.6	83.3	2.13	1.48	1.37	1.30	1.34	1.40
Italy	72.1	77.3	78.6	80.2	81.5	82.8	2.32	1.27	1.22	1.30	1.42	1.43
Austria	70.7	76.0	77.4	78.8	80.1	81.1	2.04	1.48	1.39	1.38	1.40	1.47
Germany	71.2	75.9	77.2	78.6	79.8	80.6	1.71	1.30	1.35	1.35	1.36	1.39
Finland	70.8	75.7	77.0	78.3	79.5	80.5	1.62	1.82	1.74	1.75	1.84	1.75
Ukraine	70.6	68.7	67.4	67.5	67.9	70.7	2.08	1.62	1.24	1.15	1.38	1.49

Source: UN (2015).

health-adjusted life expectancy (Institute of Demography and Social Studies 2007a; World Bank 2009).

8.2.2 Implications of Demographic Change for the Labor Market

Demographic change can have direct implications for labor markets through three primary channels: labor supply, labor productivity, and labor demand (Chawla et al. 2007). Population aging can lead to a decrease in labor supply through the increase in the share of older workers, who have lower rates of labor force participation than younger workers. If aging is accompanied by large population losses, as in Ukraine, it also directly affects labor supply through the falling numbers of total workers.

Average labor productivity can decline as older workers might be less productive than their younger colleagues because of declining cognitive performance and physical strength with age. Besides, older workers might be less responsive to economic opportunities because of lower mobility, innovation, and entrepreneurship. However, recent evidence collected in Bussolo et al. (2015) provides a mixed picture, showing that if aging economies shift toward industries that are relatively intensive in age-appreciating skills (e.g., improved verbal and non-cognitive, especially social, skills) and if new technologies reinforce work experience among aging workforces, aging does not necessarily impair productivity.

Labor demand can change because of shifts in the structure of aggregate demand. For example, an aging population will increase demand for long-term and formal care with the result that health and social care sectors are those with high employment potential (European Commission 2012a).

In order to assess the impacts of demographic trends for the future labor supply in Ukraine, we examine labor force projections for 2013–60, starting from the base scenario with constant gender- and age-specific labor force participation rates at 2012 levels. According to this scenario, Ukraine is expected to lose over 8.5 million workers aged 15 years and above between 2010 and 2060, or 37 percent of its 2010 level. In the early part of this period, the younger labor force (15–39 years) dominates the decline in labor supply, peaking in the 2020s (Figure 8.2). In the later part of the period, the decline of the labor force will be larger in the age group from 40 to 64 years as more and

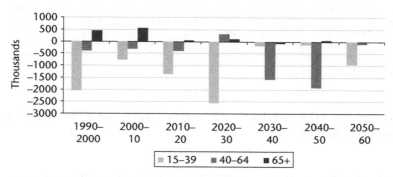

Figure 8.2. Changes in labor supply by age group (base scenario), 1990–2060

Note: the simulation for 2013–60 assumes that labor force participation rates to 2060 are kept at the level that was observed in 2012 for each five-year age group. The size of the labor force is estimated by multiplying these labor force participation rate data with the population data from the UN by five-year age groups and then summing up data for the three broad age groups.

Source: author's calculations based on population projections from UN (2015), medium variant, and gender-specific labor force participation rates from ILO (2013a), series "Estimates and projections," for ten five-year age groups from 15 to 64 years and one group of 65+ years.

more workers from populous cohorts born before the 1990s demographic crisis retire or die.

Following the methodology applied by Gill and Raiser (2012) and Bussolo et al. (2015), we also ran five alternative labor force projection scenarios that modify labor force participation rates in various ways to assess the potential to reverse the shrinking labor force.

- **ILO and constant participation rate scenario (Scenario 1)**: as with all the alternative scenarios, ILO projections of age- and gender-specific labor force participation rates in 2013–30 (ILO 2013a) are used; then this scenario assumes that these participation rates stay constant from 2030 onwards, and combines the 2030 participation rates with the UN demographic projections until 2060 (UN 2015).

- **Convergence to the best performers in Europe (Scenario 2)**: this scenario assumes that participation rates for all age–gender groups in Ukraine will converge by 2060 to respective age- and gender-specific participation rates of Iceland, which is taken as the benchmark country with the highest participation rate for those aged 50+ years in 2030. For the years between 2031 and 2060, this scenario, as well as the next three scenarios, assumes a linear adjustment over time.

- **Female-to-male convergence (Scenario 3)**: this scenario assumes that age-specific participation rates of Ukrainian women converge to those of men between 2031 and 2060.

- **Increased participation rates in older age groups (Scenario 4)**: this scenario simulates an increase in the labor force participation rates in the three oldest age groups (55–59, 60–64, and 65+ years) between 2031 and 2060 to the average levels between the rates in these older age groups and those ten years younger in 2030 as forecast by the ILO.

- **The maximum variant (Scenario 5)**: this combines the effects of the latter three variants.

Table 8.3 summarizes the projection results by presenting changes in the labor force in the three broad age groups between 2010 and 2060. It shows that even under the most optimistic assumptions (Scenario 5), where labor force participation rates would exceed 90 percent in all adult age groups (25 to 64 years) as shown in Table 8A.1 in Appendix 8A, Ukraine is not likely to counter a shrinking and aging labor force. Under all scenarios, the labor force is projected to decline considerably.

However, projected labor force declines are the lowest in Scenarios 2 and 5 involving convergence to the best performing European country (Iceland). Comparing labor force participation rates under these two scenarios with the base scenario (Table 8A.1 in Appendix 8A), the largest adjustments will need to

Table 8.3. Projected changes in the Ukrainian labor force between 2010 and 2060 by scenario and age group

Age group	Indicator	Projected changes in the labor force between 2010 and 2060					
		Base scenario	Scenario 1	Scenario 2	Scenario 3	Scenario 4	Scenario 5
15–39	Absolute change (thousands)	–5,097.9	–4,936.9	–3,430.2	–4,514.9	–4,936.9	–3,167.9
	Percentage change (%)	–45.8	–44.3	–30.8	–40.5	–44.3	–28.4
40–64	Absolute change (thousands)	–3,626.9	–3,274.4	–1,587.1	–3,003.2	–2,714.4	–1,139.8
	Percentage change (%)	–34.8	–31.4	–15.2	–28.8	–26.1	–10.9
65+	Absolute change (thousands)	178.2	308.4	324.9	431.8	1,776.4	3,517.0
	Percentage change (%)	12.2	21.2	22.3	29.7	122.0	241.6
Total (15+)	Absolute change (thousands)	–8,546.5	–7,903.0	–4,692.5	–7,086.3	–5,874.9	–790.7
	Percentage change (%)	–37.1	–34.3	–20.4	–30.8	–25.5	–3.4

Source: author's calculations based on population projections from UN (2015), medium variant, and gender-specific labor force participation rates from ILO (2013a), series "Estimates and projections," for ten five-year age groups from 15 to 64 years and one group of 65+ years.

be made among older workers (55 years and older). Achieving these increases in participation rates would involve confronting a number of challenges, discussed later in the chapter. In any case, this would not make up for the demographically driven declines in labor supply.

This raises the question of whether increasing immigration of younger people could be large enough to compensate for declines in the labor force, as in developed European countries (Pozniak 2012). As long as its richer neighbors, such as Russia, Belarus, Poland, or Hungary, provide better employment and income opportunities for immigrant workers, it is quite unlikely that Ukraine would be able to attract immigrant workers in large numbers. At the same time, Ukraine is losing thousands of its able-bodied workers annually as they head abroad in search of better jobs and better lives.[3] Meanwhile, migration does not seem to benefit those workers who are left behind and the Ukrainian economy as a whole (Kupets 2012a, b; Pozniak 2012).

[3] Of the Ukrainian population aged 15–70, 1.2 million, or 3.4 percent were identified as labor migrants from January 2010 until June 2012, according to the Labor Migration Survey 2012, carried out by the State Statistics Service of Ukraine in the framework of the ILO-EU Project "Effective Governance of Labor Migration and its Skills Dimensions" (ILO 2013b). Unfortunately, there have not been reliable surveys on labor migration from or to Ukraine conducted since 2012. Official statistics on permanent migration flows report positive net migration (i.e., the difference between the number of registered immigrants and emigrants during a year) since 2005, with 54,100 people moving into Ukraine compared to 22,187 people moving from Ukraine abroad in 2013. As regards other important types of migration, the military conflict in Crimea and Eastern Ukraine in 2014–15 increased the number of Ukrainians seeking asylum or other forms of stay in neighboring countries only to 353,600 and 570,700 people, respectively, as of July 24, 2015 (see http://unhcr.org.ua/en/2011-08-26-06-58-56/news-archive/1244-internal-displacement-map).

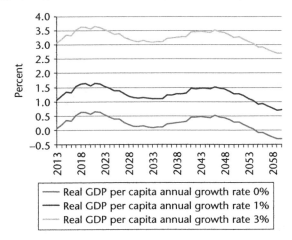

Figure 8.3. Projected annual changes in labor productivity necessary to achieve selected real GDP per capita growth rates, 2013–60

Note: the simulation assesses changes in the labor productivity measured as real GDP per person in the labor force necessary to maintain constant or increasing GDP per capita between 2011 and 2060, given the expected decline in the labor force due to aging. Age-specific labor force participation rates are assumed to be constant between 2013 and 2060 at the 2012 level as in the base scenario used above. The basic equation for simulation is the following: annual percentage change in GDP per person in the labor force is equal to the sum of annual percentage changes in GDP per capita and in the ratio of total population to the labor force.

Source: author's calculations based on population projections from UN (2015), medium variant, and gender-specific labor force participation rates from ILO (2013a), series "Estimates and projections," for ten five-year age groups from 15 to 64 years and one group of 65+ years.

This labor supply story means that improvements in the living standards of Ukrainians will increasingly have to come from productivity growth. To assess how much labor productivity (measured here as real GDP per person in the labor force) would need to grow to cushion the impact of aging on average incomes, three simulations have been carried out to capture different scenarios for GDP per capita growth to 2060 (Figure 8.3). Each assumes constant age-specific labor force participation rates in 2012–60. In order to keep real GDP per capita constant (zero growth), labor productivity would need to grow on average by 0.3 percent annually during this period, with particularly pronounced growth needed in 2017–24 and 2041–48. If the goal is to reach a GDP per capita annual growth rate of 3 percent, the required productivity growth would be much more substantial (average annual growth of 3.3 percent in 2013–60).

Although Ukraine did have strong productivity growth in 2000–07 (Figure 8.4), it was driven mainly by factors that are not likely to persist at the same order of magnitude over the longer term, such as financial stabilization efforts and privatization of loss-making state-owned enterprises, fast-growing export prices, idle industrial capacity utilization without significant

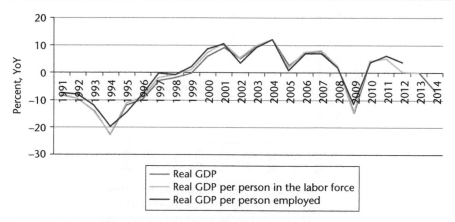

Figure 8.4. Real GDP and labor productivity growth rates, 1991–2014

Source: author's calculations of growth rates based on World Development Indicators data on GDP at PPP (in constant 2011 international $), GDP per person employed (in constant 1990 PPP $), and total labor force.

investments and innovation, and a surge of capital inflows and credit growth fueled by commercial banks' external borrowing (World Bank 2010). Therefore, other channels for sustaining productivity growth will need to be found.

If the necessary productivity gains do not materialize, Ukraine will not be able to cushion the negative impact of aging on output and income, and the living standards of many Ukrainians will inevitably fall. Public retirement schemes and the social welfare system will become unsustainable if their parameters are not adjusted to meet the aging challenges. The inability of the state to provide pension and other benefits to an aging population would be a source of social tension stretching social cohesion to the limit.

Aging can also make the labor force less mobile, creating a barrier to achieving required employment and productivity levels and for fostering structural transformation. The spatial mobility of Ukrainians within the country is already low, inefficient, and constrained by many factors (Koettl et al. 2014). Comparing Ukraine with other European countries (controlling for the average size and number of geographical units), registered internal migration rates in Ukraine are about half of those that would be expected (World Bank 2012a). Not only are actual migration rates low when compared to other countries, but so were intentions to migrate within the country. In view of high migration costs and other barriers to permanent residential migration, temporary labor migration and commuting become an increasingly important substitute, but these flows are often undocumented and biased to the capital city and the nearby region. Evidence also shows that some Ukrainians living in border regions are more inclined to find temporary employment abroad than within Ukraine as there is no sense in "trading bad for worse" by moving to some other part of Ukraine.

8.3 Jobs Through the Lens of Living Standards, Productivity, and Social Cohesion

8.3.1 *Recent Labor Market Developments*

Total employment increased steadily during 2001–08, and the share of employed persons in the adult population increased from 55.4 to 59.3 percent (Figure 8.5).[4] Unemployment rates fell from over 10 percent in the early 2000s to 6.4 percent in 2008 (Figure 8.6). The economic and financial crisis, which reached Ukraine in late 2008, resulted in significant employment losses but moderate increases in unemployment as many displaced people moved to inactivity. Despite a slight increase in 2010–13, total employment has not yet recovered to the levels in 2008. At the same time, due to a rapidly shrinking working-age population, the employment rate reached 60.3 percent in 2013, the highest rate since 2000 when comparable data became available. After the onset of the conflict with Russia in February 2014 and a concurrent economic downturn, employment severely decreased (Figure 8.5), mostly due to the exclusion of the population from Crimea and part of the Donbas region, which cannot be covered by the LFS, but also due to employment losses in the rest of Ukraine.

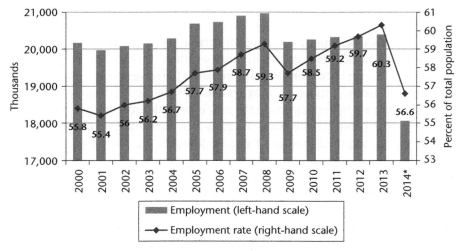

Figure 8.5. Employment levels and rates, population aged 15–70 years, 2000–14

Note: * data for 2014 do not include occupied territories in Crimea and Donbas.

Source: Labor Force Survey, State Statistics Service of Ukraine.

---

[4] Key labor market indicators in Ukraine are defined according to the ILO methodology on the basis of the Labor Force Survey (LFS) data and, following the ILO recommendations, refer to individuals aged 15–70 years.

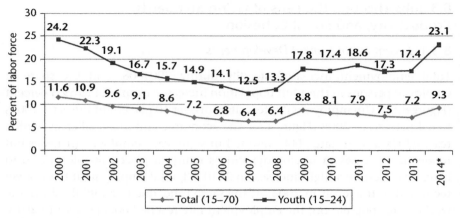

Figure 8.6 Total and youth unemployment rate, 2000–14

Note: * data for 2014 do not include occupied territories in Crimea and Donbas.

Source: Labor Force Survey, State Statistics Service of Ukraine.

As in many other countries, some groups are more excluded from the Ukrainian labor market than others and have lower participation and employment rates. These are youth, older workers, women, rural workers, and those living in lagging regions (see Table 8A.2 in Appendix 8A).

In 2014, 23.1 percent of economically active people aged 15–24 years were unemployed, which is significantly higher than in the other age groups (Figure 8.6). Youth transitions to work and adult life have become more difficult for several reasons. Although young people are supposed to acquire education and skills that are better tailored to the new economic environment than those held by their older counterparts, there is a serious mismatch between the competencies acquired through formal education and the actual needs of employers due to poor career guidance, the slow responsiveness of the education and training system to the changing labor market needs, and the generally low quality of education in Ukraine. Besides, even high and matching qualifications are no longer a guarantee for finding a decent job, particularly in times of economic crisis when the number of job offers declines and the competition for open positions increases. Many young people are disadvantaged in this competition by lack of relevant work experience and weak bargaining power. The lack of flexible and reliable contractual arrangements and significant obstacles to self-employment for youth may also be factors explaining high youth unemployment and over-qualification (European Training Foundation 2008; Institute of Demography and Social Studies 2010).

Therefore, many young people appear to be trapped at the lower end of the labor market, with little security, low wages, few on-the-job training opportunities, and weak long-term career prospects. This increases their risk of exclusion and poverty and negatively affects social cohesiveness of the society, as political upheavals in the MENA region have shown. Poor labor outcomes for youth are particularly serious in the aging context because of the importance of scarce young cohorts in eventually driving the productivity growth needed to compensate for the lack of labor supply.

Labor force participation rates of older workers (50 years and over) have slightly increased in recent years as people of pre-retirement and retirement age have become more active, probably due to decreasing pensions in real terms and increasing pressure to support the younger generations (children and grandchildren). However, as focus group discussions conducted for this study (Box 8.1) show, once these workers lose their jobs they experience

---

Box 8.1 FOCUS GROUP DISCUSSIONS: THE UKRAINIAN CASE STUDY

Focus groups collected qualitative data on the attitudes of Ukrainians toward work, labor mobility, and informality; their general vision of good jobs from individual and broader perspectives; the availability of such jobs and the barriers to accessing them; the main problems they might face in the Ukrainian labor market; and issues of trust and inter-generational relations with the emphasis on support of the elderly through tax payments and social security contributions.

Seventeen focus groups (with 163 informants) were formed to reflect diversity regarding location, employment status, informality, age, and skill level. Four localities were selected to cover differences in labor market structure and economic development:

- *Eastern* (Donetsk and the region): a heavily industrialized region with a high urban concentration and a lot of mono-industrial towns; relatively high productivity levels and good employment opportunities but with a high level of labor conflict, including coal-mining protests and large factory strikes to protect workers' rights.

- *Western* (Lviv and the region): a developed urban service sector but high import-ance of agriculture and international labor migration from small towns and rural areas because of poor employment opportunities.

- *Southern* (Crimea): a high incidence of seasonal jobs, including wage employment in tourism, hotels, and restaurants; agricultural employment; and self-employment in non-agricultural sectors (renting, catering, transport, communication, etc.).

- *Kyiv* (the capital city): the best income and employment opportunities in Ukraine, attracting a lot of workers from elsewhere.

A significant share of the participants were employed informally, that is, with no written contract (46 of 163) or were non-registered self-employed (13 of 163). Fifty-eight informants had casual work and were not registered as unemployed. Thirty-two had an official employment contract.

Six in-depth interviews with private recruiting agency managers were also conducted.

The fieldwork was done by the Kyiv International Institute of Sociology in March–April 2012.

Source: Kupets et al. (2012).

significant difficulties in finding another. A specific feature of the Ukrainian labor market is that the probability of re-employment is low not only for older cohorts, whose skills were largely built for a different kind of economic system and whose productivity might be low, but also for people aged 40–45 years who have lived most of their work life in the new economic environment. Focus group participants attribute this phenomenon to age discrimination in hiring and an insufficient number of decent jobs in Ukraine. Under such circumstances, the major motivation for older workers is to keep their current job at whatever cost, rather than to invest in human capital and personal development in order to move to more productive jobs. These behavioral patterns clearly restrain productivity growth and effective labor reallocation between the sectors. In addition, they constrain workers from moving up the career ladder and improving their incomes. Those who do not manage to keep their jobs are confined to low-productivity work or discouragement and inactivity.

Overall, about 2.2 million working-age people who would most likely be able and ready to work under favorable conditions did not work in 2014 because of unsuccessful job searching (unemployment and discouragement) (Table 8.4). Over 2.4 million people were inactive because of engagement in household work or being dependent on income of the other household members, and even more people were inactive students in 2014. In addition, according to the payroll employment statistics based on the survey of enterprises and organizations with at least ten employees, on average 90,500 employees were on unpaid administrative leave in 2014, and 888,100 workers were employed part-time for economic reasons. Huge labor underutilization seriously affects the growth and development potential of the Ukrainian economy. On the other hand, this labor reserve could help meet the aging challenge through increasing employment and productivity levels by bringing hitherto inactive youths and adults into the workplace and better utilizing their knowledge and skills.

Table 8.4. Unemployed and able-to-work inactive workers (thousands), population aged 15–70 years, 2010–14*

Year	Unemployed	Discouraged	Engaged in household work and dependents	Inactive students	Total
2010	1,713.9	346.4	2,329.3	3,069.9	7,459.4
2011	1,661.9	291.4	2,401.4	2,914.4	7,269.1
2012	1,589.8	240.6	2,348.7	2,818.4	6,997.5
2013	1,510.4	214.1	2,276.6	2,795.0	6,796.1
2014	1,847.6	324.6	2,404.6	2,609.0	7,185.8

Note: * data do not include occupied territories in Crimea and Donbas (the latter in 2014 only). "Discouraged" includes jobless workers who have given up looking for a job as well as those who did not know how or where to look for a job, believed that there were no suitable jobs, or those who hoped to come back to previous work, including seasonal workers.

Source: Labor Force Survey, State Statistics Service of Ukraine.

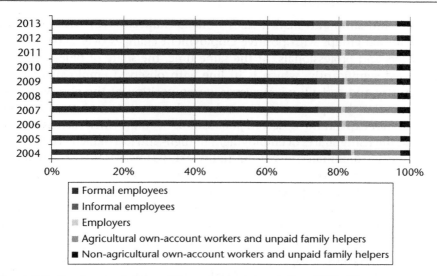

Figure 8.7. Employment status of the employed population, 2004–13

Note: the category of agricultural own-account workers and unpaid family helpers includes only those who are engaged in subsistence agriculture, i.e., it does not include farmers with large operations and their family members.

Source: author's calculations based on the LFS data.

As we saw before, employment indicators somewhat improved before 2014 (see Figure 8.5), but the quality of jobs remained quite low.[5] Many Ukrainian wage and salaried workers work informally and many of the others are engaged in low-productive employment in subsistence agriculture (Figure 8.7). Employers and non-agricultural own-account workers account for less than 5 percent of total employment.

Widespread informal employment contributes to the violation of important workers' rights in such areas as job security, timely and reasonable remuneration for work done, access to fringe benefits, age and gender equality, initial employment for young people, and employment of individuals according to their skills and qualifications. But formal employment does not always guarantee higher stability and better working conditions due to an extensive use by private employers of various schemes to cheat workers and ignore their core rights, as documented by numerous examples given by the focus group participants.

Another worrisome trend in the Ukrainian labor market is a high and growing share of unskilled jobs in total employment. Between 2000 and 2013, it increased from 17.7 percent to 23.7 percent. The largest employment growth and fastest increase in the employment shares was among service

---

[5] When discussing the quality of jobs based on the LFS data, the important aspects of wages and wage arrears are omitted because this information is not included in the survey.

workers and shop and market sales workers (Kupets 2016). The other two occupational groups with positive employment changes over 2004–13 were managers and professionals. At the same time, the share of blue-collar jobs decreased significantly, which is in line with observed employment losses in industry and agriculture. However, decomposition of the observed shifts in occupational employment shares shows that shifts in industrial composition do not explain the observed polarization of employment across occupations as the rising shares of employment in high- and low-skilled occupational categories are dominated by within-industry shifts towards these occupational categories (Kupets 2016). A slow adjustment in the relative demand for highly educated workers compared to the growth in their supply contributes to widespread and long-term overeducation and structural unemployment, which coexist with skills shortages reported by local employers (World Bank 2016). Significant imbalances between skill demand and supply, along with an aging and shrinking workforce, threaten Ukraine's international competitiveness and the much-needed transition toward higher-value-added, knowledge-intensive activities.

Therefore, the quantitative achievements before 2014—a slight rise in the employment rate and a relatively low unemployment rate—mask negative qualitative changes. Formal full-time jobs, which have been continuously destroyed in many economic sectors, are being replaced by temporary jobs created in less knowledge-intensive services and medium- or low-technology manufacturing sectors with high pollution externalities. Labor demand in higher-productivity jobs in the formal private sector remains very limited and mainly confined to the capital city and several agglomerations and large firms with foreign investors. The expected transformation of the labor market in favor of higher-skilled jobs is very slow.

Moreover, new jobs do not always provide income opportunities that are sufficient to measurably increase living standards. Specific adjustment mechanisms frequently used by Ukrainian employers, such as wage arrears and "envelope wages," accentuate the problem of fairly low wages and income inequality. At the same time, income from business activities is significantly less important for Ukrainian households than wages and various transfers due to a low share of employers and own-account workers outside subsistence agriculture (see Figure 8.7 for employment) and the fairly low earnings of small and medium-scale businesses. As a consequence, employment does not always provide a solid pathway out of poverty, and households with a working member can face even more severe economic hardship and social deprivation than households relying on social assistance, pensions, and other non-labor income. This may discourage many able-bodied individuals from participating in the labor force and finding work, which is not a healthy sign for an economy with a shrinking and aging population.

Few Ukrainians are satisfied with their jobs and financial situation, and this occurs not only because of low wages per se, but also because the pay is perceived as unjust given the workers' skills and efforts (Kupets et al. 2012). Focus group discussions and sociological surveys show that Ukrainians put a much lower priority on the social value of job (i.e., a job that is useful for society) and individual performance on the job when they decide on their profession/job and work effort compared to workers in Western European countries. Most care about the salary level and its timely payment, job security, fringe benefits, and a healthy work environment (i.e., friendly relations with management and colleagues). Young people give high preference to career opportunities, work prestige, and interesting work, but very low preference to the social value of jobs. The prevalence of survival attitudes toward jobs over their development value does not allow Ukrainians to see the broad perspective of "good jobs for development" and limits the possibility for effective application of this concept in Ukraine in the near future.

Being employed is positively related to the level of trust, civic engagement, and people's subjective wellbeing in Ukraine. But the level of generalized trust, life satisfaction, and evaluation of democratic developments in Ukraine is much lower than in Europe (Kupets et al. 2012). Furthermore, regardless of employment status, Ukrainians demonstrate low trust in social and political institutions, both public (president, government, parliament, police, tax authorities, court, political parties, and public employment services) and private (banks, insurance companies, and employers).

Focus group discussions and sociological surveys analyzed in detail in Kupets et al. (2012) show that limited and unfair access to good jobs remains a key problem for many groups, especially youth and older workers, lower-skilled workers, and residents of rural areas, small towns, and economically depressed regions. Education, skills, and personal attributes—which are considered the individual's "employability assets" in developed countries—appear to be less important for gaining and maintaining employment in Ukraine than personal connections and social status (often defined by family background). Bribery and other forms of corruption are quite widespread phenomena in the employment sphere: in order to get a job in the public sector (local authorities, tax administration, internal affairs, railway, education, health care, etc.), a worker often should pay a sizeable bribe or trade in favors, with no guarantee that he/she will be able to keep that job for a relatively long time. Unfairness in the labor market is one of the biggest threats to trust, civic engagement, subjective wellbeing, and therefore social cohesion in Ukraine.

The Ukrainian labor market seems to be in a bad equilibrium, which is suboptimal from a social point of view: private firms create jobs that are not as good as they should be; many people are forced to take up these jobs, even if they are overqualified; many others prefer not to work at all; and existing jobs connect people less than would be socially desirable. Without important policy changes, Ukrainians will continue to give high preference to a close social network (relatives, friends, colleagues, and neighbors) and to the exit option by evading taxes, social security contributions, and regulations, moving abroad, or withdrawing from the labor force. In 2012, at the time we were conducting the qualitative research reported in this chapter, we conjectured that dissatisfied Ukrainians could also search for new forms of voice to influence formal institutions in a new direction bringing more instability to the system, with important implications for the investment climate and the overall economic situation in Ukraine. The civil unrest and political crisis in 2013–14 supported our argument.

8.3.2 Trade-offs between Living Standards, Productivity, and Social Cohesion in an Aging Society

Aging increases significantly the pressure on productivity, labor force participation, and the overall efficiency of the labor market. Without substantial productivity gains and an increase in employment rates, living standards could decline rapidly, and indicators of social cohesion, which are already low in Ukraine, may become even worse. In order to cushion the Ukrainian economy and society against shortfalls in the supply of labor and the increased burden of the aging population, it is particularly important to create more jobs that positively contribute to living standards, productivity, and social cohesion. But there could be important trade-offs across these three transformations that should be also taken into account.

8.3.2.1 PRODUCTIVITY AND LIVING STANDARDS

The benefits of recent waves of productivity growth and technological innovation appear to accrue disproportionately to the most talented and well-educated workers living in large cities, leaving many others without jobs and adequate means of subsistence. Given high migration costs and institutional barriers to internal mobility, low-wage workers and the unemployed are likely to be locked in the lagging regions with high job destruction and low job creation, having no possibility to escape to the regions with higher-productivity jobs and better wages and employment opportunities (Koettl et al. 2014).

An uneven distribution of winners and losers from productivity and employment growth leads to huge regional and sectoral imbalances and the existence of geographic "pockets" of poverty, deprivation, and social exclusion. In view of the persistent demand for Ukrainian workers in the European Union, Russia, and other countries, the better-off residents of such spatial poverty traps, who are dissatisfied with their living conditions and future prospects at home, may take advantage of working abroad.[6] Migrants' remittances and earnings improve households' welfare, help smooth household consumption, and bring some other value for migrants and their families (the individual perspective). But they still have a limited impact on key aspects of Ukraine's development, including investment, human capital formation, macroeconomic stability, spatial inequality reduction, and political change (Kupets 2012b).

8.3.2.2 LIVING STANDARDS AND SOCIAL COHESION

The mobility of some categories of the population to improve their living standards[7] may lead to greater income inequality and to disruption of traditional social networks as these people may be perceived as *parvenus* by the others in their former neighborhood. These developments might also adversely affect intergenerational solidarity and relationships at both the individual and societal levels.

Besides, there are not always direct spillovers from individual income gains to poverty reduction because tax payments and social insurance contributions by employers and employees are not always made in full due to widespread informality and tax avoidance schemes. Acting as a buffer, informal employment helps lift many individuals and their households out of extreme poverty, but this is only a short-term solution. As workers employed in the informal sector are very reluctant to make voluntary contributions to the social insurance funds and the Pension Fund, or at least to save some income for the future needs, they are very likely to encounter severe poverty outcomes in the case of job loss and particularly when they approach the retirement age.

8.3.2.3 SOCIAL COHESION AND PRODUCTIVITY

Strong social connections may go hand in hand with the unwillingness of their members to move professionally or geographically in order to reap the benefits from a better match to more productive and more rewarding jobs, so they "do not rise above the crowd." As one illustration, anecdotal evidence suggests that the entrenched habits of excessive alcohol consumption and the "crowd effect" were serious impediments to the launch and further development of agricultural companies with foreign investment in Ukraine.

---

[6] Although the costs of international migration are usually much greater than the costs of mobility within Ukraine, people often prefer international migration because of its much higher expected payoffs, including prospects for permanent settlement in a developed country with a more secure and comfortable life.

[7] These include youth moving from rural areas and small towns to cities for employment; IT specialists and other highly skilled professionals moving from standard employment to outsourced or freelance work; women moving to work in top management and politics; and Ukrainians moving to Western countries for temporary employment.

Those who value personal achievement more than social capital—usually better educated and more productive workers—are also more individualistic. Such individuals tend to participate in professional networks of similar highly skilled individuals, but they find it difficult to mix in other communities. The closeness of such professional communities limits the possibility of upward social mobility among outsiders as it becomes more difficult to join such communities without specific personal attributes and social connections. As a result, a natural divide between the representatives of different social groups of the population is often drawn along productivity and income lines (Kupets et al. 2012).

Age is also important, as the ability to develop new network connections with positive implications for productivity deteriorates with age. Social networks among the elderly workers are usually smaller in size, more stable, and tend to pursue more conservative values. This adversely affects the propensity of older workers to change profession, sector, or location and to integrate into a new work environment.

8.4 Examples of Good Jobs for Development in Ukraine

To confront the challenges of aging in the Ukrainian context, jobs that increase productivity and employment levels of prime-age and young workers, improve their living standards, and retain them in Ukraine will have a positive development impact. More specifically, it is necessary: (i) to boost labor productivity through exploiting learning spillovers (e.g., from FDI or cross-border movement of workers), and through investing in skills and technology; (ii) to raise the activity and productivity levels of underemployed categories of the population, including rural residents, youth, women with small children, the elderly, return migrants, and residents of lagging regions; (iii) to enhance innovation and entrepreneurship; and (iv) to invest in environmentally friendly and energy saving technologies.

8.4.1 *Boosting Labor Productivity via Learning Spillovers and Technology Transfer*

Foreign companies bring to Ukraine not only advanced technological and managerial knowledge, but also Western standards of work ethics and corporate social responsibility, which are very important for an economy in transition. Foreign companies and organizations usually pay higher salaries that are officially declared, and therefore they contribute disproportionately to the budget, the Pension Fund, and social insurance funds. Moreover, they usually provide more fringe benefits to their employees, are more likely to support core workers' rights and comply with employment protection legislation and environmental standards, offer more training and employment opportunities for youth, demonstrate greater tolerance to workers from disadvantaged groups including older and disabled workers, and therefore provide more grounds for trust and social cohesion than domestic firms. These virtues spill over to the rest of the economy, particularly export-oriented local companies, through horizontal and vertical linkages and knowledge diffusion by demonstration effects and movement of employees (Liebscher et al. 2007; Akulava and Vakhitova 2010).

Attracting foreign companies can also have direct and indirect effects on the country's economic development through their greater ability to attract further capital via agglomeration effects, fostering financial sector development, encouraging specialization, export diversification and involvement of local companies in transnational distribution networks, and putting external discipline on local governments (OECD 2002; Liebscher et al. 2007). Foreign companies may also be a potential source of "greening" effects as they directly transfer more energy efficient and environmentally friendly technologies and indirectly facilitate spillovers to domestic firms.

However, these positive spillovers from foreign companies are not guaranteed. Foreign investors in Ukraine most often are motivated by access to markets and natural resources, leaving efficiency-seeking factors—such as looking for labor-productivity advantages or access to local research and technological expertise—as much less important. Furthermore, these companies are less likely to enter backward areas because of poor infrastructure and low human capital stock, and are reluctant to work with local suppliers. There are also strong institutional barriers to the operation of foreign firms in Ukraine, including the high level of corruption and bureaucracy, the ambiguity of the legal system, political and economic instability, and weak contract enforcement and property rights protection (Kudina and Jakubiak 2008; OECD 2011, 2012). Shrinking cohorts of adequately skilled and mobile young workers, which tend to have higher "absorptive capacity" than their older counterparts, may further reduce the attractiveness of Ukraine for efficiency-seeking foreign investors.

8.4.2 Increasing employment and productivity levels of the rural population

Creation of more and better jobs for rural residents, for example in agriculture, food processing, recreation, tourism, and personal services, would have many benefits. It would contribute to higher living standards in rural areas and to productivity gains in agriculture and the allied food-processing industry. It would also lead to better human development outcomes in agrarian regions through higher tax revenues to local budgets that could then be spent on schools, hospitals, and public infrastructure and could provide incentives for highly educated rural youth to return. In view of Ukraine's comparative advantage in agriculture (an abundance of high-quality agricultural land, favorable climatic conditions, and low labor costs) and the expected increase in the global demand for food, agricultural business is one of the three high-potential sectors for investment and development defined by the OECD Sector Competitiveness Strategy for Ukraine (2012).

But the development of high-productivity, mid-size farms is hampered in Ukraine by the ongoing processes of capitalization and land consolidation, with the dominance of domestic, vertically-integrated and export-oriented agro-holdings, primarily specialized in crop production and poultry farming. The major difficulty for small and medium-size farmers is accessing external finance; this limits their ability to invest in fixed assets, such as machinery and storage facilities, and to buy high-quality inputs, such as seeds, fertilizers, livestock, and feed. Strategic investment in agriculture, including foreign investment, is discouraged by existing limitations on ownership of agricultural land and usage of land assets as collateral, ad hoc implementation of export quotas on selected products, and increasing state intervention in the agricultural business (OECD 2012). The other sector challenges are poor yields and the low quality of products (particularly of milk, with 80 percent of production coming from households that own fewer than five cows, which does not meet the quality standards of neighboring countries), monopolized market structure in storage and distribution, and lack of technical skills in the fields of agronomy, financial literacy, and entrepreneurship abilities (OECD 2012).

Non-farming jobs in nearby urban or rural settlements present another opportunity to increase employment and productivity levels of rural residents. But this requires improvements in the rural road infrastructure and in extending and diversifying transport routes (Institute of Demography and Social Studies 2007b). There are other barriers to internal labor mobility that need to be addressed, including limited access of job-seekers to information about vacancies outside their own locality; lack of appropriate skills (both technical and soft); social factors such as "binding" social capital (family, kinship, networks) and locational inertia; and possible discrimination and exploitation, particularly in the case of informal or casual employment (Koettl et al. 2014).

8.4.3 Attracting Return Migrants through Enhanced Entrepreneurial Opportunities

Jobs created by small entrepreneurs among return migrants may also have positive development impacts by increasing employment levels, boosting productivity and investment in lagging areas, and changing the attitudes and voting behavior of their neighborhood through "remitting" democratic values and attitudes from abroad. Entrepreneurship among return migrants is more likely to be "opportunity entrepreneurship" by nature, that is, based on new business ideas and profit opportunities, rather than "necessity entrepreneurship" in which individuals are forced to create small businesses due to lack of wage employment, as often happens in Ukraine. Entrepreneurship created from opportunity rather than necessity would be expected to generate higher knowledge spillovers and attract further capital via agglomeration and cluster effects (EBRD 2011).There are also possible positive effects of entrepreneurship among migrants in terms of additional job creation, more tax revenues, and fewer payments to the unemployed (Pozniak 2012).

Another positive externality from such business start-ups is that they could set an example for other migrants who stay abroad for a long time and are afraid of coming back because of uncertainty about their employment prospects upon return to Ukraine. The return of such migrants, seen as "the agents of development and innovation," is particularly important for Ukraine's development, given the challenges of its aging and shrinking population.

A major challenge to entrepreneurship, which was frequently mentioned by migrants during in-depth interviews and focus group discussions, is the invisible barriers, particularly in small towns and villages, created by public agencies (police, tax authorities, public administration, sanitary and epidemiological services, etc.), local competitors, and business rackets. These barriers are seen as more important among return migrants than among other Ukrainians, probably because migrants working in more advanced market economies get used to civilized business conduct and a business-friendly environment, and because they lose the necessary social connections in Ukraine, which are very important for a successful start-up.[8] In addition, "opportunity" entrepreneurs are probably "more likely to attract the attention of corrupt officials since they are more worthwhile targets for extracting bribes" (EBRD 2011: 86).

8.4.4 *Investing in Environmentally-Friendly and Energy-saving Technologies*

In view of the fact that Ukraine is one of the most energy-intensive economies in the world, development of renewable and environment-friendly energy resources, along with improvements in energy efficiency, are important steps to promote environmental sustainability (OECD 2011). This would create jobs with positive externalities through reducing greenhouse gas emissions and through vertical linkages with local suppliers, with likely increases

[8] According to the EBRD–World Bank Life in Transition Survey in 2010, 11.5 percent of all adult Ukrainian respondents had tried to set up a business, but 53.5 percent of them failed. Of those who failed, 49.5 percent listed "lack of capital" as the main reason; 25.6 percent mentioned "too much bureaucracy/red tape"; 18.9 percent mentioned "change in personal situation"; 2.7 percent mentioned "competitors threatened me"; 2.1 percent mentioned "couldn't afford the bribes"; and 1.2 percent mentioned "couldn't afford protection payments."

in productivity and employment growth in allied industries.[9] Furthermore, people's involvement in such socially important jobs gives them the feeling that they are contributing to the "greener" future of Ukraine and a better environment for future generations. Besides, jobs in renewable energy created in rural or mountain areas with low-productivity land or unfavorable climates may be an alternative to employment in agriculture and small-scale activities.

The main problems common to all energy subsectors in Ukraine are low average tariff levels that make "green" energy production economically unviable; nontransparent price-setting mechanisms and related uncertainties concerning future price levels; a nontransparent system of state subsidies and privatization schemes in the sector; payment arrears by consumers; and decreasing efficiency in transmission and distribution infrastructures (OECD 2011, 2012). Lack of technical skills needed to design and launch new plants in the renewable energy sector is also a serious impediment to the sector's growth. An aging population in a poor country such as Ukraine poses further challenges for the growth of expensive renewable energy production, as older persons are less inclined to adopt new technologies and accept higher energy prices for the benefit of future generations.

8.5 Obstacles to Doing Business and Creating Jobs in Ukraine

The 2013 round of the Business Environment and Enterprise Performance Survey (BEEPS) found that the top five business environment obstacles reported by Ukrainian firms were political instability, corruption, competitors' practices in the informal sector, access to finance, and tax administration (EBRD 2014). According to the recent survey of Ukrainian firms in four economic sectors—agricultural food growers, agricultural food processors, renewable energy, and information communication technology—conducted within the World Bank's Skills toward Employment and Productivity (STEP) project in 2014, the overwhelming majority of surveyed firms reported economic and financial instability, political uncertainty, corruption and high tax rates, and administration costs to be more serious constraints to doing business in Ukraine than any labor-related issue (World Bank 2016).

Hence, growth of firms in Ukraine is primarily impeded by political instability. And the issue is not so much in the frequently changing policies or rules as in the different implementation of the same policies and rules by different

---

[9] For example, four large-scale solar photovoltaic power stations installed by the company Activ Solar in Crimea in 2011–12 are able to save around 230,000 tons of carbon emissions each year on the peninsula (http://activsolar.at). In 2008, Activ Solar launched a comprehensive modernization program for its semiconductor plant based in Zaporizhia, with a long history of polysilicon production dating back to 1964.

governments and fragmentation of the policy-making process in general. Political instability and uncertainty generate uncertainty about the future course of economic policies (including tax and exchange rates, inflation, international trade, foreign investment, privatization, industrial, regional, labor market, and social policies) and the security of property rights (Carmignani 2003). Weak property rights protection calls for offshoring of firms' activities and adversely affects long-term investment decisions. State capture by narrow interest groups and crony capitalism, which are widespread in Ukraine, constrain the entry and growth of new firms in the privileged sectors with high returns and significant state support, and leave room for the development of small and medium-sized enterprises only in less attractive, low-productivity sectors. Small businesses in Ukraine also suffer a lot from a limited access to finance and high social security contributions.

Despite some important reforms since 2010, and particularly since 2014, corruption and poor governance remain serious problems in Ukraine. Therefore, pursuing political stability and improving the country's business and investment environment should remain a top policy priority to promote employment and productivity growth.

As regards labor-related obstacles to firm growth in Ukraine, most of the employers in the STEP survey reported being constrained by high payroll taxes and social security contributions. A widening gap between employers' needs for a workforce with particular job-specific technical and soft skills (such as communication skills, conscientiousness, the ability and willingness to learn, decision-making, etc.) and the quite inflexible supply of academically trained specialists create another obstacle for doing business in Ukraine (World Bank 2016). Meanwhile, high labor turnover, financial challenges, and the absence of incentives such as tax benefits for employer-provided training inhibit the effective implementation of comprehensive on-the-job training programs and lifelong learning schemes by employers, especially in the SME sector.

Labor regulations are viewed by Ukrainian employers as one of the least significant obstacles to their firms' operation and growth, probably because these regulations are often evaded or violated or because there are more important concerns. However, the creation of jobs in the formal sector through the violation of key labor regulations (e.g., regarding probation time, remuneration, vacation, sick leave, layoffs, and special working conditions for women, youth, the disabled, and other vulnerable categories) is not an optimal outcome because it undermines the rule of law, exposes firms to costly uncertainty, and leaves workers without adequate protection. Furthermore, such practices erode the trust of Ukrainians in private businesses and the market economy as a whole, strengthen nostalgia for the Soviet past, and reinforce people's calls for more jobs to be created in the public sector and more aggressive state intervention in the private sector.

8.6 Policy Implications

Faced with a rapidly aging population, Ukraine's jobs challenge is to encourage the creation of jobs that boost productivity, support the labor force participation of more Ukrainians able to work, and ensure long-term sustainability of public finances and social programs. In this way, Ukraine can avoid the need for drastic actions in the future, such as significant tax increases or reductions in public spending, in order to meet the demands of an aging society. Furthermore, policies to achieve these goals may reinforce each other over time, and therefore the payoff from an early intervention is potentially very large.

The Jobs WDR offers a good framework for organizing these policies (World Bank 2012b). Given the obstacles to doing business and creating jobs discussed in this chapter, a prerequisite for Ukraine's job policy is to create an environment conducive to higher productivity growth, job creation, and reallocation starting from the *fundamentals*: ensuring macroeconomic and political stability; promoting the rule of law and protection of rights through an effective and depoliticized judicial system; improving the efficiency of the business tax system and functioning of capital markets; investing in a modern world-class infrastructure; and removing the other structural obstacles to investing, innovating, and creating more jobs in the formal sector. The current context of an aging society also calls for modernization of the education and training systems to equip people with broad, flexible, and transferable skills that would enable them to progress in their working lives and to adapt quickly to a rapidly changing economic environment. Sound public policies aimed at improving health and nutrition in a cost-effective manner are also of critical importance for building up human capital, increasing activity rates, and improving productivity performance.

In order to avoid the skills mismatches and labor underutilization that are especially unwelcome in an economy with a rapidly shrinking and aging population, effective *labor policies and institutions* are needed to address labor market imperfections without reducing efficiency. More specifically, it is important to improve labor market information and provide career guidance; remove excessive labor market rigidity supported by the outdated (1971) Labor Code; encourage flexible work arrangements in the formal sector, including part-time work and distance work; strengthen the capacity of Public Employment Service and private employment agencies to better match workers to jobs; and assist vulnerable people in finding a suitable job and in fighting discriminatory practices in hiring and pay.

Finally, policy-makers should respond to the *specific country priority* of addressing population aging, namely through the creation of jobs that maximize the years of activity of skilled workers. It is necessary, then, to develop a comprehensive approach to promoting active aging and extending working-life careers as has been recently done in many developed countries facing the aging challenge.[10] Three broad areas where policy actions are necessary to encourage labor force participation among older workers include the following:

- *Tackling labor demand barriers.* This could include reduced or reimbursed social security contributions for older workers, subsidized employment targeted specifically at the older age groups, reduced payment of sickness benefits by employers, or other policy measures to decrease labor costs for them. Effective enforcement of labor legislation banning age limits on job offers and discrimination on the grounds of age and the implementation of projects aimed at changing negative employer attitudes toward older workers would also be useful.

- *Improving the employability of older workers.* First of all, it is necessary to strengthen the Public Employment Service and better align its information, occupational guidance, and job-placement services to the needs of older workers. Older workers also need training to upgrade their skills to match the changing needs of the labor market.[11] Other policy measures may include programs that encourage employers to invest continuously in skills of their workers, including lifelong learning schemes. Taking into account the poor health and premature mortality of Ukrainians that are often linked to poor working conditions and significant stress at work, it is important to implement effective policy measures aimed at improving the health status of individuals through positive changes in their lifestyles, reforms in the health care system, and significant improvement of the quality of jobs in the labor market.

- *Encouraging older workers to work longer.* Although controversial and often unpopular, Ukraine needs to adjust the age of retirement in accordance with changes in life expectancy and demographic trends, remove early retirement privileges for large groups of workers, and tighten the conditions for unemployment pathways into retirement. These changes may be effectively combined with financial incentives to work longer. Policies adapting working conditions to changing needs of older workers and encouraging part-time or distance work are also of increasing importance.

It is important to ensure, however, that these reforms targeted at older workers do not crowd out measures to foster the employment of youth and other vulnerable categories of workers who are also key to increasing the labor supply.

---

[10] See the OECD review of aging and employment policies and recent reforms and measures to stimulate employment of older workers in OECD countries at http://www.oecd.org/employment/ageingandemploymentpolicies.htm. Also see European Commission (2012b).

[11] One such program is the education and training benefit (voucher) for individuals aged 45 years and over who have a social insurance period of at least fifteen years, which was introduced in 2013 through the Law on Employment. Unlike standard labor market training provided by the Public Employment Service, it subsidizes training efforts while giving participants some freedom to choose the type of training that they want.

As has been repeatedly stressed in this chapter, the ultimate priority has to be placed on increases in labor productivity, professional and geographical labor mobility, and trust in government and other public institutions. Since the option of offsetting some of the decline in the labor force and its aging through increased immigration of skilled young workers is less feasible in Ukraine than in richer countries, more efforts should be spent on retaining Ukrainians at home and on increasing positive development effects from emigration of Ukrainian workers through remittances, return migration, and diaspora involvement.

Appendix 8A: Additional Tables

Table 8A.1. Projected age-specific labor force participation rates under alternative scenarios

Age group	Year	Labor force participation rate (%)					
		Base scenario	Scenario 1	Scenario 2	Scenario 3	Scenario 4	Scenario 5
15–19	2010	14.7	14.7	14.7	14.7	14.7	14.7
	2030	15.0	17.8	17.8	17.8	17.8	17.8
	2060	15.0	17.8	68.0	19.2	17.8	67.0
20–24	2010	60.5	60.5	60.5	60.5	60.5	60.5
	2030	60.6	61.7	61.7	61.7	61.7	61.7
	2060	60.6	61.7	81.1	69.0	61.7	81.5
25–29	2010	79.9	79.9	79.9	79.9	79.9	79.9
	2030	80.2	82.4	82.4	82.4	82.4	82.4
	2060	80.3	82.5	84.0	89.3	82.5	90.7
30–34	2010	83.4	83.4	83.4	83.4	83.4	83.4
	2030	83.7	85.7	85.7	85.7	85.7	85.7
	2060	83.8	85.7	89.7	90.2	85.7	93.8
35–39	2010	86.0	86.0	86.0	86.0	86.0	86.0
	2030	86.2	86.9	86.9	86.9	86.9	86.9
	2060	86.2	86.9	92.6	90.2	86.9	96.8
40–44	2010	86.1	86.1	86.1	86.1	86.1	86.1
	2030	86.3	87.7	87.7	87.7	87.7	87.7
	2060	86.3	87.7	92.3	89.2	87.7	95.3
45–49	2010	83.4	83.4	83.4	83.4	83.4	83.4
	2030	83.6	85.3	85.3	85.3	85.3	85.3
	2060	83.6	85.3	92.2	86.2	85.3	95.4
50–54	2010	76.7	76.7	76.7	76.7	76.7	76.7
	2030	77.0	79.7	79.7	79.7	79.7	79.7
	2060	77.0	79.7	91.3	81.3	79.7	94.3
55–59	2010	51.3	51.3	51.3	51.3	51.3	51.3
	2030	52.7	59.6	59.6	59.6	59.6	59.6
	2060	53.4	60.3	89.2	69.3	72.8	93.8
60–64	2010	28.4	28.4	28.4	28.4	28.4	28.4
	2030	29.2	36.1	36.1	36.1	36.1	36.1
	2060	29.4	36.3	79.6	39.0	58.0	89.9
65+	2010	20.0	20.0	20.0	20.0	20.0	20.0
	2030	20.2	21.8	21.8	21.8	21.8	21.8
	2060	20.3	21.9	22.1	23.4	40.1	61.6

Source: author's calculations based on population projections from UN (2015), medium variant, and gender-specific labor force participation rates from ILO (2013a), series "Estimates and projections," for ten five-year age groups from 15 to 64 years and one group of 65+ years.

Table 8A.2. Labor market indicators by sex, place of residence, and age group, 2014*

Indicator	Category	Total	By age group						
			15–24	25–29	30–34	35–39	40–49	50–59	60–70
Labor force	Total	62.4	38.4	80.5	82.6	84.8	84.6	63.2	15.5
participate rate	Female	56.1	32.5	69.4	73.3	80.2	83.3	57.1	13.8
	Male	69.3	44.0	91.3	91.7	89.5	86.0	70.7	18.1
	Urban	62.6	37.0	82.8	84.3	85.9	85.6	62.5	12.5
	Rural	61.8	41.3	75.0	77.3	82.0	82.4	64.8	22.9
Employment rate	Total	56.6	29.5	71.6	74.9	77.9	78.4	59.4	15.5
	Female	51.9	25.2	62.7	67.7	74.6	78.7	54.6	13.8
	Male	61.8	33.6	80.2	81.9	81.2	78.2	65.3	18.1
	Urban	56.9	28.4	74.2	76.6	78.9	79.3	58.6	12.5
	Rural	55.9	31.8	65.2	69.8	75.4	76.6	61.2	22.9
Unemployment	Total	9.3	23.1	11.1	9.3	8.1	7.3	6.0	0.1
rate	Female	7.5	22.4	9.7	7.6	6.9	5.6	4.4	0.1
	Male	10.8	23.7	12.2	10.6	9.3	9.1	7.6	0.0
	Urban	9.2	23.2	10.4	9.1	8.2	7.4	6.2	0.1
	Rural	9.5	23.1	13.1	9.7	8.0	7.1	5.6	0.0

Source: Labor Force Survey, State Statistics Service of Ukraine.

Note: * data for 2014 do not include occupied territories in Crimea and Donbas.

References

Akulava, M. and Vakhitova, G. (2010). The Impact of FDI on Firms' Performance across Sectors: Evidence from Ukraine. KEI Discussion Paper No. 26. Kyiv: Kyiv Economics Institute.

Bussolo, M., Koettl, J., and Sinnott, E. (2015). *Golden Aging: Prospects for Healthy, Active, and Prosperous Aging in Europe and Central Asia.* Europe and Central Asia Studies. Washington, DC: World Bank.

Carmignani, F. (2003). "Political instability, uncertainty and economics." *Journal of Economic Surveys*, 17(1):1–54.

Chawla, M., Betcherman, G., and Banerji, A. (2007). *From Red to Gray. The "Third Transition" of Aging Populations in Eastern Europe and the Former Soviet Union.* Washington, DC: World Bank.

European Bank for Reconstruction and Development (EBRD) (2011). Transition Report 2011. Crisis and Transition: The People's Perspective. London: European Bank for Reconstruction and Development.

European Bank for Reconstruction and Development (EBRD) (2014). Business Environment and Enterprise Performance Survey (BEEPS) V Country Profile. URL: http://ebrd-beeps.com/countries/ukraine. [Accessed May 2016.]

European Commission (2012a). Communication from the Commission to the European Parliament, the Council, the European Economic and Social Committee and the Committee of the Regions "Towards a Job-rich Recovery." COM (2012) 173 final, 18.04.2012, Strasbourg: European Commission.

European Commission (2012b). European Employment Observatory Review: Employment Policies to Promote Active Ageing. Luxembourg: European Union.

European Training Foundation (ETF) (2008). Transition from Education to Work in EU Neighbouring Countries. Results of an ETF Innovation and Learning Project. Turin: European Training Foundation.

Gill, I.S. and Raiser, M. (2012). *Golden Growth: Restoring the Lustre of the European Economic Model*. Washington, DC: World Bank.

Institute of Demography and Social Studies (IDSS) (2007a). *Mortality of Working Age Population in Ukraine*. Edited by Ella Libanova. Kyiv: IDSS (in Ukrainian: Смертність населення України у трудоактивному віці/Відпов. ред. Е. М. Лібанова. —— К.: Ін-т демографії та соціальних досліджень НАН України, 2007).

Institute of Demography and Social Studies (IDSS) (2007b). *Population of Ukraine. Social and Demographic Problems of Ukrainian Countryside*. Kyiv: IDSS (in Ukrainian: Населення України. Соціально-демографічні проблеми українського села. —— К.: Ін-т демографії та соціальних досліджень НАН України, 2007).

Institute of Demography and Social Studies (IDSS) (2010). *Youth and Youth Policy in Ukraine: Social and Demographic Aspects*. Edited by Ella Libanova. Kyiv: IDSS (in Ukrainian: Молодь та молодіжна політика в Україні: соціально-демографічні аспекти/ Відпов. ред.Е. М. Лібанова. —— К.:Ін-т демографії та соціальних досліджень НАН України, 2010).

International Labour Organization (ILO) (2013a). Estimates and Projections of the Economically Active Population, 1990–2030 (7th edition). Geneva: International Labour Office. URL: http://www.ilo.org/ilostat/. [Accessed May 2016.]

International Labour Organization (ILO) (2013b). Report on the Methodology, Organization and Results of a Modular Sample Survey on Labour Migration in Ukraine. Decent Work Technical Support Team and Country Office for Central and Eastern Europe (DWT/CO-Budapest). Budapest: ILO.

Koettl, J., Kupets, O., Olefir, A., and Santos, I. (2014). "In search of opportunities? The barriers to more efficient internal labor mobility in Ukraine." *IZA Journal of Labor & Development*, 3(21):1–28. doi: 10.1186/s40175-014-0021-3.

Kudina, A. and Jakubiak, M. (2008). The Motives and Impediments to FDI in the CIS. CASE Network Studies & Analyses No. 370/2008. Warsaw: Centre for Economic and Social Research.

Kupets, O. (2012a). The Economic and Demographic Effects of Labour Migration in the EU Eastern Partners and Russia: A Synthesis Report. Research Report 2012/26, Consortium for Applied Research on International Migration (CARIM-East), Robert Schuman Centre for Advanced Studies, Florence: European University Institute. URL: http://www.carim-east.eu/media/CARIM-East-2012-RR-26.pdf. [Accessed May 2016.]

Kupets, O. (2012b). The Development and the Side Effects of Remittances in the CIS Countries: The Case of Ukraine. Research Report 2012/02, Consortium for Applied Research on International Migration (CARIM-East), Robert Schuman Centre for Advanced Studies, Florence: European University Institute. URL: http://www.carim-east.eu/media/CARIM-East-2012-02.pdf. [Accessed May 2016.]

Kupets, O. (2016). "Education-job mismatch in Ukraine: Too many people with tertiary education or too many jobs for low-skilled?" *Journal of Comparative Economics*, 44(1):125–47.

Kupets, O., Vakhitov, V., and Babenko, S. (2012). Ukraine Case Study: Jobs and Demographic Change. Background paper for the World Development Report 2013. URL: http://siteresources.worldbank.org/EXTNWDR2013/Resources/8258024-1320950747192/8260293-1320956712276/8261091-1348683883703/WDR2013_bp_Jobs_And_Demographic_Change.pdf. [Accessed May 2016.]

Liebscher, K., Christl, J., Mooslechner, P., and Ritzberger-Grünwald, D. (2007). *Foreign Direct Investment in Europe: A Changing Landscape*. Cheltenham: Edward Elgar Publishing Limited.

Organisation for Economic Co-operation and Development (OECD) (2002). *Foreign Direct Investment for Development: Maximising Benefits, Minimising Costs*. Paris: OECD.

Organisation for Economic Co-operation and Development (OECD) (2011). *OECD Investment Policy Reviews: Ukraine 2011*. Paris: OECD.

Organisation for Economic Co-operation and Development (OECD) (2012). *Ukraine Sector Competitiveness Strategy. Competitiveness and Private Sector Development*. Paris: OECD.

Pozniak, A. (2012). External Labour Migration in Ukraine as a Factor in Socio-Demographic and Economic Development. Research Report 2012/14, Consortium for Applied Research on International Migration (CARIM-East), Robert Schuman Centre for Advanced Studies, Florence: European University Institute. URL: http://www.carim-east.eu/media/CARIM-East-2012-RR-14.pdf. [Accessed May 2016.]

United Nations (UN) (2015). World Population Prospects: The 2015 Revision. New York: United Nations, Department of Economic and Social Affairs, Population Division. URL: http://esa.un.org/unpd/wpp/DVD. [Accessed May 2016.]

World Bank (2009). An Avoidable Tragedy: Combating Ukraine's Health Crisis. Lessons from Europe. Kyiv: Verso 04 for the World Bank.

World Bank (2010). Ukraine Country Economic Memorandum: Strategic Choices to Accelerate and Sustain Growth. Washington, DC: World Bank.

World Bank (2012a). In Search of Opportunities. How a More Mobile Workforce Can Propel Ukraine's Prosperity. Washington, DC: World Bank.

World Bank (2012b). World Development Report 2013: Jobs. Washington, DC: World Bank.

World Bank (2016). Skills for a Modern Ukraine. Diagnostic and Policy Options. Washington, DC: World Bank.

Index

Index

Index

productivity (*cont.*)
and social protection systems 180, 205
South Korea 180–1
St Lucia 162–3, 164–5, 168, 173
Tunisia 238–49, 250
Ukraine 256, 263–4, 267–8, 272–6,
279–80, 282
demographic change 259, 260
Programa de Apoya al Empleo (PAE), Mexico 194
Programme de mise à niveau (PMN) 251–2
Program to Support Employment, Mexico 194
Progresa program, Mexico 184
property rights
Papua New Guinea 117
Tunisia 251
Ukraine 275, 279
Prospera program, Mexico 184, 185
public economics 7
public–private partnerships (PPPs),
Mozambique 50
public sector
Bangladesh 91
Mexico 202
Papua New Guinea 132, 133
small-island nations 142
St Lucia 153
Tunisia 223, 227
Ukraine 279
Puga, D. 41

quality certification, Mozambique 51
quality of jobs 1
quality of life
Tunisia 230

Rahman, H.Z.R. 73, 81
Raiser, M. 261
Rama, M. 91 n. 38
Ramsaran, D. 165
Ramskogler, P. 199 n. 9
Rashid, S. 75
Ravallion, M. 75
Ray, D. 87 n. 30
readymade garments (RMG) sector
Bangladesh 63, 67, 78–81, 93, 94, 95
human capital 84–5
social cohesion 90
Tunisia 252
real effective exchange rate (REER),
St Lucia 149
redundancy pay, St Lucia 158
regulations
consequences of inefficient 182
good jobs for development 181
Mexico 179, 207
Reilly, B. 163
religious issues, Bangladesh 85, 86, 89, 90, 95

remittances *see* domestic remittances; overseas
remittances
renewable energy
St Lucia 141
Ukraine 277–8
Republic of Korea *see* South Korea
Reshaping Economic Geography WDR 8
resilience, economic 165
resource-rich countries
jobs challenges 3
see also Papua New Guinea
retail sector
Mexico 196
Tunisia 232
Ukraine 270
retirement age, Ukraine 281
Rhoades, S.A. 39
rice production, Bangladesh 68–9, 73, 74–5, 92
rickshaw pullers, Bangladesh 84, 94
Rijkers, B. 239 n. 8, 241
Rio Tinto 48 n. 18
Roberts, J. 141
Rodríguez-Oreggia, E. 202 n. 15
Rodrik, D. 47, 47 n. 16, 87 n. 30
Rofman, R. 187
Rokeya, Begum 90
Roodman, D. 74 n. 9
Rosenfeld, D. 48, 48 n. 19, 51 n. 21
rural areas
Bangladesh 66
migration flows 76, 77
non-farm self-employment 73, 74, 92
poverty 65, 66
wellbeing, and urban growth 82–5
Mexico 192
Mozambique 53
determinants of jobs choices 40, 41, 42,
43, 44
education 24–5
employment status 28
employment type 29
good jobs for development 45–7
household-based production 31
labor force participation 27
living standards 32, 33
policy recommendations 49, 53
poverty 20, 32
sectoral allocation of labor 29–30
social cohesion 36, 37
trust in President 36, 37
Papua New Guinea 102, 106, 135
changing patterns of employment 111
domestic remittances 121
job creation policies 118
poverty 107
projected job growth 117
social protection systems 181

298